Megalithic Astronomy

A new archaeological and statistical study of 300 western Scottish sites

C. L. N. Ruggles

with contributions by
P. N. Appleton, S. F. Burch, J. A. Cooke, R. W. Few,
J. G. Morgan and R. P. Norris

BAR British Series 123
1984

B.A.R.

122 Banbury Road, Oxford OX2 7BP, England

GENERAL EDITORS

A.R. Hands, B.Sc., M.A., D.Phil.
D.R. Walker, M.A.

B.A.R. -123,1984 : 'Megalithic Astronomy'.

Price £ 15.00 post free throughout the world. Payments made in currency other than sterling must be calculated at the current rate of exchange. Cheques should be made payable to B.A.R. and sent to the above address.

ISBN 0 86054 253 X

For details of all BAR publications in print please write to the above address. Information on new titles is sent regularly on request, with no obligation to purchase.

Volumes are distributed direct from the publisher. All BAR prices are inclusive of postage by surface mail anywhere in the world.

Printed in Great Britain

CONTENTS

LIST OF CONTRIBUTORS

Dr C.L.N. Ruggles, Computing Studies Unit, University of Leicester,
   LEICESTER LE1 7RH.

***

Dr P.N. Appleton, Department of Astronomy, University of Manchester,
   MANCHESTER M13 9PL.

Dr S.F. Burch, Atomic Energy Research Establishment, Harwell, DIDCOT,
   Oxon. OX11 ORA.

Dr J.A. Cooke, 6 Greenbank Terrace, EDINBURGH EH10 6ER.

Dr R.W. Few, 147 Girton Road, Girton, CAMBRIDGE CB3 OPQ.

Dr J.G. Morgan, "Cedars", Springhill, Longworth, ABINGDON, Oxon. OX13
   5HL.

Dr R.P. Norris, CFIRO Division of Radio Physics, P.O. Box 78, EPPING,
   New South Wales, 2121, AUSTRALIA.

PREFACE AND ACKNOWLEDGEMENTS

This volume is something between a monograph and an edited volume of separate papers. It is completely written by CR, but represents the outcome of a project first conceived and undertaken by the various contributors during the years 1973 - 1978. The project was subsequently brought to completion by CR during the period 1979 - 1983. Jointly-attributed chapters present the fruits of collaborative work, and may be regarded as multi-author papers. Other chapters represent the work of CR alone.

The contributions of a number of individuals and institutions have been invaluable both before and during the project, and all are very gratefully acknowledged. Foremost in the list must be Alexander Thom himself, whose extensive work in megalithic astronomy (Thom 1955; 1967; 1971) motivated the project in the first place, and who has helped, even in the face of criticism of some of his conclusions, by making available unpublished material, particularly his full site list.

The project would never initially have been undertaken but for the enthusiasm, active encouragement and advice of Douglas Heggie. He has remained on hand throughout to give helpful advice and criticism whenever it was needed.

In its early stages the work was carried out as a spare time project largely without financial aid. However we were grateful for grants towards field trips, which were obtained from Merton College, Oxford (CR), Jesus College, Cambridge (JGM) and Trinity College, Cambridge (JAC & SFB). Our thanks are due to the following departments for the loan of theodolites between 1973 and 1978: Dept. of Engineering, University of Cambridge; Dept. of Geography, University of Cambridge; and Dept. of Surveying and Geodesy, University of Oxford.

In 1979 CR was awarded the first of a series of grants which enabled him to continue and complete this project, and to undertake research in related areas (Ruggles 1981; 1982b; 1983; 1984). He is especially grateful to Barry Cunliffe and to Richard Atkinson, whose active encouragement during 1977 and 1978 helped to bring this about. The grants have taken the form of an SERC-sponsored Research Assistantship (1979-80) and a University of Wales Research Fellowship (1980-82), both tenable in the Department of Archaeology, University College, Cardiff, and an SERC Research Fellowship (1982-83), tenable in the Department of Mathematics at the University of Leicester. A lightweight theodolite was purchased out of the 1979 SERC grant, and two extensive seasons of fieldwork were undertaken in 1979 and 1981, thanks to financial assistance from the SERC (1979) and the Leverhulme Trust (1981). The following survey assistants were employed on this and two related projects which were undertaken concurrently: Kim Bramley, Sheila Brookes, Sal Brown, Clare Huxley, Chris Jennings, Colin Martin, Gordon Moir, Cilla Norris, Oliver Strimpel, Mari Williams and Mary Wilson. Phil Appleton, Roger Few and Ray Norris also helped with parts of this later survey work.

Computer programs for the reduction of the survey data were developed using the facilities of the Universities of Cambridge and Oxford and University College, Cardiff. Graphics packages were developed in Cardiff and at the University of Leicester. The graphical output in this volume was produced using the facilities of the Computer Graphics Centre at Leicester, and the text has been produced using the word-processing facilities there. The assistance of many staff at these institutions, and particularly at Cardiff and Leicester, is gratefully acknowledged.

The bulk of the reduction work for this project was completed during 1982-83, with the aid for a short period in 1982 of Kim Bramley, whose main contribution was in producing the calculated horizon profiles. Financial assistance towards the reduction work on this and other projects was obtained from the British Academy Small Grants Research Fund.

The project is cross-disciplinary, and owes much to helpful advice archaeological, astronomical, computational and statistical. In this context the contributions of Patrick Ashmore, Richard Atkinson, Peter Freeman, Douglas Heggie, Leslie Morrison, Henry Neave, Jon Patrick, Graham Ritchie, Alasdair Whittle and many others are gratefully acknowledged. Patrick Ashmore, Richard Atkinson, Douglas Heggie and Graham Ritchie also read sections of the text and made a great many helpful suggestions. Henry Neave made available preprints of a publication concerning a new statistical test, and checked over an additional argument presented here (Appendix II). No blame attaches to these people for any faults that remain.

The staff of a number of institutions have been particularly helpful: the Ordnance Survey, Southampton, for giving access to essential triangulation information at only a nominal charge; the Royal Commission on Ancient and Historical Monuments (Scotland), Edinburgh, for giving access to inventory information in advance of publication; and the staff of the Bodleian Library Map Room, Oxford, and the Ordnance Survey, Edinburgh, for their co-operation and patience. Thanks are also due to Margaret and Gerald Ponting for supplying survey information at a site in the Callanish area.

Finally, a number of people helped with the practical aspects of the surveying trips during 1979 and 1981. Particular thanks are due to Colin Martin and to Cecilia and David Taylor.

Some passages in Chapters 1 and 13 repeat, with only minor alterations, what has been said in a previous publication (Ruggles 1982a). CR is grateful to Cambridge University Press for permission to reproduce them.

LIST OF TABLES

LIST OF FIGURES

1   INTRODUCTION

1.1   The role of ethnoastronomy and archaeoastronomy

Recent years have seen an explosion of interest in ethno-astronomy (defined as the study of astronomical practice amongst contemporary societies) and its sister archaeoastronomy (the same amongst past societies). Both subdisciplines have acquired considerable momentum: there are two publications entirely devoted to archaeoastronomy (the _Archaeoastronomy_ supplement to _Journal for the History of Astronomy_ and the bulletin of the Center for Archaeo-astronomy, University of Maryland), and in September 1983 the first international conference on ethnoastronomy was held in the USA.

Ethno- and archaeoastronomy, though of particular interest to astronomers and historians of science, form merely one aspect of the study of human societies in general. The anthropologist and arch-aeologist are entitled to ask why astronomy merits being concentrated upon to the apparent exclusion of the many other facets of these societies, and to point out the dangers of ethnocentrism in inter-pretation. Much work exists, however, in which other facets are not excluded and the problems of ethnocentrism are recognised and tackled. Urton's (1981) examination of a contemporary Andean community is a particularly fine example of the study of astronomical practice in its social context, and one which is also relevant to the astronomy of the Inca, from whom the community being studied is descended. Turton & Ruggles (1978) have attempted to use a study of a contemporary Ethi-opian community to counter certain assumptions in the astronomical interpretation of the archaeological record. Many further examples may be found amongst the bibliographies of Baity (1973), Urton (1981) and Thorpe (1981), and within the 1983 ethnoastronomy conference proceedings (Carlson & von del Chamberlain 1985). Given that the pitfalls are recognised and that such work does exist, the question still remains as to why astronomical practice should be of such particular interest, especially where (as in archaeological applic-ations, and especially in prehistoric archaeology) a thorough study of related aspects of society is not possible.

Firstly, astronomy is intimately related to the development of human conceptualisation of space and time, and its study can give val-uable insights into the latter. The heavenly bodies are beyond reach, everywhere present yet imperturbable; they form the basis of cosmo-logical frameworks. The cycles of the sun, moon, planets and stars are also by far the most dependable regularly recurring natural events. Anthropological work on the conceptualisation of duration shows that the boundaries between well-defined time periods tend to be marked off by ritual activities such as seasonal festivals (Leach 1961: 124-36; see also Thorpe 1983). Astronomical observations provide a reliable way of demarcating these time intervals (i.e. of determining the timing of festivals), and hence astronomical symbolism features in the ritual activities themselves. Tedlock (1984) provides an example of particular interest; for others see Carlson & von del Chamberlain (1985).

Secondly, the fact that the movements of the heavenly bodies are of almost universal concern, even amongst the most technologically primitive of hunter-gatherer societies, gives the anthropologist some hope of correlating astronomical practice with other facets of society. Leach (1954), for example, has suggested that increasing complexity of ways of thinking about time (hence more systematic observations of the heavens) is correlated with the emergence of a priestly class of time-keepers (i.e. with increasing social stratification). An such view may of course be oversimplistic (see, e.g., Thorpe 1981) and can only be developed with the aid of ethnographic fieldwork of sufficient methodological rigour (for an attempt in this direction see Turton & Ruggles 1978). However in the light of such correlations ethno- and archaeoastronomy acquire a valuable role in extrapolating from astronomical evidence to facets of the society in question which may be less directly observable. This remark has particular force in archaeological applications, where facets of great interest may leave no direct trace in the archaeological record.

Archaeoastronomical evidence nonetheless suffers, in common with archaeological evidence in general, from the limitations of the archaeological record. It is clear from ethnographic work that a variety of widespread practices, such as the recognition and naming of stars and constellations, and even the use of heliacal risings and settings to determine seasonal activities (e.g. Turton & Ruggles 1978: 590), tend to leave no trace in the archaeological record. However astronomical symbolism featuring in ritual activities may be incorporated in the design of centres where such activities were performed, and hence may well be recoverable. Our best hope of success lies where we have extensive remains of burial and (presumably) ceremonial sites, as in the megalithic period of British prehistory. Indeed, albeit perhaps for the wrong motives, it was upon the design of British megalithic monuments that archaeoastronomical investigations concentrated during the earliest emergence of the subject (e.g. Lockyer 1909).

1.2 Astronomy and prehistoric British archaeology

Archaeoastronomy originally emerged in Britain as the study of orientations, alignments and putative horizon indications at megalithic sites: burial sites such as chamber tombs, sites presumed ceremonial such as stone rings, and the enigmatic stone alignments, pairs and single standing stones which are particularly abundant in northern and western Britain. It has since been suggested that astronomical considerations entered into the construction of a range of non-domestic pre- and proto-historic sites in many parts of the world. In some countries, archaeoastronomical studies benefit from evidence other than just the present disposition of archaeological remains: in Mesoamerica for instance (Aveni 1980) there exists ethnohistoric evidence (accounts by Spanish invaders of practices current when the sites were in use), ethnographic material which is clearly relevant (present-day practices by descendants of the groups being studied) and first-hand written accounts (Maya and Aztec codices). However none of these other sources is available in British work.

Despite their potential interest and value for archaeological research, studies of orientations and alignments at megalithic sites manifest a continuing lack of communication (and at times much contention) between those workers with backgrounds in the numerate disciplines such as astronomy or surveying, who tend to undertake the archaeoastronomical field work and provide the astronomical conclusions, and those with backgrounds in archaeology and the social sciences who try to place them in the context of prehistoric society. Hereinafter, and purely for convenience, I shall refer to the two groups respectively as "the archaeoastronomers" and "the archaeologists".

The main problem is that the archaeoastronomers have effectively been doing no more for some years than arguing amongst themselves about what constitutes reliable archaeoastronomical evidence. They are not yet ready to supply archaeologists with dependable evidence which can be considered in its social context alongside more conventional data.

The reason for this is straightforward. A single alignment of apparent astronomical significance, unlike an artefact, is ambiguous; it might have arisen through the interaction of factors quite unrelated to astronomy. It is an insufficient, indeed futile, yet nonetheless overworked practice in archaeoastronomy simply to seek out examples of astronomical alignments and to lay great emphasis upon them. Instead, we must first examine enough archaeological structures to permit a statistical examination. By this means we can compare the actual number of astronomical alignments obtained with that which would have been expected by chance (i.e. by the interaction of factors unrelated to astronomy). This immediately raises numerous questions of the fair selection of data, which, if we do not pay full attention to them at the outset, will introduce the possibility of bias, and thus invalidate any statistical conclusions. Only if the data can be seen to have been selected fairly (that is without regard for the astronomical possibilities), and the presence of significantly more astronomical alignments than would have been expected by chance can be demonstrated statistically, can the archaeoastronomer present the archaeologist with reliable evidence that astronomical considerations did affect site design.

The objection might be raised here that orientations and alignments are not the only conceivable way in which astronomical practice might have left its mark at ceremonial sites. Burl (1980), for example, has cited cup-markings and quartz assemblages as evidence in support of lunar ritual at the Aberdeenshire Recumbent Stone Circles. Might not a more wide-ranging approach, paying more attention to artefactual and depositional evidence, prove more fruitful? A further objection might be that to concentrate upon surface features alone risks being very misleading. Excavations have been carried out by Euan MacKie at two Argyllshire sites in order to test astronomical hypotheses — at Kintraw (MacKie 1974) and at Minard, or Brainport Bay (MacKie 1981) — but these are isolated cases. Might not conclusions based on apparently deliberate structure orientations lead us astray when we are in fact, and unknowingly, dealing with partially destroyed, altered or multi-phase sites?

Unfortunately all supporting evidence, such as Burl's quartz assemblages, has until now been highly interpretative and tentative, and it is difficult to envisage discoveries that could change this. Furthermore excavation is expensive and (as far as astronomical evidence is concerned) at present largely shooting in the dark. MacKie's efforts at Kintraw, for example, have sadly proved inconclusive (Heggie 1981a: S29-31 and references therein). Non-destructive analysis is the obvious way forward. This of necessity involves the statistical approach described above, an approach which actually helps to counter the vagaries of the surface record. For although we need to consider a large quantity of data, we aim solely at determining an overall probability level in favour of a particular hypothesis (astronomical or otherwise). A significant result will have succeeded in isolating an overall trend amongst a group of sites. Any anomalous data that have been introduced unknowingly, owing to misleading surface evidence, will merely have added to the background "random noise". At the end of the day, examination of the statistical results can hopefully be used to suggest sites where excavation might be of most value. The statistical approach and non-destructive analysis thus go hand-in-hand. In British prehistory the only promising path towards reliable astronomical evidence, at least for the foreseeable future, is the statistical one.

It is the numerous problems needing to be clarified in the statistical approach that have recently caused such vigorous debate (see, e.g., papers in Ruggles & Whittle (1981) and recent issues of the Archaeoastronomy supplement to Journal for the History of Astronomy). This prepossession leaves megalithic archaeoastronomy (hereinafter, by convention, "megalithic astronomy") open to the charge that it is a study "conducted .. up to now, separately from consideration of the society in which it operated" (Thorpe 1982). Yet any attempt to interpret existing astronomical evidence in its social context has risked being considerably misleading: obvious examples are MacKie's work (1977) based largely on Thom's conclusions (1967; 1971), and Thorpe's own recent work (1983) based largely on Burl's (1980; 1981; 1982).

Unfortunately the important issues are obscured, and the differences between the archaeoastronomy and archaeology camps exacerbated, by the many misleading pronouncements made on both sides of the fence. Thus on the one hand some leading archaeoastronomers, notably Alexander Thom (whose extensive and high-quality fieldwork has formed the backbone of British archaeoastronomy for many years), refuse to accept that their evidence is in question at all, and go on to interpret it themselves in manifestly ethnocentric terms quite unrelated to current thought about the social context (hence talk of "Megalithic Man"; see also Thom 1971: chs. 1 & 10; Thom & Thom 1978a: 181-182). On the other hand archaeologists have been keen to interpret and discuss what astronomical evidence there is (e.g. MacKie 1977; 1981; Burl 1980; 1981; 1983; Thorpe 1981; 1983), and some have tended in an equally high-handed way to select certain astronomical evidence as reliable and to dismiss the rest. The choice is clearly influenced by their own ideas of the social context in the first place, and largely or completely ignores the relevant archaeoastronomical and statistical arguments.

In this atmosphere of confusion, it is clear that a reasoned approach is urgently needed to investigating possible astronomical influences on the design of megalithic sites. Apt methods of analysis of putative astronomical orientations and alignments need to be formulated by the archaeoastronomers and presented clearly to the archaeological community at large for constructive criticism. Only when a reliable basic approach has been accepted can meaningful astronomical evidence be incorporated into theories of prehistoric society.

Hopefully this volume will go some way towards establishing guidelines both acceptable (if restricting) to the archaeoastronomers and reassuring, as well as comprehensible, to the archaeologists. In an attempt to do this we present an investigation of a certain group of megalithic monuments, the free-standing megalithic sites of the Highlands and Islands of western Scotland. Our reasons for this choice are elaborated in Section 1.4 below. The motive for the volume is methodological, but an important subsidiary aim is to present data which may be of more general value in other discussions. For this reason archaeological information, horizon profile diagrams and tabular data are presented in detail. While the archaeological implications are discussed in the closing chapters, this investigation will deliberately stop short of any detailed interpretation of the evidence in its social context.

1.3   The analysis of structure orientations – basic remarks

At the outset we must attempt to identify some of the general problems involved in analysing the orientations of archaeological structures. This will provide necessary groundwork for the methodological approach that follows.

Three general classes of factor which might have influenced structure orientations are:

(i) Astronomical considerations. Structures might be aligned upon the heavenly bodies, e.g. towards the horizon rising or setting points of the sun at a solstice or other significant time in the year.
(ii) Azimuthal directions. Structures might be deliberately or preferentially aligned north-south, or in some other direction.
(iii) Features on the ground. Structure orientations might be towards nearby sites of a certain type, natural features such as distant mountains, or directions of local significance (e.g. whence ancestors came); or else they might depend upon the local lie of the land (e.g. tomb entrances downhill).

Any given orientation will, presumably, actually have resulted from any number of different factors, acting together or vying against one another in importance. For example, it might have been desired to situate a ceremonial site in a position with wide views, within the restriction of the builders' available territory and avoiding prime agricultural land; a desired solar or lunar rising or setting alignment behind a distant mountain, for example, might have been secondary to the other requirements, and a compromise reached. In the absence of independent evidence, we can never prove that any particular structure orientation was motivated by a single overriding consideration: it might have arisen through the chance combination of other factors, many of which are inaccessible to us. Even sheer human perversity might have prevailed, as is known from some ethnographic cases (e.g. Burl 1981: 250-51). Thus we are of necessity forced to seek a large data sample and to hope that the causal factor being tested will lead to trends distinguishable at high significance levels from the effects of other causal factors.

In practice one tests any particular orientation hypothesis against the alternative that the orientations in question were randomly distributed. It is essential, then, to check (as far as is possible) that other causal factors would merely lead to random background noise amongst the data being tested. There may, of course, be many possible causal factors not now apparent to us, which we would never think of testing; however any reasonable possibilities must be examined. If this check is not made, demonstrably invalid conclusions can result. As an example, consider the group of earthen long barrows on Cranborne Chase examined by Ashbee (1970: 23-24). Three quarters of them face south-easterly directions, a fact which would undoubtedly show up as significant under a type (ii) hypothesis, and possibly under a type (i) hypothesis as well. However a type (iii) hypothesis explains the orientation trend quite simply: it is that the builders were compelled to lay out the mounds along the ridges upon which they were erected (ibid.: 24). This causal factor does not produce random azimuths because the sites all lie on predominantly NW-SE ridges.

The testing of any particular causal hypothesis must depend upon a number of directions being deemed "significant". Our first procedural problem, then, is to decide how great this number should be. If too few, then trends of possible importance may be missed. If too many, then so many fortuitous orientations will be considered significant that they will inevitably overwhelm any genuine trends in the data. In case (iii) significant directions under any particular hypothesis need to be identified for each site individually. For example, in order to test the hypothesis that structures are preferentially aligned upon distant mountains, we must first define what constitutes a distant mountain, and then identify all candidates at each site.

In cases (i) and (ii) we can surmount the problem of how many directions to consider significant, achieving considerable simplification in field procedure. This arises because any significant directions can be defined in terms of the universal concepts of declination and azimuth respectively. Azimuth is defined as the clockwise bearing from true north: thus due east corresponds to an azimuth of 90°, due south 180°, due west 270° and so on. Declination is related to the rising and setting paths of celestial objects: its value depends upon the altitude as well as the azimuth of the horizon, and also upon the latitude of the site. It is easily calculated from a standard formula (Thom 1967: ch. 3). The concept is explained in more detail in Appendix I. At each site, any range of horizon "indicated" by a structure orientation can be defined in terms of azimuth or declination. When data are accumulated from a number of sites, the observed distribution of indicated declinations or azimuths can be compared statistically with the expected distribution given random structure orientations. A significant accumulation of declinations around a particular value, say, can be related to a particular celestial object or objects.

In what follows we shall consider both declinations and azimuths, because the former are directly related to particular celestial objects, whereas the latter are more useful in considering whether ground-based hypotheses could in fact explain any observed trends just as well as astronomical ones. However in view of the considerable additional work involved, no type (iii) hypotheses have been considered methodically in any detail.

1.4   The selection of data

The result of a statistical test on any particular accumulation of data is a simple overall answer: a probability that random orientation can account for the distribution of declinations or azimuths observed. If this probability is very small, we must ask whether the non-randomness can be accounted for by any non-astronomical hypothesis; if not, we are forced to accept an astronomical explanation. In this case, and at this stage, we can return to the data in more detail and investigate possible variations in astronomical precision with site type or geographical location, in the hope of correlating evidence on variations in astronomical orientation with other facets of archaeological evidence about the sites.

Before there is any point in carrying out a statistical test, we need to accumulate enough data, and from a sufficiently promising group of sites, to give a reasonable hope of a definitive result. We also need to select the data in a demonstrably unbiased manner, otherwise the result of the statistical test will be questionable.

How, then, do we identify a sufficiently promising group of sites? In an ideal case we might be provided with a well-defined group of manifestly similar sites confined to a given area, but sufficient in number to provide a reasonable data base, and with a design such that, say, one direction at each site (e.g. that of the entrance of a chamber tomb) seems of special importance. Two intriguing groups have been investigated by Burl on the basis of existing survey data: the Recumbent Stone Circles (Burl 1980) and the Clava cairns (Burl 1981: Section 7.5) of north-eastern Scotland. Both groups exhibit clear orientation trends (Burl 1976: fig. 25) which demand explanation. Further investigation clearly being called for, resurveys of the RSCs were undertaken by the present author in 1981, using a rigorous hypothesis-testing approach. This sort of data set might well provide important astronomical insights, although Burl's particular conclusions about the RSCs (Burl 1980), formulated before the new survey work was undertaken, are now in question. Publication of the recent work is anticipated shortly (Ruggles 1984; Ruggles & Burl 1985).

Unfortunately few groups of sites exist that are as ideally suited to orientation analysis as the Recumbent Stone Circles; to restrict ourselves to these might be to pass over important evidence about prehistoric astronomy. There remain large numbers of British megalithic monuments, such as stone rings, alignments of standing stones and isolated menhirs, which do not fall into well-defined geographical groups. They may represent a variety of motivations and span a long period in terms of culture change. Many of them are of a design (e.g. three or four stones, not in line) which does not suggest any unique, overridingly important, site orientation. Some of them may be partially destroyed, further standing stones having vanished without trace. Finally some may not be genuinely prehistoric, such as single standing stones erected in more recent times as trackway markers, boundary stones or cattle rubbing posts. A rigorous statistical approach provides the only possible means of isolating any overall trends; but given such a diverse group of sites, are any such trends really likely?

Fortunately the answer is yes, owing to the early work of Thom (1955; 1967), which considers a selection of free-standing megalithic sites from throughout Britain and obtains positive results. Thus free-standing megalithic sites have been chosen as the data input for this volume. We have limited our investigation to the Highlands and Islands of western Scotland, as this is an area very rich in this type of site, and one which has been of particular interest to Thom. The project described here can thus be regarded as a reassessment of Thom's early work; it complements other recently-published reassessments concentrating upon his later work (Ruggles 1981; 1982b; 1983). A comparison of the results of this project and of Thom's early work forms part of the discussion in Chapter 13.

We now turn to the problem of selecting data in a demonstrably unbiased manner. In order that our selection decisions are open to full discussion and criticism, we need to present them in detail, and to reveal information about the data we have rejected as well as that which we have included for analysis. One of the author's chief criticisms of Thom's early work is that much vital information on selection decisions and rejected data is lacking in his publications. This is a matter for concern as there are many ways in which bias might unwittingly have entered into his data selection (Ruggles 1981: 155-158 & 172-174; 1982a: 92-96).

Where we are dealing with a variety of site configurations, very great care is needed in deciding at each site what constitutes an orientation worthy of consideration (and, indeed, what sets of structures constitute a "site" in the first place). We must at all costs avoid making a series of individual decisions in the field, decisions which might vary from site to site and might be influenced by our own predilections and prejudices regarding astronomy. For example, Patrick (1979) has pointed out that while great emphasis has been placed upon lunar alignments at the site at Kilmartin (Temple Wood), Argyll, the nearby and architecturally somewhat similar site at Barbreck is hardly ever mentioned by archaeoastronomers. He could find no lunar alignments at Barbreck. Our data selection process must ensure that we include (or reject) similar alignments from architecturally similar sites.

One way to achieve this end is to lay down, prior to any field work, an explicit code of practice governing all stages in the data selection process. This code of practice is then strictly adhered to in making selection decisions on site. It must be flexible enough to cope with each different type of site encountered: it must also be just sufficiently selective so as to provide enough data for the analysis, while at the same time not allowing any potentially significant evidence to be submerged and lost amidst a welter of data which is patently irrelevant to the hypothesis. As an example, consider the following selection criterion: "the orientations of all lines joining two standing stones at a site are to be included in the analysis (in both directions)". At a site consisting only of two menhirs this is a good criterion, as these are the most obvious ways in which an orientation at the site might be significant. However now consider a circle of 20 stones: the criterion would have us include from the site some 380 orientations, virtually all without a doubt of no particular significance. The code of practice adopted in this volume attempts to classify likely structures for deliberate astronomical orientation into an order of preference. We then only consider those structures with the highest classification that exist at any particular site. There are a number of associated problems, such as procedure at sites where we find fallen stones whose original position is unknown, or partially submerged stones which may or may not be fallen menhirs. In order to prevent our being left to make subjective judgements in individual cases, the code of practice must cater for these situations also. One possibility is to attach lower statistical weight to indications involving fallen or dubious stones, another to give them a lower classification on the classification scale, and another to give equal likelihood to the full range of declinations or azimuths that might, conceivably, originally have been intended. A combination of the second and third options is favoured in this volume.

In practice, prior to field work we lack knowledge of the full range of possible site designs, and the code of practice may need to be modified when unanticipated configurations are encountered. We can ensure that additions and amendments to the code of practice are not influenced by predilections about individual sites by leaving the reduction of the survey data until the entire programme of field work has been completed. This procedure has been strictly adhered to in the project described here.

A preliminary set of selection criteria were developed in 1975 and tested at the group of sites around Callanish, Lewis (Cooke et al. 1977). They have since been modified, in order to take account both of new types of site which have been encountered, and of criticisms by other authors (e.g. Heggie 1981a: S19; 1981b: 141). Surveys were completed in 1981: reduction work proceeded during 1981-82, following earlier developmental work on computer software and reduction work on other projects. Profile diagrams and details of indicated declinations and azimuths only became available during 1983. Where survey data were not available but were required by the final selection criteria, data calculated from Ordnance Survey maps have been used instead. Variations in the reliability of the data (reliable and less reliable surveys, and calculated data) are clearly identified in what follows, and the variations are taken into account in the subsequent analysis.

Chapters 2 and 3 present detailed explanations of selection procedures, and contain several examples similar to that above. At each stage a code of practice is laid down consisting of arbitrary but fixed rules, which are then rigidly adhered to in the subsequent data selection. The merits and inadequacies of particular rules might of course be argued at great length, but to do so might be to miss the entire point of the statistical exercise. Minor adjustments are unlikely to alter in any substantial way the overall results of the statistical tests. More important are questions of the whole methodological approach, major strategies in the data selection, the statistical analysis itself and the interpretation of the results. Hopefully these questions are presented clearly enough in this volume to permit adequate criticism and discussion.

2 THE SELECTION OF SITES FOR CONSIDERATION

2.1 The initial site list

In preparing a list of sites for initial consideration, three problems immediately arise:

(I) Which types of feature do we include?
(II) What combinations of features comprise a site?
(III) Which geographical areas do we consider and how do we extract data on sites within these areas?

We respond as follows.

(I). We consider only monuments consisting of free-standing megaliths, that is stone rings, settings, alignments and single standing stones, as opposed to those standing stones erected as part of more complex architectural structures, such as orthostats and peristaliths of chamber tombs. The decision to concentrate on free-standing sites is elaborated in Section 1.4.

(II). In general we define a SITE as any collection of megalithic rings, standing or fallen menhirs and sites of menhirs, such that each of these features is within 300m of at least one of the others. If, however,

(i) two features are separated by a sea channel, or
(ii) natural rises in intervening ground level prevent them being intervisible,

then the features are counted as separate sites.

It might be pointed out here that although we may be on safe statistical ground, our criteria are obviously naive in terms of any realistic social models. After all, we can not expect different sites to cover similar extents on the ground: furthermore in the absence of excavation we are totally ignorant of the actual relative chronology of adjacent structures, their interconnection, their phases of construction and use, and so on. Here, as elsewhere in this and the following chapter, we would merely draw attention to the aims and limitations of the statistical method as set out in Chapter 1, and particularly in Section 1.2.

(III). The Highlands and Islands of western Scotland have been chosen as the general region for study, for reasons described in Section 1.4 above. Within this region, geographical boundaries such as islands tend to provide a natural and convenient means of subdividing sites by area. With a few exceptions, notably Skye and Colonsay, all the Hebridean Islands have been considered together with mainland Argyll, from North Argyll down to Kintyre. The Isles of Bute and Arran have not been included.

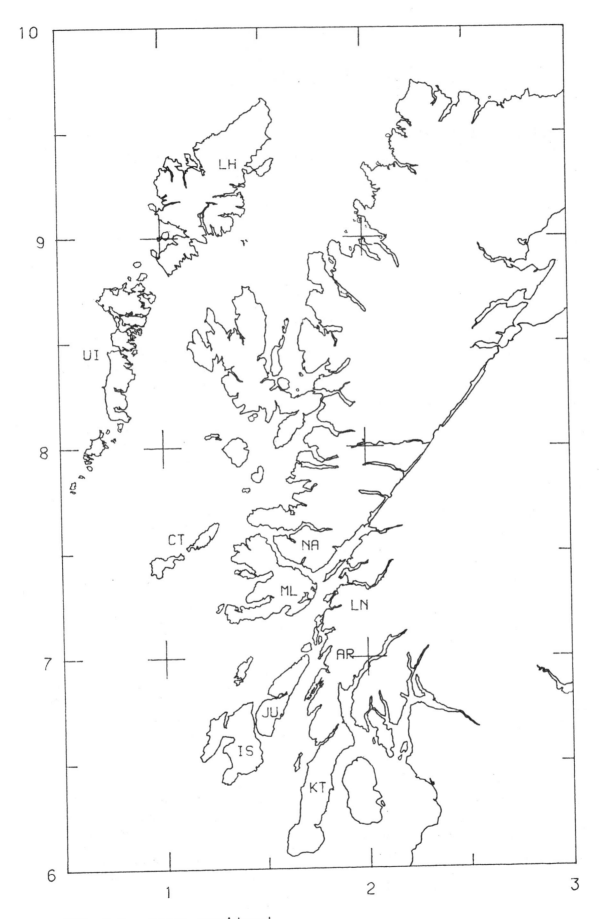

FIG. 2.1. Areas considered.

The region chosen for study has been subdivided into the following areas (Fig. 2.1): Lewis and Harris, including associated smaller islands such as Great Bernera and Ensay (LH); North and South Uist, Benbecula, Barra, etc. (UI); North Argyll, i.e. Ardnamurchan, Sunart and Morvern (NA); Coll and Tiree (CT); Mull (ML); Lorn, including Appin, Benderloch and Lismore (LN); Mid-Argyll, including northern Knapdale (AR); Jura (JU); Islay (IS); and Kintyre, including southern Knapdale (KT).

Within the areas chosen, the following five major sources have been consulted as reference lists of reported megalithic sites:

(1) A. Thom. Thom has been kind enough to let the author have a copy of his original, unpublished, full site list (FSL), the relevant parts of which appear in this book for the first time. It includes 207 sites in the regions we have considered. His fullest published site list (1967: Table 12.1) contains only some 86 of these sites.

(2) Ordnance Survey Archaeological Record cards, Southampton and Edinburgh (OSAR). (N.B. These records have now been transferred respectively to Fortress House, London and RCAHMS, Edinburgh.)

(3) Royal Commission on the Ancient and Historical Monuments of Scotland (RCAHMS) inventories. These are available for all areas considered, with the exception of mid-Argyll; in this case the list published by Campbell and Sandeman (1961) was used instead. Coverage of the relevant areas by the RCAHMS has been carried out within the last twenty years, with the notable exception of the outer Hebrides, where site visits and surveys date back to around 1920.

(4) H. A. W. Burl. Burl's "The Stone Circles of the British Isles" (Burl 1976) lists in Appendix 1 some 33 reported stone circles and rings in the regions considered.

(5) "Discovery and Excavation in Scotland". This annual publication contains reports of new discoveries. Issues before 1970 were disregarded, since any sites appearing in these earlier issues have now been included in the Ordnance Survey lists. The latest issue examined was that of 1980.

An initial site list, comprising 322 reported sites, has been compiled from the various reference lists available. It is given in full in Table 2.1. All reports of free-standing megalithic sites by each of the five sources are included. Since Thom's full site list (FSL) has not been published elsewhere, we have also included all of Thom's sites within the relevant areas (apart from a few unavoidable exceptions - see Section 2.2), even though some are identified by Thom himself as tumuli or natural features rather than free-standing megaliths. These data provide invaluable information on Thom's own selection decisions which is not readily available elsewhere. Thus, for example, cairns and chamber tombs have been included where they are listed by Thom, whether or not he has recognised them as such, but otherwise omitted wherever they are clearly and consistently identified by the other sources. Where opinions differ, a valuable additional source is the work on Scottish chamber tombs by Henshall (1972), and this source is also referenced in Table 2.1.

Each source has its own convention for ordering and classifying sites, and its own reference system. Two or more names are frequently used for the same site, and interpretations differ, sometimes widely. For these reasons we have introduced an independent reference numbering system of our own, with sites ordered geographically rather than alphabetically, and we have chosen one site name which is used throughout this volume. Cross-references to the major sources and principal alternative site names are given in Table 2.1, which thus serves as a full reference list of reported megalithic sites in the areas considered. Grid references are taken from the most reliable source available, usually the Ordnance Survey, but although they are mostly quoted to 10m they may not always be dependable to this accuracy.

There follow some examples of where our criteria for defining a site lead in practice. Two stone rings at Hough, Tiree (CT7) some 150m apart are counted as one site, whereas those at Cnoc Fillibhir Bheag and Cnoc Ceann a'Gharaidh in Lewis (LH18 & LH19), which are some 320m apart, are counted as separate. The remains of two stone alignments near Dunamuck (AR29 & AR30), although only some 150m apart, are counted as separate because they are not intervisible. While the Temple Wood stone circle in Argyll and a group of menhirs a little under 300m away (AR13) are counted as a single site, the semi-circular setting at Bernera Bridge, Great Bernera (LH8) and the fallen menhir some 150m away at Aird a'Chaolais, Lewis (LH9), now moved from its original position, are counted as different sites because they are separated by the Bernera Straits. The pair of menhirs 200m apart at Knockrome, Jura (JU4) are counted as a single site, and a third stone 700m away at Ardfernal (JU3) as a separate site, even though the three form a long alignment. At Strontoiller in Lorn (LN17), a stone ring is hidden from a standing stone (and nearby ring cairn) some 200m away by intervening rocky ground. From the centre of the stone ring the menhir is also entirely hidden, but from eye level (1.7m above present ground level) at the far side of the ring, its tip is visible. In this borderline case the structures have been counted as a single site.

2.2   Thom sites not listed

A small number of sites listed in Thom's full site list (FSL) have not been included in Table 2.1. They represent

(i) sites for which no accurate grid reference (or latitude and longitude) has been given by Thom;
(ii) sites we have included as part of another site; and
(iii) accidental duplications by Thom.

They are as follows:

H5/7 (S Uist). Described by Thom as a large natural rock. No name, position or further details given.

A1/11 - Connel, Lorn. This is apparently an accidental duplication of A1/9 (LN12).

A2/4 - Barbreck, Argyll. Described by Thom as "suspected stones", this appears to refer to the alignment of two stones at Barbreck

(ctd. on page 44

TABLE 2.1. Full reference list of reported sites of free-standing
megaliths in the areas considered.

<u>Column headings</u>

1   All-figure National Grid reference
2   Site reference number*
3   Site name and location
4   Site reference used by Thom
5   Ordnance Survey Archaeological Records card number
6   Royal Commission Inventory entry number
7   Site reference number used by Burl (1976: Appendix 1)
8   Site reference number used by Henshall (1972)
9   Year and page number in 'Discovery and Excavation in Scotland'
         between 1970 and 1980
10   Latest year of visit by the author
11   Reason for exclusion of site from further consideration
12   Alternative name(s) for site

<u>Key to column 6 (Royal Commission Inventory letter codes)</u>

A**   Campbell and Sandeman (1961)
H   RCAHMS (1928)
I   RCAHMS (1984)
K   RCAHMS (1971)
L   RCAHMS (1975)
M   RCAHMS (1980)
O   RCAHMS (1946a)
Z   RCAHMS (1946b)
−   Not in the appropriate list

<u>Key to column 11 (Sites excluded from further consideration)</u>

D   Highly dubious contender for a prehistoric site (see Section
         2.3.1)
F   Site considered not to have been constructed as free-standing
         menhirs (see Section 2.3.2)
G   Documented site which has been moved, removed, re-erected or
         destroyed (see Section 2.4.1)
N   Documented site which was not located (see Section 2.4.2)
T   Site in a remote location which could not be visited in the time
         available (see Section 2.5)
U   Site unknown to us at the time of our visit(s) (see Section 2.6)
X   Site already excavated in order to test an astronomical
         hypothesis (see Section 2.7)

- - - - -

* Note that in two earlier publications (Ruggles 1981; 1982b), where
    our reference numbers were cited in advance of this public-
    ation, Unival was given erroneously as UI30 rather than UI28,
    and Ballinaby as IS11 rather than IS15.
** Referenced in place of the RCAHMS Inventory, as none yet exists for
    this area

Table 2.1

NGR	Site	Name and location		Thom	OS Card
15349 96417	LH1	Port of Ness	,Lewis;	–	NB56SW12
13970 95456	LH2	Shader N	,Lewis;	H1/9	NB35SE03
1401 9543	LH3	Shader E	,Lewis;	H1/11	–
13962 95407	LH4	Shader S	,Lewis;	H1/10	NB35SE02
13755 95377	LH5	Ballantrushal	,Lewis;	H1/12	NB35SE01
12041 94295	LH6	Carloway	,Lewis;	H1/16	NB24SW01
11775 93459	LH7	Kirkibost	,Gt Bernera;	–	
11642 93424	LH8	Bernera Bridge	,Gt Bernera;	H1/8	NB13SE02
1165 9341	LH9	Aird a'Chaolais	,Lewis;	H1/8a	–
12223 93568	LH10	Beinn Bheag	,Lewis;	–	–
12155 93496	LH11	Stonefield	,Lewis;	–	NB23SW05
1215 9341	LH12	Sgeir nan Each	,Lewis;	–	–
12137 93381	LH13	Cliacabhaidh	,Lewis;	–	–
12297 93362	LH14	Druim nan Eun	,Lewis;	–	NB23SW06
12182 93312	LH15	Buaile Chruaidh	,Lewis;	–	–
12130 93300	LH16	Callanish	,Lewis;	H1/1	NB23SW01
12270 93296	LH17	Cnoc Sgeir na h-Uidhe	,Lewis;	–	–
12281 93291	LH17		;	–	–
12250 93269	LH18	Cnoc Fillibhir Bheag	,Lewis;	H1/3	NB23SW02
12220 93260	LH19	Cnoc Ceann a'Gharaidh	,Lewis;	H1/2	NB23SW03
12367 93199	LH20	Garynahine	,Lewis;	–	–
12297 93042	LH21	Ceann Hulavig	,Lewis;	H1/4	NB23SW04
12465 93034	LH22	Cul a' Chleit	,Lewis;	H1/6	NB23SW07
1232 9302	LH23	Cnoc Dubh	,Lewis;	H1/7	–
12342 92989	LH24	Airigh nam Bidearan	,Lewis;	H1/5	NB22NW01
12338 92976	LH25	Druim nam Bidearan	,Lewis;	–	–
1244 9292	LH26	Loch Crogach	,Lewis;	–	–
14132 93565	LH27	Newmarket	,Lewis;	–	NB43NW04
14111 93519	LH28	Priests Glen	,Lewis;	–	NB43NW01
15281 93340	LH29	Dursainean NE	,Lewis;	H1/15	NB53SW07
15238 93307	LH30	Dursainean SW	,Lewis;	H1/13	NB53SW02
15165 93174	LH31	Lower Bayble	,Lewis;	H1/14	NB53SW05
1031 9198	LH32	Aird Sleitenish	,Lewis;	–	NB01NW02
12781 91662	LH33	Sideval	,Lewis;	–	NB21NE01
0989 9119	LH34	Husinish	,Harris;	H2/4	–
10128 90077	LH35	Loch na h-Uidhe	,Harris;	H2/1	NB00SW04
10408 89727	LH36	Horgabost	,Harris;	H2/2	NG09NW04
10202 89392	LH37	Scarista	,Harris;	H2/3	NG09SW02
09803 88667	LH38	Ensay	(Harris);	H2/5	NF98NE03
01506 90499	UI1	Boreray	(St Kilda);	–	NA10SE02
00886 89943	UI2	Gleann Mor	,St Kilda;	–	NF09NE10
09242 88288	UI3	Bhruist	,Berneray;	–	NF98SW06
09230 88187	UI4	Bays Loch	,Berneray;	–	NF98SW02
09101 88155	UI5	Scalabriag	,Berneray;	–	NF98SW05
09122 88068	UI6	Borve	,Berneray;	H3/1	NF98SW07

RCAHMS	Burl	Henshall	D&E	Visit	Ex	Alternative name
H(19)	–	–	–	;79:	–:	Clach Stein
H(18)	–	–	–	;79:	D:	Clach Stei Lin
–	–	–	–	;81:	D:	Tom Naobhe
H(17)	–	LWS6a	–	;79:	D:	Stein-a-Cleit
H(16)	–	–	–	;81:	–:	Clach an Trushal
H(87)	–	–	–	;81:	–:	Clach an Tursa
–	–	–	D(76:59)	;81:	–:	Callanish XV
H(86)	–	–	D(76:57)	;81:	–:	Callanish VIII
–	–	–	D(76:58)	;81:	G:	Callanish VIIIa
–	–	–	D(76:58)	;81:	–:	Callanish XI
H(88)	–	–	–	;81:	G:	Callanish XII
–	–	–	D(76:58)	;81:	D:	Callanish XIII
–	–	–	D(76:59)	;81:	D:	Callanish XVI
H(92)	Lew6	–	D(76:58)	;80:	F:	Callanish X
–	–	–	D(77:32)	;80:	D:	Callanish XIX
H(89)	Lew3	LWS3	D(77:32)	;81:	–:	Callanish I
–	–	–	D(76:59)	;80:	D:	Callanish XIV
–	–	–	D(76:59)	;80:	D:	Callanish XIV
H(91)	Lew4	–	D(76:57)	;80:	–:	Callanish III
H(90)	Lew8	–	D(76:57)	;80:	–:	Callanish II
–	–	–	D(76:59)	;80:	G:	Callanish XVII
H(93)	Lew7	–	D(76:57)	;80:	–:	Callanish IV
H(95)	Lew5	–	D(76:57)	;75:	–:	Callanish VI
–	–	–	D(73:48)	;81:	D:	Callanish VII
H(94)	Lew2	–	–	;81:	–:	Callanish V
–	–	–	D(76:58)	;81:	D:	Callanish IX
–	–	–	D(76:59)	;81:	D:	Callanish XVIII
–	–	–	–	;81:	–:	
H(56)	Lew10	–	–	;81:	–:	
–	–	–	–	;81:	–:	Allt na Muilne
H(54)	–	LWS6	–	;79:	F:	Garrabost
H(57)	–	–	–	;79:	–:	Clach Stein
–	Lew1	–	D(73:48)	;--:	T:	
–	Lew9	–	–	;79:	–:	Loch Seaforth
–	–	–	–	;--:	N:	
H(116)	–	–	–	;--:	D:	Clach an Teampuill
H(135)	–	–	–	;79:	–:	Clach Mhic Leoid
H(136)	Har1	–	–	;79:	–:	Borvemore
H(137)	–	–	–	;--:	T:	
–	StK1	–	–	;--:	T:	
–	–	–	–	;--:	T:	
H(132)	Ber1	–	–	;79:	D:	
H(134)	–	HRS2	–	;79:	F:	Cnoc na Greana
H(127)	–	–	–	;81:	F:	
H(133)	–	–	–	;81:	–:	Cladh Maolrithe

Table 2.1 (continued)

NGR		Site	Name and location		Thom	OS Card
085	881	UI7	Boreray	(N Uist);	H3/10	-
08242	87843	UI8	Udal	,N Uist;	-	NF87NW01
08937	87818	UI9	Newtonferry	,N Uist;	H3/22	NF87NE08
09044	87795	UI10	Beinn a'Chaolais	,N Uist;	-	NF97NW04
07907	87650	UI11	Vallay	(N Uist);	-	NF77NE19
08785	87605	UI12	Clachan Sands	,N Uist;	H3/2	NF87NE14
08050	87495	UI13	Middlequarter	,N Uist;	-	NF87SW08
088	873	UI14	Loch an Duin	,N Uist;	-	NF87SE17
08645	87292	UI15	Maari	,N Uist;	-	NF87SE23
08598	87221	UI16	Bogach Maari	,N Uist;	-	NF87SE09
08567	87207	UI17	Barpa nam Feannag	,N Uist;	H3/6	NF87SE13
085	872	UI18	Loch nan Geireann	,N Uist;	-	NF87SE24
08875	87176	UI19	Blashaval	,N Uist;	H3/8	NF87NE14
0728	8738	UI20	Balelone	,N Uist;	-	-
073	873	UI21	Balmartin	,N Uist;	-	NF77SW05
07501	87118	UI22	South Clettraval	,N Uist;	H3/3	NF77SE13
07516	87101	UI22		;	H3/4	NF77SE14
07700	87029	UI23	Toroghas	,N Uist;	H3/5	NF77SE12
08324	86952	UI24	Marrogh	,N Uist;	H3/13	NF86NW02
07956	86938	UI25	Marrival	,N Uist;	-	NF76NE02
07863	86909	UI26	Beinn a'Charra	,N Uist;	H3/9	NF76NE01
08366	86878	UI27	Loch Scadavay	,N Uist;	H3/7	NF86NW08
08003	86685	UI28	Unival	,N Uist;	H3/11	NF86NW04
08031	86651	UI29	L na Buaile Iochdrach	,N Uist;	-	NF86NW17
0740	8670	UI30	Craig Hasten	,N Uist;	H3/21	-
07700	86619	UI31	Claddach Kyles	,N Uist;	H3/12	NF76NE02
08381	86571	UI32	Barpa Langass	,N Uist;	H3/16	NF86NW06
08427	86502	UI33	Ben Langass	,N Uist;	H3/17	NF86NW07
08152	86451	UI34	Cringraval E	,N Uist;	H3/14	NF86SW21
08116	86447	UI35	Cringraval W	,N Uist;	-	-
08046	86431	UI36	Claddach Illeray	,N Uist;	H3/15	NF86NW34
08289	86302	UI37	Loch a'Phobuill	,N Uist;	H3/18	NF86SW28
08384	86290	UI38	Loch Glen na Feannag	,N Uist;	H3/19	NF86SW11
08417	86247	UI39	Oban nam Fiadh	,N Uist;	H3/20	NF86SW12
08321	86021	UI40	Carinish	,N Uist;	-	NF86SW01
079	856	UI41	Aerodrome	,Benbecula;	H4/3	-
08250	85614	UI42	Gramisdale N	,Benbecula;	H4/1	NF85NW02
08247	85522	UI43	Gramisdale S	,Benbecula;	H4/2	NF85NW03
08445	85381	UI44	Hacklett	,Benbecula;	H4/6	NF85SW03
07664	85379	UI45	Nunton	,Benbecula;	H4/7	NF75SE04
08142	85315	UI46	Stiaraval	,Benbecula;	H4/4	-
08170	85247	UI47	Loch Ba Una	,Benbecula;	H4/5	NF85SW05
07340	83366	UI48	Stoneybridge	,S Uist;	H5/2	NF73SW03
07703	83211	UI49	Beinn a'Charra	,S Uist;	H5/1	NF73SE01
07273	82860	UI50	Ru Ardvule	,S Uist;	H5/3	NF72NW03

RCAHMS	Burl	Henshall	D&E	Visit	Ex	Alternative name
H(259)	-	-	-	;--:	T:	
-	-	-	-	;81:	N:	
H(243)	-	-	-	;81:	-:	Crois Mhic Jamain
H(241)	NUi1	-	-	;81:	D:	
H(258)	-	-	-	;81:	F:	
H(170)	-	-	-	;81:	D:	Clach an't Sagairt
H(264)	-	-	-	;81:	F:	Clach na Croise
-	-	-	-	;--:	N:	
-	-	-	-	;81:	-:	
-	-	-	-	;81:	D:	
H(238)	-	UST7	-	;81:	F:	
-	-	-	-	;--:	N:	
H(246)	-	-	-	;81:	-:	Na Fir Bhreige
H(257)	-	-	-	;79:	G:	
-	-	-	-	;--:	N:	
H(256)	-	-	-	;77:	-:	
H(234)	-	UST28	-	;77:	-:	Tigh Cloiche (W)
H(255)	-	-	-	;81:	-:	Fir Bhreige
H(242)	-	-	-	;79:	-:	Tigh Cloiche (E)
H(232)	-	UST20	-	;81:	F:	Guala na h-Imrich
H(253)	-	-	-	;81:	-:	
H(226)	-	UST2	-	;--:	F:	Airigh nam Seilicheag
H(228)	-	UST34	-	;79:	-:	Leacach an Tigh Cloiche
H(254)	-	-	-	;79:	-:	
-	-	-	-	;--:	D:	
H(252)	-	-	-	;79:	-:	Clach Mhor a Che
H(224)	-	UST6	-	;81:	F:	
H(250)	NUi5	-	-	;81:	-:	Sornach Coir Fhinn
H(229)	-	UST34c	-	;81:	F:	
H(251)	NUi3	-	-	;81:	-:	
-	-	-	-	;81:	D:	
H(249)	NUi4	-	-	;81:	-:	Sornach a'Phobuill
H(219)	-	UST23	-	;81:	F:	
H(218)	-	UST25	-	;81:	F:	
H(248)	NUi2	-	-	;81:	-:	
-	-	-	-	;--:	G:	
H(353)	Ben1	-	-	;77:	F:	North Ford
H(352)	Ben2	UST31	-	;77:	F:	Suidheachadh Sealg
H(355)	-	-	-	;--:	-:	
H(340)	-	-	-	;--:	D:	Cladh Mhuire
-	-	-	-	;81:	-:	Rueval
H(350)	-	UST1	-	;--:	F:	Airidh na h-Aon Cloiche
H(408)	-	UST34b	-	;81:	-:	Crois Chnoca Breaca
H(407)	-	-	-	;81:	-:	An Carra
H(406)	-	-	D(77:18)	;81:	-:	Kildonan

Table 2.1 (continued)

NGR	Site	Name and location		Thom	OS Card
0736 8277	UI51	Loch Kildonan	,S Uist;	H5/6	-
07469 82689	UI52	Mingary	,S Uist;	H5/4	NF72NW05
08117 82248	UI53	Loch nan Arm	,S Uist;	H5/9	NF82SW02
07963 81998	UI54	Lochboisdale	,S Uist;	H5/5	NF71NE01
07538 81495	UI55	Layaval	,S Uist;	-	NF71SE10
07459 81439	UI56	Pollachar	,S Uist;	H5/8	NF71SW01
06527 80144	UI57	Borve	,Barra;	H6/1	NF60SE10
0684 8008	UI58	Beul a'Bhealaich	,Barra;	H6/2	-
06890 79903	UI59	Brevig	,Barra;	H6/3	NL69NE01
06277 79389	UI60	Ben Rulibreck	,Vatersay;	H6/4	NL69SW02
05626 78021	UI61	Leac a'Langich	,Berneray;	H6/5	NL58SE04
15268 76950	NA1	Branault	,Ardnamurchan;	-	NM56NW02
14767 76396	NA2	Kilchoan	,Ardnamurchan;	M5/1	NM46SE01
15605 76184	NA3	Camas nan Geall	,Ardnamurchan;	-	NM56SE02
18154 76136	NA4	Strontian	,Sunart;	-	NM86NW01
15868 74969	NA5	Killundine	,Morvern;	M6/1	NM54NE02
162 748	NA6	Sallochan Burn	,Morvern;	-	NM64NW04
16591 74926	NA7	Beinn Bhan	,Morvern;	-	NM64NE08
16922 74740	NA8	Kinlochaline	,Morvern;	M6/2	NM64NE05
11860 75674	CT1	Acha	,Coll;	-	NM15NE17
11665 75594	CT2	Totronald	,Coll;	M3/1	NM15NE15
11519 75329	CT3	Breachacha	,Coll;	-	NM15SE15
1122 7532	CT4	Caolas	,Coll;	-	NM15SW16
10776 74833	CT5	Caoles	,Tiree;	M4/1	NM04NE14
10240 74565	CT6	Gott	,Tiree;	-	NM04NW21
10227 74551	CT6		;	-	NM04NW20
09588 74518	CT7	Hough	,Tiree;	-	NL94NE20
09580 74505	CT7		;	-	NL94NE23
09468 74300	CT8	Barrapoll	,Tiree;	M4/3	NL94SW11
09731 74258	CT9	Balinoe	,Tiree;	M4/2	NL94SE04
14347 75715	ML1	Glengorm	,Mull;	M1/7	NM45NW02
14134 75524	ML2	Quinish	,Mull;	M1/3	NM45NW05
1492 7550	ML3	Newdale	,Mull;	-	NM45NE02
14996 75413	ML4	Balliscate	,Mull;	M1/8	NM45SE01
1348 7543	ML5	Caliach Point	,Mull;	M1/1	NM35SW01
13626 75331	ML6	Lag	,Mull;	-	NM35SE23
13773 75348	ML7	Cillchriosd	,Mull;	M1/2	NM35SE05
13849 75231	ML8	Calgary	,Mull;	-	NM35SE22
14355 75311	ML9	Maol Mor	,Mull;	M1/4	NM45SW05
14390 75202	ML10	Dervaig N	,Mull;	M1/5	NM45SW04
14385 75163	ML11	Dervaig S	,Mull;	M1/6	NM45SW07
15422 74915	ML12	Ardnacross	,Mull;	M1/9	NM54NW03
15040 74632	ML13	Tenga	,Mull;	M1/10	NM54NW04
13917 74561	ML14	Tostarie	,Mull;	M1/11	NM34NE03
15401 74193	ML15	Killichronan	,Mull;	M2/15	NM54SW01

RCAHMS	Burl	Henshall	D&E	Visit	Ex	Alternative name
-	-	-	-	;81:	N:	
H(415)	-	-	-	;--:	D:	Cladh Ard an Dugain
H(399)	-	-	-	;--:	G:	Carragh Broin
H(411)	-	-	-	;--:	D:	
-	-	UST21	-	;81:	D:	
H(401)	-	-	-	;81:	G:	
H(461)	-	-	-	;81:	-:	
-	-	-	-	;81:	-:	
H(460)	-	-	-	;79:	-:	
H(462)	-	-	-	;81:	-:	Cuithe Heillanish
-	-	-	-	;--:	T:	
M(99)	-	-	-	;81:	-:	Cladh Chatain
-	-	ARG39	-	;81:	F:	Greadal Fhinn
M(263)	-	-	-	;81:	-:	Cladh Chiarain
M(115)	-	-	-	;81:	G:	Clach a'Bhranguis
M(43)	-	-	-	;--:	F:	
-	-	-	-	;--:	N:	
M(93)	-	-	-	;81:	-:	
M(45)	-	-	-	;--:	F:	
M(50)	-	-	-	;79:	-:	Loch nan Cinneachan
M(120)	-	-	-	;79:	-:	
M(94)	-	-	-	;79:	-:	
M(95)	-	-	-	;79:	-:	
M(96)	-	-	-	;79:	-:	
-	Tir2	-	-	;--:	D:	Loch a Chapuil
-	Tir1	-	-	;--:	D:	Loch a'Bhleoghan
M(107)	Tir3a	-	-	;79:	-:	Moss A
M(107)	Tir3b	-	-	;79:	-:	Moss B
M(91)	-	-	-	;79:	-:	
M(89)	-	-	-	;79:	-:	Balemartin
M(105)	-	-	-	;76:	-:	
M(111)	-	-	-	;79:	-:	Mingary
-	-	-	-	;--:	D:	Sgriob-Ruadh
M(90)	Mul1	-	-	;76:	-:	Tobermory
-	-	-	-	;--:	D:	
M(109)	-	-	-	;79:	-:	Mornish
M(98)	-	-	-	;79:	-:	
M(104)	-	-	-	;79:	-:	Frachadil
M(101)	Mul4	-	-	;76:	-:	Dervaig A
M(101)	Mul2	-	-	;76:	-:	Dervaig B
M(101)	-	-	-	;79:	-:	Dervaig C
M(10)	-	-	-	;76:	-:	
M(117)	Mul5	-	-	;76:	-:	Loch Frisa
M(119)	-	-	-	;76:	-:	
M(108)	-	-	-	;76:	-:	Torr nam Fiann

Table 2.1 (continued)

NGR	Site	Name and location	Thom	OS Card
15437 73977	ML16	Gruline	,Mull; M2/16	NM53NW03
15456 73960	ML16		; M2/1	NM53NW01
14256 73928	ML17	Ormaig	,Ulva; –	NM43NW03
14028 73901	ML18	Cragaig	,Ulva; –	NM43NW09
14969 73574	ML19	Dishig	,Mull; –	NM43NE03
14387 73549	ML20	Inch Kenneth	(Mull); M2/12	NM43NW02
16999 73827	ML21	Scallastle	,Mull; –	NM63NE02
17265 73525	ML22	Torosay	,Mull; M2/3	NM73NWm1
17260 73425	ML23	Duart	,Mull; M2/2	NM73SW02
17275 73425	ML23		; M2/2	NM73SW04
17368 72932	ML24	Port Donain	,Mull; –	NM72NW04
15469 73004	ML25	Uluvalt I	,Mull; –	NM53SW02
15463 73002	ML25		; –	NM53SW02
15468 72996	ML25		; –	NM52NW03
1546 7293	ML26	Uluvalt II	,Mull; –	NM52NW04
15434 72820	ML27	Rossal	,Mull; –	NM52NW06
16163 72543	ML28	Lochbuie	,Mull; M2/14	NM62NW03
16141 72524	ML28		; M2/14	NM62NW04
16178 72512	ML28		; M2/14	NM62NW01
16175 72507	ML28		; M2/14	NM62NW02
16169 72506	ML28		; M2/14	NM62NW05
14199 71890	ML29	Scoor	,Mull; M2/11	NM41NW03
13973 72239	ML30	Taoslin	,Mull; M2/8	NM32SE01
13916 71961	ML31	Uisken	,Mull; M2/10	NM31NE02
13890 72171	ML32	Assapol Cottage	,Mull; –	NM32SE04
13784 71888	ML33	Ardalanish	,Mull; M2/9	NM31NE01
13706 72185	ML34	Suie	,Mull; M2/7	NM32SE07
13531 72240	ML35	Tirghoil	,Mull; M2/6	NM32SE06
134 723	ML36	Ardfenaig	,Mull; –	NM32SW10
13251 72216	ML37	Poit na h-I	,Mull; M2/5	NM32SW02
131 723	ML38	Aridghlas	,Mull; –	NM32SW11
13133 72331	ML39	Achaban House	,Mull; M2/4	NM32SW01
130 723	ML40	Catchean	,Mull; –	–
12720 72372	ML41	Cnoc an t-Sidhein	,Iona; M2/13	NM22SE30
19866 75455	LN1	Acharra	,Appin; M7/1	NM95SE03
19583 74503	LN2	Inverfolla	,Appin; M7/2	NM94NE01
19636 74214	LN3	Barcaldine	,Benderloch; M8/2	NM94SE03
1956 7416	LN4	Home Farm	,Benderloch; M8/3	NM94SE01
19444 74075	LN5	Achacha	,Benderloch; M8/1	NM94SW09
19105 74030	LN6	Barcaldine Castle	,Benderloch; –	NM94SW10
19117 74027	LN6		; –	NM94SW03
19062 73865	LN7	Benderloch N	,Benderloch; –	NM93NW03
1906 7386	LN7		; –	NM93NW10
19033 73802	LN8	Benderloch S	,Benderloch; M8/4	NM93NW09
1903 7379	LN8		; M8/4	NM93NW28

RCAHMS	Burl	Henshall	D&E	Visit	Ex	Alternative name
M(106)	-	-	-	;76:	-:	
M(106)	-	-	-	;76:	-:	
M(122)	-	-	-	;79:	-:	
M(100)	-	-	-	;79:	-:	
M(102)	-	-	-	;76:	-:	
-	-	-	-	;--:	G:	
M(113)	-	MUL1c	-	;76:	-:	
-	-	-	-	;--:	N:	Clach Nighean a Mhoraire
M(92)	-	-	-	;76:	-:	Barr Leathan
M(92)	-	-	-	;76:	-:	Barr Leathan
M(52)	-	-	-	;--:	-:	
M(121)	-	MUL1a	-	;79:	-:	
M(121)	-	-	-	;79:	-:	
M(121)	-	-	-	;79:	-:	
-	-	-	-	;--:	G:	
M(54)	-	-	-	;76:	-:	Breac Achadh
M(110)	-	-	-	;76:	-:	
M(49)	-	-	-	;76:	-:	
M(110)	Mul3	-	-	;76:	-:	
M(110)	-	-	-	;76:	-:	
M(110)	-	-	-	;76:	-:	
M(114)	-	-	-	;76:	G:	
M(116)	-	-	-	;79:	-:	Bunessan
M(103)	-	-	-	;76:	-:	Druim Fan/ Am Fan
-	-	-	-	;--:	G:	
M(88)	-	-	-	;76:	-:	
M(61)	-	MUL1b	-	;76:	-:	Dail na Carraigh
M(118)	-	-	-	;79:	-:	Ross of Mull
-	-	-	-	;--:	N:	
M(112)	-	-	-	;76:	-:	Torr Mor
-	-	-	-	;--:	N:	
M(87)	-	-	-	;76:	-:	
M(97)	-	-	-	;--:	G:	
-	-	-	-	;--:	N:	Cnoc nam Aingeal
L(110)	-	-	-	;81:	-:	
L(118)	-	-	-	;81:	-:	
L(111)	-	-	-	;81:	-:	
-	-	-	-	;--:	D:	
L(10)	-	-	-	;81:	-:	
L(32)	-	-	-	;81:	G:	
L(32)	-	-	-	;81:	G:	
L(113)	-	-	-	;81:	-:	
-	-	-	-	;--:	-:	
L(112)	-	-	-	;81:	-:	
-	-	-	-	;--:	-:	

Table 2.1 (continued)

NGR		Site	Name and location	Thom	OS Card
18609	74342	LN9	Clachan	,Lismore; M9/1	NM84SE17
1779	7351	LN10	Eilean Musdile	(Lismore); —	NM73NE04
19169	73409	LN11	Connel	,Lorn; A1/1	NM93SW05
18978	73382	LN12	Dunstaffnage House	,Lorn; A1/9	NM83SE22
20051	73109	LN13	Airdsbay House	,Lorn; A1/12	NN03SW12
20120	73115	LN14	Taynuilt	,Lorn; —	NN03SW14
19155	73124	LN15	Black Lochs	,Lorn; —	NM93SW04
18524	73097	LN16	Oban Esplanade	,Lorn; A1/3	NM83SE17
19067	72914	LN17	Strontoiller	,Lorn; A1/2	NM92NW08
19076	72897	LN17		; A1/2	NM92NW02
19078	72896	LN17		; A1/2	NM92NW07
19250	72854	LN18	Glenamacrie	,Lorn; —	NM92NW01
20628	72457	LN19	Allt an Dunain	,Lorn; A1/7	NN02SE01
20539	72358	LN20	Kilchrenan	,Lorn; A1/6	NN02SE13
18250	72207	LN21	Kilninver	,Lorn; A1/5	NM82SW13
18014	72052	LN22	Duachy	,Lorn; A1/4	NM82SW01
19658	71423	LN23	Kilmun	,Lorn; A1/10	NM91SE08
18013	70773	AR1	Barrichbeyan	,Argyll; —	NM80NW10
18405	70762	AR2	Sluggan	,Argyll; A2/2	NM80NW06
18403	70757	AR2		; A2/2	NM80NW04
18315	70641	AR3	Barbreck	,Argyll; A2/3	NM80NW19
1810	7055	AR4	Ardlarich	,Argyll; —	NM80NW09
18305	70498	AR5	Kintraw	,Argyll; A2/5	NM80SW01
18405	70403	AR6	Salachary	,Argyll; A2/26	NM80SW16
18788	70488	AR7	Torran	,Argyll; A1/8	NM80SE37
18668	70333	AR8	Ford	,Argyll; A2/22	NM80SE42
18595	70157	AR9	Glennan N	,Argyll; A2/23	NM80SE29
18573	70113	AR10	Glennan S	,Argyll; A2/24	NM80SE28
18014	70173	AR11	Eilean Righ	(Argyll); —	NM80SW07
18345	70080	AR12	Carnasserie	,Argyll; A2/6	NM80SW22
18263	69783	AR13	Kilmartin	,Argyll; A2/8	NR89NW06
18279	69774	AR13		; A2/8	NR89NW44
18282	69760	AR13		; A2/8	NR89NW03
18283	69761	AR13		; A2/8	NR89NW45
18252	69761	AR13		; A2/8	NR89NW73
18203	69721	AR14	Tayness	,Argyll; A2/10	NR89NW35
18337	69641	AR15	Duncracaig	,Argyll; A2/12	NR89NW14
18205	69585	AR16	Rowanfield	,Argyll; A2/11	NR89NW47
18034	69561	AR17	Duntroon	,Argyll; —	NR89NW57
18083	69410	AR18	Crinan Moss	,Argyll; A2/7	NR89SW05
20947	70905	AR19	Inverary	,Argyll; A2/1	NN00NE06
19325	69809	AR20	Carron	,Argyll; A2/18	NR99NW02
1973	6950	AR21	Minard	,Argyll; —	—
18668	69703	AR22	Kirnan Hill	,Argyll; —	NR89NE07
18757	69550	AR23	Lechuary	,Argyll; A2/17	NR89NE08

RCAHMS	Burl	Henshall	D&E	Visit	Ex	Alternative name
L(267)	–	–	–	;–:	D:	
L(117)	–	–	–	;–:	G:	
L(115)	–	–	–	;–:	G:	
L(51)	–	–	–	;–:	F:	
L(121)	–	–	–	;–:	G:	Taynuilt 1
L(122)	–	–	–	;81:	–:	Taynuilt 2
–	–	–	–	;81:	–:	
L(109)	–	–	–	;–:	F:	
L(120)	Arg1	–	–	;81:	–:	Loch Nell
L(78)	–	–	–	;81:	–:	Loch Nell/ Clach na Carraig
L(78)	–	–	–	;81:	–:	Loch Nell
L(114)	–	–	–	;81:	–:	
–	–	–	–	;–:	D:	
L(105)	–	–	–	;–:	F:	
L(119)	–	–	–	;–:	G:	
L(116)	–	–	–	;81:	–:	Loch Seil
L(209)	–	–	–	;–:	D:	Loch Avich
A(164)	–	–	–	;–:	G:	Caisteal nan Coin Duibh
–	–	–	–	;79:	–:	
A(190)	–	–	–	;79:	–:	
A(159)	–	–	–	;81:	–:	
A(156)	–	–	–	;–:	G:	
A(174)	–	–	–	;81:	X:	
A(162)	–	–	–	;79:	–:	
A(193)	–	–	–	;79:	–:	
A(181)	–	–	–	;79:	–:	
A(171)	–	–	–	;79:	–:	Creagantairbh
A(182)	–	–	–	;79:	–:	
A(180)	–	–	–	;–:	D:	
A(166)	–	–	–	;79:	–:	
A(122)	Arg2	–	–	;81:	–:	Temple Wood
A(187)	–	–	–	;81:	–:	Nether Largie
A(187)	–	–	–	;81:	–:	Nether Largie
–	–	–	–	;81:	–:	
–	–	–	D(73:13)	;81:	–:	
A(163)	–	–	–	;79:	G:	Brouch an Drummin
A(158)	–	–	–	;79:	–:	Ballymeanach
A(189)	–	–	–	;81:	–:	Poltalloch
A(179)	–	–	–	;79:	–:	
A(173)	–	–	–	;79:	–:	
A(169)	–	–	–	;–:	–:	
A(167)	–	–	–	;–:	T:	Meall Reamhar
–	–	–	D(80:32)	;83:	X:	Brainport Bay
A(184)	–	–	–	;–:	D:	
A(165)	–	–	–	;79:	–:	An Car

Table 2.1 (continued)

NGR	Site	Name and location	Thom	OS Card
18548 69509	AR24	Loch na Torrnalaich	,Argyll; A2/16	NR89NE10
18639 69449	AR25	Torbhlaran N	,Argyll; A2/15	NR89SE03
18607 69428	AR26	Torbhlaran S	,Argyll; –	NR89SE12
18386 69362	AR27	Dunadd	,Argyll; A2/13	NR89SW35
18397 69343	AR27		; A2/13	NR89SW25
18471 69290	AR28	Dunamuck I	,Argyll; A2/21	NR89SW28
18484 69248	AR29	Dunamuck II	,Argyll; A2/14	NR89SW27
18484 69233	AR30	Dunamuck III	; A2/20	NR89SW24
18554 69018	AR31	Achnabreck	,Argyll; A2/19	NR89SE13
18563 68993	AR31		; A2/19	NR88NE16
18572 68852	AR32	Oakfield	,Argyll; –	NR88NE15
18674 68652	AR33	Kilmory	,Argyll; –	NR88NE14
17828 69070	AR34	Barnluasgan	,Knapdale; A3/3	NR79SE19
180 690	AR35	Dunans	,Knapdale; –	NR89SW08
17443 68766	AR36	Tayvallich	,Knapdale; A3/10	NR78NW08
17298 68640	AR37	Barnashaig	,Knapdale; A3/4	NR78NW01
17280 68614	AR38	Upper Fernoch	,Knapdale; A3/4	NR78NW06
17269 68594	AR38		; A3/4	NR78NW07
17772 67801	AR39	Lochead	,Knapdale; A3/9	NR77NE04
16062 68231	JU1	Tarbert	,Jura; A6/5	NR68SW01
16089 68221	JU1		; A6/5	NR68SW02
15505 67192	JU2	Knockrome N	,Jura; –	NR57SE02
15601 67171	JU3	Ardfernal	,Jura; A6/4	NR57SE01
15503 67148	JU4	Knockrome	,Jura; A6/4	NR57SE03
15484 67144	JU4		; A6/4	NR57SW03
15387 67128	JU5	Leargybreck	,Jura; –	NR57SW02
15128 66648	JU6	Craighouse	,Jura; A6/6	NR56NW02
15184 66480	JU7	Sannaig	,Jura; A6/3	NR56SW04
15078 66375	JU8	Strone	,Jura; A6/2	NR56SW03
14641 66477	JU9	Camas an Staca	,Jura; A6/1	NR46SE01
12732 67326	IS1	Druim nan Crann	,Islay; A7/22	NR27SE10
12852 67150	IS2	Kilnave	,Islay; A7/23	NR27SE01
13475 66978	IS3	Beinn a'Chuirn	,Islay; A7/2	NR36NW01
13927 66856	IS4	Finlaggan	,Islay; A7/24	NR36NE03
14108 66724	IS5	Scanistle	,Islay; –	NR46NW06
13492 66793	IS6	Beinn Cham	,Islay; A7/3	NR36NW02
13636 66762	IS7	Ballachlavin	,Islay; A7/4	NR36NE16
13792 66662	IS8	Kepollsmore	,Islay; A7/9	NR36NE19
1406 6656	IS9	Lossit Lodge	,Islay; –	–
13958 66560	IS10	Suidh' an Eoin Mor	,Islay; –	NR36NE10
13989 66483	IS11	Knocklearoch	,Islay; –	NR36SE01
14037 66410	IS12	Mullach Dubh	,Islay; A7/10	NR46SW01
12166 66774	IS13	Smaull	,Islay; A7/7	NR26NW03
12296 66754	IS14	An Carnan	,Islay; A7/6	NR26NW17
1222 6676	IS15	Ballinaby	,Islay; –	NR26NW15

RCAHMS	Burl	Henshall	D&E	Visit	Ex	Alternative name
A(186)	-	-	-	;81:	-:	
A(192)	-	-	-	;79:	-:	
-	-	-	D(78:23)	;--:	G:	Kilmichael Glassary
-	-	-	-	;81:	-:	
A(175)	-	-	-	;81:	-:	
A(178)	-	-	-	;81:	-:	
A(177)	-	-	-	;81:	-:	
A(176)	-	-	-	;81:	-:	
A(155)	-	-	-	;79:	-:	
A(191)	-	-	-	;79:	-:	
A(188)	-	-	-	;79:	-:	Auchendarroch
A(183)	-	-	-	;79:	-:	
A(161)	-	-	-	;79:	D:	Bellanoch
A(170)	-	-	-	;--:	G:	Clach na Beithir
-	-	-	-	;--:	D:	
A(160)	-	-	-	;81:	-:	Tayvallich
A(194)	-	-	-	;81:	-:	Tayvallich
A(195)	-	-	-	;81:	-:	Tayvallich
A(185)	-	-	-	;79:	-:	
I(122)	-	-	-	;79:	-:	
I(328)	-	-	-	;79:	-:	
I(109)	-	-	-	;79:	-:	
I(75)	-	-	-	;79:	-:	
I(109)	-	-	-	;79:	-:	
I(109)	-	-	-	;79:	-:	
I(111)	-	-	-	;79:	-:	
I(83)	-	-	-	;79:	-:	Carragh a'Ghlinne
I(116)	-	-	-	;79:	-:	
I(120)	-	-	-	;79:	-:	
I(81)	-	-	-	;79:	-:	
-	-	-	-	;--:	D:	Ardnave
-	-	-	-	;--:	D:	
I(86)	-	-	-	;79:	-:	Clach an Tiampain
I(97)	-	-	-	;78:	-:	
I(119)	-	-	-	;78:	-:	
I(80)	-	-	-	;79:	-:	
I(78)	-	-	-	;79:	-:	Baile Tharbhach
I(105)	-	-	-	;78:	G:	
-	-	-	D(72:04)	;--:	N:	
I(121)	-	-	-	;--:	U:	
I(108)	-	-	-	;78:	-:	
I(113)	-	-	-	;79:	-:	
-	-	-	-	;--:	D:	Tobar Haco
-	-	-	-	;--:	D:	Cladh Dhubhain
-	-	-	-	;--:	-:	

Table 2.1 (continued)

NGR		Site	Name and location		Thom	OS Card
12210	66738	IS15		;	A7/5	NR26NW14
12200	66719	IS15		;	A7/5	NR26NW13
12735	66735	IS16	Aoradh	,Islay;	A7/1	NR26NE01
1246	6645	IS17	Sunderland	,Islay;	—	NR26SW11
12692	66429	IS18	Foreland House	,Islay;	—	NR26SE03
12938	66335	IS19	Uisgeantsuidhe	,Islay;	A7/20	NR26SE03
13101	66341	IS20	West Carrabus	,Islay;	—	NR36SW15
13360	66423	IS21	Knockdon	,Islay;	A7/8	NR36SW12
12197	66314	IS22	Kilchoman	,Islay;	A7/11	NR26SW01
12135	66301	IS22		;	A7/11	NR26SW09
12527	66137	IS23	Gartacharra	,Islay;	A7/13	NR26SE08
12241	66041	IS24	Carn Mor	,Islay;	A7/12	NR26SW32
12317	66000	IS25	Cnoc Thornasaig	,Islay;	—	NR26SW23
12106	65938	IS26	Droighneach	,Islay;	A7/14	NR25NW11
1197	6573	IS27	Cnoc Mor	,Islay;	—	NR15NE12
11956	65697	IS28	Cultoon	,Islay;	A7/15	NR15NE01
12105	65642	IS29	Beinn Tart a'Mhill	,Islay;	A7/16	NR25NW03
1202	6560	IS30	Lossit Burn	,Islay;	—	NR25NW20
11901	65561	IS31	Kelsay	,Islay;	—	NR15NE08
13582	66137	IS32	Gortanilivorrie	,Islay;	—	NR36SE07
13595	66053	IS33	Neriby	,Islay;	—	NR36SE11
14658	65457	IS34	Ardtalla	,Islay;	—	NR45SE16
14618	65372	IS35	Claggain Bay	,Islay;	A7/21	NR45SE02
14630	65290	IS36	Trudernish	,Islay;	—	NR45SE09
14426	64919	IS37	Ardilistry	,Islay;	—	NR44NW27
14369	64832	IS38	Cnoc Rhaonastil	,Islay;	—	NR44NW06
13954	64621	IS39	Lagavulin N	,Islay;	—	NR34NE09
13972	64592	IS40	Lagavulin S	,Islay;	—	NR34NE15
13895	64607	IS41	Laphroaig	,Islay;	A7/19	NR34NE07
13838	64657	IS42	Kilbride	,Islay;	A7/18	NR34NE05
13826	64595	IS43	Druim nam Madagan	,Islay;	—	NR34NE35
13714	64603	IS44	Port Ellen III	,Islay;	—	NR34NE21
13726	64581	IS45	Port Ellen II	,Islay;	—	NR34NE22
13715	64559	IS46	Port Ellen I	,Islay;	—	NR34NE12
13283	64781	IS47	Kintra	,Islay;	A7/17	NR34NW07
13109	64721	IS48	Cnoc Mor Ghrasdail	,Islay;	—	NR34NW24
13264	64600	IS49	Cornabus	,Islay;	—	NR34NW11
12975	64315	IS50	Kinnabus	,Islay;	—	NR24SE02
17072	66689	KT1	Cretshengan	,Knapdale;	A3/5	NR76NW03
17414	66166	KT2	Carse	,Knapdale;	A3/6	NR76SW01
17425	66163	KT2		;	A3/6	NR76SW01
17573	66014	KT3	Ardpatrick	,Knapdale;	A3/7	NR76SE03
18391	66746	KT4	Avinagillan	,Knapdale;	A3/8	NR86NW01
18464	66678	KT5	Escart	,Kintyre;	A4/1	NR86NW02
19063	65876	KT6	Skipness	,Kintyre;	—	NR95NW01

RCAHMS	Burl	Henshall	D&E	Visit	Ex	Alternative name
I(79)	-	-	-	;79:	-:	
I(79)	-	-	-	;79:	-:	
-	-	-	-	;78:	D:	Clach Mhic-Illean
I(63)	-	-	-	;--:	G:	
I(98)	-	-	-	;78:	-:	
I(124)	-	-	-	;78:	-:	
-	-	-	-	;--:	U:	
I(107)	-	-	-	;78:	-:	
-	-	-	-	;--:	D:	
-	-	-	-	;78:	D:	
I(99)	-	-	-	;78:	-:	
I(91)	-	-	-	;78:	-:	Cnoc nan Guaillean
I(90)	-	-	-	;78:	-:	Cnoc a'Charraigh
I(102)	-	-	-	;78:	-:	
-	-	-	-	;--:	D:	
I(94)	Isl2	-	D(75:08)	;78:	-:	
-	-	ILY2	-	;--:	F:	Slochd Measach
-	Isl3	-	-	;--:	D:	
I(104)	-	-	-	;78:	-:	
I(103)	-	-	-	;--:	U:	
I(114)	-	-	-	;78:	G:	
I(77)	-	-	D(76:09)	;78:	-:	
I(88)	-	-	-	;79:	-:	
I(123)	-	-	-	;79:	-:	
I(76)	Isl1	-	-	;--:	-:	
I(85)	-	-	-	;79:	-:	Clachan Ceann Ile
I(110)	-	-	-	;79:	-:	
I(28)	-	-	-	;78:	F:	Druim Mor
I(74)	-	-	-	;78:	-:	Achnancarranan
I(106)	-	-	-	;78:	-:	
I(95)	-	-	-	;--:	U:	
-	-	-	-	;--:	U:	
-	-	-	D(76:09)	;--:	D:	
I(115)	-	-	-	;78:	-:	
I(84)	-	-	-	;78:	-:	Druim an Stuin/Carragh Bhan
I(92)	-	-	-	;--:	U:	Coille a'Chnoic Mhoir
I(93)	-	-	-	;78:	-:	Cnoc Ard
I(101)	-	-	-	;78:	-:	Glac a'Charraigh
A(172)	-	-	-	;79:	-:	
A(168)	-	-	-	;79:	-:	Loch Stornoway
A(168)	-	-	-	;79:	-:	Loch Stornoway
A(154)	-	-	-	;79:	-:	Achadh-Chaorun
A(157)	-	-	-	;79:	-:	
K(143)	-	-	-	;79:	-:	
-	-	-	-	;81:	D:	

Table 2.1   (continued)

NGR	Site	Name and location	Thom	OS Card
18648 65825	KT7	Glenreasdale	,Kintyre; A4/3	NR85NE04
17624 65704	KT8	Dunskeig	,Kintyre; A4/23	-
17802 65479	KT9	Loch Ciaran	,Kintyre; -	NR75SE01
17309 65241	KT10	Ballochroy I	,Kintyre; A4/4	NR75SW03
17348 65214	KT11	Ballochroy II	,Kintyre; -	NR75SW11
16555 65227	KT12	Tarbert	,Gigha; A4/17	NR65SE22
16427 64818	KT13	Achamore House	,Gigha; A4/18	NR64NW02
16420 64806	KT13		; A4/18	NR64NW03
17141 64893	KT14	Rhunahaorine	,Kintyre; -	NR74NW01
16926 64330	KT15	Beacharr I	,Kintyre; A4/5	NR64SE02
16952 64295	KT16	Beacharr II	,Kintyre; -	NR64SE09
16963 64218	KT17	Allt Achapharick	,Kintyre; -	NR64SE11
17937 64187	KT18	Brackley	,Kintyre; A4/22	NR74SE01
16792 63914	KT19	South Muasdale	,Kintyre; A4/6	NR63NE20
16938 63777	KT20	Killmaluag	,Kintyre; -	NR63NE05
16616 63707	KT21	Barlea	,Kintyre; A4/7	NR63NE18
16703 63545	KT22	Barr Mains	,Kintyre; A4/8	NR63NE19
17349 63506	KT23	Beinn an Tuirc	,Kintyre; A4/9	NR73SW07
16641 62898	KT24	Tighnamoile	,Kintyre; -	NR62NE03
16609 62756	KT25	Drumalea	,Kintyre; -	NR62NE19
16667 62563	KT26	Drum	,Kintyre; -	NR62NE08
16577 62445	KT27	Clochkeil	,Kintyre; -	NR62SE15
17094 62701	KT28	Skeroblingarry	,Kintyre; A4/11	NR72NW13
16950 62572	KT29	High Park	,Kintyre; A4/2	NR62NE18
16935 62406	KT30	Glencraigs N	,Kintyre; -	NR62SE16
16902 62362	KT31	Craigs	,Kintyre; -	NR62SE05
16932 62354	KT32	Glencraigs S	,Kintyre; A4/13	NR62SE06
17765 62727	KT33	Ballochgair	,Kintyre; -	NR72NE19
17638 62570	KT34	Peninver Bridge	,Kintyre; -	NR72NE08
17614 62541	KT35	Glenlussa Lodge	,Kintyre; A4/10	NR72NE13
17238 62123	KT36	Campbeltown	,Kintyre; A4/14	NR72SW03
16995 61982	KT37	Stewarton	,Kintyre; -	NR61NE12
16446 62065	KT38	Machrihanish	,Kintyre; A4/15	NR62SW02
16533 61940	KT39	Mingary	,Kintyre; -	NR61NE07
16657 61546	KT40	Lochorodale	,Kintyre; -	NR61NE10
17026 61240	KT41	Knockstapple	,Kintyre; A4/19	NR71SW10
16517 61192	KT42	Culinlongart	,Kintyre; A4/16	NR61SE04
17365 60927	KT43	Macharioch	,Kintyre; A4/20	NR70NW05
16976 60787	KT44	Southend	,Kintyre; -	NR60NE06

RCAHMS	Burl	Henshall	D&E	Visit Ex	Alternative name
K(6)	-	ARG26	-	;--: F:	Skipness
-	-	-	-	;79: -:	Clach Leth Rathad
K(150)	-	-	-	;79: -:	
K(57)	-	-	-	;81: -:	
-	-	-	-	;81: D:	
K(136)	-	-	-	;81: -:	Carragh an Tarbert
K(244)	-	-	-	;--: G:	
K(138)	-	-	-	;--: G:	Cnoc na Carraigh
-	-	-	-	;81: -:	
K(134)	-	ARG27	-	;79: -:	
-	-	-	-	;--: D:	
-	-	-	-	;--: D:	
K(5)	-	ARG28	-	;--: F:	
K(153)	-	-	-	;81: -:	Carragh Muasdale
-	-	-	-	;--: D:	
K(132)	-	-	-	;79: -:	Glenbarr
K(133)	-	-	-	;--: G:	
K(130)	-	-	-	;81: -:	Arnicle / Crois Mhic Aoida
-	-	-	-	;81: -:	
K(142)	-	-	-	;79: -:	
K(141)	-	-	-	;--: G:	
K(137)	-	-	-	;79: -:	
K(152)	-	-	-	;79: -:	Pobull Burn
K(148)	-	-	-	;79: -:	
K(145)	-	-	-	;--: G:	
K(139)	-	-	-	;79: -:	
K(144)	-	-	-	;79: -:	
-	-	-	-	;81: D:	
-	-	-	-	;81: G:	
K(146)	-	-	-	;81: -:	Peninver
K(131)	-	-	-	;79: -:	Balegreggan
K(147)	-	-	-	;79: -:	
-	-	-	-	;--: F:	Cnocan Sithein
K(34)	-	-	-	;79: -:	
K(151)	-	-	-	;79: -:	
K(149)	-	-	-	;79: -:	
K(140)	-	-	-	;79: -:	
K(11)	-	ARG34	-	;--: F:	
K(135)	-	-	-	;79: -:	Brunerican

(AR3). Thom's site A2/3, described as a single stone, appears to refer only to the isolated slab. In fact, the two sites are only some 20m apart.

A2/9 - Rowanfield (Poltalloch), Argyll. Described as a circle, no position is given. This may refer to the cairn at 826 971 (Campbell & Sandeman 1961: no. 119).

A2/25 - Crinan Moss, Argyll. This is apparently an accidental duplication of A2/7 (AR18).

A3/1 & A3/2 -Bellanoch Hill area, Knapdale. Both sites are described as poor circles, with the comment that there seem to be several in the district. No exact positions are given. These sites are probably amongst the homesteads listed by the Ordnance Survey (OSAR: NR 79 SE, 3-5).

A4/12 - High Park, Kintyre. This is apparently an accidental duplication of A4/2 (KT29).

A4/21 - "Carskey", Kintyre. No description of this site is given, and the grid reference (1652 6120) corresponds to KT42 (Culinlongart) rather than to the site name; Carskey is around 1655 6081.

2.3 Sites excluded on archaeological grounds

Most of the 322 sites in the initial site list (Table 2.1) have been visited by the author between 1973 and 1981, often more than once. The year of the latest visit is given in that table. These first-hand examinations, as well as the descriptions and interpretations of other authors, have provided the basis of reassessments of the status of each site as a contender for a site of free-standing megaliths erected in prehistoric times. These have resulted in 133 of the sites being dismissed from further consideration on various grounds, none of which was related to their possible astronomical significance. Details of each of these sites and the reasons for its exclusion are given in the remainder of this chapter.

Of the 322 sites, 75 have been excluded from further consideration on archaeological grounds. Of these 75, 47 are highly dubious contenders for prehistoric sites. They consist of natural rocks and stone settings, more modern structures such as enclosures and shielings, and the like. In the remaining 28 cases there is convincing evidence that the sites were not constructed as free-standing megaliths. Most of them apparently represent the remains of more complex structures such as megalithic chamber tombs. A small number represent natural boulders which have been cup-marked.

Some borderline cases occur where standing stones have been erected near to the peripheries of chamber tombs. Although arguably they should be considered as part of the chamber tomb structure and thus excluded from further consideration, we have counted them as structures which possibly have an independent motivation, and thus have not done so. Examples are the single menhirs standing in the vicinity of the chamber tombs at South Clettraval (UI22) and Unival

(UI28), North Uist; and the two menhirs standing very close to the edge of the chamber tomb at Suie, Mull (ML34). This decision is consistent with our not excluding all those menhirs standing near to kerb cairns, as at Strontoiller, Lorn (LN15), and close to long cairns, as at Beacharr, Kintyre (KT15). The standing stone at Lagavulin S (IS40), on the other hand, has been excluded because it actually protrudes above the top of a small cairn; then again the menhir at Stoneybridge, North Uist (UI48) is not excluded because it has been erected on the summit of a mound which is not thought to be a cairn.

A full list of sites excluded on archaeological grounds is given below. Descriptions are compiled from first-hand site visits and measurements, and any comments are our own, except where references are cited, in which case they are taken from the sources quoted. Dimensions of standing stones are taken at the base unless otherwise stated. We emphasize that these details are meant to be sufficient merely to justify our subsequent rejection of the sites from further consideration. Fuller descriptions are available in the references cited in Table 2.1, for example the RCAHMS inventories.

2.3.1 Highly dubious contenders for prehistoric sites

LH2 - Shader N (Clach Stei Lin), Lewis. NB 3970 5456. Although listed by Thom (FSL: H1/9) and the RCAHMS (1928: no. 18) as a single standing stone, there are in addition a number of smaller stones and a peaty bank. According to the Ordnance Survey in 1969 (NB 35 SE, 3), when taken together these form part of a sub-circular drystone enclosure of indeterminate date.

LH3 - Shader E (Tom Naobhe), Lewis. NB 401 543. Marked on the 1:10000 Ordnance Survey map as a "pile of stones", Thom (FSL: H1/11) describes this site as unimpressive. It is merely a collection of small boulders, the four largest being about 0.6m long, confined to an area about 2m by 1m.

LH4 - Shader S (Stein-a-Cleit), Lewis. NB 3962 5407. Although listed by the RCAHMS (1928: no. 17) as a stone circle and denuded chambered cairn, more recent interpretations suggest that this is more likely a settlement site. The reported stone circle may be a ruined field or enclosure wall of indeterminate age (OSAR: NB 35 SE, 2) and the reported cairn a ruined building (Henshall 1972: 465) or central homestead.

LH12 - Sgeir nan Each ("Callanish XIII"), Lewis. NB 215 341. This reported stone setting conforms to the descriptions given by Ponting & Ponting (D & E 1976: 58; 1981: 88). It consists merely of a thin prostrate slab 1.3m x 0.6m x 0.1m thick lying on a pile of small rounded stones, and three similar piles of stones.

LH13 - Cliacabhaidh ("Callanish XVI"), Lewis. NB 2137 3381. The two small erect stones here (D & E 1976: 59; 1977: 32; see also 1981: 89) are less than 1m tall. They appear to have been artificially erected but are of indeterminate date; one is in the line of a field wall.

LH15 - Buaile Chruaidh ("Callanish XIX"), Lewis. NB 2182 3312.
Described by the Pontings (D & E 1977: 32) as a possible stand-
ing stone, this site comprises a rounded block only 0.7m high.
There are three outcrops and several loose stones nearby.

LH17 - Cnoc Sgeir na h-Uidhe ("Callanish XIV"), Lewis. NB 2270 3296 &
2281 3291. At the first location is a setting of small stones
on a hilltop as described by the Pontings (D & E 1976: 59) which
might be the remains of a cist, but certainly were not standing
stones. At the second location, the flat summit of another
small hilltop 100m away, is a boulder about 0.8m long and 0.5m
high, which appears to be natural.

LH23 - Cnoc Dubh ("Callanish VII"), Lewis. NB 232 302. Although described by Thom (FSL: H1/7; 1967: 128, unnumbered) as a circle,
this site is in fact a shieling (D & E 1973: 48).

LH25 - Druim nam Bidearan ("Callanish IX"), Lewis. NB 2338 2976. Two
prostrate slabs each about 1.3m long, near the summit of a rocky
ridge (D & E 1976: 58) were discovered by the Glasgow University
survey team (Tait 1978), but appear indistinguishable from a
number of natural stones in the area.

LH26 - Loch Crogach ("Callanish XVIII"), Lewis. NB 244 292. A tiny
slab 0.6m high (D & E 1976: 59) is wedged into a cleft in the
outcrop on a rocky knoll, and is unstable.

LH35 - Loch na h-Uidhe (Clach an Teampuill), Harris. NB 0128 0077.
This site is listed as a standing stone by Thom (1967: Table
12.1, H2/1), but is in fact a post-Roman cross-incised stone
(OSAR: NB 00 SW, 4).

UI3 - Bhruist, Berneray (N). NF 9242 8288. This site comprises an
erect stone 1.2m high, irregularly shaped, and four large
boulders, including one leaning against the erect stone.
Although listed as the remains of a stone circle by the RCAHMS
(1928: no. 132), there is no evidence relating to the original
positions of the stones. The erect stone may be deliberately
placed, at an indeterminate date, but the others may represent
field clearance.

UI10 - Beinn a'Chaolais, North Uist. NF 9044 7795. Listed by the
RCAHMS (1928: no. 241) and by Burl (1976: 358) as a possible
stone circle, the six stones (two "standing" up to 0.6m in
height, and four prostrate) described by the RCAHMS were located
in 1981 on a summit amidst an area strewn with boulders and outcrops. There is no apparent reason why they should be singled
out as possible menhirs. The site is some 100m to the NNE of
two further reported standing stones (Beveridge 1911: 258). However these are in fact situated in the westernmost of a group of
six shielings noted by the Ordnance Survey (OSAR: NF 97 NW, 4).

UI12 - Clachan Sands (Clach an't Sagairt), North Uist. NF 8785 7605.
Although listed by Thom (1967: Table 12.1, H3/2) as a standing
stone (see also Thom 1966: fig. 8), this is a large natural
block with a Latin cross incised near one corner (RCAHMS 1928:
no. 170; OSAR: NF 87 NE, 14).

UI16 - Bogach Maari, North Uist. NF 8598 7221. Although this site is listed by the RCAHMS (1928: no. 244) as "stone circle (very doubtful)", it is simply a natural setting of eight irregular stones, five of which tend towards a rough circle, enclosing a natural peaty mound (OSAR: NF 87 SE, 9).

UI30 - Craig Hasten, North Uist. NF 740 670. Listed by Thom (1967: Table 12.1, H3/21), this is a natural rock and is described by him as such (1967: 130).

UI36 - Claddach Illeray, North Uist. NF 8046 6431. Although described by Thom (1967: Table 12.1, H3/15) as a circle and two standing stones, the site consists of a small erect slab only 0.8m high, an adjacent block 1.0m long, and a "ring" of outcrops and boulders which form an entirely natural setting (OSAR: NF 86 SW, 34).

UI45 - Nunton (Cladh Mhuire), Benbecula. NF 7664 5379. Listed by Thom (FSL: H4/7) without description, the site is the remains of a chapel (RCAHMS 1928: no. 340).

UI52 - Mingary (Mill Loch; Cladh Ard an Dugain), South Uist. NF 7469 2689. Although listed by Thom (1967: Table 12.1, H5/4) as four kists, according to the Ordnance Survey (OSAR: NF 72 NW, 5) the site consists of old walls and buildings in the vicinity of a former burial ground.

UI54 - Lochboisdale (Cladh Choinnich), South Uist. NF 7963 1998. Listed by Thom (FSL: H5/5) without description and marked "disappointing", the location is the site of a chapel and burial ground (OSAR: NF 71 NE, 1).

UI55 - Layaval, South Uist. NF 7538 1495. Some 160m WNW of a ruined cairn listed by Henshall (1972: UST 21) are two recumbent stones up to 4m long. Some 30m to their SE is a large 4m-long boat-shaped stone. The origin of these stones is uncertain, although the latter may be a "rocking stone" (OSAR: NF 71 SE, 10).

CT6 - Gott (Loch a'Bhleoghan & Loch a Chapuil), Tiree. NM 0240 4565 & 0227 4551. Although described by Beveridge (1903: 130-1) as two stone circles, according to the Ordnance Survey (OSAR: NM 04 NW, 20 & 21) they are both similar in construction to several old field walls in the area and are almost certainly the remains of enclosures associated with them.

ML3 - Newdale (Sgriob-Ruadh), Mull. NM 492 550. A stone circle was reported here by Major MacLachlainn (D & E 1958: 8). The Ordnance Survey (OSAR: NM 45 NE, 2) report merely: "Major Mac-Lachlainn is now dead. There is no circle of stones in the area indicated."

ML5 - Caliach Point, Mull. NM 348 543. This site was described by Orr (1937: 132) as standing stones, and subsequently listed by Thom (FSL: M1/1). However according to the Ordnance Survey (OSAR: NM 35 SW, 1) there are only several upright stones and boulders in old dykes, and the RCAHMS do not include it in their inventory.

LN4 - Home Farm, Barcaldine, Benderloch. NM 956 416. Although listed as a possible cromlech by Thom (FSL: M8/3), and reported as a cairn by Leckie (D & E 1968: 6), the Ordnance Survey in 1971 (OSAR: NM 94 SE, 1) report only modern clearance in the area.

LN9 - Clachan, Lismore. NM 8609 4342. Although listed as a standing stone by Thom, this site was apparently a mediaeval cross marking a sanctuary boundary. It stands about 60m from the east wall of the Cathedral of St. Moluag (RCAHMS 1975: no. 267).

LN19 - Allt an Dunain, Lorn. NN 0628 2457. The "poor circle" noted by Thom (FSL: A1/7) to the north of the Holystone (LN20) probably corresponds to a 5m-diameter hut circle of indeterminate date (OSAR: NN 02 SE, 1) situated some 50m to the east of a 10m-diameter ruined cairn at 0623 2457 (RCAHMS 1975: no. 15), or possibly to the cairn itself.

LN23 - Kilmun (Larach na Iobairte; Loch Avich), Lorn. NM 9658 1423. Although listed by Thom (FSL: A1/10; see also Thom, Thom & Burl 1980: 143, remarks by Thom) as a crude stone ring, this appears to be a homestead similar to those in central Perthshire (OSAR: NM 83 SE, 22; see also Thom, Thom & Burl 1980: 143, remarks by Burl). Site plan: Thom, Thom & Burl (1980: 142).

AR11 - Eilean Righ (Argyll). NM 8014 0173. The stone alignment and possible cairn listed by Campbell & Sandeman (1961: no. 180) are probably no more than the remains of an old field wall and the residue of material used to build it (OSAR: NM 80 SW, 7).

AR22 - Kirnan Hill, Argyll. NR 8668 9703. Although listed by Campbell & Sandeman (1961: no. 184) as a stone projecting above a surrounding cairn, the site is in fact no more than a clearance heap (OSAR: NR 89 NE, 7).

AR34 - Barnluasgan (Bellanoch), Knapdale. NR 7828 9070. This site consists of two upright stones about 1.5m tall, linked by an arc of earthfast boulders up to 20m in diameter. Although listed by Thom (FSL: A3/3; see also Thom, Thom & Burl 1980: 149) and Campbell & Sandeman (1961: no. 161) as the remains of a stone circle, its east side would not fall within the area which has been levelled. It is more likely the remains of a badly ruined homestead (OSAR: NR 79 SE, 19; Thom, Thom & Burl 1980: 149, remarks by Burl). Site plan: Thom, Thom & Burl (1980: 148).

AR36 - Tayvallich, Argyll. NR 7443 8766. This site is listed by Thom (A3/10) as a stone circle, but in fact consists of a group of large boulders which appear to have occurred naturally (OSAR: NR 78 NW, 8).

IS1 - Druim nan Crann (Carn Bhuaile Corc; Ardnave), Islay. NR 2732 7326. Although listed by Thom (FSL: A7/22; see also Thom, Thom & Burl 1980: 151, remarks by Thom) as a stone ring, this site is not prehistoric. It consists of a shelter with adjacent stock pen built at the foot of a cliff (OSAR: NR 27 SE 10). Burl speculates that it might be a fisherman's bothy (Thom, Thom & Burl 1980: 151, remarks by Burl). Site plan: Thom, Thom & Burl (1980: 150).

IS2   -   Kilnave, Islay.   NR 2852 7150.   Thom (FSL: A7/23) lists "stone crosses"; the Ordnance Survey (OSAR: NR 27 SE, 1) note a reported 8th Century "high cross" standing in a burial ground.

IS13   -   Smaull (Tobar Haco), Islay.   NR 2166 6774.   Listed by Thom (FSL: A7/7) but with description marked "unknown", the site is that of a reported ancient burial ground, although in 1978 the Ordnance Survey (OSAR: NR 26 NW, 3) found only fragmentary earth and stone field banks in the area.

IS14   -   An Carnan (Cladh Dhubhain), Islay.   NR 2296 6754.   Listed by Thom (FSL: A7/6) but with description marked "unknown", the site is that of a reported old burial ground (OSAR: NR 26 NW, 17).

IS16   -   Aoradh (Clach mhic-Illean), Islay.   NR 2735 6735.   Listed by Thom (FSL: A7/1) as a standing stone, this is a tiny erect stone slab only 0.6m high x 0.5m x 0.2m (OSAR: NR 26 NE, 1).

IS22   -   Kilchoman, Islay.   NR 2197 6314 & 2135 6301.   The two standing stones listed by Thom (FSL: A7/11) are in fact two sculptured stones thought to date to the 8th and 9th Centuries (OSAR: NR 26 SW, 1 & 9).

IS27   -   Cnoc Mor, Islay.   NR 197 573.   Although documented as a standing stone, this is in fact a natural boulder (OSAR: NR 15 NE, 12).

IS30   -   Lossit Burn, Islay.   NR 202 560.   This reported stone circle (D & E 1961: 19) is actually one of a number of ruined structures enclosed by earth and stone walls, probably dating to the 18th or 19th century (OSAR: NR 25 NW, 20).

IS45   -   Port Ellen II, Islay.   NR 3726 4581.   A reported standing stone here (D & E 1976: 9) is in fact a small, almost portable, boulder (OSAR: NR 34 NE, 22).

KT6   -   Skipness, Kintyre.   NR 9063 5876.   This site is not included in Thom's original list.   In more recent work, Thom and Thom (1979a; 1979b: 8) mention it as an unimpressive stone, and assume that it has fallen or been knocked over since the Ordnance Survey reported it on the 6" County Series map as a standing stone.   However many of the designations on early O.S. maps were inaccurate, and the stone is undoubtedly a natural erratic boulder (OSAR: NR 95 NW, 1).   It is rounded, of maximum dimensions about 1.0m, and approximately 0.3m thick.   The Thoms refer to a socket adjacent to the stone on its west side; although there is a marked depression here there are also depressions in the ground on two other sides of the stone.

KT11   -   Ballochroy II, Kintyre.   NR 7348 5214.   This upright stone is only 0.9m tall x 1.1m x 0.3m, and it is probably a boundary stone of some description (OSAR: NR 75 SW, 11).

KT16   -   Beacharr II, Kintyre.   NR 6952 4295.   This reported standing stone is in fact a remnant from a largely-destroyed stone wall (OSAR: NR 64 SE, 9).

KT17 - Allt Achapharick, Kintyre. NR 6963 4218. This is a small upright stone 0.7m high x 0.6m x 0.3m, and is unlikely to be an antiquity (OSAR: NR 64 SE, 11).

KT20 - Killmaluag, Kintyre. NR 6938 3777. This reported standing stone is incorporated into a stone dyke. Similar (although somewhat smaller) stones can be seen in the dyke at regular intervals (OSAR: NR 63 NE, 5).

KT33 - Ballochgair, Kintyre. NR 7765 2727. This reported standing stone is a small slab 1.0m high x 0.5m x 0.2m situated immediately adjacent to an existing field wall and oriented at right angles across the line of it. Similar stones have been encountered in the area (OSAR: NR 72 NE, 19), and it is probably the remains of an earlier wall.

2.3.2 Sites not constructed as free-standing megaliths

LH14 - Druim nam Eun (Na Drommanan; "Callanish X"), Lewis. NB 2297 3362. Although described as a destroyed stone circle by various authors (RCAHMS 1928: no. 92; Ponting & Ponting, D & E 1976: 58; Curtis 1979), there is no evidence that any of these loose slabs atop a rocky knoll has ever been set upright. However it does seem likely they were prised by human hand from the level outcrop here (OSAR: NB 23 SW, 6).

LH30 - Dursainean SW (Garrabost), Lewis. NB 5238 3307. Although described by Thom (1967: Table 12.1, H1/13) as a possible stone circle, this site is in fact a ruined chambered cairn (Henshall 1972: no. LWS 6).

UI4 - Bays Loch (Cnoc na Greana), Berneray (N). NF 9230 8187. This site consists of a large boulder, probably a glacial erratic, two small erect stones and a prone slab. Although listed as "standing stones" by the RCAHMS (1928: no. 134), if the latter features are prehistoric at all they probably represent the remains of the chamber of a cairn (Henshall 1972: HRS 2), even though no trace remains of the cairn itself (OSAR: NF 98 SW, 2).

UI5 - Scalabraig, Berneray (N). NF 9101 8155. This site consists of a cairn 5.5m in diameter listed by the RCAHMS (1928: no. 127), now completely grass-covered (OSAR: NF 98 SW, 5). Nearby are a number of small earthfast stones apparently set on edge and a chair-shaped stone 1.3m long.

UI11 - Vallay (North Uist). NF 7907 7650. An alignment of two slabs, the northernmost 1.6m high by 1.1m x 0.2m and the other 1.4m high x 0.9m x 0.2m, as described by the Ordnance Survey (OSAR: NF 77 NE, 19). They appear to represent the remains of one side of a burial chamber, although no trace of a chambered cairn remains.

UI13 - Middlequarter (Clach na Croise), North Uist. NF 8050 7495. This is a natural outcrop containing traces of an incised cross and two groups of cupmarks (RCAHMS 1928: no. 264; OSAR: NF 87 NW, 8).

UI17 - Barpa nam Feannag, North Uist. NF 8567 7207. Listed by Thom (1967: Table 12.1, H3/6) as a large tumulus, this site is a chambered long cairn (Henshall 1972: UST 7).

UI25 - Marrival (Guala an h-Imrich), North Uist. NF 7956 6938. Although listed by the RCAHMS (1928: no. 232) as a chambered cairn surrounded by a ruined stone circle, the site consists of a setting which appears to have been quadrangular with concave sides (Henshall 1972: UST 20), and the cairn lies on the eastern side of the setting rather than within it. Despite the RCAHMS giving the height of one stone as 5 ft. (1.5m), none was taller than 1.0m in 1981.

UI27 - Loch Scadavay (Airigh nam Seilicheag), North Uist. NF 8366 6878. Listed by Thom (1967: Table 12.1, H3/7) as a tumulus and two standing stones, this site is a Hebridean group long cairn (Henshall 1972: UST 2). Thom's stones appear to be two remaining passage orthostats noted by Henshall.

UI32 - Barpa Langass, North Uist. NF 8381 6571. Listed by Thom (1967: Table 12.1, H3/16) as a tumulus, this is a Hebridean group round cairn (Henshall 1972: UST 6).

UI34 - Cringraval E, North Uist. NF 8152 6451. Although there are two large slabs here set on edge, described by Thom (1967: Table 12.1, H3/14) as standing stones, there are in addition several other features as described by the Ordnance Survey (OSAR: NF 86 SW, 21) and Henshall (1972: 534). Henshall interprets them as a ruined circular house; the O.S. think the site was more probably a cairn. In either case the site does not represent isolated standing stones.

UI38 - Loch Glen na Feannag, North Uist. NF 8384 6290. Listed by Thom (1967: Table 12.1, H3/19) as a tumulus, this is a Hebridean group round cairn (Henshall 1972: UST 23).

UI39 - Oban nam Fiadh, North Uist. NF 8417 6247. Listed by Thom (1967: Table 12.1, H3/20) as a tumulus, this is a Hebridean group round cairn (Henshall 1972: UST 25).

UI42 - Gramisdale N (North Ford), Benbecula. NF 8250 5614. Although listed by the RCAHMS (1928: no. 353) as a stone circle, the site is badly ruined. Its diameter of only about 27m is small for stone circles in the area, and the presence of a 2.5m-long prostrate slab near its centre suggests that the site represents the remains of a chambered cairn (see Henshall 1972: addendum to no. UST31). Site plan: Thom, Thom & Burl (1980: 314).

UI43 - Gramisdale S (Suidheachadh Sealg), Benbecula. NF 8247 5522. Although listed by the RCAHMS (1928: no. 352) as a stone circle, the site is badly ruined. Its diameter of around 27m is small for stone circles in the area, and the presence of two parallel prostrate slabs on the SW side which appear to represent the remains of a chamber or cist, suggests that the site is in fact the remains of a chamber tomb (see Henshall 1972: no. UST31). Site plan: Thom, Thom & Burl (1980: 316).

UI47 - Loch ba Una (Airidh na h-Aon Oidhche), Benbecula. NF 8170
5247. Thom's site H4/5 (FSL) is described as a complex cairn,
and is probably to be identified as this chambered long cairn
(Henshall 1972: UST 1).

NA2 - Kilchoan (Greadal Fhinn), Ardnamurchan. NM 4767 6396. Described by Thom (FSL: M5/1) as "stones, etc.", this is in fact a
Hebridean group round cairn (Henshall 1972: ARG 39).

NA5 - Killundine, Morvern. NM 5868 4969. Although described by Thom
(FSL: M6/1) as three circles, and elsewhere (1967: Table 12.1)
as four stones, the site consists, according to the Ordnance
Survey (OSAR: NM 54 NE, 2), of two heavily robbed cairns with
their kerbstones surviving relatively intact.

NA8 - Kinlochaline, Morvern. NM 6922 4740. Although listed by Thom
(FSL: H6/2) as a stone circle, according to the Ordnance Survey
(OSAR: NM64 NE, 5) this site consists of a remaining arc of the
kerbstones originally surrounding a cairn.

LN12 - Dunstaffnage House, Lorn. NM 8978 3382. Listed by Thom (FSL:
A1/9) as a stone circle, this site was described as such by the
Ordnance Survey in 1870, but is now thought to have been a cairn
with a massive stone kerb. It was destroyed during the second
half of the 18th century, and its site is indicated by a slight,
amorphous, turf-covered mound of small stones (OSAR: NM 83 SE,
22).

LN16 - Oban Esplanade, Lorn. NM 8524 3097. Thom's site A1/3 (FSL) is
described as a suspected stone on the roadside in Oban on the
Connel Road. There are no stones listed by other sources on the
Connel Road, but the site may correspond to a cup-marked granite
boulder on the roadside in the Esplanade, 2.9m high x 1.8m x
1.5m, as listed by the RCAHMS (1975: no. 109). It was moved some
7m to its present position around the end of the 19th century
(RCAHMS, ibid.)

LN20 - Kilchrenan, Lorn. NN 0539 2358. Known locally as the "Holy
Stone" or "Slaughter Stone", this is a large boulder 1m high x
2.6m x 1.8m bearing numerous plain cup marks (RCAHMS 1975: no.
105).

IS29 - Beinn Tart a'Mhill (Slochd Measach), Islay. NR 2105 5642.
Listed by Thom (FSL: A7/16) but with description marked "unknown", this is a chambered cairn of the Clyde group (Henshall
1972: ILY 2).

IS40 - Lagavulin S (Druim Mor), Islay. NR 3972 4592. This standing
stone protrudes 1.0m above the top of a small cairn (RCAHMS
1984: no. 28).

KT7 - Glenreasdale, Kintyre. NR 8648 5825. This site is listed by
Thom (FSL: A4/3) under the name "Skipness", but is distinct from
the stone KT6, which is discussed only in more recent work (Thom
& Thom 1979a; 1979b: 8). It is described as a ruined stone
circle, but is in fact a Clyde group round cairn (Henshall 1972:
ARG26).

KT18 - Brackley, Kintyre. NR 7937 4187. Listed by Thom (FSL: A4/22) with no description given, this is the remains of a Clyde group chambered cairn (Henshall 1972: ARG28) excavated by J.G.Scott in 1952-3 (Scott 1955).

KT38 - Macrihanish (Cnocan Sithein), Kintyre. NR 6446 2065. Thom's site A4/15 (FSL), described as a standing stone with earthworks, appears to correspond to this cairn. It is 2.4m in diameter and 3,5m in height with a central hollow containing a stone slab about 1m long (OSAR: NR 62 SW, 2).

KT43 - Macharioch, Kintyre. NR 7365 0927. Thom's site A4/20 (FSL), a "reported circle", appears to correspond to a setting of stones described by Henshall (1972: ARG34). They may represent the remains of a chambered cairn, but this interpretation is uncertain.

2.4 Documented sites whose exact (original) position could not be determined

Of the remaining 247 sites in the initial list, 43 have been excluded from further consideration on the grounds that their exact (original) position could not be determined. Of these 43, 31 have either been completely destroyed or (in the case of single menhirs) removed intact from their original positions, which can only be established with varying degrees of certainty. (We include re-erected menhirs in this category, unless prior to re-erection their original position was determined by excavation.) In order to avoid making decisions from site to site about the reliability of the original position, we have excluded all such sites from further consideration. The remaining 12 sites could not be located by us, or else could not be located by other sources and we made no fresh attempt to do so. A list of the sites in each category is given below.

2.4.1 Sites moved, removed, re-erected or destroyed

LH9 - Aird a'Chaolais ("Callanish VIIIa"), Lewis. NB 165 341. A former standing stone, recently moved, as per the Pontings' description (D & E 1976: 58).

LH11 - Stonefield ("Callanish XII"), Lewis. NB 2155 3496. A standing stone 1.3m tall x 0.7m x 0.2m set in a concrete plinth in the middle of a small housing development. According to local information it is in its original position (Ponting & Ponting 1981: 88).

LH20 - Garynahine (Druim na h-Aon Chloich; "Callanish XVII"), Lewis. NB 2367 3199. This is a prostrate slab 1.7m long (D & E 1976: 59) known to have been standing (Ponting & Ponting 1981: 90). It is probably to be identified with a standing stone marked some 50m away on the 1853 6" Ordnance Survey map, but it is unknown whether the O.S. marked its position erroneously or whether it has been moved.

UI20 - Balelone, North Uist. NF 728 738. A standing stone listed by the RCAHMS (1928: no. 257) had been removed by 1979.

<u>UI41</u> - <u>Aerodrome, Benbecula.</u> NF 79 56. Listed by Thom (FSL: H4/3) without description, this site is marked "removed for aerodrome". We made no attempt to locate the site.

<u>UI53</u> - <u>Loch nan Arm (Carragh Broin), South Uist.</u> NF 8117 2248. Listed by Thom (FSL: H5/9) but with description marked 'unknown', this site consisted of a small block of stone (RCAHMS 1928: no. 399) which was destroyed in fencing operations (D & E 1965: 21). We made no attempt to visit this site.

<u>UI56</u> - <u>Pollachar, South Uist.</u> NF 7459 1439. A standing stone 1.7m high which has been re-erected. Thom's reference number for the site has changed (FSL: H5/8; 1967: Table 12.1, H5/9).

<u>NA4</u> - <u>Strontian (Clach a'Bhranguis), Sunart.</u> NM 8154 6136. A standing stone 1.6m high as described by the RCAHMS (1980: no. 115), which appears to have been moved to its present position from 8154 6136 (OSAR: NM 86 NW, 1) where it might have been erected in antiquity.

<u>ML20</u> - <u>Inch Kenneth (Mull).</u> NM 4387 3549. A standing stone 1m tall which was re-erected shortly before 1967. Before that it was built into a nearby wall (OSAR: NM 43 NW, 2).

<u>ML26</u> - <u>Uluvalt II, Mull.</u> NM 546 293. A possible standing stone 0.8m high (D & E 1958: 8) was not located by the Ordnance Survey (OSAR: NM 52 NW, 4) in 1972, and appeared to have been moved in the construction of a new road. We made no attempt to locate the site.

<u>ML29</u> - <u>Scoor, Mull.</u> NM 4199 1890. A recorded standing stone at this location had been removed by 1972 (RCAHMS 1980: no. 114). The present farmer located its probable position for us in 1976.

<u>ML32</u> - <u>Assopol Cottage, Mull.</u> NM 3890 2171. A reported standing stone had been removed by 1961 (OSAR: NM 32 SE, 4). We did not attempt to locate this site.

<u>ML40</u> - <u>Catchean, Mull.</u> NM 30 23. A standing stone at this location was destroyed in the 1860's (RCAHMS 1980: no. 97). We made no attempt to locate the site.

<u>LN6</u> - <u>Barcaldine Castle, Benderloch.</u> NM 9105 4030 & 9117 4027. This 2.1m-tall standing stone has been moved to its present position some 120m E of three cairns (RCAHMS 1975: no. 32).

<u>LN10</u> - <u>Eilean Musdile (Lismore).</u> NM 779 351. A standing stone recorded in 1784 has since disappeared (RCAHMS 1975: no. 117).

<u>LN11</u> - <u>Connel, Lorn.</u> NM 9169 3409. A reported standing stone at this location was presumably removed shortly before 1880 when the railway was being constructed (RCAHMS 1975: no. 115).

<u>LN13</u> - <u>Airdsbay House (Taynuilt 1), Lorn.</u> NN 0051 3109. A standing stone 1.2m high was moved over 1 km. to its present location in 1805 (RCAHMS 1975: no. 121).

LN21 - Kilninver, Lorn. NM 8250 2207. A standing stone recorded here had been destroyed by 1970 (RCAHMS 1975: no. 119).

AR1 - Barrichbeyan (Caisteal nan Coin Duibh), Argyll. NM 8013 0773. According to the Ordnance Survey (OSAR: NM 80 NW, 10) there is a prostrate stone here conforming to Campbell & Sandeman's description (1961: no. 164) which was quite possibly once a standing stone. However if so it has probably been moved here as part of clearance operations and its original position is unknown.

AR4 - Ardlarich, Argyll. NM 810 055. Campbell & Sandeman (1961: no. 156) record "large stones" recently removed for gateposts.

AR14 - Tayness (Brouch an Drummin), Argyll. NR 8203 9721. A stone which stood 1.7m tall x 0.6m x 0.4m (Campbell & Sandeman 1961: no. 163) was moved between 1973 and 1977 (OSAR: NR 89 NW, 35) and is now recumbent.

AR26 - Torbhlaran S (Kilmichael Glassary), Argyll. NR 8607 9428. The Ordnance Survey (OSAR: NR 89 SE, 12) list a former standing stone 3.4m long, now used as a footbridge across a ditch, which according to the farmer lies not far from its original position. A note from the Natural History and Antiquarian Society of mid-Argyll (D & E 1978: 23) lists a second former standing stone, 1.5m long, now lying alongside the same ditch.

AR35 - Dunans (Clach na Beithir), Knapdale. NR 80 90. Campbell & Sandeman (1961: no. 170) list a standing stone which fell before 1830. There is now no trace of it (OSAR: NR 89 SW, 8).

IS8 - Kepollsmore, Islay. NR 3792 6662. We were unable in 1978 to locate the standing stone listed by Thom (A7/9). We now learn (RCAHMS 1984: no. 105) that it has fallen and lies intact by a boundary wall.

IS17 - Sunderland, Islay. NR 246 645. A large standing stone was blasted and removed in 1838, and a cist found beneath it (OSAR: NR 26 SW, 11; RCAHMS 1984: no. 63).

IS33 - Neriby, Islay. NR 3595 6053. This standing stone, recorded in 1878, had disappeared without trace by the time of our visit in 1978.

KT13 - Achamore House (Cnoc na Carraigh), Gigha. NR 6427 4818 & 6420 4806. Of two reported standing stones, some 130m apart, one was removed at the beginning of the 19th Century (RCAHMS 1971: no. 138) and the other is in fact an Ogam-inscribed stone, not re-erected in its original position (RCAHMS 1971: no. 244).

KT22 - Barr Mains, Kintyre. NR 6703 3545. This standing stone was removed to the side of the field in 1950 (RCAHMS 1971: no. 133).

KT26 - Drum, Kintyre. NR 6667 2563. This standing stone was removed by blasting in about 1910 (RCAHMS 1971: no. 141).

KT30 - Glencraigs N., Kintyre. NR 6935 2406. This standing stone has been removed to the edge of the field (RCAHMS 1971: no. 145).

KT34 - Peninver Bridge, Kintyre. NR 7638 2570. This is a stone 2.4m
      long lying on the edge of a rocky outcrop, which may have been
      standing, but there is no information on its original position
      (OSAR: NR 72 NE, 8).

2.4.2 Sites not located

LH34 - Husinish, Harris. NA 989 119. Listed as a single standing
      stone by Thom (FSL: H2/4), no exact position is given for this
      site. It does not correspond to any sites recorded on the other
      available lists, and, when the settlement at Husinish was vis-
      ited in 1981, there was no local knowledge of a standing stone.

UI8 - Udal, North Uist. NF 8242 7843. According to the Ordnance
      Survey (OSAR: NF 87 NW, 1) an orthostatic circle was discovered
      during the 1964 excavation of the nearby mediaeval settlement,
      but excavation of the circle was abandoned. We could not find
      any trace of a circle at the given grid reference when visiting
      the site in 1981.

UI14 - Loch an Duin, North Uist. NF 88 73. A site consisting of a
      standing stone 1.0m high and a prostrate slab 1.2m long was
      recorded by Beveridge (1911: 153), but was not located by the
      Ordnance Survey in 1965 (OSAR: NF 87 SE, 17). We did not
      attempt to locate this site.

UI18 - Loch nan Geirann, North Uist. NF 85 72. Two large prone slabs
      described by Beveridge (1911: 262) were not located by the
      Ordnance Survey (OSAR: NF 87 SE, 24) in 1965. We made no
      attempt to locate the site.

UI21 - Balmartin (Carra-Crom), North Uist. NF 73 73. A large
      standing stone referred to by Martin Martin (c. 1695: 59) could
      not be traced by the Ordnance Survey in 1965 (OSAR: NF 77 SW,
      5). We did not attempt to locate it.

UI51 - Loch Kildonan, South Uist. NF 736 277. Thom (1967: Table
      12.1, H5/6) lists at 736 277 a site which "looks like a poor
      circle". On visiting the location in 1981, no trace was found
      of a site at this grid reference; merely a few grass-covered
      rocky hillocks amidst low-lying peaty ground. It is conceivable
      that one of the hillocks could have been mistaken for a possible
      stone ring, but it seems unlikely.

NA6 - Sallochan Burn, Morvern. NM 62 48. The Ordnance Survey (OSAR:
      NM 64 NW, 4) list a documented stone circle which they failed to
      locate in 1970. We did not attempt to locate the site.

ML22 - Torosay (Clach Nighean a'Mhoraire), Mull. NM 7265 3525.
      Thom's site M2/3 (FSL) corresponds to a "large stone" listed by
      the Ordnance Survey (OSAR: NM 73 NW, misc. 1). We could not
      locate the site in 1976.

ML36 - Ardfenaig, Mull. NM 34 23. A standing stone listed by the
      Ordnance Survey (OSAR: NM 32 SW, 10) was not located by them in
      1972. We made no attempt to locate this site.

ML38 - Aridghlas, Mull. NM 31 23. A standing stone listed by the Ordnance Survey (OSAR: NM 32 SW, 1) was not located by them in 1972. We made no attempt to locate this site.

ML41 - Cnoc an t-Sidhein, Iona. NM 2720 2372. A cairn and circle of stones reported by Pennant (1774: 297), whose location is probably (but not certainly) the hill of Cnoc an t-Sidhein (Crawford 1933: 459), could not be located by the Ordnance Survey in 1972 (OSAR: NM 22 SE, 30). We made no attempt to locate the site.

IS9 - Lossit Lodge, Islay. NR 406 656. We were unable to locate this standing stone (D & E 1972: 4), and it is not listed by the RCAHMS (1984).

2.5 Sites excluded because they could not be visited in the time available

Every effort was made to visit all sites, however remote. However seven of the remaining 204 sites in the initial list (mostly on small islands) could not be reached, either because of lack of available time or sufficient funds, and have not been considered further. They are as follows:

LH32 - Aird Sleitenish, Lewis. NB 031 198. The possible remains of a stone circle are documented in D & E (1973: 48) and by the Ordnance Survey (OSAR: NB 01 NW, 2). This site is situated on the remote Western coast of Lewis.

LH38 - Ensay (Harris). NF 9803 8667. Standing stone. Island not visited.

UI1 - Boreray (St. Kilda). NA 1506 0499. Possible stone circle. Island not visited.

UI2 - Gleann Mor, St. Kilda. NF 0886 9943. Possible stone circle. Island not visited.

UI7 - Boreray (North Uist). NF 85 81. Standing stone. Island not visited.

UI61 - Leac a'Langich, Berneray (S). NL 5626 8021. Standing stone, probably now removed, and possible stone circle. Island not visited.

AR20 - Carron, Argyll. NR 9325 9809. Standing stone. This site is situated in a remote part of Kilmichael forest.

2.6 Sites unknown to us at the time of our visits

The Ordnance Survey and RCAHMS have been carrying out surveys of Jura and Islay since 1978. Six sites included in their lists, and included among the remaining 197 sites in our initial list, were however unknown to us at the time of our visits to these islands in 1978 and 1979. We have not considered any of these sites further. They are:

IS10 - Suidh' an Eoin Mor, Islay. NR 3958 6560. Possible standing
stone.

IS20 - West Carrabus, Islay. NR 3101 6341. A prostrate slab,
probably a fallen standing stone.

IS32 - Gortanilivorrie, Islay. NR 3582 6137. Standing stone.

IS43 - Druim nam Madagan, Islay. NR 3826 4595. Standing stone.

IS44 - Port Ellen III, Islay. NR 3714 4603. Standing stone.

IS48 - Cnoc Mor Ghrasdail (Coille a'Chnoic Mhoir), Islay. NR 3109
4721. Standing stone.

2.7 Excavated sites

Finally, two sites in Argyll have been excavated with a view to
testing the hypothesis that astronomical considerations were relevant
to the design of the site. Since our approach is designed to try to
deal with the much larger mass of data from unexcavated sites, and
ultimately to suggest hypotheses testable by excavation (see Section
1.2), it is unnecessary, and might perhaps be misleading, to include
in our analysis sites which have already been excavated in order to
test an astronomoical hypothesis. The two sites concerned are:

AR5 - Kintraw, Argyll. NM 8305 0498. A menhir 4m tall x 1.0m x 0.3m,
which fell during the winter of 1978-79 and was subsequently re-
erected after excavation of the socket-hole (Cowie 1979). It is
situated between two cairns investigated by Simpson (1967: 54).
A small prostrate slab some 8m to its NW, described as a fallen
stone by Thom (1971: 38, fig. 4.3, stone S2), appears to be the
only remaining part of a further structure, possibly a cairn,
marked in a sketch plan made by Edward Lhuyd in 1699 (Campbell &
Thomson 1963; see also Burl 1983: 45). A further stone (S3)
noted by Thom is an irregular block measuring about 1.9m x 1.3m
x at least 0.5m, and situated some 50m to the NE of the standing
stone. It appears to be natural. A hill platform on the far
side of a gorge some 100m to the NE of the standing stone has
been excavated by MacKie (1974), but the question as to whether
it was artificially constructed remains unresolved (Heggie
1981a: S29-31).

AR21 - Minard (Brainport Bay), Argyll. NR 973 950. This site has
been excavated by Col. P. Fane-Gladwin and Euan MacKie. For
details see MacKie (1981: 128-37).

2.8 The site source list

We are left with 189 sites from our initial site list which are
considered to represent genuine or possible sites of free-standing
megaliths constructed in prehistoric times. These sites comprise our
site source list and are carried forward to the analyses that follow.

3   THE CLASSIFICATION AND SELECTION OF SITE DATA

3.1   Archaeological status

The 189 sites comprising the site source list were examined archaeologically prior to surveys being undertaken. Structures at the sites have been divided into two categories on the basis of first-hand examinations as well as the examinations and reports of other investigators. Standing stones which can reasonably be assumed to have been erected in prehistoric times, and to have been little disturbed since by human hand, are designated high status stones. Throughout the remainder of the volume the term "menhir" is assumed to refer to a high status stone. It may be standing or leaning, but not fallen.

We define a low status stone to be one of the following:

  (i) Possible menhir. A somewhat dubious contender for a prehistoric standing stone, for example an erect stone less than about 1m high which might have occurred naturally, or an isolated standing stone for which some other hypothesis (e.g. constructed in later times as a trackway marker) is especially plausible.
 (ii) Boulder. A non-erect stone whose possible significance would not be considered but for its association with other, apparently authentic, prehistoric standing stones. Given the presence of these other features, it is considered possible that the boulder was placed in its present position during prehistoric times.
(iii) Fallen menhir. A stone which is known or can reasonably be assumed to be a fallen menhir which has not been moved from the position where it fell.

Thus for example the five small upright slabs about 0.5m high at Airigh nam Bidearan, Lewis (LH24) are designated possible menhirs and given low status under (i). A boulder situated within an alignment of three prostrate stones at Uluvalt, Mull (ML25) is considered to be a low status stone under (ii), while the prostrate stones themselves are considered to be low status stones under (iii).

We define the archaeological status of a site as follows:

  (A) A site is of archaeological status "A" if it contains at least one high status stone.
  (B) A site is of archaeological status "B" if it consists only of low status stones.

Full details of structures at the 189 sites are given in the area-by-area chapters that follow (Chs. 5 - 10): their designation as of high or low status is implicit in the descriptions. The archaeological status of the sites is also given.

3.2   Oriented structures and horizon indications

We shall consider any given oriented structure as constituting an indication of two ranges of horizon, one in each direction. In

order to calculate the azimuth or declination of a point on an indicated horizon we need to postulate an <u>observing position</u> (OP). The
assumed OPs for different indications need to be chosen in a consistent manner and stated explicitly if we are to ensure that the quoted
values of azimuths and altitudes, and hence of declinations, are
fairly chosen for the purposes of the statistical analysis. (For
examples of how the non-explicit and subjective choice of OPs can
affect quoted declinations see Ruggles 1983: Section 5.) This is the
case even though in practice an equally tenable "observing position"
might have been any place from which the azimuths or declinations were
unaffected within the required level of precision.

For the purposes of our computations we shall always take the OP
to be at a distance of 2m directly behind the indicating structure,
i.e. near enough to ensure that local ground level at the OP is
similar to that at the indicating structure itself, and at a height of
1.5m above present ground level.

Taking into account the highest level of astronomical precision
that we wish to test in this analysis, we shall not consider azimuths,
altitudes or declinations to an accuracy greater than $0°.1$. In view
of the uncertainties involved in the use of nearby horizons, such as
significant changes brought about by the growth of vegetation on the
horizon itself, we do not consider horizons nearer than 1 km (see Section 3.4 below). Thus even in the most unfavourable case a lateral or
height shift of 1.75m in the position of the observer would be needed
in order to affect the value of the indicated azimuth or declination,
and in most cases the required shift would be considerably greater
than this. This means that there is no implication at this level of
precision that people always stood at exactly the same position in
order to view any phenomena important in the construction of an oriented structure, and also means that any changes in the original ground
level in the vicinity of the site will have a negligible effect upon
the declinations quoted. Thus although the OP is implicit in our computations, we shall not need to enter into any more discussion of it.

We define the <u>indicated azimuth range</u> (IAR) as that range of
horizon which can reasonably be supposed to have been indicated by a
given configuration on the ground, taking into account

(i) different possible ways of providing the indication, e.g. in the
case of an alignment of menhirs, lining up the uppermost points
of the menhirs or lining up their sides; and
(ii) possible changes in the direction indicated due to movement of
individual menhirs.

We shall only quote the edges of an IAR to an accuracy of $0°.2$.
Greater accuracy is seldom justified because of uncertainties in the
deterioration of an indicating structure since its erection. Thus no
IAR can have a width in azimuth of less than $0°.2$.

Suppose that the width of the IAR is I. We define the <u>adjacent
azimuth range</u> (AAR) as a range of horizon extending for an azimuth A
on either side of it, where
A = $1°$ when I is up to $1°$;
A = I   when I is between $1°$ to $2°$; and
A = $2°$ when I is above $2°$.

3.3   Selection criteria for oriented structures

We wish to classify megalithic structures in an attempt to order them qualitatively in terms of their inherent likelihood as astronomical indicators. In constructing our selection criteria for possible indications we have concentrated on alignments of stones, giving greatest preference to alignments of three or more menhirs or two oriented slabs. Next in the order of preference come various situations where such an alignment includes low status stones. After this we have considered lines between stone pairs where they are not known once to have formed part of a larger setting, and finally, following Thom, we consider the flat sides of single slabs. Throughout the system structures are assigned a lower classification if low status stones are present. Thus the archaeological status of the site features implicitly in the classification assigned to any structures there.

An earlier attempt to lay down an order of preference was made in 1975 (Cooke et al. 1977) and used in a preliminary study of the sites near Callanish, Lewis (LH10–LH24). It is hoped that the present modified criteria answer various criticisms raised against the earlier ones (e.g. Heggie 1981a: S19; 1981b: 141).

We have dismissed from further consideration any on-site indications involving stone rings. Astronomical hypotheses involving sighting across stone rings, for example those proposed by Thom at Castle Rigg (Thom 1967: 145-51), have to be approached with particular caution, as they are often dependent upon the secondary hypothesis that the site fits a particular geometrical construction. Such problems are discussed elsewhere in relation to the Aberdeenshire Recumbent Stone Circles (Ruggles 1984; Ruggles & Burl 1984). We have not, however, dismissed inter-site lines between stone rings, as is explained in Section 3.5.

We have also excluded lines between the centres of stone rings and outlying stones, a significant departure from the classification system of Cooke et al. and from the early work of Thom, since very few cases occur amongst the western Scottish sites where there is a stone ring together with only one outlier. In addition most stone rings are not perfectly circular and in a good state of repair, which means that there can be considerable uncertainty in determining the centre unless geometrical assumptions are made. The orientations of stone rings and outliers should, it is felt, form the basis of a separate study in areas where such structures are more common.

We define a slab to be a menhir which has opposite faces both of which are of maximum width at least twice that of the other faces. Likewise a possible menhir may be a possible slab. Whether fallen menhirs were in fact slabs has no effect upon our site procedure and we do not try to determine this.

We specify the following proviso relating to the classification of indications:

(i) no standing menhir or stone involved in defining the indication can be, or known from documentary evidence to have been, part of a megalithic ring.

Subject to this proviso we now define six <u>classes of indication</u> as follows:

CLASS 1 - One of the following:

(1a) An alignment of three or more menhirs, possibly with further low status stones which stand or could have stood in the line.
(1b) Two slabs which are, or can reasonably be assumed to have been, oriented along the line joining them; possibly with further low status stones which stand or could have stood in the line.

CLASS 2 - One of the following:

(2a) Two menhirs (not both slabs oriented along the line joining them) together with one or more low status stones which stand or could have stood in the line (in which case the IAR is taken as that defined by the two standing menhirs);
(2b) A slab together with two or more low status stones which stand or could have stood in line with its orientation (in which case the IAR is taken as that defined by the orientation of the slab);
(2c) A menhir (not a slab) and two or more low status stones, which form or could have formed an alignment; or
(2d) A slab and two or more low status stones, which form or could have formed an alignment which is not in the direction of orientation of the slab.

CLASS 3 - One of the following:

(3a) Two menhirs, not both slabs oriented along the line joining them;
(3b) A slab together with a low status stone which stands or could have stood in line with its orientation (in which case the IAR is taken as that defined by the orientation of the slab);
(3c) Three or more low status stones which form or could have formed an alignment; or
(3d) Two possible slabs which are, or can reasonably be assumed to have been, oriented along the line joining them.

CLASS 4 - One of the following:

(4a) A menhir, not a slab, together with a low status stone; or
(4b) A slab together with a low status stone which does not stand and does not appear to have stood in line with the orientation of the slab.

CLASS 5 - One of the following:

(5a) One or both of the wider faces of a slab.
(5b) Two low status stones.

CLASS 6 -

One or both of the wider faces of a possible slab.

We now define eight <u>types of site</u> as follows:

TYPE 1 - A site containing at least one CLASS 1 indication.
TYPE 2 - A site containing no CLASS 1 indications but at least one CLASS 2 indication.
TYPE 3 - A site containing no CLASS 1 or 2 indications but at least one <u>and no more than six</u> CLASS 3 indications.
TYPE 4 - A site containing no CLASS 1, 2 or 3 indications but at least one <u>and no more than six</u> CLASS 4 indications.
TYPE 5 - A site containing no CLASS 1, 2, 3 or 4 indications but at least one <u>and no more than six</u> CLASS 5 indications.
TYPE 6 - A site containing no CLASS 1, 2, 3, 4 or 5 indications but at least one CLASS 6 indication.
TYPE 7 - A site consisting of at least one menhir which either contains no CLASS 1-5 indications, or more than six indications of CLASS 3 or 4.
TYPE 8 - A site consisting of at least one low status stone which either contains no CLASS 1-6 indications, or more than six indications of CLASS 5(b).

Details of the classification of each of the 189 sites in the site source list are given in the area-by-area chapters (Chs. 5 - 10). Some examples follow of the use of these classification criteria.

An alignment consisting of three standing menhirs, as at Dervaig S, Mull (ML11), is of Class (1a) and the site is Type 1. An alignment of two standing menhirs and one fallen one, as at Duachy (LN22), is of Class (2a) and the site is Type 2. A standing slab and several fallen ones which appear to have formed an alignment, as at Quinish, Mull (ML2), give an indication of Class (2b), and the site is again of Type 2. An alignment consisting entirely of low status stones, for example the three prostrate stones (assumed to be fallen menhirs) and boulder at Uluvalt, Mull (ML25), form an indication of Class (3c) and the site is Type 3.

Two aligned slabs, as at Carnasserie, Argyll (AR12), form an indication of Class (1b) and the site is Type 1. A slab together with a single fallen menhir which appears to have stood in line, as at Lagavulin N, Islay (IS39), is of Class (3b) and the site is Type 3. An alignment of two possible slabs (there are no examples in our sample of sites) would be of Class (3d).

The line joining two standing stones other than aligned slabs, as at Cul a'Chleit, Lewis (LH22), is of Class (3a) and the site is Type 3. That joining a menhir (not a slab) and a possible menhir or boulder, as at Glenamacrie, Lorn (LN18), is of Class (4a) and the site is Type 4. That joining two possible menhirs, as at Dunskeig, Kintyre (KT8) is of Class (5b) and the site is Type 5.

The flat side(s) of a slab, as at many sites in Kintyre (e.g. KT28, KT29, KT36) form indications of Class (5a) and the sites are Type 5. In some cases where the flat sides of a slab are nowhere near parallel, as at Knockstapple, Kintyre (KT41), they define two completely separate indications in each direction. In such cases the flattest side (narrowest indication) only is selected. However where a stone is not even rectangular but triangular, as at Beinn a'Charra, North Uist (UI26), we do not count it as a slab. The flat side(s) of a possible slab, as at Dursainean NE, Lewis (LH29) or Stiaraval, Ben-becula (UI46), form indications of Class 6 and the sites are Type 6.

Three menhirs not forming an alignment, and no two of which form an aligned pair of slabs, produce six Class (3a) indications and the site is Type 3. An example is Carse, Knapdale (KT2), although this is in fact a borderline case: two of the menhirs form an aligned pair, but their wider faces are not quite twice as wide as the other faces, and so they are not counted as slabs. Four menhirs not forming an alignment, and no two of which form an aligned pair of slabs, as at Tenga, Mull (ML13), produce twelve Class (3a) indications. However this is greater than the limit allowed and the site is Type 7. Stone rings occurring in isolation can contain no Class 1-6 indications owing to proviso (i), and hence these are also Type 7. A site consisting of a single menhir, not a slab, as at Beinn a'Charra, North Uist (UI26), is of Type 7 as well. A site consisting of a single low status stone, for example the fallen menhir at Lower Bayble, Lewis (LH31) or the possible menhir at Loch na Buaile Iochdrach, North Uist (UI29), is of Type 8.

The upper limit of six lines between pairs of stones prevents our having to consider large numbers of lines, most of which are un-doubtedly of no special orientational significance, at sites where there are a number of stones and no alignments or rings. It also circumvents the problem of defining in borderline cases when exactly a setting of stones constitutes a stone ring. Burl (1971) has identified a class of stone ring, the "four-poster", consisting of only four stones: should all four-stone settings apart from alignments be treat-ed as stone rings? Under our classification system, no lines will be considered between pairs of stones in settings of four stones of equal status, whether they are considered to constitute a stone ring or not. Thus at Port of Ness, Lewis (LH1) no lines are considered because the two stones once formed part of a four-stone setting. Similarly no pairwise alignments are considered between the central four stones at Cnoc Fillibhir Bheag (LH18), regardless of whether they are considered to form an internal stone ring or not. On the other hand the site at Bernera Bridge (LH8) consists of only three stones (two standing and one prostrate) which can with impunity be said to have formed an original megalithic setting: a fourth stone at the site is very much smaller, and unlikely to have been erected in antiquity. In this case the site is treated as a three stone setting, and pairwise lines are considered between the two high status (standing) stones.

There is a further reason for the limit of six lines which concerns the need for independent data: this point is elaborated in Chapter 12.

3.4 Exclusion criteria for selected indications

Of the highest class indications existing at a site, those falling into either of the following categories have been excluded from further consideration:

(L) the indicated horizon is less than 1 km distant;
(W) the IAR exceeds 5° in width.

Suppose that some structures were deliberately astronomically aligned to a precision of around $0°.1$ in declination (the greatest precision in which we are interested here). For any indication, the declination(s) that we select for analysis on the basis of its present state will inevitably differ from the original intended declination, owing to changes in ground level and vegetation on the indicated horizon, and to the deterioration of the site. If in particular cases a probable error is introduced which is considerably greater than $0°.1$, then sufficient random noise may be introduced into the data as a whole to hamper, or even thwart completely, our efforts to detect any deliberate alignments of this precision. Criteria (L) and (W) exclude cases where the probable error is considered to be sufficiently large for this effect to be important. Should evidence of deliberate orientations emerge from our analysis, but only at a precision substantially lower than $0°.1$, then we should consider reinstating the excluded indications. Evidence for lower precision alignments may still be recoverable from them.

Criterion (L) assumes that changes in ground level and vegetation since prehistoric times may alter the height of a horizon by up to about 2m. When the horizon is nearer than 1 km this will result in the declination being altered by at least $0°.1$.

The statistical test used in Section 12.2, which involves nearest-neighbour analysis, depends only upon the central azimuth within each IAR. The intended indication, however, might lie anywhere within the limits of the IAR, this being how the IAR was originally defined (see Section 3.2 above). For IARs in excess of $5°$ in width (criterion W) the probable error introduced by analysing the central azimuth rather than the true indicated declination becomes significantly large.

The other tests described in Chapter 12 consist of spreading a fixed probability for each indication over the entire IAR or AAR. For sharply-defined indications (narrow IARs) this will produce a concentration of probability around a certain azimuth or declination. However for very wide IARs and AARs the probability will be so diffused that to omit the indication completely will have negligible effect on the statistical result.

We have disregarded two further exclusion criteria used in an earlier code of practice (Cooke et al. 1977: 115-17), since they were motivated by considerations of even higher-precision astronomy than we are investigating here. The detection of deliberate astronomical alignments of a precision higher than $0°.1$ is considered extremely unlikely following the author's reassessments of Thom's later work (Ruggles 1981; 1982b; 1983). However should evidence emerge from this analysis of deliberate orientations at a precision of around $0°.1$, then we should re-consider the possibility of even higher precision alignments.

3.5   Inter-site indications

In his early statistical work Thom (1955; 1967: ch. 8) included a number of inter-site indications - indications formed by standing at one site and using another as foresight. The fact that he obtained positive results motivates us to consider inter-site indications also: however in doing so we risk, rather more obviously than in the case of on-site ones, associating structures which are in fact of very different dates and purposes. Where sites are in fact culturally unrelated, the orientations of inter-site alignments will be random, unless a pattern is enforced by geographical constraints (a possibility that must be checked if apparently significant statistical results emerge). However if some sites were culturally related then there is certainly a possibility that astronomical symbolism might have influenced their relative siting.

Inter-site lines also act as somewhat of a buffer if decisions about what constitutes a single site - decisions dictated by the (arbitrary) 300m distance criterion (Section 2.1) - go the wrong way in individual cases and lead us to separate features more than 300m apart which were in fact related. Provided that they are intervisible, alignments between such features will still be included in the data set as inter-site indications.

In what follows we have considered any intervisible pairs of sites that occur within our region of interest. Although examples are found throughout the region, there are three notable concentrations: one, around Callanish in Lewis (LH10 - LH24), consists mainly of stone rings; another, in the flat neck of Kintyre between Machrihanish and Campbeltown (KT27 - KT39), consists almost entirely of single stone slabs; and the last, in North Uist (UI22 - UI37), consists of a greater diversity of types of site. Perhaps the concentrations of similar sites provide the best chance of inter-site indications being astronomically significant; certainly many examples from around Callanish were included in Thom's list of 262 alignments (1967: Table 8.1). However even in these areas, and especially overall, we should expect much random noise to be introduced into the data through our inevitable inclusion of many pairings of sites which were in fact unrelated.

We select data for consideration using a code of practice similar to that for on-site indications, and one which is again derived from that laid down by Cooke et al. (1977). As with oriented structures at single sites, two sites form an indication of two ranges of horizon, one in each direction. We assume that the indicated horizon was directly above the foresight as viewed from the backsight.* We take the observing position (OP) to be the centre of the backsight if it consists of more than one stone, or 2m behind a single stone.

We define the indicated azimuth range (IAR) as that range of horizon which can reasonably be supposed to have been indicated by one site as viewed from another, taking into account

   (i) any uncertainty in defining the OP at the centre of the rear
      site; and
  (ii) the difficulty in defining a vertical line by eye when the far
      site is situated considerably below the horizon.

- - - - - -

* We follow Thom in using the "foresight/backsight" terminology both for our own convenience and for clarity in the explanations that follow. However we risk, and wish to discourage, overtones associated with Thom's particular interpretations.

Where the backsight is a stone ring or a site of more complex design, there may be considerable uncertainty as to where to define its centre. A lateral shift in OP will produce a horizontal shift in the position of the foresight with respect to the horizon (unless it itself forms the horizon) as well as altering the azimuth or declination of any particular range of horizon. Where the OP is uncertain, both effects must be taken into account. However the former effect is limited since the foresight must be at least 300m distant (see Section 2.1). As with IARs for on-site indications, we shall only quote their limits to an accuracy of $0°.2$. We define the adjacent_azimuth_range (AAR) as for on-site lines.

We define classes_of_inter-site_indication as follows:

CLASS 1 - The foresight is nearer than 6 km and on the horizon as seen from the backsight, or on the crest of a ridge with more distant horizon beyond. At least one menhir projecting above the horizon or ridge must subtend at least 1' (i.e. approximately 1m for each 3 km distance).

CLASS 2 - The indication is not Class 1 and the foresight is nearer than 3 km.

CLASS 3 - The indication is not of Class 1 or 2 and the foresight is nearer than 6 km.

As with on-site indications, this classification is an attempt to order indications qualitatively in terms of their inherent likelihood of being astronomically significant. The visual prominence of the foresight is an important factor to be considered, but one which may change markedly in differing atmospheric conditions (Cooke et_al. 1977: 117). Hence Class 1 indications incorporate a qualitative estimate of prominence, the 1' criterion being suggested by the resolution of the human eye. The other classes, together with the overall inclusion criterion, are determined by distance considerations only. We also note an "archaeological status" for the indication, which is "A" if the archaeological status of both sites concerned is "A", but "B" if either site is "B".

Any indications falling into categories (L) or (W), as defined in Section 3.4 above, have been excluded from further consideration.

4   THE RECOVERY OF SITE DATA

C.L.N.Ruggles, J.G.Morgan, R.W.Few & J.A.Cooke

4.1   Surveying technique

Sites have been surveyed during the years between 1973 and 1981 using the following theodolites:

(1973- 1975): Hilger & Watts 20" Vernier theodolite;
(1976   ): Cooke, Troughton & Simms 20" optical theodolite;
(1977- 1978): Hilger and Watts 1" microptic theodolite;
(1979- 1981): Kern DKM-1 10" lightweight microptic theodolite.

Fieldwork during the 1975 - 1978 seasons lasted from three to four weeks, enabling theodolite adjustment errors to be determined from measurements repeated on both theodolite faces throughout the expeditions. During 1979 and 1981, fieldwork by CR on this and other projects lasted for more than three months, allowing the theodolite adjustment errors to be regularly monitored.

The selection criteria set out in Chapter 3 dictated which horizon profiles were to be surveyed at each site, and laid down the observing position (OP) for each profile. In practice it was not always possible or convenient to place the theodolite at the exact OP: for example

  (i) when nearby trees obscured the profile when viewed from the OP, but not from nearby; or
 (ii) when it was necessary to survey several profiles, with several different OP's, from the same site, and considerable time could be saved by setting up the theodolite only once or twice.

In these cases a correction can be applied to the measurements at a later stage (see below).

At each theodolite station it is necessary to determine Plate Bearing Zero (PBZ), the true azimuth of the zero graduation on the horizontal circle of the theodolite. When weather permitted, this was achieved by taking observations of the sun, timed by the following methods:

(1973- 1978): The MSF Rugby standard time signal, using a receiver taken on site.
(1979   ): A quartz crystal wristwatch, calibrated using GPO telephone time signals.
(1981   ): Various digital timers, calibrated as above.

A series of twelve observations (three on each combination of solar limb and theodolite face) typically gave PBZ to ±10". In other cases, PBZ was determined from sightings of three or more Ordnance Survey triangulation stations. In the case of the sites in the vicinity of Callanish, Lewis, data were taken from the Glasgow University survey (Tait 1978). Thanks to information supplied for this project by the

Ordnance Survey, Southampton, the positions of the relevant Ordnance Survey triangulation stations were known sufficiently accurately that PBZ could be determined by the triangulation method to the nearest 1' or better. Exceptionally, other triangulation points (such as church spires) had to be used, and PBZ was determined less reliably. At a number of sites both sun-azimuth and triangulation station observations were available, allowing consistency checks to be made.

On each horizon profile, theodolite readings were taken of relocatable points, at least once on each theodolite face. When we take into account errors in determining PBZ, scale reading errors for individual measurements, and the uncertainties in the astronomical refraction correction to the measured altitude needed to calculate declinations (which may be 0'.5 or even larger at low altitudes), we expect that for relocatable points our azimuths will be reliable to about 0'.5, our altitudes to about 1', and hence our declinations to about 1'.

Intervening, non-relocatable points were often also surveyed. A 400mm or 200mm photograph of the horizon was then obtained from the theodolite station, to enable the horizon profile to be reconstructed between the surveyed points (see Section 4.3 below).

Surveys of the sites themselves, using theodolite and steel measuring tape, were strictly only necessary in order to determine the corrections from theodolite stations to OP's. However they were often undertaken for the sake of completeness at sites where no existing surveys were available. The method employed was to determine directly the position of one or more primary points on each stone using theodolite and tape, taking distance measurements between adjacent primary points as a consistency check. The shapes and orientations of individual stones were then determined relative to primary points using magnetic compass and tape. For further details and an example of a survey of a complex site, see Ruggles & Norris (1980).

4.2   Computer programs for the reduction of the survey data

A number of computer programs have been written in FORTRAN in order to facilitate the reduction of the survey data. These have been considerably updated by CR in recent years and form a library about which more details are available on request. Brief details follow.

For the statistical analysis, and where standard packages were not available, programs have been written in PASCAL. It is anticipated that updates of some or all of the programs described below will eventually be available in PASCAL.

4.2.1 Megaliths package (MEGPAK)

(i) PBERRS.   Calculates theodolite plate bearing errors. Input: a set of pairs of horizontal scale readings on both faces. Output: collimation error, maximum centring error, plate bearing of zero centring error, and standard deviation of one observation.

(ii) STIMES. Calculates plate bearing minus azimuth (PB-AZ) from sun observations. Input: (i) Approximate National Grid reference (NGR) of station to within 1 km, date, plate bearing errors, series of observations (time recorded, calibration correction, theodolite face, horizontal scale reading, alidade tilt). (ii) Astronomical ephemeris data for date concerned. Output: table of universal time (UT), observed plate bearing, calculated azimuth, and PB-AZ; mean PB-AZ.

(iii) TRIGPT. Calculates accurate station position and PB-AZ from three or more triangulation station (TS) observations. Input: Accurate NGR's of TS's, plate bearing errors, vertical scale type, series of observations (TS observed, theodolite face, horizontal and vertical scale readings). Output: data for each TS (mean plate bearing, convergence (i.e. difference of grid north from true north), line-of-sight correction); station NGR and PB-AZ as determined from each combination of three TS's; mean station NGR and PB-AZ.

(iv) TRGFID. Converts horizontal and vertical scale theodolite readings of points at known distance to azimuth and altitude values as seen from nearby observing positions. Input: NGR of station, plate bearing errors, vertical scale type, PB-AZ, profile identifier, distance units (metric or imperial); observations (point identifier, theodolite face, horizontal and vertical scale readings, distance of point); plate bearing, horizontal and vertical distance of OP from theodolite. Output: (i) List of azimuths and altitudes, from theodolite and OP. (ii) Corrected azimuths and altitudes, together with appropriate header information, for immediate input to CALDEC.

(v) CALDEC. Calculates declinations for the sun and/or moon of points on a horizon profile. Input: Header information and observed azimuths and altitudes of horizon points. Output: list of observed azimuths and altitudes, altitudes corrected for mean astronomical refraction and solar and/or lunar parallax (for more detail see Ruggles 1983), declination of sun and/or moon.

(vi) PLAN2D. Produces plane co-ordinates of points from theodolite readings and measured distances. Input: Co-ordinates of theodolite, PBZ (e.g. (0,0) and PB-AZ for true co-ordinates relative to theodolite; NGR of theodolite and plate bearing minus grid azimuth for plan in National Grid co-ordinates), plate bearing errors, observations (point, theodolite face, horizontal reading, distance). Output: list of co-ordinates of surveyed points; table of distances between them, for comparison with direct measurements.

(vii) PLAN3D. Produces spatial co-ordinates of points from theodolite readings and measured distances. Input: Co-ordinates of theodolite, PBZ as above, plate bearing errors, vertical scale type, observations (point, theodolite face, horizontal and vertical scale readings, distance). Output: list of co-ordinates of surveyed points, table of distances between them.

4.2.2 Subroutines of stand-alone value

(i) GRIDLA.   Converts a National Grid easting and northing to latitude and longitude. Input: Easting and northing. Output: Latitude and longitude, convergence (difference between grid north and true north), and bending (related to line-of-sight correction).

(ii) LAGRID.   Converts a latitude and longitude to National Grid easting and northing. Input: Latitude and longitude. Output: Easting, northing, convergence and bending (see above).

(iii) IPTANG.   Input time or angle. Converts a string of characters representing a time or angle, in any reasonable format, to a value in hours/degrees/radians. For example, "-0 10 0" is recognised as -10'.

(iv) OPTANG. Output time or angle. Reverse of IPTANG.

(v) SUNNAZ.   Calculates the azimuth and altitude of the centre of the sun, and its semidiameter, from a given place at a given time. Input: Date, UT, National Grid Easting and Northing, astronomical ephemeris information for date concerned. Output: Azimuth and altitude of centre of sun, solar semidiameter.

4.2.3 Graphics programs (using GINO and GINOGRAF routines)

(i) PROPIC.   Plots a profile diagram with declination lines plotted on at half-degree intervals. Input: Graph specifications, latitude of site, parameters of surveyed points, parameters of calculated points, digitised parameters of profile points, character strings for comments to be included on the graph. Examples: Figs. 5.2 - 5.14 (etc.) of this volume.

(ii) MAP.   Draws a geographical map from digital data in National Grid co-ordinates, with sites, etc. marked on as desired. Input: (i) Graph specifications, including instructions for interpreting the site list. (ii) Digital map data (e.g. coastline, rivers). (iii) Site list in any format. Grid references must be included at a fixed position in each line of the list, as must numbers determining symbols or character strings to be plotted at the position of the site. Examples: Figs. 2.1, 5.1 (etc.) of this volume.

(iii) TRNSFM.   Transforms a series of number pairs representing the plane co-ordinates of a digitised map, horizon profile, etc., into a new co-ordinate system. Uses specified reference points in order to calculate the transformation. If more than two reference points are specified, performs a least-squares fit to the points.

(iv) CURVIG.   Plots a cumulative gaussian probability histogram, or "curvigram", as used by Thom (1967: Figs. 8.1 & 10.1; 1971: Fig. 7.1); see also Ruggles (1981: 155-6). Input: Graph spec-

ifications, mean and standard deviation of each hump. Exam‑
ples: Ruggles 1981: Figs. 4.1 & 4.2; figures in Chapter 12 of
this volume.

4.3   Reduction of the survey data

Theodolite readings of horizon points were converted to
azimuths, altitudes and declinations using various programs in the
"MEGPAK" package. Although we generally expect our azimuths and dec‑
linations as determined from the theodolite station to be reliable to
1', the greatest accuracy required for the analyses in this volume is
$0°.1$, or 6'. Where the parallax correction from the theodolite to the
OP would amount to less than half this, the theodolite readings were
left uncorrected for this effect in order to simplify the analysis.
Thus although with more thorough analysis our survey measurements are
capable of giving azimuths and declinations reliable to about 1',
those quoted in the chapters that follow are only generally reliable
to $0°.1$.

In a few cases where the theodolite station was situated at some
distance from the OP, a large parallax correction was applied using
program "TRGFID". This introduces the possibility of some error into
the quoted azimuths and altitudes, owing to

   (i) perspective effects (i.e. profiles not being two-dimensional);
  (ii) notches which are formed by the junctions between hills at
       different distances closing or opening up; and
 (iii) the difficulty in determining accurately from maps the distance
       of the profile, which is necessary for the calculation of the
       correction.

The size of the uncertainties in azimuth and altitude will depend upon
the distance of the profile and the size of the parallax correction
involved. These cases are noted, and the uncertainties estimated,
where they occur in the chapters that follow.

The full horizon profiles shown in the diagrams in this volume
were constructed by digitising 200 mm and 400 mm photographs taken on
site. These were calibrated by performing a least-squares fit of
relocatable points to their surveyed azimuths and altitudes, using
program "TRNSFM". Vertical lines underneath points on the profiles
denote surveyed points, not all of which may have been relocatable and
hence included in the least squares fit. Lines of constant declin‑
ation are plotted above the profile at half-degree intervals.

While we attempted to survey all the horizon profiles dictated
by our selection criteria, surveys were sometimes not possible owing
to time constraints, persistent bad weather or trees or buildings
obscuring the relevant horizon profile. In these cases the profiles
have been calculated from 1:50000 (or occasionally 1:10000) Ordnance
Survey maps broadly following the methods suggested by Thom (1971:
123). Calculated points are shown by crosses on the profile diagrams.
They are as close together as the scale of the maps used would allow.

Profiles have been classified into three categories depending
upon the reliability of the survey, as follows.

(A) Surveyed; survey considered reliable to $0^{o}.2$ in azimuth.

(B) Surveyed; a continuous horizon is displayed in the profile diagrams but some error is possible for one or more of the following reasons:

  (e) The horizon profile has been extended well beyond the surveyed points using photographs only;

  (p) A large parallax correction was necessary from the theodolite to the observing position;

  (t) There are trees at some distance which obscure the exact profile; or

  (v) Visibility during the survey was poor. In some of these cases surveyed points are available, but not photographs: here the surveyed points have been marked by crosses on the diagrams, in contrast to the normal convention.

(C) Calculated profiles.

Each profile has been numbered, in order to facilitate cross-referencing between the profile data and diagrams, which are presented in Chs. 5 - 10, and the analyses in subsequent chapters.

5   <u>SITES IN LEWIS AND HARRIS (LH)</u>

C.L.N.Ruggles, J.G.Morgan, R.W.Few & J.A.Cooke

5.1   <u>Introduction</u>

In 1975, several sites in the vicinity of Callanish, Lewis, were
visited and surveyed by the authors. Some of the results quoted here
have already been published as part of a preliminary investigation
along the lines adopted in this volume (Cooke <u>et al</u>. 1977); where this
is the case the reduction of the original data has now been reworked
using procedures and computer programs updated since 1979.

The remaining sites in Lewis and Harris, including several
further reported sites in the Callanish area, have been visited by CR
during 1979, 1980 and 1981. Surveys were undertaken by CR both in
1979, with the assistance of Phil Appleton and Ray and Cilla Norris,
and in 1981, with the assistance of Kim Bramley. Some 1975 surveys
were repeated and checked. The locations of the sites considered are
shown in Fig. 5.1.

Sites in the vicinity of Callanish have been designated "Callanish I", "Callanish II" and so on by various authors (Thom 1967;
1971; Cooke <u>et al</u>. 1977; Tait 1978; Ponting & Ponting 1981). Although
we do not adopt this nomenclature here, principally because it carries
premature overtones of a cultural connection between all of the sites
involved, we do list the alternative site names both in column 12 of
Table 2.1 and in the following section.

5.2   <u>Descriptions and classification of sites</u>

The descriptions that follow are compiled from first-hand site
visits and measurements, and any comments are our own, except where
references are cited, in which case they are taken from the sources
quoted. Dimensions of standing stones are taken at the base unless
otherwise stated. We emphasize that these details are meant merely to
provide basic background information for the analyses that follow.
Fuller descriptions are available in the references cited in Table
2.1.

<u>LH1 - Port of Ness (Clach Stein), Lewis.</u> NB 5349 6417. Two erect
     stones, irregularly shaped, 1.5m and 1.0m high, some 3m apart.
     A prostrate boulder, not in line with the other two (RCAHMS
     1928: no. 19) was broken up and removed at least forty years ago
     (local knowledge), and an Ordnance Survey name book of 1852
     reports "four standing stones .. about 6 ft. apart .. forming a
     rectangular figure" (OSAR: NB 56 SW, 12). Arch. status = A;
     type = 7.

<u>LH5 - Ballantrushal (Clach an Trushal), Lewis.</u> NB 3755 5377. A
     standing stone more than 5.5m tall, approximately 2m wide and
     0.8m thick. Its longer faces are convex. Arch. status = A;
     type = 5.

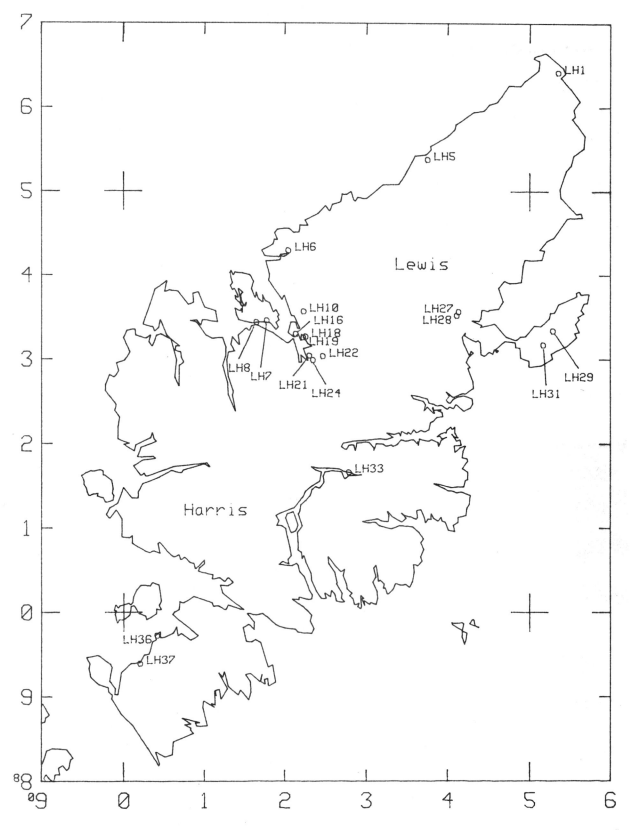

FIG. 5.1. Sites considered in Lewis and Harris (LH).

LH6 - Carloway (Clach an Tursa), Lewis. NB 2041 4295. An upright slab about 2.5m tall x 1.5m x 0.6m, oriented NNW-SSE; two large fallen stones, both split in two and originally about 4m long. If both the fallen stones stood at their SW ends it is quite possible that the three formed an alignment about 5m long and oriented roughly NW-SE, but the exact azimuth is uncertain within wide bounds. Thom's reference number for this site has changed (FSL: H1/16; 1967: Table 12.1, H1/8). Site plan: Thom, Thom & Burl (1984). Arch. status = A; type = 2.

LH7 - Kirkibost (Airigh Mhaoldonuich; "Callanish XV"), Great Bernera. NB 1775 3459. As described by Ponting & Ponting (1981: 93), this is a recumbent menhir, 3.5m long, which appears to have stood at its SW end. Arch. status = A; type = 8.

LH8 - Bernera Bridge (Cleiter; "Callanish VIII"), Great Bernera. NB 1642 3424. Two large standing slabs, heights about 2m and 3m, a small erect slab less than 1m tall, and a large prostrate stone 2.5m long. Situated on a cliff edge, the site has been reported as the remains of a stone circle about 20m in diameter whose other half has fallen away; however the size and anomalous orientation of the small erect stone make this unlikely. Thom's reference number for this site has changed (FSL: H1/8; 1967: Table 12.1, H1/7). Site plans: Thom (1967: 126); Tait (1978); Ponting & Ponting (1981: 81); Thom, Thom & Burl (1984). Arch. status = A; type = 3.

(ctd. on page 80

- - - - - -

TABLE 5.1. List of on-site indications in Lewis and Harris (LH).

Column headings

1   Site reference number
2   Site name
3   Description of the indication
4   Classification of the indication (see Section 3.3)
5   Distance of the horizon profile
6   Survey status (see Sections 4.3 & 3.4):
        A Reliably surveyed
        B Less reliably surveyed
        C Calculated
        L Dismissed because horizon is local
        W Dismissed because IAR is too wide
7   Comment: reason that profile survey is less reliable
        e Horizon profile extended using photographs only
        p Large parallax correction
        t Trees obscure the exact profile
        v Poor visibility during survey
        (for further details see Section 4.3)
        o Survey data from other authors (see Section 5.3)
8   Date of latest survey
9   Indication reference number
10   Azimuth limits of the indication, accurate to $0°.2$

Table 5.1

Site	Name	Indication	Class	Dist	St	Com	Survey	No.	Az limits	
LH5	Ballantrushal	To W	5a	–	W					
LH5	Ballantrushal	To E	5a	–	W					
LH6	Carloway	abc (To NW)	2d	–	W					
LH6	Carloway	cba (To SE)	2d	–	W					
LH8	Bernera Bridge	ab (To NE)	3a	0.0 km	L					
LH8	Bernera Bridge	ba (To SW)	3a	14.5 km	A		810724;	2:	219.4	223.6
LH10	Beinn Bheag	ba (To NW)	4a	0.1 km	L					
LH10	Beinn Bheag	ab (To SE)	4a	10.0 km	B	o	–;	4:	146.0	147.0
LH16	Callanish	av W to N	1a	3.5 km	A		750711;	11:	7.6	10.8
LH16	Callanish	av W to S	1a	0.1 km	L					
LH16	Callanish	av E to N	1a	3.5 km	A		750711;	12:	9.8	12.0
LH16	Callanish	av E to S	1a	0.1 km	L					
LH16	Callanish	S row to N	1a	3.0 km	A		750711;	13:	359.4	0.0
LH16	Callanish	S row to S	1a	0.1 km	L					
LH16	Callanish	W row to W	1a	1.5 km	A		750711;	14:	266.0	268.6
LH16	Callanish	W row to E	1a	6.0 km	C		–;	15:	86.0	88.6
LH16	Callanish	E row to W	1a	1.5 km	C		–;	16:	258.8	259.6
LH16	Callanish	E row to E	1a	9.0 km	A		750629;	17:	78.8	79.6
LH22	Cul a'Chleit	ba (To NNE)	3a	9.5 km	C		–;	37:	33.0	35.8
LH22	Cul a'Chleit	ab (To SSW)	3a	14.0 km	A		750718;	38:	213.0	215.8
LH24	Airigh nam Bid.	bcd(To NNW)	3c	8.0 km	C		–;	44:	342.0	344.0
LH24	Airigh nam Bid.	dcb(To SSE)	3c	16.5 km	A		810726;	45:	162.0	164.0
LH29	Dursainean NE	To NW	6	12.5 km	A		810722;	52:	305.4	307.2
LH29	Dursainean NE	To SE	6	0.5 km	L					
LH36	Horgabost	To WNW	5a	5.0 km	A		790801;	53:	284.4	289.0

Table 5.1 (continued)

Site	Name	Indication	Class	Dist	St	Com	Survey No.	Az limits
LH36	Horgabost	; To ESE	; 5a	0.1 km	L			
LH37	Scarista	; ba (To WNW)	; 3b	-Sea-	C	-	; 55:	302.0 305.0
LH37	Scarista	; ab (To ESE)	; 3b	0.5 km	L			

LH10 - Beinn Bheag (Airigh na Beinne Bige; "Callanish XI"), Lewis. NB
     2223 3568.   A menhir 1.5m tall x 0.5m x 0.5m, as described by
     Ponting & Ponting (1981: 82). Of the other features described by
     them and shown on their site plan (1981: 85) one appears to be a
     fallen menhir at least 1.9m long, 0.8m wide tapering to a
     pointed top, and 0.2m thick. It is some 50m from the standing
     stone.   However the other reported stumps and fallen stones are
     smaller fragments and seem unlikely to be prehistoric; moreover,
     as noted by the Pontings, they do not lie in the arc of a ring.
     Some metres to the east of the stones are two stony mounds which
     appear to be ruined cairns. Site plans: Tait (1978) (but see
     Ponting & Ponting 1981: 107, note 2); Ponting & Ponting (1981:
     85). Arch. status = A; type = 4.

LH16   - Callanish, Lewis. NB 2130 3300. A 13m-diameter ring of large
     menhirs, with heights about 3m to 4m, surrounding a cairn and
     great menhir (4.5m); five radial lines of menhirs, two ("the
     avenue") approx. northwards and one each approx. east, west and
     south. Excavations prior to site repairs were undertaken during
     1980-81 by P.J. Ashmore of the Scottish Development Department.
     Although it seems likely that the construction of the radial
     alignments was either roughly contemporary with, or else post-
     dated, that of the central ring, the possibility that the radial
     alignments predated the ring can not yet be formally excluded.
     We can however now at least say that the alignments did not
     originally extend across the central area, and the results of
     pollen analysis from the excavation may well cast further light
     upon the relative chronology of the site (P.J. Ashmore, priv.
     comm.; eventual publication of the excavation is envisaged in
     Proceedings of the Society of Antiquaries of Scotland).   In the
     absence of such further information, we include in our analysis
     all ten Class (1a) indications at the site, that is each way
     along each of the five alignments. Site plans: Tait (1978);
     Ponting & Ponting (1981: 80). Arch. status = A; type = 1.

LH18   - Cnoc Fillibhir Bheag ("Callanish III"), Lewis. NB 2250 3269.
     A 17m-diameter ring of menhirs up to about 2.5m in height,
     surrounding four menhirs which appear to be the remains of an
     internal ring.   Site plans: Thom (1967: 126); Cooke et al.
     (1977: 118); Tait (1978); Ponting & Ponting (1981: 81). Arch.
     status = A; type = 7.

LH19   - Cnoc Ceann a'Gharaidh ("Callanish II"), Lewis. NB 2220 3260.
     Five menhirs from 2m to 3m tall in a 21m-diameter ring surround-
     ing a cairn. Site plans: Thom (1967: 126); Cooke et. al. (1977:
     118); Tait (1978) (but see Ponting & Ponting 1981: 107, note 2);
     Ponting & Ponting (1981: 81). Arch. status = A; type = 7.

LH21   - Ceann Hulavig ("Callanish IV"), Lewis. NB 2297 3042. Five
     large menhirs from 2m to 3.5m high in a 13m-diameter ring
     surrounding a cairn.   Site plans: Thom (1967: 126); Cooke et.
     al. (1977: 118); Tait (1978); Ponting & Ponting (1981: 81).
     Arch. status = A; type = 7.

LH22   - Cul a'Chleit ("Callanish VI"), Lewis. NB 2465 3034. Two
     standing stones, 1.5m and 0.8m tall, some 10m apart upon a small
     rocky knoll.   The site is listed by the RCAHMS (1928: no. 95)

and by Burl (1976: 358) as the remains of a stone circle. Although there are three prostrate slabs to the west (D & E 1976: 57), the ground is so uneven that the circle interpretation seems extremely unlikely. This opinion is shared by the Ordnance Survey (OSAR: NB 23 SW, 7). Arch. status = A; type = 3.

LH24 – Airigh nam Bidearan ("Callanish V"), Lewis. NB 2342 2989. Five small upright slabs around 0.5m high, three of which are close (within 10m) and in line. The site is described by the RCAHMS (1928: no. 94) and listed by Burl (1976: 358) as the remains of a stone circle. However the irregular spacing of the stones and the fact that the diameter of such a circle would need to be very large (over 100m) make this interpretation extremely unlikely. The stones forming the alignment may represent no more than the remaining grounders of a field or enclosure wall (OSAR: NB 22 NW, 1), but they may well be sunken prehistoric menhirs. Site plans: Thom (1967: 128); Cooke et al. (1977: 118); Tait (1978); Ponting & Ponting (1981: 84); Thom, Thom & Burl (1984). Arch. status = B; type = 3.

LH27 – Newmarket, Lewis. NB 4132 3565. Three small erect stones about 1m high and spaced about 6m apart, which are possibly menhirs, forming the northern arc of a ring about 45m in diameter. A fourth stone only 0.4m high and other possible buried

(ctd. on page 84

– – – – – –

TABLE 5.2. List of inter-site indications in Lewis and Harris (LH).

Column headings

1   Site reference number
2   Site name
3   Site reference number of foresight
4   Distance of foresight
5   Archaeological status of the indication (see Section 3.5)
6   Classification of the indication (see Section 3.5)
7   Distance of the horizon profile
8   Survey status (see Sections 4.3 & 3.5):
        A Reliably surveyed
        B Less reliably surveyed
        C Calculated
        L Dismissed because horizon is local
        W Dismissed because IAR is too wide
9   Comment: reason that profile survey is less reliable
        e Horizon profile extended using photographs only
        p Large parallax correction
        t Trees obscure the exact profile
        v Poor visibility during survey
        (for further details see Section 4.3)
        o Survey data from other authors (see Section 5.3)
10   Date of latest survey
11   Indication reference number
12   Azimuth limits of the indication, to $0°.2$

Table 5.2

Site	Name	F/s & dist		St	CL	Dist	St	Com	Survey	No.	Az limits	
LH7	Kirkibost	; LH8	1.4 km;	B	1	8.0 km	A		810724;	1:	251.6	251.8
LH8	Bernera Bridge	; LH7	1.4 km;	B	1	1.5 km	A		810724;	3:	71.6	71.8
LH10	Beinn Bheag	; LH16	2.8 km;	A	2	29.0 km	A		750717;	5:	194.8	195.0
LH10	Beinn Bheag	; LH18	3.0 km;	A	1	27.0 km	A		750717;	6:	170.2	170.4
LH10	Beinn Bheag	; LH19	3.1 km;	A	1	16.0 km	A		750717;	7:	176.0	176.2
LH10	Beinn Bheag	; LH21	5.3 km;	A	3	27.0 km	A		750717;	8:	167.6	167.8
LH10	Beinn Bheag	; LH22	5.9 km;	A	3	22.5 km	B	o	-	9:	151.4	151.6
LH10	Beinn Bheag	; LH24	5.9 km;	B	3	22.0 km	A		750717;	10:	164.2	164.4
LH16	Callanish	; LH10	2.8 km;	A	2	3.0 km	A		790803;	18:	14.8	15.0
LH16	Callanish	; LH18	1.2 km;	A	1	10.5 km	A		750717;	19:	99.8	100.8
LH16	Callanish	; LH19	1.0 km;	A	1	2.5 km	A		750717;	20:	109.6	111.4
LH16	Callanish	; LH21	3.1 km;	A	3	6.5 km	A		790803;	21:	143.0	143.2
LH16	Callanish	; LH22	4.3 km;	A	1	4.5 km	A		790803;	22:	124.0	124.6
LH16	Callanish	; LH24	3.8 km;	B	3	6.5 km	A		790803;	23:	141.6	141.8
LH18	Cnoc Fillibhir	; LH10	3.0 km;	A	2	3.5 km	A		790803;	24:	350.2	350.4
LH18	Cnoc Fillibhir	; LH16	1.2 km;	A	1	12.0 km	A		750716;	25:	278.8	283.6
LH18	Cnoc Fillibhir	; LH19	0.3 km;	A	1	6.0 km	A		750708;	26:	247.2	251.0
LH18	Cnoc Fillibhir	; LH21	2.3 km;	A	1	19.5 km	A		790803;	27:	164.2	164.4
LH18	Cnoc Fillibhir	; LH24	2.9 km;	B	2	21.0 km	A		790803;	28:	157.8	158.2
LH19	Cnoc Ceann	; LH10	3.1 km;	A	3	3.5 km	A		790803;	29:	356.0	356.2
LH19	Cnoc Ceann	; LH16	1.0 km;	A	1	1.0 km	W		750709;	-:	287.4	292.6
LH19	Cnoc Ceann	; LH18	0.3 km;	A	1	0.3 km	L		-	-:	67.4	70.8
LH19	Cnoc Ceann	; LH22	3.3 km;	A	1	8.5 km	A		750709;	30:	128.8	129.2
LH19	Cnoc Ceann	; LH24	3.0 km;	B	2	19.5 km	A		790803;	31:	152.0	152.2
LH21	Ceann Hulavig	; LH10	5.3 km;	A	3	5.5 km	C		- ;	32:	347.6	347.8

Table 5.2 (continued)

Site	Name	F/s & dist	St	CL	Dist	St	Com	Survey	No.	Az limits	
LH21	Ceann Hulavig	; LH16 3.1 km;	A	1	4.0 km	A		750714;	33:	322.6	324.0
LH21	Ceann Hulavig	; LH18 2.3 km;	A	2	3.5 km	A		750714;	34:	344.0	344.4
LH21	Ceann Hulavig	; LH22 1.7 km;	A	2	7.5 km	A		750714;	35:	88.6	89.0
LH21	Ceann Hulavig	; LH24 0.7 km;	B	2	3.0 km	A		750714;	36:	134.8	135.4
LH22	Cul a'Chleit	; LH10 5.9 km;	A	3	6.0 km	C		- ;	39:	331.4	331.6
LH22	Cul a'Chleit	; LH16 4.3 km;	A	1	8.0 km	A		750718;	40:	304.2	304.8
LH22	Cul a'Chleit	; LH19 3.3 km;	A	3	13.5 km	A		750718;	41:	308.8	309.2
LH22	Cul a'Chleit	; LH21 1.7 km;	A	2	17.0 km	A		750718;	42:	268.0	268.4
LH22	Cul a'Chleit	; LH24 1.3 km;	B	2	25.0 km	A		750718;	43:	243.8	247.8
LH24	Airigh nam Bid.	; LH10 5.9 km;	B	3	8.0 km	C		- ;	46:	344.2	344.4
LH24	Airigh nam Bid.	; LH16 3.8 km;	B	3	4.5 km	A		750715;	47:	321.4	322.0
LH24	Airigh nam Bid.	; LH18 2.9 km;	B	2	7.5 km	A		750707;	48:	337.8	338.2
LH24	Airigh nam Bid.	; LH19 3.0 km;	B	2	14.0 km	A		750707;	49:	332.0	332.2
LH24	Airigh nam Bid.	; LH21 0.7 km;	B	2	8.0 km	A		750715;	50:	313.4	314.8
LH24	Airigh nam Bid.	; LH22 1.3 km;	B	2	14.0 km	A		750707;	51:	65.2	65.6
LH27	Newmarket	; LH28 0.5 km;	B	1	0.5 km	L		- ;	-:	201.6	207.4
LH28	Priests Glen	; LH27 0.5 km;	B	2	14.5 km	W		- ;	-:	21.8	27.2
LH36	Horgabost	; LH37 3.9 km;	A	3	8.0 km	A		790801;	54:	207.6	207.8
LH37	Scarista	; LH36 3.9 km;	A	3	17.5 km	A		790801;	56:	27.6	27.8

stones appear also to lie in the ring, although the situation is confused by what may be an old field wall to the east. If this is a stone ring, the nearby road will have destroyed its southern part. Arch. status = B; type = 8.

LH28 - Priests Glen, Lewis. NB 4111 3519. Three prostrate stones, between 1.5m and 2m long, located in the S-SW arc of a ring about 50m in diameter. A further stone of similar length lies on the northern arc, and the Ordnance Survey (OSAR: NB 43 NW, 1) note five in all. A central mound 0.7m high and about 15m across is probably not a central cairn (ibid.). Arch. status = A; type = 8.

LH29 - Dursainean NE, Lewis. NB 5281 3340. An erect block 1.7m high x 1.8m x 0.5m which may be a standing stone (OSAR: NB 53 SW, 7). According to Thom (1967: 129) it stands on a long mound; however this could not be identified either by us or by the Ordnance Survey in 1971. Arch. status = B; type = 6.

LH31 - Lower Bayble (Clach Stein), Lewis. NB 5165 3174. A prostrate menhir, broken into two parts some 1.5m long. Arch. status = A; type = 8.

LH33 - Sideval (Loch Seaforth), Lewis. NB 2781 1662. Two standing stones some 1.5m high and other prostrate stones which appear to form the remains of a stone circle about 17m in diameter. Arch. status = A; type = 7.

LH36 - Horgabost (Clach Mhic Leoid), Harris. NG 0408 9727. A fine standing slab 3.5m tall x 1.4m x 0.4m. Some small stones nearby (RCAHMS 1928: no. 135) may represent the remains of a cairn (OSAR: NG 09 NW, 4). Arch. status = A; type = 5.

LH37 - Scarista (Borvemore), Harris. NG 0202 9392. A standing slab 2.0m tall x 0.8m x 0.3m and two prostrate stones, possibly fallen menhirs, of which one is 2.5m long and could have stood in line with the slab. The three stones form a triangle of sides some 13m x 10m x 7m. The RCAHMS (1928: no. 136) list two further prostrate stones, and assuming all four to have been moved, classify the site as the remains of a stone circle. Some 20m to the NNW of the site is a mound which may represent the remains of a cairn, but is more likely due to field clearance (ibid.). Arch. status = A; type = 3.

5.3 Remarks on the surveys and survey data

The data for the surveys are presented in full in Tables 5.1 and 5.2, for on-site and inter-site lines respectively. Profile diagrams are presented in Figs. 5.2 - 5.14.

No surveying difficulties arose in this geographical area from profiles being obscured by trees and buildings; and (thanks to repeated visits) there were few problems due to poor visibility and lack of time. One necessary remark, however, concerns the application

(ctd. on page 98

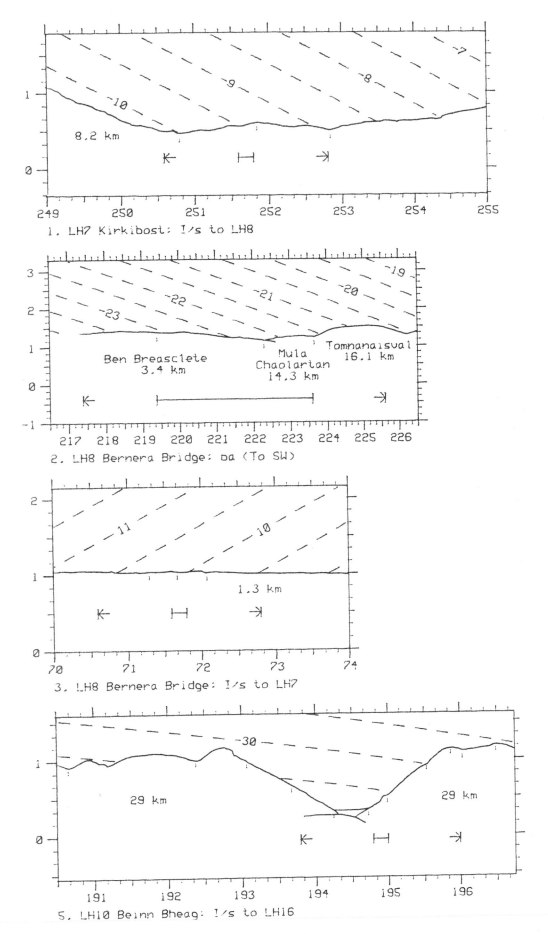

1. LH7 Kirkibost: 1/s to LH8

2. LH8 Bernera Bridge: Da (To SW)

3. LH8 Bernera Bridge: 1/s to LH7

5. LH10 Beinn Bheag: 1/s to LH16

FIG. 5.2.

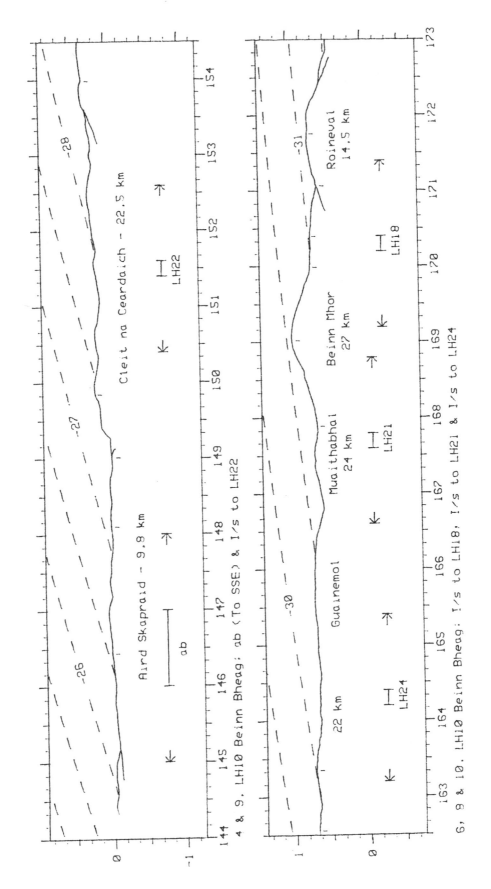

FIG. 5.3.

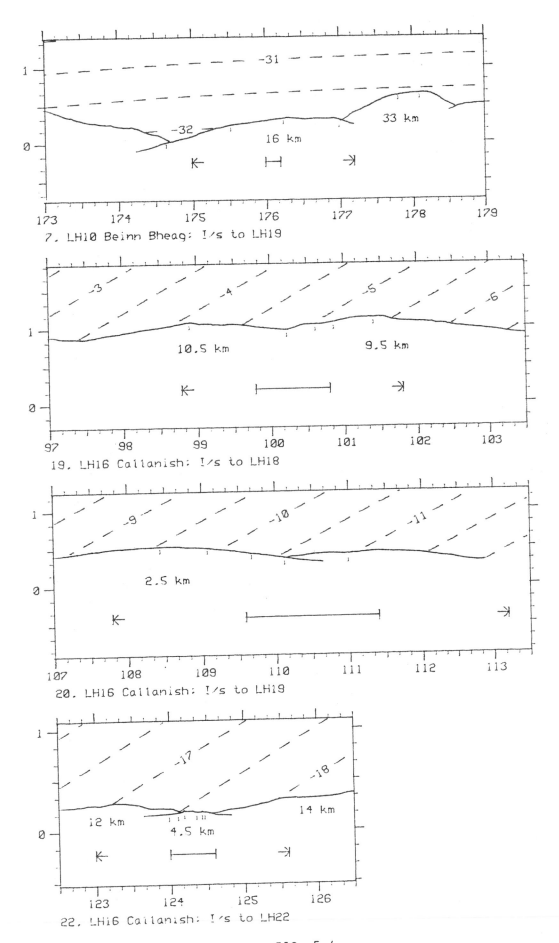

7. LH10 Beinn Bheag: I's to LH19

19. LH16 Callanish: I's to LH18

20. LH16 Callanish: I's to LH19

22. LH16 Callanish: I's to LH22

FIG. 5.4.

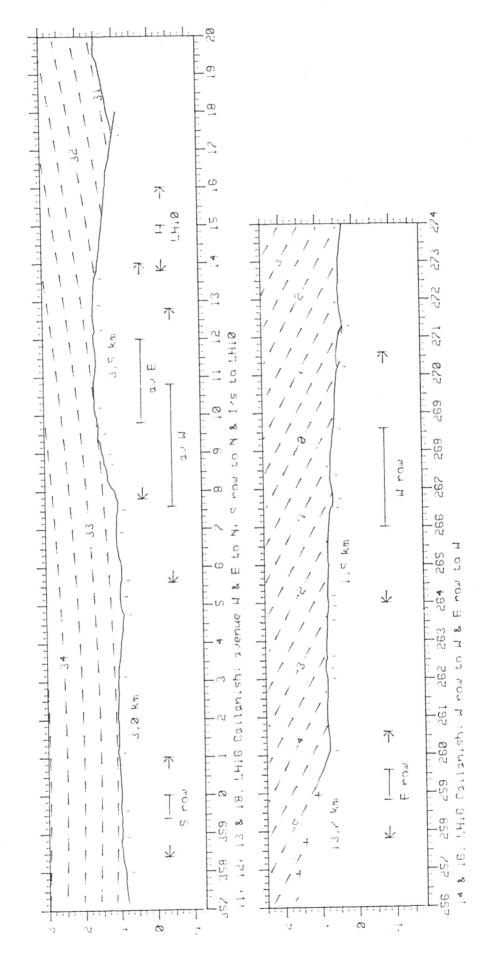

FIG. 5.5.

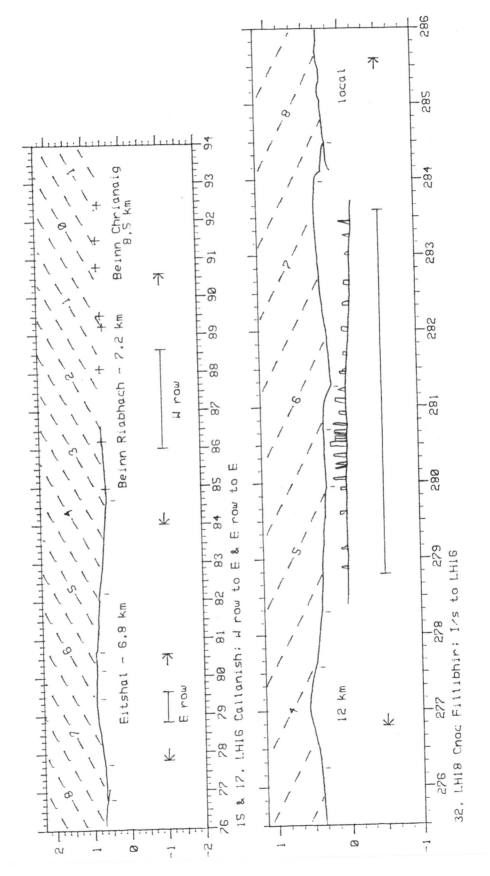

FIG. 5.6.

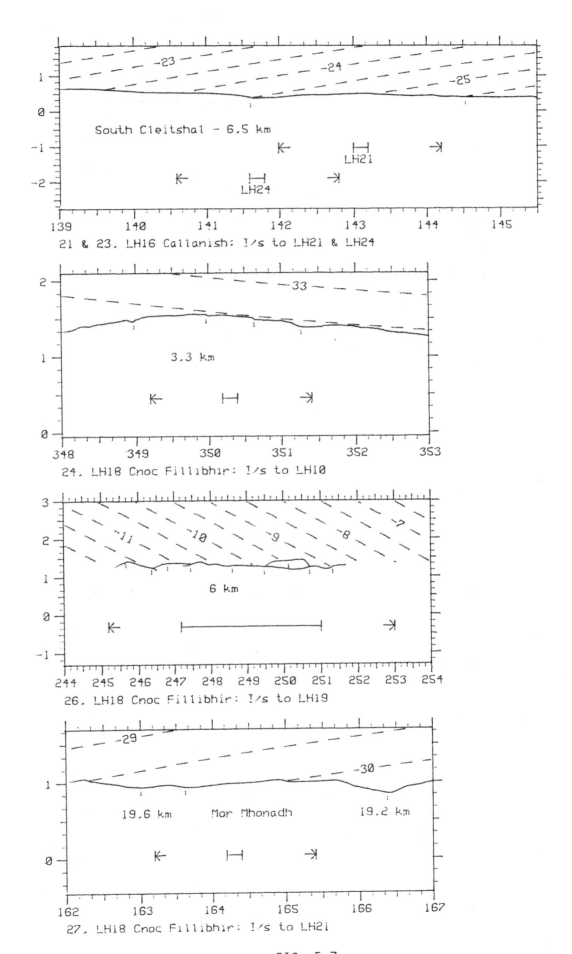

21 & 23. LH16 Callanish: l/s to LH21 & LH24

24. LH18 Cnoc Fillibhir: l/s to LH10

26. LH18 Cnoc Fillibhir: l/s to LH19

27. LH18 Cnoc Fillibhir: l/s to LH21

FIG. 5.7.

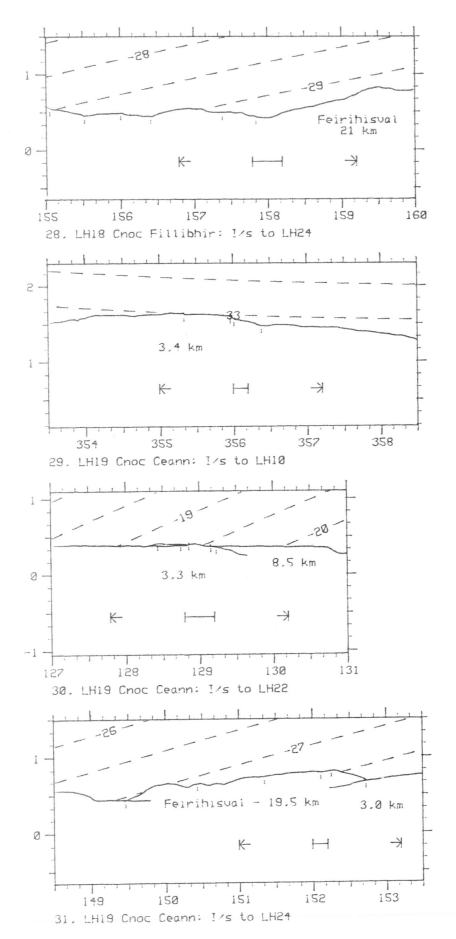

28. LH18 Cnoc Fillibhir: l/s to LH24

29. LH19 Cnoc Ceann: l/s to LH10

30. LH19 Cnoc Ceann: l/s to LH22

31. LH19 Cnoc Ceann: l/s to LH24

FIG. 5.8.

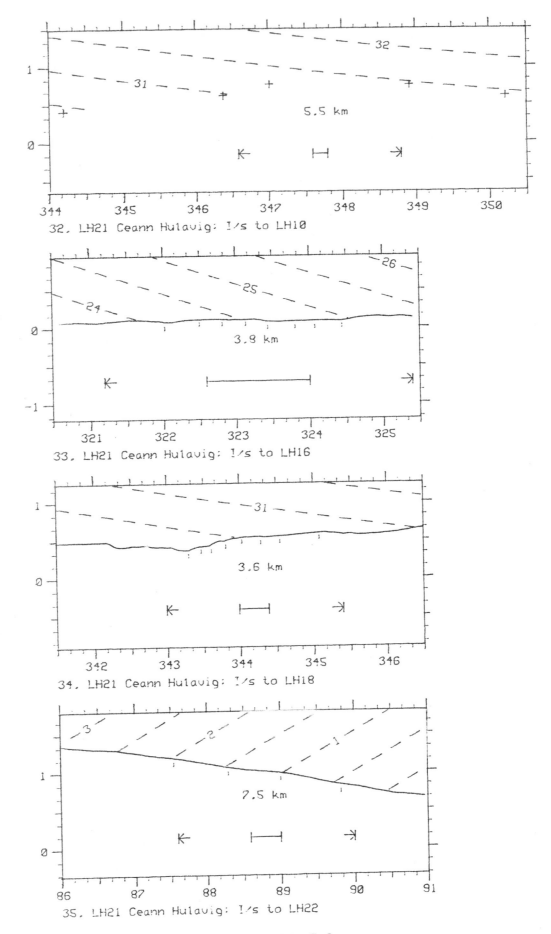

32. LH21 Ceann Hulavig: I/s to LH10

33. LH21 Ceann Hulavig: I/s to LH16

34. LH21 Ceann Hulavig: I/s to LH18

35. LH21 Ceann Hulavig: I/s to LH22

FIG. 5.9.

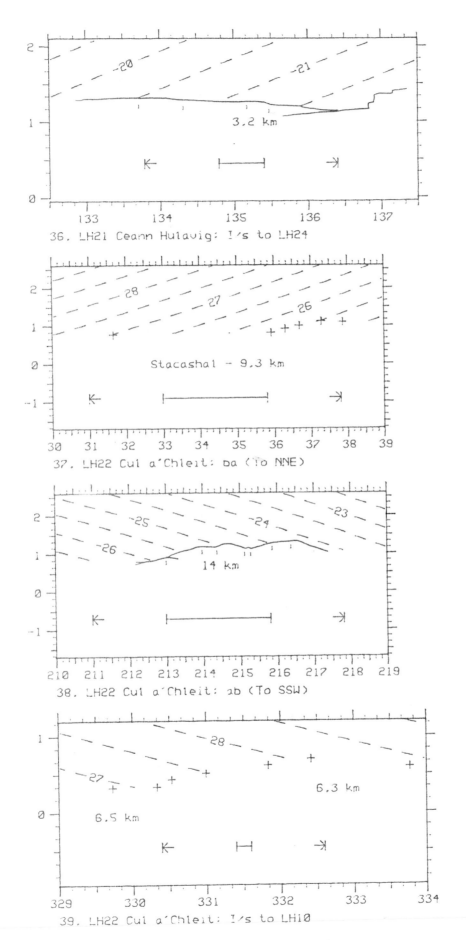

36. LH21 Ceann Hulavig: I's to LH24

37. LH22 Cul a'Chleit: ɔa (To NNE)

38. LH22 Cul a'Chleit: ɔb (To SSW)

39. LH22 Cul a'Chleit: I's to LH10

FIG. 5.10.

- 93 -

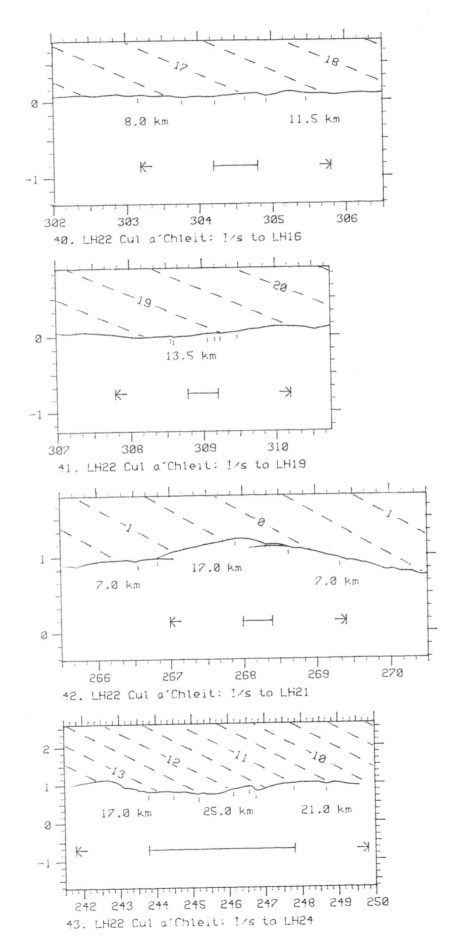

40. LH22 Cul a'Chleit: I/s to LH16

41. LH22 Cul a'Chleit: I/s to LH19

42. LH22 Cul a'Chleit: I/s to LH21

43. LH22 Cul a'Chleit: I/s to LH24

FIG. 5.11.

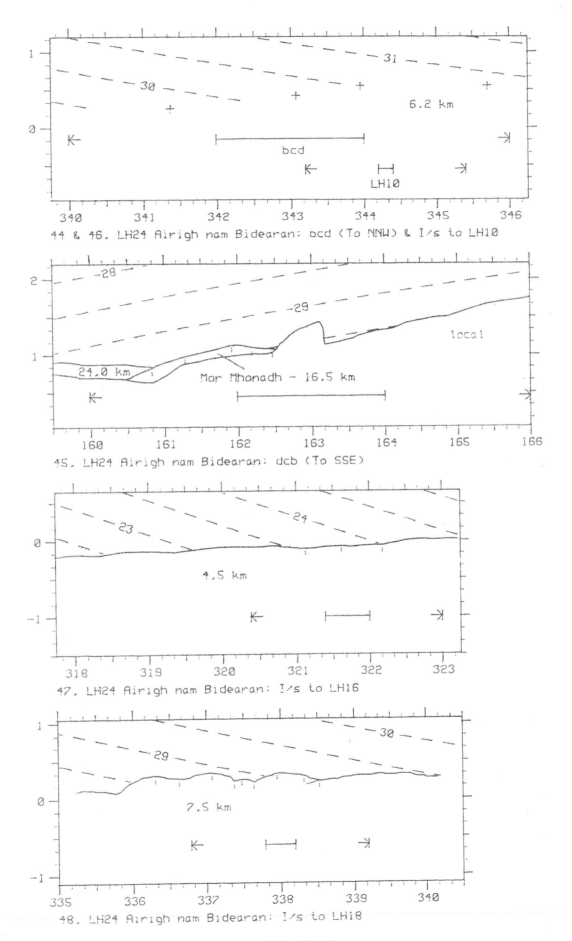

44 & 46. LH24 Airigh nam Bidearan: bcd (To NNW) & I/s to LH10

45. LH24 Airigh nam Bidearan: dcb (To SSE)

47. LH24 Airigh nam Bidearan: I/s to LH16

48. LH24 Airigh nam Bidearan: I/s to LH18

FIG. 5.12.

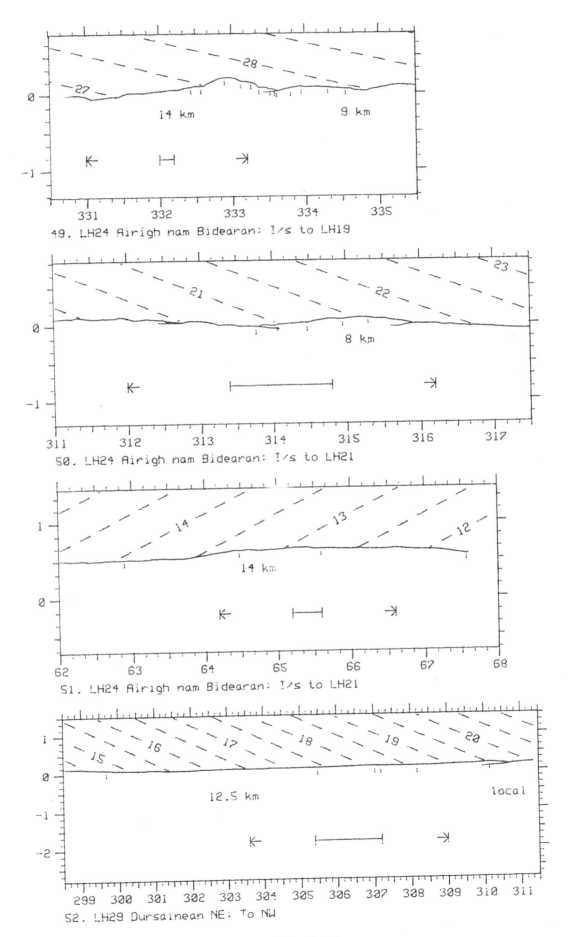

49. LH24 Airigh nam Bidearan: I/s to LH19

50. LH24 Airigh nam Bidearan: I/s to LH21

51. LH24 Airigh nam Bidearan: I/s to LH21

52. LH29 Dursainean NE: To NW

FIG. 5.13.

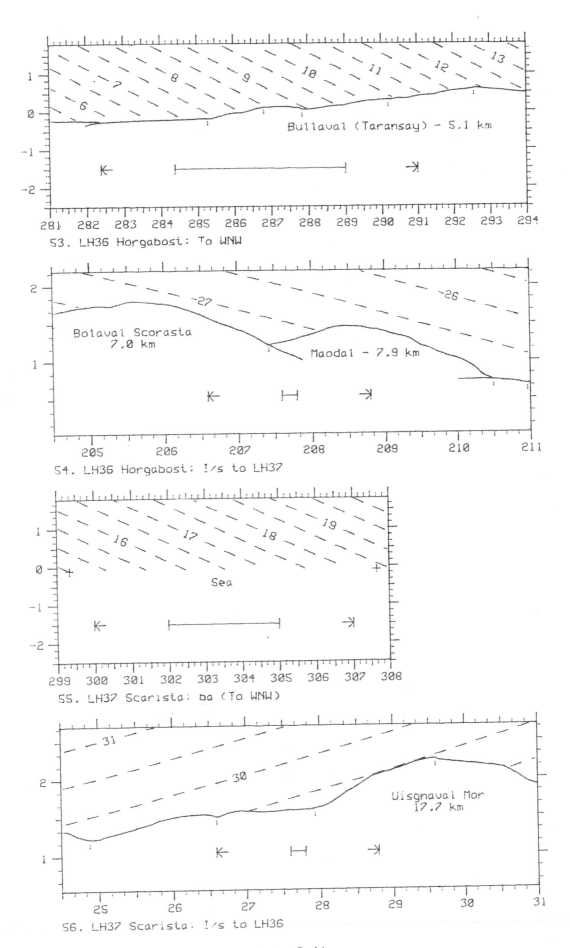

53. LH36 Horgabost: To WNW

Bullaval (Taransay) - 5.1 km

54. LH36 Horgabost: l/s to LH37

Bolaval Scorasta 7.0 km

Maodal - 7.9 km

55. LH37 Scarista: ba (To WNW)

Sea

56. LH37 Scarista: l/s to LH36

Uisgnaval Mor 17.7 km

FIG. 5.14.

of the selection criteria to inter-site lines involving Callanish (LH16). In defining the OP for lines from Callanish, a natural choice for the 'centre of the site' (Section 3.5) was the centre of the stone ring; however this is some 30m to the south of the point mid-way between the farthest (known) extents of the northern and southern rows. For lines to Callanish the entire extent of the site was considered in defining the IAR. The result is that the mean indicated azimuths quoted for corresponding inter-site alignments to and from Callanish will be found not to be exactly 180°.0 apart, as might have been expected.

Data have kindly been provided by M.R. & G.H. Ponting for two indications which were not surveyed owing to lack of time (Lines 4 & 9). These cases are marked 'o' in the comment columns of Tables 5.1 & 5.2.

6   SITES IN THE UISTS (UI)

C.L.N.Ruggles, J.G.Morgan, R.W.Few, J.A.Cooke, R.P.Norris &
S.F.Burch

6.1   Introduction

Most of the sites in North and South Uist and Benbecula were
visited, and as many as possible of the necessary surveys completed,
by the authors during 1977. Further surveys were undertaken by CR and
RPN in 1979, with the assistance of Cilla Norris, and by CR in 1981,
with the assistance of Kim Bramley. Some 1977 surveys were later repeated and checked. During the latter years the islands of Berneray
(N) and Vatersay were also covered. The locations of the sites considered are shown in Figs. 6.1 & 6.2.

6.2   Descriptions and classification of sites

For general notes on the descriptions that follow, see Section
5.2 (page 75).

UI6 - Borve (Cladh Maolrithe), Berneray (N). NF 9122 8068. A fine
        slab 2.5m tall x 1.2m x 0.3m. It stands adjacent to the remains
        of a rectangular enclosure (RCAHMS 1928: no. 133). Arch. status
        = A; type = 5.

UI9 - Newtonferry (Crois Mhic Jamain), North Uist. NF 8937 7818. Two
        standing stones, one a slab between 0.9m and 1.5m above present
        ground level x 0.5m x 0.2m, the other 0.5m tall x 0.4m x 0.3m,
        set into the summits of a mound some 6m apart. According to the
        lady in the house next to the site, the slab fell over during
        the spring of 1981 and was re-erected by her husband and son.
        Its position in summer 1981 was not measurably different from
        that in 1979, but its northern end had been propped up with
        several small stones. Arch. status = A; type = 3.

UI15 - Maari, North Uist. NF 8645 7292. A standing stone, measuring
        2.2m from top to bottom but now leaning by some 45° out of the
        vertical, and 0.5m x 0.4m in cross-section. Arch. status = A;
        type = 7.

UI19 - Blashaval (Na Fir Bhreige), North Uist. NF 8875 7176. Three
        stones standing only about 0.5m above present peat level, spaced
        at intervals of about 15m and 35m in almost a straight line.
        Site plan: Thom, Thom & Burl (1984). Arch. status = A; type = 1.

UI22 - South Clettraval, North Uist. NF 7501 7118 & 7516 7101. At
        the first location is a standing stone 1.5m tall x 1.0m x 0.8m
        (Thom's site H3/3).   At the second, 220m to the SE, is Tigh
        Cloiche (W), a chambered cairn of the Hebridean group (Henshall
        1972: no. UST 28; Thom's site H3/4).   Some 150m from the
        standing stone in the opposite direction is a Clyde group long
        cairn (Henshall 1972: no. UST12). Arch. status = A; type = 7.

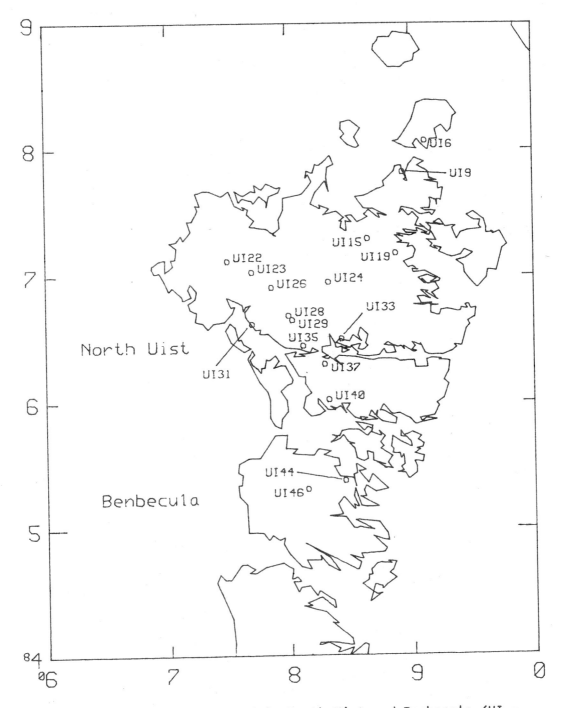

FIG. 6.1. Sites considered in North Uist and Benbecula (UI —
northern part).

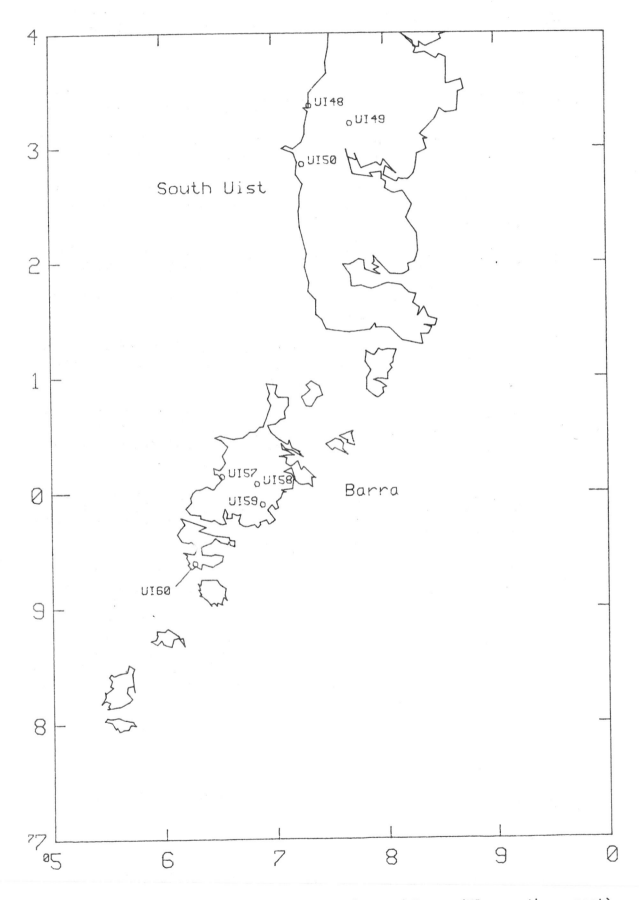

FIG. 6.2. Sites considered in South Uist and Barra (UI - southern part).

UI23 – Toroghas (Fir Bhreige), North Uist. NF 7700 7029. Two stones standing about 1.0m above present peat level and about 35m apart. Site plan: Thom, Thom & Burl (1984). Arch. status = A; type = 3.

UI24 – Marrogh (Tigh Cloiche (E)), North Uist. NF 8324 6952. A small erect stone 1.0m high, possibly a standing stone, triangular in cross-section at the base and tapering to a top only about 0.3m x 0.2m. Some 100m to the NE is a Hebridean group round cairn (Henshall 1972: no. UST24). Arch. status = B; type = 8.

UI26 – Beinn a'Charra, North Uist. NF 7863 6909. A menhir 2.8m tall x 1.5m x 0.6m, triangular in cross-section, leaning to the south. Arch. status = A; type = 7.

UI28 – Unival (Leacach an Tigh Cloiche), North Uist. NF 8003 6685. A slab 2.5m tall x 1.5m x 0.3m, standing some 10m to the SW of a Hebridean group chamber tomb (Henshall 1972: no. UST34). Further ref: Moir (1980: 38-9). Site plan: Ruggles & Norris (1980: 41). Arch. status = A; type = 5.

UI29 – Loch na Buaile Iochdrach, North Uist. NF 8031 6651. A small slab 1.0m high x 0.7m x 0.3m, which may represent a standing stone. Arch. status = B; type = 6.

UI31 – Claddach Kyles (Clach Mhor a Che), North Uist. NF 7700 6619. A slab 2.5m tall x 1.2m x 0.4m, standing some 20m to the north of Dun na Carnaich, a ruined chambered cairn (Henshall 1972: no. UST16). Arch. status = A; type = 5.

UI33 – Ben Langass (Pobull Fhinn; Sornach Coir Fhinn), North Uist. NF 8427 6502. A 35m-diameter ring of menhirs up to 2.1m in height. Site plans: RCAHMS (1928: fig. 141); Thom, Thom & Burl (1980: 310). Arch. status = A; type = 7.

UI35 – Cringraval W, North Uist. NF 8116 6447. Five stones lie in the eastern arc of a ring about 35m in diameter. One of them is a small erect slab 0.7m high, and the others (which are up to 1.5m long) are possibly prostrate menhirs. The stones lie on the eastern side of an edge formed by peat clearance; a stone in the side of this edge on the northern arc of the ring is of uncertain status. A further stone, possibly a prostrate menhir, lies in the uncut area to the west, quite possibly in the western arc of the ring. Arch. status = B; type = 8.

(ctd. on page 106

– – – – – –

TABLE 6.1. List of on-site indications in the Uists (UI).

Column headings are as for Table 5.1 (see page 77).

TABLE 6.2. List of inter-site indications in the Uists (UI).

Column headings are as for Table 5.2 (see page 81).

Table 6.1

Site	Name	Indication	Class	Dist	St	Com Survey	No.	Az limits
UI6	Borve	; To WNW	5a	-Sea-	A	810718;	57:	293.0 294.0
UI6	Borve	; To ESE	5a	63.5 km	A	810718;	58:	113.0 114.0
UI9	Newtonferry	; ab (To NE)	3a	0.9 km	L			
UI9	Newtonferry	; ba (To SW)	3a	8.0 km	A	810717;	60:	229.0 232.4
UI19	Blashaval	; abc(To WNW)	1a	2.5 km	A	770628;	63:	288.8 290.6
UI19	Blashaval	; cba(To ESE)	1a	0.1 km	L			
UI23	Toroghas	; ba (To W)	3a	0.2 km	L			
UI23	Toroghas	; ab (To E)	3a	4.0 km	A	770701;	67:	94.0 96.0
UI28	Unival	; To NNW	5a	0.1 km	L			
UI28	Unival	; To SSE	5a	22.0 km	A	790726;	75:	154.8 156.4
UI29	L na Buaile I	; To NW	6	0.1 km	L			
UI29	L na Buaile I	; To SE	6	0.5 km	L			
UI31	Claddach Kyles	; To WNW	5a	0.5 km	L			
UI31	Claddach Kyles	; To ESE	5a	14.5 km	A	770701;	81:	107.4 108.8
UI46	Stiaraval	; To NW	6	84	A	770713;	96:	303.6 304.4
UI46	Stiaraval	; To SE	6	120 km	A	770713;	97:	123.6 124.4
UI49	Beinn a'Charra	; To NE	5a	5.5 km	A	790727;	100:	51.2 52.0
UI49	Beinn a'Charra	; To SW	5a	-Sea-	C	- ;	101:	231.2 232.0
UI57	Borve	; ab (To NE)	3b	1.5 km	A	790722;	106:	33.4 37.6
UI57	Borve	; ba (To SW)	3b	3.0 km	A	790723;	107:	213.4 217.6
UI59	Brevig	; ab (To WNW)	4a	1.0 km	A	790723;	108:	298.6 300.6
UI59	Brevig	; ba (To ESE)	4a	110 km	A	790723;	109:	118.6 120.6

Table 6.2

Site	Name	F/s & dist	St	CL	Dist	St	Com	Survey	No.	Az limits
UI6	Borve	UI9 3.1 km;	A	3	13.5 km	A		810718;	59:	212.0 212.4
UI9	Newtonferry	UI6 3.1 km;	A	3	6.0 km	A		810717;	61:	32.0 32.4
UI15	Maari	UI19 2.6 km;	A	2	3.0 km	C		- ;	62:	111.8 112.8
UI19	Blashaval	UI15 2.6 km;	A	2	2.5 km	C		- ;	64:	292.0 292.6
UI22	S Clettraval	UI26 4.2 km;	A	3	83 km	A		770713;	65:	115.2 115.6
UI22	S Clettraval	UI31 5.4 km;	A	3	19.5 km	A		770713;	66:	153.4 153.8
UI23	Toroghas	UI26 2.0 km;	A	1	80 km	A		770701;	68:	120.4 120.8
UI23	Toroghas	UI28 4.6 km;	A	1	4.5 km	A		770701;	69:	133.6 133.8
UI23	Toroghas	UI31 4.1 km;	A	3	55.0 km	A		770701;	70:	175.2 175.4
UI26	Beinn a'Charra	UI22 4.2 km;	A	1	4.0 km	A		770630;	71:	295.2 295.6
UI26	Beinn a'Charra	UI23 2.0 km;	A	2	4.5 km	A		770630;	72:	300.4 300.8
UI26	Beinn a'Charra	UI28 2.6 km;	A	1	2.5 km	A		770630;	73:	143.8 144.2
UI26	Beinn a'Charra	UI31 3.3 km;	A	3	-Sea-	A		770630;	74:	204.8 205.2
UI28	Unival	UI23 4.6 km;	A	3	5.0 km	A		790726;	76:	313.6 313.8
UI28	Unival	UI26 2.6 km;	A	2	4.5 km	A		790726;	77:	323.8 324.2
UI28	Unival	UI33 4.6 km;	A	3	12.0 km	A		790726;	78:	108.8 109.2
UI28	Unival	UI35 2.6 km;	B	2	14.5 km	C		- ;	79:	150.0 150.2
UI28	Unival	UI37 4.8 km;	A	3	6.5 km	C		- ;	80:	138.4 138.8
UI31	Claddach Kyles	UI22 5.4 km;	A	3	6.0 km	C		- ;	82:	333.4 333.8
UI31	Claddach Kyles	UI23 4.1 km;	A	3	4.5 km	A		790731;	83:	355.2 355.4
UI31	Claddach Kyles	UI26 3.3 km;	A	3	5.5 km	A		770701;	84:	24.8 25.2
UI31	Claddach Kyles	UI35 4.5 km;	B	3	14.0 km	C		- ;	85:	107.6 108.2
UI33	Ben Langass	UI28 4.6 km;	A	1	4.5 km	A		810713;	86:	288.8 289.2
UI33	Ben Langass	UI37 2.4 km;	A	2	3.5 km	A		810713;	87:	210.0 211.0
UI35	Cringraval W	UI28 2.6 km;	B	1	2.5 km	A		810715;	88:	330.0 330.2

Table 6.2 (continued)

Site	Name	F/s & dist	St	CL	Dist	St	Com	Survey	No.	Az limits
UI35	Cringraval W	UI31 4.5 km;	B	3	8.0 km	A		810715;	89:	287.6 288.2
UI35	Cringraval W	UI37 2.3 km;	B	2	2.5 km	A		810715;	90:	125.0 126.0
UI35	Cringraval W	UI40 4.7 km;	B	3	5.0 km	C		–;	91:	149.2 149.6
UI37	Loch a'Phobuill	UI28 4.8 km;	A	1	5.0 km	A		770704;	92:	318.4 318.8
UI37	Loch a'Phobuill	UI33 2.4 km;	A	2	3.0 km	A		770704;	93:	30.0 31.0
UI37	Loch a'Phobuill	UI35 2.3 km;	B	2	2.5 km	C		–;	94:	305.0 306.0
UI40	Carinish	UI35 4.7 km;	B	3	7.5 km	A		810715;	95:	329.2 329.6
UI48	Stoneybridge	UI49 3.9 km;	A	3	9.0 km	A		810711;	98:	108.4 108.6
UI48	Stoneybridge	UI50 5.1 km;	A	3	–Sea–	C		–;	99:	182.8 183.2
UI49	Beinn a'Charra	UI48 3.9 km;	A	1	–Sea–	C		–;	102:	288.4 288.6
UI49	Beinn a'Charra	UI50 5.6 km;	A	3	–Sea–	C		–;	103:	226.0 226.4
UI50	Ru Ardvule	UI48 5.1 km;	A	1	5.0 km	C		–;	104:	2.8 3.2
UI50	Ru Ardvule	UI49 5.6 km;	A	3	5.5 km	C		–;	105:	46.0 46.4

UI37 - Loch a'Phobuill (Sornach a'Phobuill), North Uist. NF 8289
6302. A 40m-diameter ring of stones up to 1.0m in height. Thom
mistakenly calls the site Sornach Coir Fhinn (1967: Table 12.1,
H3/18; and the following two references). Site plans: Thom
(1966: fig. 14); Thom, Thom & Burl (1980: 312). Arch. status =
A; type = 7.

UI40 - Carinish, North Uist. NF 8321 6021. The remains of a stone
circle about 40m in diameter, ruined since the RCAHMS' inspec-
tion (1928: no. 248) by the construction of the A865 through the
middle of it. In 1965 the Ordnance Survey (OSAR: NF 86 SW, 1)
noted seven stones to the north and two to the south of the
road; however by 1981 the road had been widened and only four
standing stones now remain to its north and one to its south.
Arch. status = A; type = 7.

UI44 - Hacklett, Benbecula. NF 8445 5381. A prostrate cup-marked
stone 3.0m long which apparently represents a fallen standing
stone. Arch. status = A; type = 8.

UI46 - Stiaraval (Rueval), Benbecula. NF 8142 5315. A small erect
slab 1.2m tall x 1.2m x 0.3m, which is possibly a standing
stone. During 1981 quarrying operations were in progress only
some 100m to the west of the stone. Arch. status = B; type = 6.

UI48 - Stoneybridge (Crois Chnoca Breaca), South Uist. NF 7340 3366.
Although marked on recent 1" Ordnance Survey maps as a chambered
cairn, this is a rectangular menhir 2.5m tall x 0.5m x 0.3m
erected on the summit of a 1m-high mound. Arch. status = A;
type = 7.

UI49 - Beinn a'Charra (An Carra), South Uist. NF 7703 3211. A fine
slab 5m high x 1.5m x 0.6m. Arch. status = A; type = 5.

UI50 - Ru Ardvule (Kildonan), South Uist. NF 7273 2860. Listed by
the RCAHMS (1928: no. 406) as a standing stone 2m high together
with two prostrate stones, and described by Thom (1967: 133) as
"several stones, only one now upright", the site lies amidst
shifting sand dunes, and only the standing stone can now be
found. By 1979 its tip had just disappeared below the sand, and
could only be located thanks to a wooden marker post which had
been erected by its side. Arch. status = A; type = 7.

UI57 - Borve, Barra. NF 6527 0144. Two stones 8m apart, one an erect
slab of height 1.5m above present ground level x 0.6m x 0.2m,
the other fallen with only its tip now showing above the grass.
Site plan: Thom, Thom & Burl (1984). Arch. status = A; type = 3.

UI58 - Beul a'Bhealaich, Barra. NF 684 008. A large prostrate stone
at the location specified by Thom (FSL: H6/2). It is at least
4.5m long and up to 1.6m wide, as described by A.S. Thom (Thom
1967: 133-34), and may be a large standing stone which has
fallen from its eastern end. Its western end tapers to 0.6m x
0.2m. It is situated some 30m to the west of the top of the
saddle at Beul a'Bhealaich. Arch. status = B; type = 8.

(ctd. on page 120

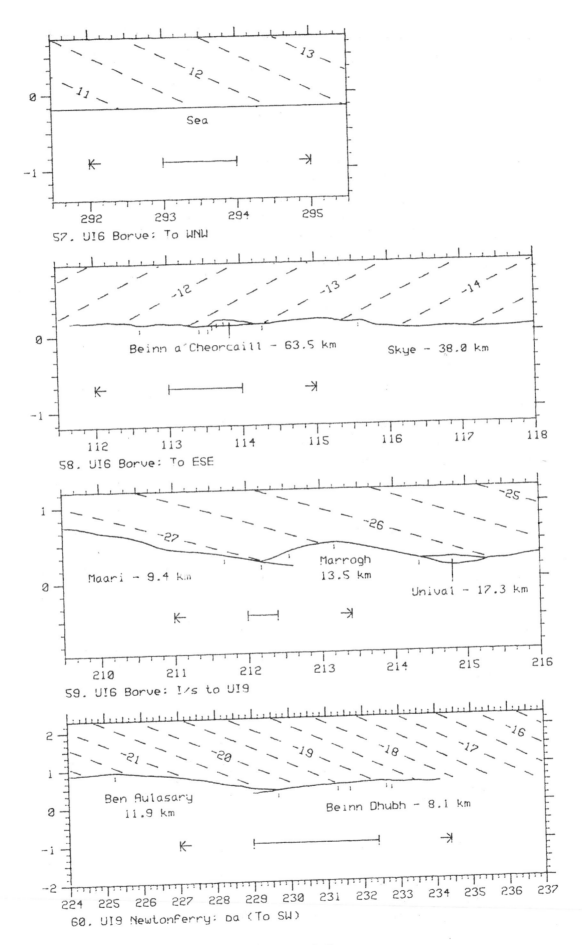

57. UI6 Borve: To WNW

58. UI6 Borve: To ESE

59. UI6 Borve: I/s to UI9

60. UI9 Newtonferry: DA (To SW)

FIG. 6.3.

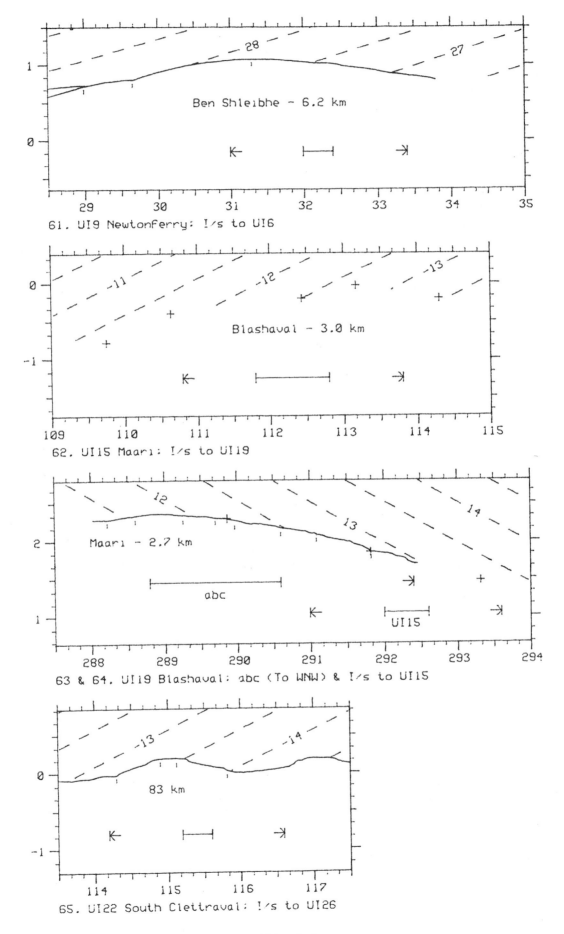

61. UI9 Newtonferry: I/s to UI6

62. UI15 Maari: I/s to UI19

63 & 64. UI19 Blashaval: abc (To WNW) & I/s to UI15

65. UI22 South Clettraval: I/s to UI26

FIG. 6.4.

- 108 -

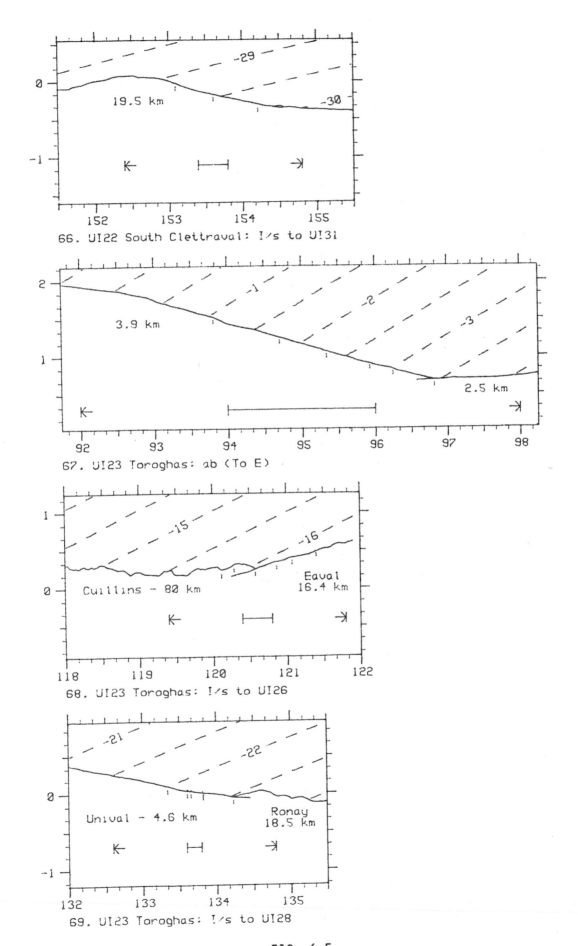

66. UI22 South Clettraval: I/s to UI31

67. UI23 Toroghas: ab (To E)

68. UI23 Toroghas: I/s to UI26

69. UI23 Toroghas: I/s to UI28

FIG. 6.5.

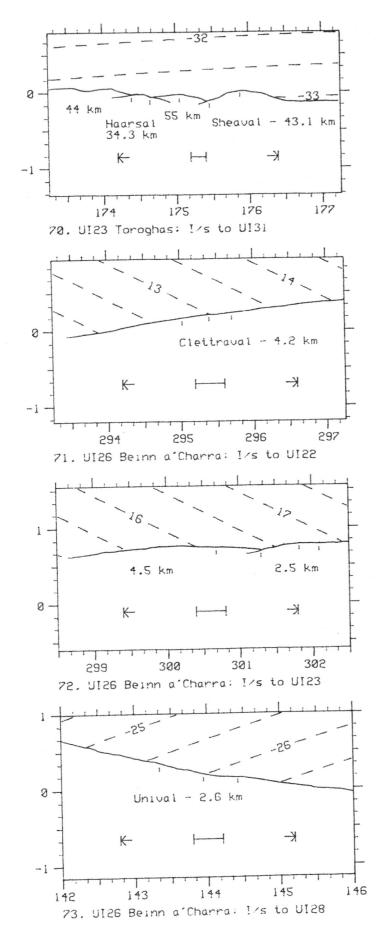

70. UI23 Toroghas: l/s to UI31

71. UI26 Beinn a'Charra: l/s to UI22

72. UI26 Beinn a'Charra: l/s to UI23

73. UI26 Beinn a'Charra: l/s to UI28

FIG. 6.6.

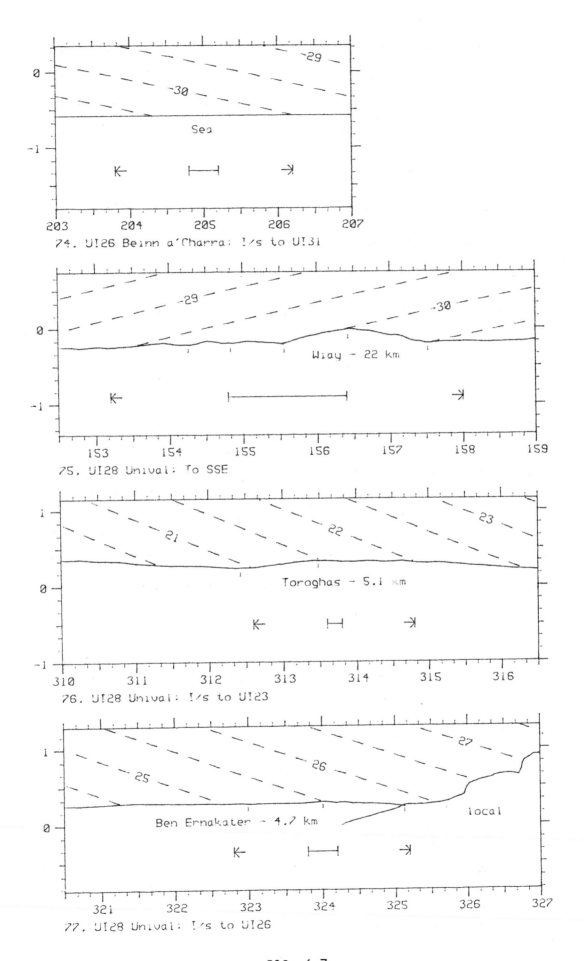

74. UI26 Beinn a'Charra: I/s to UI31

75. UI28 Unival: To SSE

76. UI28 Unival: I/s to UI23

77. UI28 Unival: I/s to UI26

FIG. 6.7.

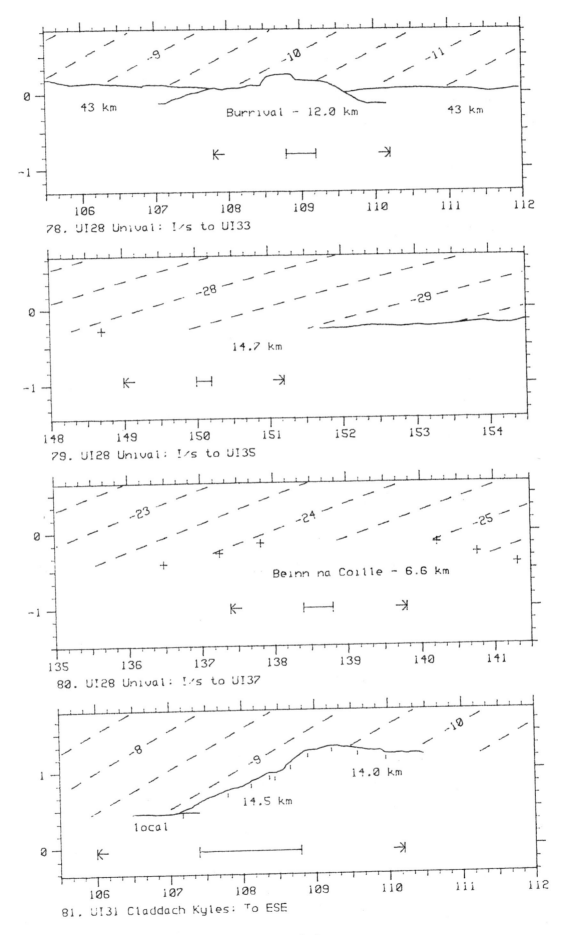

78. UI28 Unival: l/s to UI33

79. UI28 Unival: l/s to UI35

80. UI28 Unival: l/s to UI37

81. UI31 Claddach Kyles: To ESE

FIG. 6.8.

- 112 -

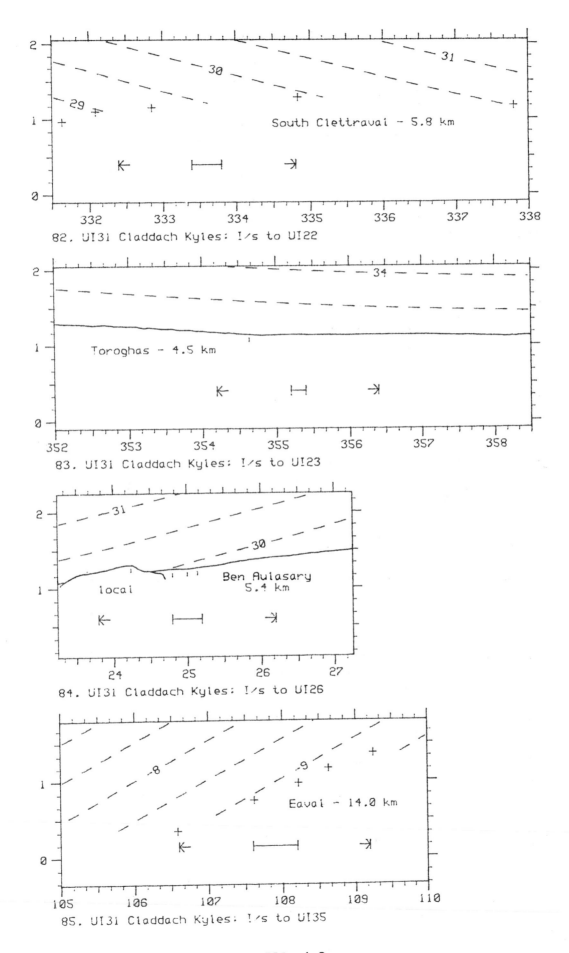

82. UI31 Claddach Kyles: I/s to UI22

83. UI31 Claddach Kyles: I/s to UI23

84. UI31 Claddach Kyles: I/s to UI26

85. UI31 Claddach Kyles: I/s to UI35

FIG. 6.9.

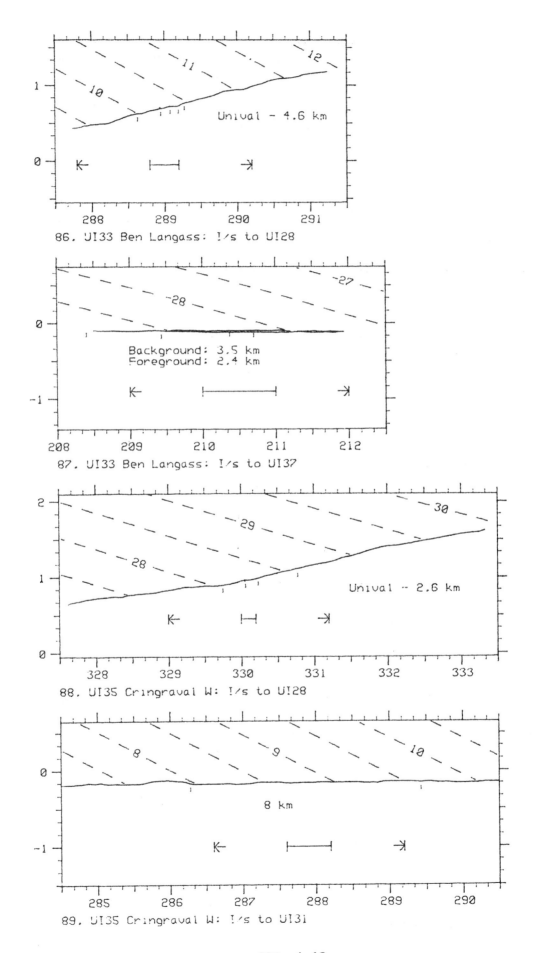

86. UI33 Ben Langass: l/s to UI28

87. UI33 Ben Langass: l/s to UI37

88. UI35 Cringraval W: l/s to UI28

89. UI35 Cringraval W: l/s to UI31

FIG. 6.10.

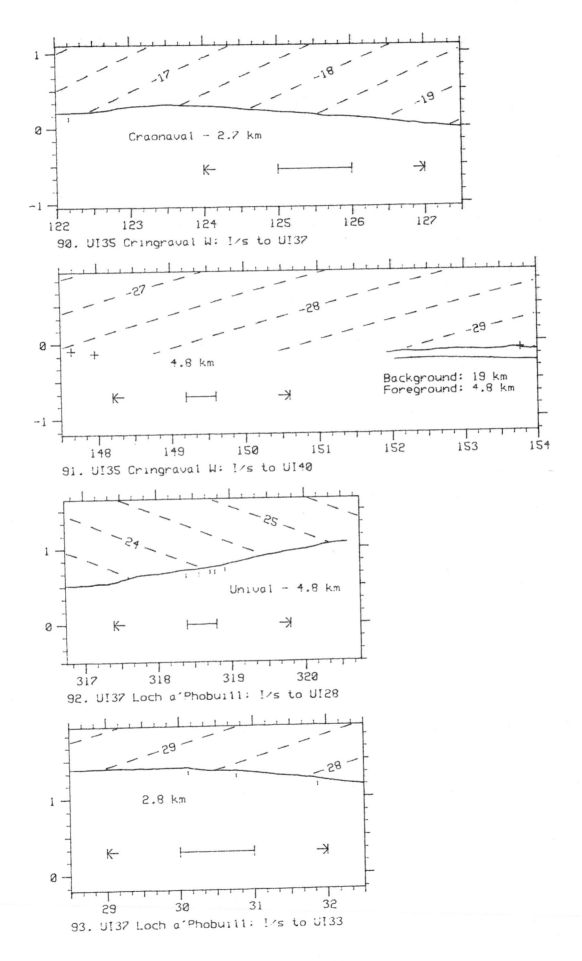

90. UI35 Cringraval W: I/s to UI37

91. UI35 Cringraval W: I/s to UI40

92. UI37 Loch a'Phobuill: I/s to UI28

93. UI37 Loch a'Phobuill: I/s to UI33

FIG. 6.11.

- 115 -

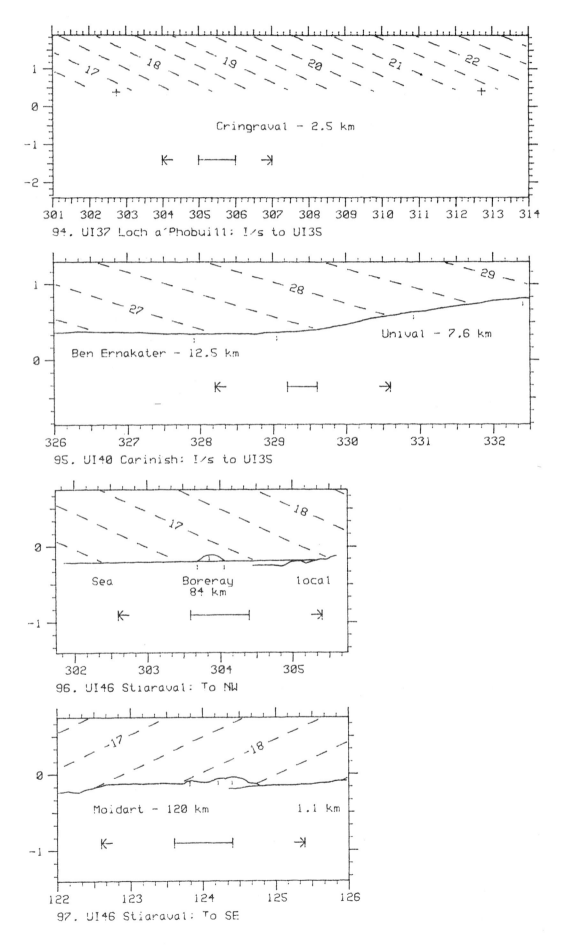

94. UI37 Loch a'Phobuill: l/s to UI35

95. UI40 Carinish: l/s to UI35

96. UI46 Stiaraval: To NW

97. UI46 Stiaraval: To SE

FIG. 6.12.

- 116 -

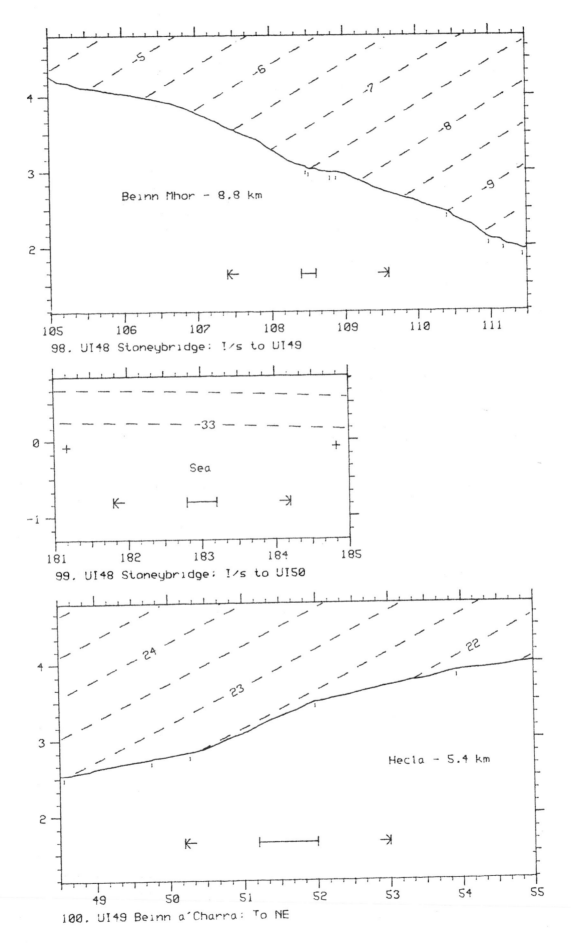

98. UI48 Stoneybridge: I/s to UI49

99. UI48 Stoneybridge; I/s to UI50

100. UI49 Beinn a'Charra; To NE

FIG. 6.13.

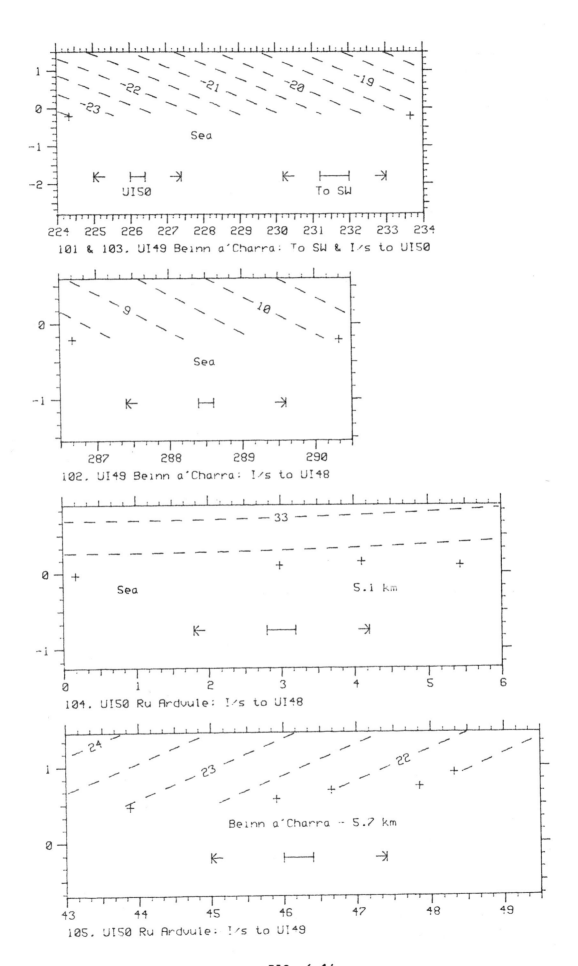

101 & 103. UI49 Beinn a'Charra: To SW & I/s to UI50

102. UI49 Beinn a'Charra: I/s to UI48

104. UI50 Ru Ardvule: I/s to UI48

105. UI50 Ru Ardvule: I/s to UI49

FIG. 6.14.

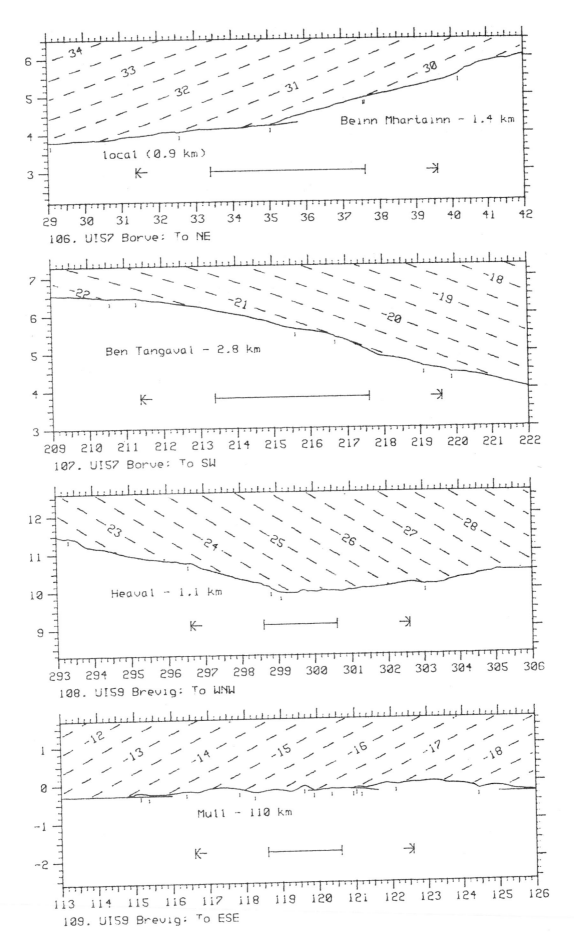

106. UIS7 Borve: To NE

107. UIS7 Borve: To SW

108. UIS9 Brevig: To WNW

109. UIS9 Brevig: To ESE

FIG. 6.15.

UI59 - Brevig, Barra. NL 6890 9903. Two menhirs some 5m apart, one triangular in cross-section and 2.5m high, the other prostrate and broken into two. We did not locate the stone alignments listed by Thom (1967: Table 12.1, H6/3; see also 134). Site plan: Thom, Thom & Burl (1984). Arch. status = A; type = 4.

UI60 - Ben Rulibreck (Cuithe Heillanish), Vatersay. NL 6277 9389. A standing stone 1.7m tall x 0.6m x 0.4m. Thom (1967: Table 12.1, H6/4; see also 134) refers to two stones forming part of an oval. The standing stone now forms one of two entrance jambs of the entrance of an old enclosure (OSAR: NL 69 SW, 2). Arch. status = A; type = 7.

6.3   Remarks on the surveys and survey data

The data for the surveys are presented in full in Tables 6.1 and 6.2, for on-site and inter-site lines respectively. Profile diagrams are presented in Figs. 6.3 - 6.15.

Surveys in this area were continually hampered by poor weather, and three expeditions had to be made here in different years before the data set was reasonably complete. No difficulties arose from profiles being obscured by trees and buildings.

7   SITES IN NORTH ARGYLL (NA), COLL AND TIREE (CT) AND MULL (ML)

C.L.N.Ruggles, J.G.Morgan, R.W.Few & S.F.Burch

7.1   Introduction

Most of the sites in Mull were visited and surveyed by the authors during 1976. Sites in Coll and Tiree were covered by CR and RWF during 1979, and the remainder in Mull (including those in Ulva) by CR during the same year, assisted by Oliver Strimpel. Sites in North Argyll were covered by CR during 1981, assisted by Colin Martin. The locations of the sites considered are shown in Fig. 7.1.

7.2   Descriptions and classification of sites

For general notes on the descriptions that follow, see Section 5.2 (page 75).

NA1 - Branault (Cladh Chatain), Ardnamurchan. NM 5268 6950. A standing stone 2.2m high together with a stone only 0.4m high which may represent the stump of another. The two are only 1m apart. Arch. status = A; type = 4.

NA3 - Camas nan Geall (Cladh Chiarain), Ardnamurchan. NM 5605 6184. A slab 2.3m tall x 0.9m x 0.2m standing adjacent to a burial ground. Although now decorated with motifs of later date (RCAHMS 1980: no. 263) the stone was probably erected in prehistoric times. Arch. status = A; type = 5.

NA7 - Beinn Bhan, Morvern. NM 6591 4926. A standing stone 1.8m tall x 0.9m at its widest x 0.5m. Arch. status = A; type = 7.

CT1 - Acha (Loch nan Cinneachan), Coll. NM 1860 5674. A small slab 1.0m tall x 0.9m x 0.3m standing some 20m from two grass-covered mounds which may (RCAHMS 1980: no. 50) or may not (OSAR: NM 15 NE, 17) be cairns. Arch. status = A; type = 5.

CT2 - Totronald, Coll. NM 1665 5594. Two slabs, 1.4m tall x 1.2m x 0.3m and 1.5m tall x 1.3m x 0.4m, standing some 14m apart and oriented across the line joining them. Arch. status = A; type = 3.

CT3 - Breacacha, Coll. NM 1519 5329. A small standing stone 1.5m tall x 1.0m x 0.6m and leaning slightly. A large slab lying some 10m to the west is probably not a fallen standing stone (OSAR: NM 15 SE, 15; RCAHMS 1980: no. 94). Arch. status = A; type = 6.

CT4 - Caolas, Coll. NM 122 532. A small erect stone about 0.8m high x 0.6m x 0.4m is possibly a standing stone. A stone 1m long and 0.5m high, situated some 6m to its SE (RCAHMS 1980: no. 95) appears to be an outcrop. Arch. status = B; type = 8.

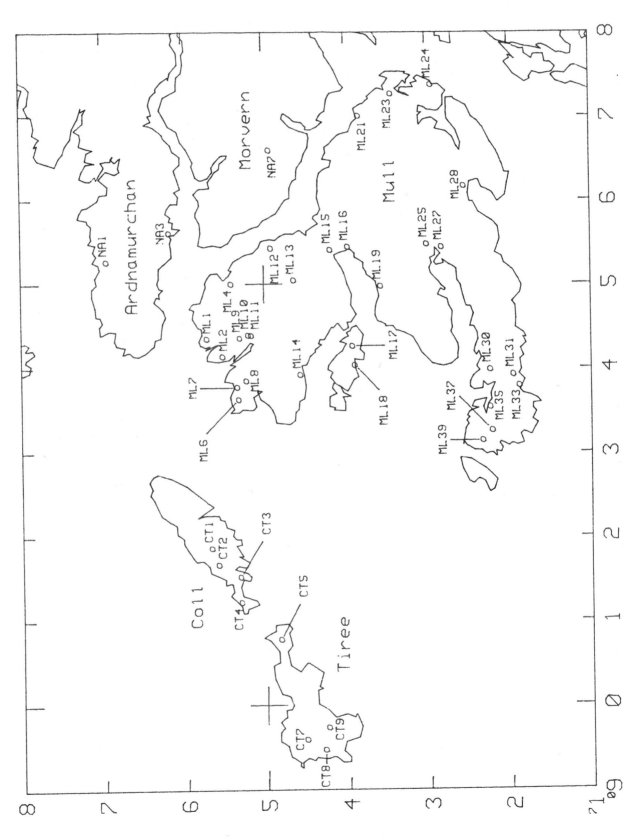

FIG. 7.1. Sites considered in North Argyll (NA), Coll and Tiree (CT), and Mull (ML).

CT5 - Caoles, Tiree. NM 0776 4833. A rectangular standing stone 3.0m
tall x 0.8m x 0.6m, now leaning at about 45° to the NW. The
cairn also listed by Thom (1967: Table 12.1, M4/1) was not
located. Arch. status = A; type = 7.

CT7 - Hough (Moss), Tiree. NL 9588 4518 & 9580 4505. Two stone rings
some 150m apart, both about 40m in diameter. The RCAHMS (1980:
no. 107) also refer to a nearby cairn. Site plan: RCAHMS (1980:
fig. 45). Arch. status = A; type = 7.

CT8 - Barrapoll, Tiree. NL 9468 4300. A standing stone of trapezoidal cross-section, 1.5m tall x 0.8m x 0.6m. Arch. status = A;
type = 7.

CT9 - Balinoe (Balemartin), Tiree. NL 9731 4258. A large standing
stone 3.5m tall x 2.0m x 1.0m, with irregular longer faces. A
stone ring 60m to the north noted by Thom (1967: Table 12.1,
M4/2; 1971: 67) appears to consist of natural boulders. Arch.
status = A; type = 5.

ML1 - Glengorm, Mull. NM 4347 5715. Three standing stones, all
around 2m in height, in a triangular setting. Two have been
re-erected (RCAHMS 1980: no. 105) and are probably not in their
original positions. The third is a slab 0.8m x 0.3m, not
aligned upon the present positions of either of the other two.
Site plans: RCAHMS (1980: fig. 44); Thom, Thom & Burl (1984).
Arch. status = A; type = 7.

ML2 - Quinish (Mingary), Mull. NM 4134 5524. A standing stone 2.8m
tall x 0.5m x 0.4m, together with three recumbent stones which
represent the remains of a group of five stones noted in the
last century (RCAHMS 1980: no. 111). The remaining four stones
appear probably to have formed an alignment some 10m long, and
the fifth stone may originally have been in the alignment. Site
plans: Ruggles (1981: 188); Thom, Thom & Burl (1984). Arch.
status = A; type = 2.

ML4 - Balliscate (Tobermory), Mull. NM 4996 5413. A 5m-long three-
stone alignment. The end stones are 2.5m and 1.8m in height;
the central one, which has fallen, is 2.8m long. Site plans:
RCAHMS (1980: fig. 39); Thom, Thom & Burl (1984). Arch. status
= A; type = 2.

(ctd. on page 127

- - - - - -

TABLE 7.1. List of on-site indications in North Argyll (NA), Coll and
Tiree (CT) and Mull (ML).

Column headings are as for Table 5.1 (see page 77).

TABLE 7.2. List of inter-site indications in North Argyll (NA), Coll
and Tiree (CT) and Mull (ML).

Column headings are as for Table 5.2 (see page 81).

Table 7.1

Site	Name	Indication	Class	Dist	St	Com	Survey	No.	Az limits	
NA1	Branault	; ab (To NNW);	4a	29.0 km	B	e	810606;	110:	328.0	329.6
NA1	Branault	; ba (To SSE);	4a	2.5 km	A		810606;	111:	148.0	149.6
NA3	Camas nan Geall;	To NNW ;	5a	1.0 km	A		810606;	112:	328.0	331.0
NA3	Camas nan Geall;	To SSE ;	5a	0.5 km	L					
CT1	Acha	; To N ;	5a	0.1 km	L					
CT1	Acha	; To S ;	5a	-Sea-	C		- ;	113:	178.0	181.4
CT2	Totronald	; ab (To NNE);	3a	3.0 km	A		790707;	114:	17.8	19.0
CT2	Totronald	; ba (To SSW);	3a	4.0 km	A		790707;	115:	197.8	199.0
CT9	Balinoe	; To NNE ;	5a	0.5 km	L					
CT9	Balinoe	; To SSW ;	5a	2.5 km	A		790704;	120:	195.0	196.6
ML2	Quinish	; To NNW ;	2c	0.2 km	L		760819;	122:	166.0	170.0
ML2	Quinish	; To SSE ;	2c	8.0 km	A			124:	4.4	6.2
ML4	Balliscate	; abc (To N) ;	2a	13.5 km	C		- ;			
ML4	Balliscate	; cba (To S) ;	2a	1.5 km	A		760821;	125:	184.4	186.2
ML6	Lag	; ab (To N) ;	4a	0.1 km	L					
ML6	Lag	; ba (To S) ;	4a	0.1 km	L					
ML7	Cillchriosd	; To NW ;	5a	0.8 km	L					
ML7	Cillchriosd	; To SE ;	5a	5.5 km	A		790710;	126:	132.6	133.4
ML8	Calgary	; ab ;	5b	-	W					
ML8	Calgary	; ba ;	5b	-	W					
ML9	Maol Mor	; To NNW ;	1a	47.0 km	C		- ;	128:	341.0	343.0
ML9	Maol Mor	; To SSE ;	1a	0.3 km	L					
ML10	Dervaig N	; To NNW ;	2a	3.0 km	B	t	760823;	130:	328.6	331.0
ML10	Dervaig N	; To SSE ;	2a	0.5 km	L					
ML11	Dervaig S	; cba(To NNW);	1a	0.3 km	L					

Table 7.1 (continued)

Site	Name	Indication Class	Dist	St	Com	Survey	No.	Az limits
ML11	Dervaig S	; abc(To SSE): 1a	8.0 km	A		760823;	131:	156.4 157.8
ML12	Ardnacross	; abc(To NNE): 2c	8.0 km	A		760824;	132:	26.0 29.2
ML12	Ardnacross	; cba(To SSW); 2c	2.0 km	A		760824;	133:	206.0 209.2
ML16	Gruline	; ba (To NW) ; 3a	4.0 km	B	p	760820;	135:	307.6 308.6
ML16	Gruline	; ab (To SE) ; 3a	10.5 km	B	p	760820;	136:	127.6 128.6
ML18	Cragaig	; ba (To ENE); 3a	9.0 km	A		790711;	138:	66.6 67.6
ML18	Cragaig	; ab (To WSW); 3a	0.5 km	L				
ML21	Scallastle	; abc (To W) ; 2c	0.4 km	L				
ML21	Scallastle	; cba (To E) ; 2c	0.8 km	L				
ML25	Uluvalt	; abc (To NW); 3c	3.5 km	A		790712;	139:	316.4 317.6
ML25	Uluvalt	; cba (To SE); 3c	4.0 km	A		790712;	140:	136.4 137.6
ML30	Taoslin	; To NNW ; 6	2.5 km	A		760826;	143:	328.2 330.4
ML30	Taoslin	; To SSE ; 6	0.2 km	L				
ML31	Uisken	; To NE ; 5a	6.5 km	A		760827;	144:	49.4 50.2
ML31	Uisken	; To SW ; 5a	4.0 km	A		760827;	145:	229.4 230.2
ML33	Ardalanish	; ba (To WNW); 3b	1.0 km	A		760827;	146:	281.6 283.2
ML33	Ardalanish	; ab (To ESE); 3b	0.5 km	L				
ML34	Suie	; ab (To NE) ; 3a	-	W				
ML34	Suie	; ba (To SW) ; 3a	-	W				

Table 7.2

Site	Name	F/s & dist	St	CL	Dist	St	Com	Survey	No.	Az limits	
CT2	Totronald	; CT3 3.0 km;	A	2	-Sea-	A		790707;	116:	204.6	205.0
CT3	Breacacha	; CT2 3.0 km;	A	1	5.5 km	A		790707;	117:	24.6	25.0
CT7	Hough	; CT8 2.5 km;	A	2	5.0 km	B	p	790705;	118:	204.0	205.2
CT8	Barrapoll	; CT7 2.5 km;	A	2	2.5 km	C		– ;	119:	24.0	25.2
ML1	Glengorm	; ML9 4.0 km;	A	3	12.0 km	C		– ;	121:	175.0	175.6
ML2	Quinish	; ML7 4.0 km;	A	3	6.0 km	C		– ;	123:	240.0	241.0
ML7	Cillchriosd	; ML2 4.0 km;	A	3	9.5 km	A		790710;	127:	60.0	61.0
ML9	Maol Mor	; ML1 4.0 km;	A	3	10.5 km	C		– ;	129:	355.0	355.6
ML15	Killichronan	; ML16 2.2 km;	A	2	5.0 km	C		– ;	134:	163.4	167.2
ML16	Gruline	; ML15 2.2 km;	A	2	3.0 km	C		– ;	137:	343.4	347.2
ML25	Uluvalt	; ML27 1.9 km;	B	2	4.5 km	A		790712;	141:	191.6	192.0
ML27	Rossal	; ML25 1.9 km;	B	2	3.0 km	C		– ;	142:	11.6	12.0

ML6 - Lag (Mornish), Mull. NM 3626 5331. A standing stone 1.6m tall x 0.7m x 0.5m, and a fallen menhir 1.4m long which appears to have stood only about 1m away from it. Two further small standing stones some 15m to the SE were noted by Orr (1937: 132-3), but they are simply the remains of a boundary wall (RCAHMS 1980: no. 109). Arch. status = A; type = 4.

ML7 - Cillchriosd, Mull. NM 3773 5348. A rectangular slab 2.6m tall x 1.4m x 0.6m. Arch. status = A; type = 5.

ML8 - Calgary (Frachadil), Mull. NM 3849 5231. Two prostrate stones 2.8m and 2.6m long, lying close together, which may represent fallen menhirs. Arch. status = B; type = 5.

ML9 - Maol Mor (Dervaig A), Mull. NM 4355 5311. A 10m-long four-stone alignment. Three stones stand, and are all about 2m tall; the fourth is prone, and 2.4m long. Site plans: Thom (1966: fig. 8); RCAHMS (1980: fig. 41); Thom, Thom & Burl (1984). Arch. status = A; type = 1.

ML10 - Dervaig N (Dervaig B), Mull. NM 4390 5202. Two standing stones, 2.5m and 2.4m tall, and three prostrate stones all about 2.3m in length, which appear to have formed an 18m-long five-stone alignment. The site is now in a clearing in thick forest. Some 250m to the SE, and also in the alignment, is an erect stone 1.0m high x 0.6m x 0.6m, which is possibly a standing stone. Site plans: Thom (1966: fig. 7); RCAHMS (1980: fig. 42); Thom, Thom & Burl (1984). Arch. status = A; type = 2.

ML11 - Dervaig S (Dervaig C), Mull. NM 4385 5163. A 15m-long three-stone alignment. The present stone heights are between 1.0m and 1.3m, although two of them appear to be broken off. The RCAHMS (1972: no. 101(3)) note a fourth stone 1.1m high which has probably been removed from its original position. Site plans: RCAHMS (1980: fig. 43); Thom, Thom & Burl (1984). Arch. status = A; type = 1.

ML12 - Ardnacross, Mull. NM 5422 4915. One standing and five prostrate stones, which appear to have formed two parallel three-stone alignments each about 10m long, in association with three kerb-cairns. The standing stone is 2.4m tall x 1.0m x 0.5m, and the prostrate stones are between about 2m and 3m long. Site plans: RCAHMS (1980: fig. 18); Thom, Thom & Burl (1984). Arch. status = A; type = 2.

ML13 - Tenga (Loch Frisa), Mull. NM 5040 4632. Four stones between 0.8m and 1.8m tall in a trapezoidal formation, which may represent the remains of a stone ring of diameter about 35m. Against this interpretation is the fact that the longer faces of the stones would not in every case lie tangential to the ring. Recently a fifth stone has been reported by the inhabitants of Tenga farm (J. Barnatt, priv. comm. 1983). Site plan: RCAHMS (1980: fig. 48). Arch. status = A; type = 7.

ML14 - Tostarie, Mull. NM 3917 4561. A standing stone 1.7m tall x 0.6m x 0.4m. Arch. status = A; type = 7.

ML15 - Killichronan (Torr nam Fiann), Mull. NM 5401 4193. A standing
        stone 2.4m tall x 0.5m x 0.3m, now leaning by about 70° from the
        vertical. Arch. status = A; type = 7.

ML16   - Gruline, Mull. NM 5437 3977 & 5456 3960. Two standing stones
        some 250m apart. One is a slab 2.3m tall x 0.8m x 0.3m oriented
        across the line joining the two stones; the other is a 2.4m-tall
        stone of lozenge-shaped cross section. The latter stands amidst
        thick wooded scrub. Arch. status = A; type = 3.

ML17 - Ormaig, Ulva. NM 4256 3928. A prostrate stone 2.6m long, for-
        merly standing. Arch. status = A; type = 8.

ML18   - Cragaig, Ulva. NM 4028 3901. Two standing stones, one 1.3m
        tall x 1.2m x 0.6m, the other 1.6m tall x 0.6m x 0.6m, placed
        about 4m apart.   Both stones appear to have been broken off.
        Arch. status = A; type = 3.

ML19   -   Dishig, Mull. NM 4969 3574. A small erect stone 1.0m tall x
        0.8m x 0.6m which is possibly a prehistoric standing stone.
        Arch. status = B; type = 8.

ML21   - Scallastle, Mull. NM 6999 3827. A standing stone 1.2m high x
        0.9m x 0.6m and two prostrate stones 1.7m and 2.0m long, which
        apparently formed a 5m-long three-stone alignment. Arch. status
        = A; type = 2.

ML23   - Duart, Mull. NM 7260 3425 & 7275 3425. A standing stone 2.5m
        tall x 0.8m x 0.7m, now leaning to the west. Some 150m to its
        east is a structure listed by Thom (1967: Table 12.1, M2/2) as a
        stone circle; however it consists of six low boulders confined
        to an area only about 10m across. While it may represent the
        disturbed remains of some sort of prehistoric structure (RCAHMS
        1980: no. 92) the boulders may just be natural (OSAR: NM 73 SW,
        4). Arch. status = A; type = 7.

ML24   - Port Donain, Mull. NM 7368 2932. A large prostrate slab 4.1m
        long x 0.6m x 0.5m may represent a fallen standing stone. It
        lies close to the perimeter of a 6m-diameter kerb cairn. Some
        100m to the SE is a Clyde group long cairn (Henshall 1972: no.
        MUL1).   Site plan: RCAHMS (1980: fig. 29). Arch. status = B;
        type = 8.

ML25   - Uluvalt I (Barr Leathan), Mull. NM 5469 3004 (A), 5463 3002
        (B) & 5468 2996 (C). At (A) are the reported remains of a cham-
        bered cairn, but they probably just represent the remains of a
        building of recent date (RCAHMS 1980: no. 121(3)). At (B) are
        three prostrate stones between 2.0m and 2.3m long, which appear
        to have stood in a line some 10m long, although their status as
        prehistoric standing stones is disputed (OSAR: NM 53 SW, 2). A
        0.5m-high boulder located between two of the prostrate stones
        may have formed part of the alignment. The RCAHMS (1980: no.
        121(4)) also note a possible fallen standing stone 2.1m long
        some 50m to the west of the alignment. At (C) is a standing
        stone 1.9m tall x 0.8m x 0.6m. This may not be prehistoric, as

(ctd. on page 139

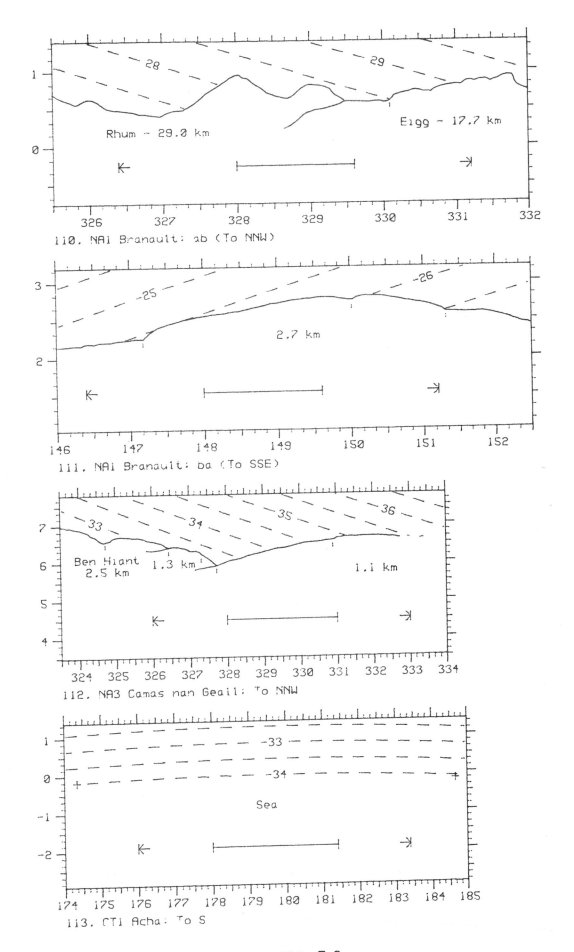

110. NA1 Branault: ab (To NNW)

111. NA1 Branault: ba (To SSE)

112. NA3 Camas nan Geail: To NNW

113. CT1 Acha: To S

FIG. 7.2.

- 129 -

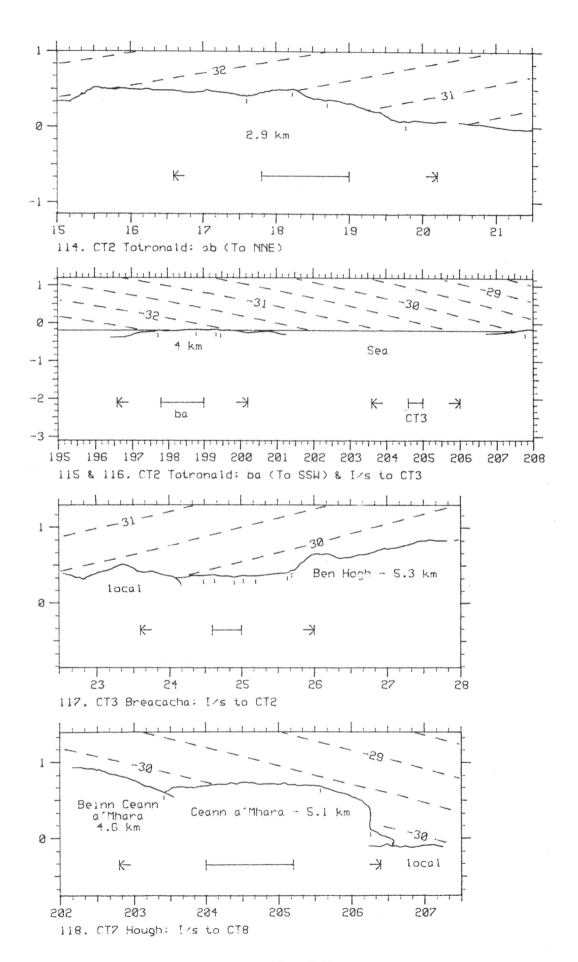

114. CT2 Totronald: ab (To NNE)

115 & 116. CT2 Totronald: ba (To SSW) & I/s to CT3

117. CT3 Breacacha: I/s to CT2

118. CT7 Hough: I/s to CT8

FIG. 7.3.

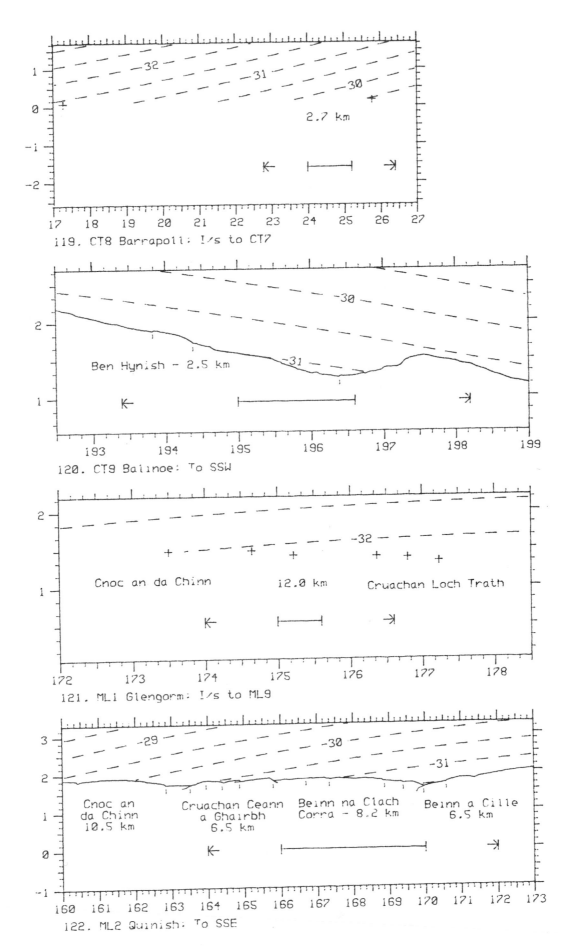

119. CT8 Barrapoll: I/s to CT7

120. CT9 Balinoe: To SSW

121. ML1 Glengorm: I/s to ML9

122. ML2 Quinish: To SSE

FIG. 7.4.

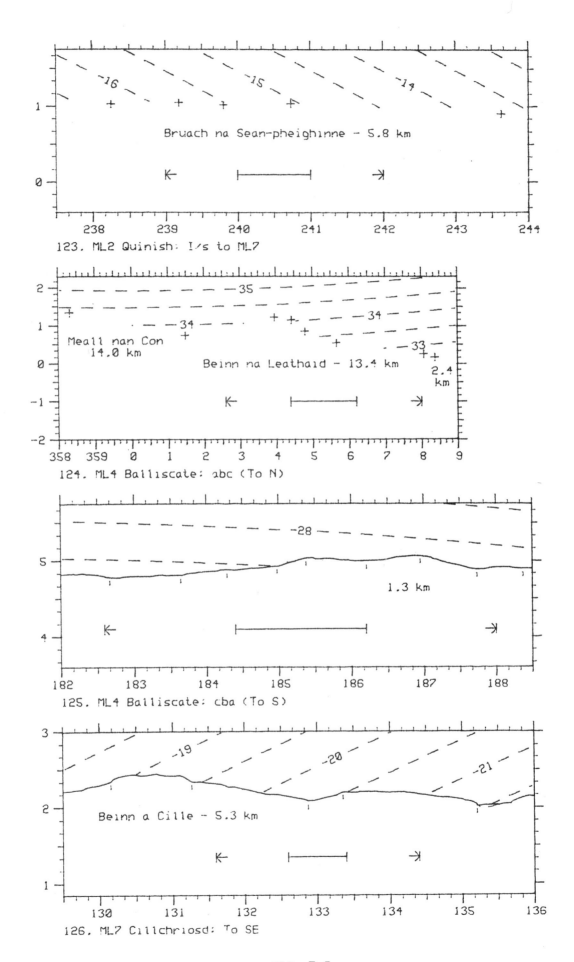

123. ML2 Quinish: I/s to ML7

124. ML4 Bailiscate: abc (To N)

125. ML4 Bailiscate: cba (To S)

126. ML7 Cillchriosd: To SE

FIG. 7.5.

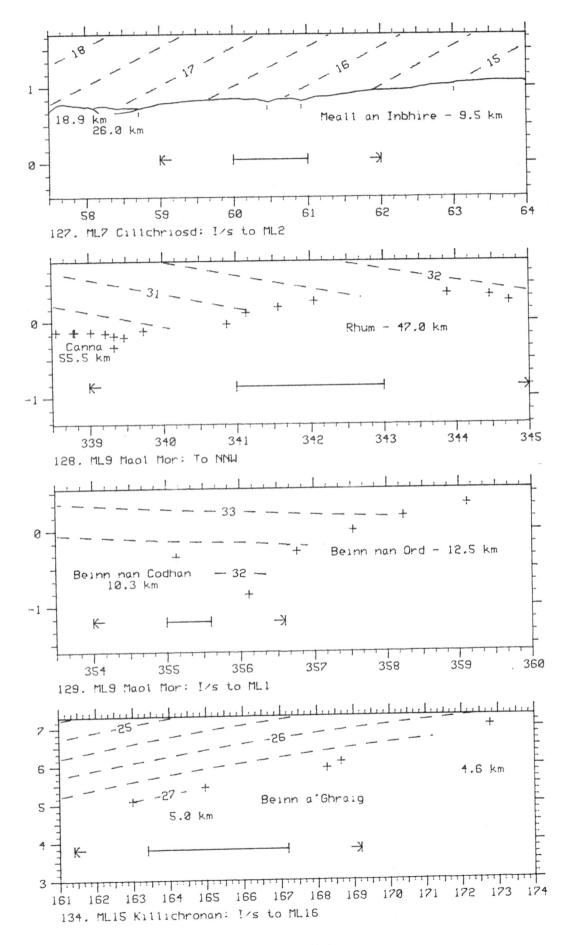

127. ML7 Cillchriosd: I/s to ML2

128. ML9 Maol Mor: To NNW

129. ML9 Maol Mor: I/s to ML1

134. ML15 Killichronan: I/s to ML16

FIG. 7.6.

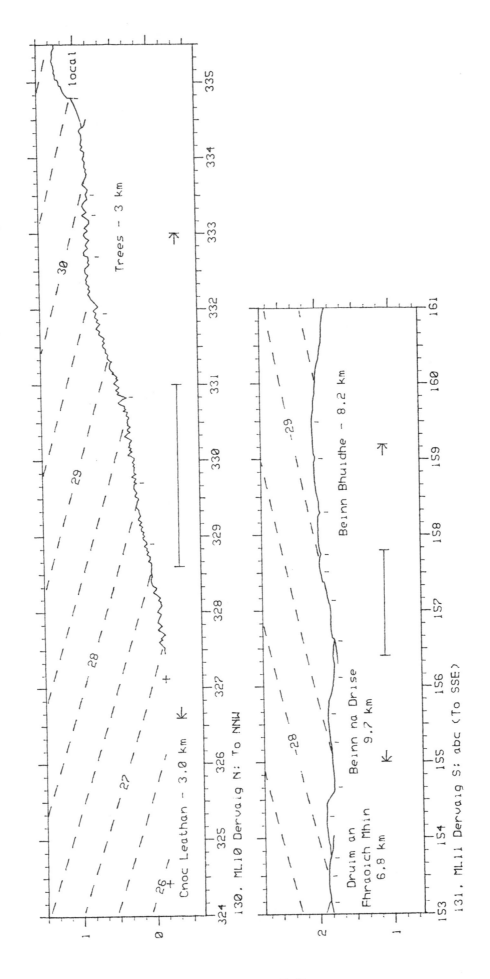

130. ML10 Dervaig N: To NNW

131. ML11 Dervaig S: abc (To SSE)

FIG. 7.7.

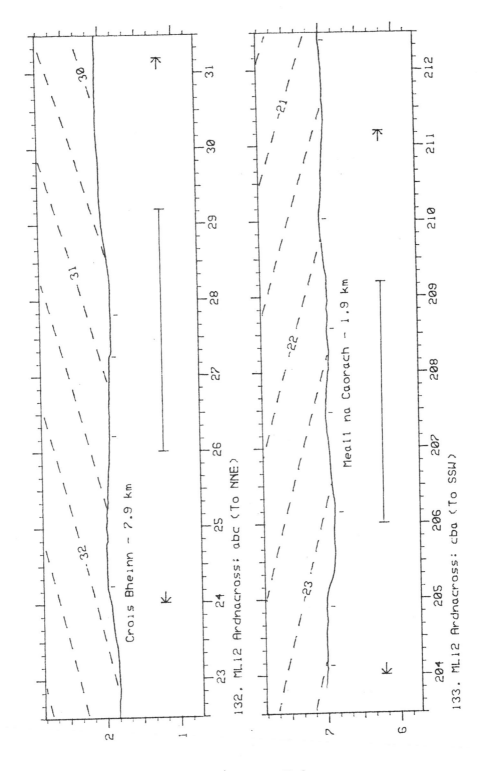

Crois Bheinn ~ 7.9 km

132. ML12 Ardnacross: abc (To NNE)

Meall na Caorach ~ 1.9 km

133. ML12 Ardnacross: cba (To SSW)

FIG. 7.8.

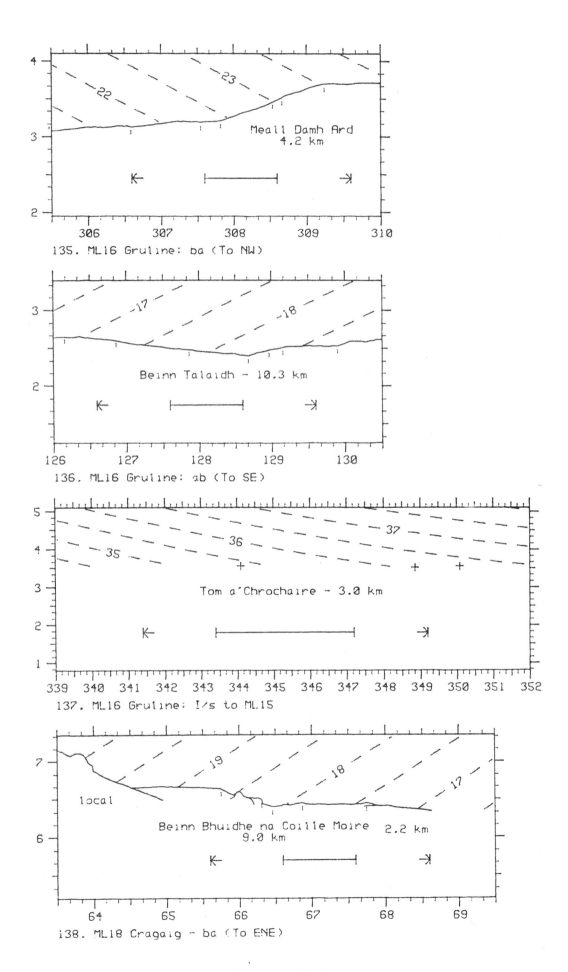

135. ML16 Gruline: ba (To NW)

136. ML16 Gruline: ab (To SE)

137. ML16 Gruline: l/s to ML.15

138. ML18 Cragaig - ba (To ENE)

FIG. 7.9.

- 136 -

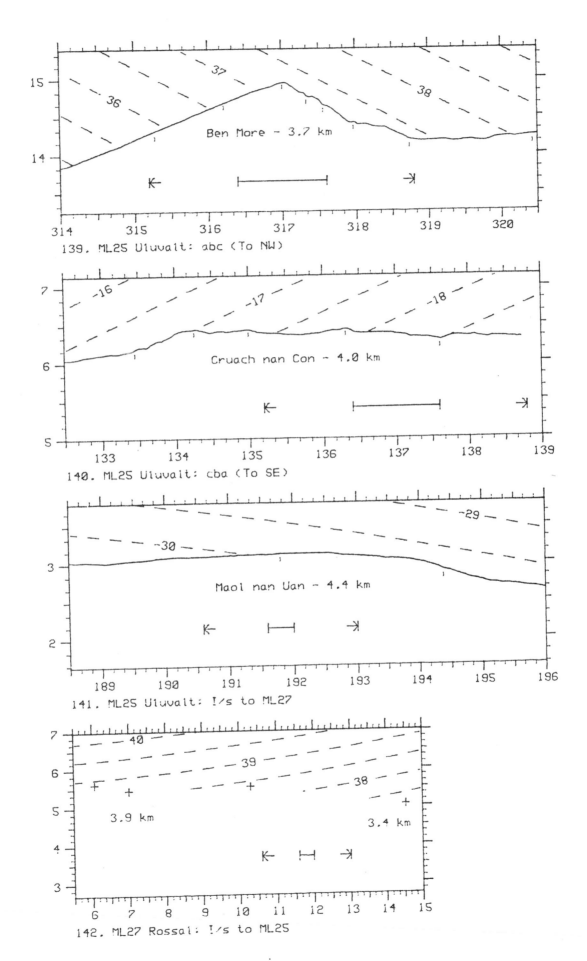

139. ML25 Uluvalt: abc (To NW)

140. ML25 Uluvalt: cba (To SE)

141. ML25 Uluvalt: l/s to ML27

142. ML27 Rossal: l/s to ML25

FIG. 7.10.

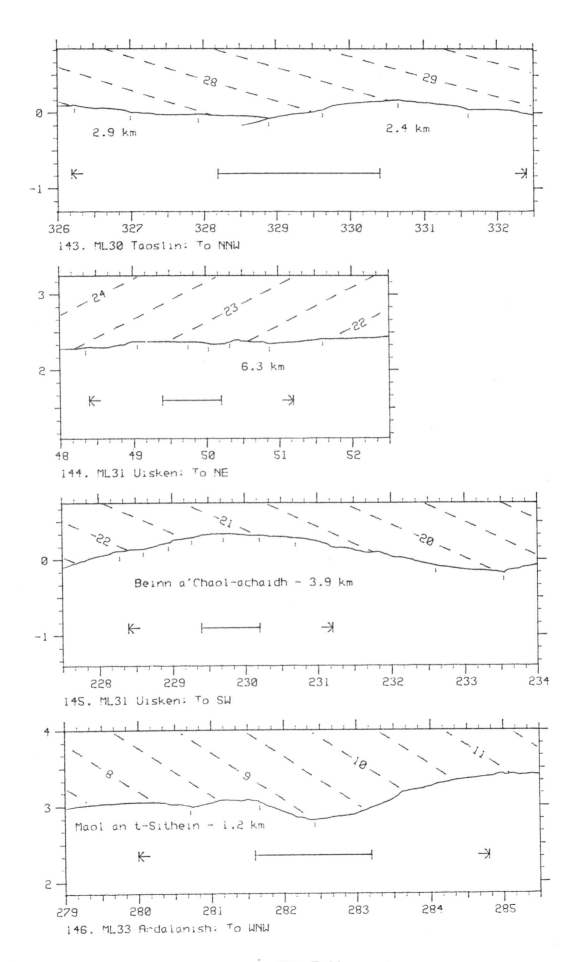

143. ML30 Taoslin: To NNW

144. ML31 Uisken: To NE

145. ML31 Uisken: To SW

146. ML33 Ardalanish: To WNW

FIG. 7.11.

it is possibly one of a series of pilgrim route marker stones
(OSAR: NM 52 NW, 3; see also site ML27 below). Site plan:
RCAHMS (1980: fig. 49). Arch. status = B; type = 3.

ML27 - Rossal (Breac Achadh), Mull. NM 5434 2820. A standing stone
2.0m tall x 0.8m x 0.5m. It is possibly one of a series of
marker stones erected along the pilgrim route from Green Point
to Iona (see M'Laughlin 1865: 49). Arch. status = B; type = 8.

ML28 - Lochbuie, Mull. NM 6163 2543 (A), 6141 2524 (B), 6178 2512
(C), 6175 2507 (D) & 6169 2506 (E). At (C) is a 13m-diameter
circle of stones up to 2m tall. Five metres to its SE is an
outlier 0.9m tall x 0.6m x 0.3m. Some 40m to its SW, at (D), is
a tall stone 3m high x 0.8m x 0.3m. Some 100m to its SW, at
(E), is a stone now 2.2m tall, which has been broken off. A
further stone 350m NNW of the circle, at (A), is 2.0m tall x
1.5m x 0.4m. The second circle listed by Thom (1967: Table
12.1, M2/14) is in fact a kerb-cairn at (B) (RCAHMS 1980: no.
49; OSAR: NM 62 NW, 4). Site plans: Thom, Thom & Burl (1980:
320); RCAHMS (1980: fig. 47). Arch. status = A; type = 7.

ML30 - Taoslin (Bunessan), Mull. NM 3973 2239. A rectangular standing stone 2.1m tall x 0.8m x 0.4m. It is possibly one of a
series of pilgrim route marker stones (see site ML27 above).
Arch. status = B; type = 6.

ML31 - Uisken (Druim Fan; Am Fan), Mull. NM 3916 1961. A slab 2.2m
tall x 1.3m x 0.3m. Arch. status = A; type = 5.

ML33 - Ardalanish, Mull. NM 3784 1888. A standing stone 1.9m tall x
0.9m x 0.3m and a prostrate stone at least 2.3m long, located
11m apart. The standing slab is roughly oriented along the line
joining the two stones. Arch. status = A; type = 3.

ML34 - Suie (Dail na Carraigh), Mull. NM 3706 2185. Two standing
stones respectively 2.0m and 1.1m high and 1.2m apart, are
situated on the NE side of a large ruined cairn as described by
Henshall (1972: 467) and the RCAHMS (1980: no. 61). A stone
alignment referred to by Thom (1967: Table 12.1, M2/7) in fact
consists of the remaining grounders of an old field dyke
(RCAHMS: priv. comm. 1976; OSAR: NM 32 SE, 7). Site plan:
RCAHMS (1980: fig. 36). Arch. status = A; type = 3.

ML35 - Tirghoil (Ross of Mull), Mull. NM 3531 2240. A slab 2.4m tall
x 0.6m x 0.5m. It is possibly one of a series of pilgrim route
marker stones (see site ML27 above). Arch. status = B; type =
8.

ML37 - Poit na h-I (Torr Mor), Mull. NM 3251 2216. A standing stone
2.4m tall x 0.6m x 0.6m. Arch. status = A; type = 7.

ML39 - Achaban House, Mull. NM 3133 2331. A standing stone 2.5m tall
x 0.6m x 0.4m. It is possibly one of a series of pilgrim route
marker stones (see site ML27 above). Arch. status = B; type =
8.

7.3   Remarks on the surveys and survey data

The data for the surveys are presented in full in Tables 7.1 and 7.2, for on-site and inter-site lines respectively. Profile diagrams are presented in Figs. 7.2 – 7.11.

Some error is possible in the case of the following surveyed profiles, for the reasons stated.

Line 110 (NA1 Branault: ab). The Rhum profile (29 km) could not be surveyed owing to poor visibility. Points on a nearer profile (Eigg, 18 km) were surveyed instead, and the more distant profile was calibrated using a photograph obtained on a subsequent visit to the site.

Line 118 (CT7 Hough: I/s to CT8). Large parallax correction. Measurements were reduced to the OP (taken between the two rings) from a point 75m behind it (the centre of the NNE ring).

Line 130 (ML10 Dervaig N: To NNW). Forestry planting on the profile itself (3 km).

Lines 135-6 (ML16 Gruline: ba & ab). Large parallax corrections (NW menhir situated in thick woodland). Measurements were reduced to the OPs from a point 115m in front and 55m off line to the right (Line 135) and 145m in front and 55m off line to the left (Line 136).

8   SITES IN LORN (LN) AND MID-ARGYLL (AR)

8.1   Introduction

Sites in Lorn and mid-Argyll were visited and surveyed by the author during 1979 with the assistance of Mari Williams and Mary Wilson, and during 1981 with the assistance of Sal Brown and Colin Martin. The sites at Strontoiller (LN17) and Duachy (LN22), which had been surveyed during 1973 by the author and his colleagues Guy Morgan, Roger Few, John Cooke and Mark Bailey (Bailey et al. 1975), were re-surveyed during 1981. The locations of the sites considered are shown in Fig. 8.1.

8.2   Descriptions and classification of sites

For general notes on the descriptions that follow, see Section 5.2 (page 75).

LN1 - Acharra, Appin. NM 9866 5455. A rectangular standing stone about 3.5m tall x 1.1m x 0.6m. Arch. status = A; type = 7.

LN2 - Inverfolla, Appin. NM 9583 4503. A prostrate stone about 3.5m in length, known to have been a standing stone (RCAHMS 1975: no. 118). Arch. status = A; type = 8.

LN3 - Barcaldine, Benderloch. NM 9636 4214. A rectangular standing stone 1.7m tall, with a second stone 1.6m tall moved to its side and propped up against it. Arch. status = A; type = 7.

LN5 - Achacha, Benderloch. NM 9444 4075. A standing stone rhomboidal in cross-section, 2.5m tall x 0.6m x 0.4m, situated 90m to the E of a cairn (RCAHMS 1975: no. 10). The latter is erroneously listed as a stone circle by Thom (1967: Table 12.1, M8/1). A second menhir listed by Thom (ibid.) is not mentioned by the RCAHMS and was not located by us. Arch. status = A; type = 7.

LN7 - Benderloch N, Benderloch. NM 9062 3865. A slab 1.5m tall x 1.0m x 0.2m. It is possible that it represents the remaining menhir of a stone circle, since the site of a stone circle was reported in this vicinity in 1871 (Smith 1872: 88-9). Arch. status = A; type = 5.

LN8 - Benderloch S, Benderloch.   NM 9033 3802. A standing stone triangular in cross-section, 2.1m tall with sides 1.1m, 1.0m and 0.5m.   Smith (1874: 80) refers to a "field with the standing stones" in this vicinity, which may indicate that there were originally more stones here. Thom describes the site as a circle and two stones (FSL: M8/4; 1967: Table 12.1, M8/3). Arch. status = A; type = 7.

LN14 - Taynuilt (Taynuilt 2), Lorn. NN 0120 3115. A squat standing stone 1.2m tall which appears originally to have been taller.

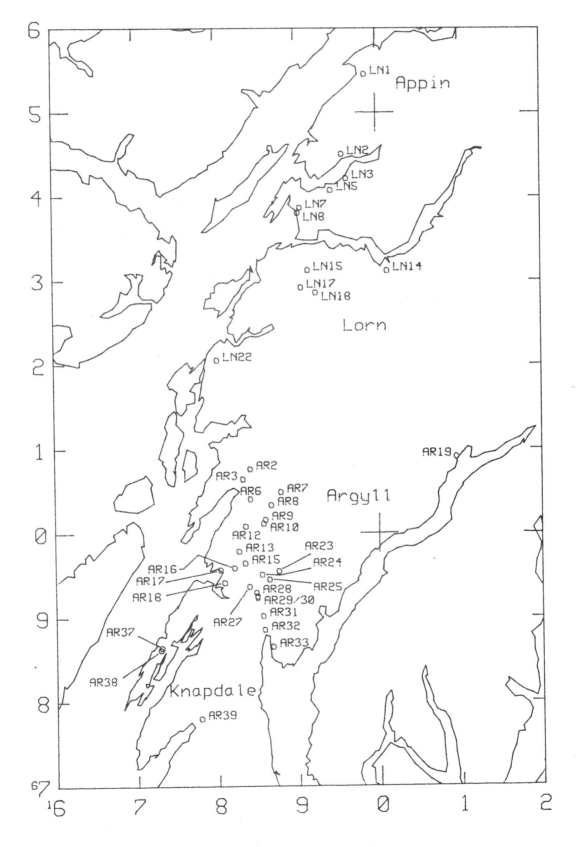

FIG. 8.1. Sites considered in Lorn (LN) and mid-Argyll and
northern Knapdale (AR).

It is roughly triangular in cross-section. Arch. status = A; type = 7.

LN15 - Black Lochs, Lorn. NM 9155 3124. An erect block of stone 1.4m tall x about 0.9m wide, which may be prehistoric (OSAR: NM 93 SW, 4). Arch. status = B; type = 8.

LN17 - Strontoiller (Loch Nell), Lorn. NM 9067 2914 (A), 9076 2897 (B) & 9078 2896 (C). At (A) is a ring of rounded boulders some 20m in diameter. At (B), some 190m to the SE, is a standing stone ("Clach na Carraig") some 4m tall x 1.2m x 1.0m. At (C), 12m ESE of the standing stone, is a ring cairn 5m across, excavated in 1967 (Ritchie 1971). This cairn is erroneously listed by Thom (1967: Table 12.1, A1/2) as a second stone ring. Site plans: RCAHMS (1975: fig. 27); Thom, Thom & Burl (1980: 140). Arch. status = A; type = 7.

LN18 - Glenamacrie, Lorn. NM 9250 2854. A standing stone 1.5m tall x 0.7m x 0.6m. Three metres to its west is a rounded boulder about 1m tall, which may be associated with it. Adjacent to the second stone is an outcropping stone which appears to be natural. Arch. status = A; type = 4.

LN22 - Duachy (Loch Seil), Lorn. NM 8014 2052. A 5m-long alignment of three stones respectively 2.8m, 1.9m and 2.2m tall, the central one now leaning at about 70° from the vertical. An isolated fourth stone some 40m from the alignment was originally 2.5m tall but was felled in 1963 (RCAHMS 1975: no. 116) and only a 0.3m-high stump now remains in situ. Site plans: Thom (1966: fig. 10); Thom, Thom & Burl (1984). Arch. status = A; type = 1.

AR2 - Sluggan, Argyll. NM 8405 0762 & 8403 0757. A possible cairn noted by Campbell & Sandeman at the first location (1961: no. 190) is in fact field clearance (OSAR: NM 80 NW, 6). A slab within the clearance may be the remains of the northernmost of two standing stones marked on the 1:10000 Ordnance Survey map. The southermost is a slab 2.5m tall x 0.8m x 0.2m standing in situ at the second location. Arch. status = A; type = 5.

AR3 - Barbreck, Argyll. NM 8315 0641. An alignment of two slabs, one 2.5m tall x 2.0m x 0.2m, the other 1.3m tall x 1.0m x 0.2m, some 3m apart. An isolated slab 2.0m tall x 1.5m x 0.3m, and oriented

(ctd. on page 148

- - - - - -

TABLE 8.1. List of on-site indications in Lorn (LN) and mid-Argyll and northern Knapdale (AR).

Column headings are as for Table 5.1 (see page 77).

Table 8.2. List of inter-site indications in Lorn (LN) and mid-Argyll and northern Knapdale (AR).

Column headings are as for Table 5.2 (see page 81).

Table 8.1

Site	Name	Indication	Class	Dist	St	Com	Survey	No.	Az limits	
LN7	Benderloch N	; To N	; 5a	24.5 km	C		-	; 147:	0.0	4.0
LN7	Benderloch N	; To S	; 5a	0.5 km	L					
LN18	Glenamacrie	; ab (To W)	; 4a	1.0 km	B	t	810529;	148:	270.2	273.8
LN18	Glenamacrie	; ba (To E)	; 4a	0.4 km	L					
LN22	Duachy	; abc(To NNW)	; 1a	1.0 km	A		810601;	149:	326.6	329.0
LN22	Duachy	; cba(To SSE)	; 1a	1.0 km	B	t	810601;	150:	146.6	149.0
AR2	Sluggan	; To N	; 5a	2.5 km	C		-	; 151:	356.0	358.0
AR2	Sluggan	; To S	; 5a	0.6 km	L					
AR3	Barbreck	; ab (To N)	; 1b	3.5 km	A		810527;	153:	6.4	7.6
AR3	Barbreck	; ba (To S)	; 1b	4.0 km	A		810527;	154:	186.4	187.6
AR6	Salachary	; abc (To N)	; 2a	2.0 km	A		790610;	156:	356.4	357.8
AR6	Salachary	; cba (To S)	; 2a	0.7 km	L					
AR9	Glennan N	; To ENE	; 5a	9.0 km	B	t	790718;	159:	69.4	71.0
AR9	Glennan N	; To WSW	; 5a	0.7 km	L					
AR10	Glennan S	; To NE	; 5a	0.4 km	L					
AR10	Glennan S	; To SW	; 5a	0.4 km	L					
AR12	Carnasserie	; To N	; 1b	0.8 km	L					
AR12	Carnasserie	; To S	; 1b	0.2 km	L					
AR13	Kilmartin	; S2-S3-S6	; 1a	2.5 km	A		790610;	162:	329.0	329.8
AR13	Kilmartin	; S6-S3-S2	; 1a	0.6 km	L					
AR13	Kilmartin	; S5-S1-S2	; 1a	6.5 km	C		-	; 163:	20.2	21.2
AR13	Kilmartin	; S2-S1-S5	; 1a	18.5 km	C		-	; 164:	200.2	201.2
AR13	Kilmartin	; S4-S1-S3	; 1a	2.5 km	C		-	; 165:	26.0	26.8
AR13	Kilmartin	; S3-S1-S4	; 1a	6.5 km	B	pt	810525;	166:	206.0	206.8
AR13	Kilmartin	; S5-S4	; 1b	2.0 km	A		810525;	167:	322.2	322.8

Table 8.1 (continued)

Site	Name	Indication	Class	Dist	St	Com	Survey	No.	Az limits
AR13	Kilmartin	; S4–S5 ;	1b	0.5 km	L				
AR15	Duncracaig	; abcd(To NW) ;	1a	4.0 km	B	p	790630;	168:	320.8 324.0
AR15	Duncracaig	; dcba(To SE);	1a	3.0 km	B	p	790630;	169:	140.8 144.0
AR15	Duncracaig	; ef (To NNW);	1b	4.0 km	B	pt	790630;	170:	333.4 335.4
AR15	Duncracaig	; fe (To SSE);	1b	5.5 km.	C		– ;	171:	153.4 155.4
AR16	Rowanfield	; To NW ;	5a	2.5 km	B	t	810526;	173:	316.8 319.6
AR16	Rowanfield	; To SE ;	5a	10.5 km	B	t	810526;	174:	136.8 139.6
AR19	Inverary	; To NE ;	5a	–	W				
AR19	Inverary	; To SW ;	5a	–	W				
AR23	Lechuary	; To NNW ;	5a	0.7 km	L				
AR23	Lechuary	; To SSE ;	5a	0.5 km	L				
AR25	Torbhlaran N	; To NW ;	5a	0.3 km	L				
AR25	Torbhlaran N	; To SE ;	5a	0.4 km	L				
AR27	Dunadd	; ab (To NNW);	4a	7.0 km	B	et	810522;	180:	327.4 329.2
AR27	Dunadd	; ba (To SSE);	4a	0.2 km	L				
AR28	Dunamuck I	; abc(To NNW);	2a	1.5 km	B	pt	810526;	181:	344.2 345.6
AR28	Dunamuck I	; cba(To SSE);	2a	2.0 km	B	pt	810526;	182:	164.2 165.6
AR29	Dunamuck II	; ab (To NW) ;	1b	1.0 km	B	p	810526;	185:	314.0 318.4
AR29	Dunamuck II	; ba (To SE) ;	1b	2.0 km	B	pt	810526;	186:	134.0 138.4
AR30	Dunamuck III	; ab (To W) ;	5b	–	W				
AR30	Dunamuck III	; ba (To E) ;	5b	–	W				
AR31	Achnabreck	; ab (To NNW);	3b	0.9 km	L				
AR31	Achnabreck	; ba (To SSE);	3b	0.3 km	L				
AR32	Oakfield	; To WNW ;	5a	2.0 km	C		– ;	189:	287.0 289.0
AR32	Oakfield	; To ESE ;	5a	3.0 km	C		– ;	190:	107.0 109.0

Table 8.1 (continued)

Site	Name	Indication	Class	Dist	St	Com	Survey No.	Az limits
AR33	Kilmory	; To WNW	; 5a	3.5 km	C	–	; 191:	299.0 302.0
AR33	Kilmory	; To ESE	; 5a	1.0 km	C	–	; 192:	119.0 122.0
AR39	Lochead	; To WNW	; 5a	–	W			
AR39	Lochead	; To ESE	; 5a	–	W			

Table 8.2

Site	Name	F/s & dist	St	Cl	Dist	St	Com	Survey	No.	Az limits	
AR2	Sluggan	; AR3 1.5 km;	A	2	65.5 km	C		–	; 152:	213.6	214.4
AR3	Barbreck	; AR2 1.5 km;	A	2	5.0 km	C		–	; 155:	33.6	34.4
AR7	Torran	; AR8 2.0 km;	A	2	3.0 km	C		–	; 157:	214.6	215.0
AR8	Ford	; AR7 2.0 km;	A	2	3.0 km	C		–	; 158:	34.6	35.0
AR9	Glennan N	; AR10 0.5 km;	A	2	1.5 km	C		–	; 160:	203.4	203.8
AR10	Glennan S	; AR9 0.5 km;	A	2	1.0 km	C		–	; 161:	23.4	23.8
AR13	Kilmartin	; AR16 1.9 km;	A	2	18.5 km	W		–	; – :	191.6	201.0
AR15	Duncracaig	; AR18 3.4 km;	B	3	6.0 km	C		–	; 172:	224.6	225.0
AR16	Rowanfield	; AR13 1.9 km;	A	2	5.5 km	W		–	; – :	11.6	21.0
AR16	Rowanfield	; AR17 1.7 km;	A	2	18.0 km	C		–	; 175:	258.8	259.4
AR17	Duntroon	; AR16 1.7 km;	A	2	4.0 km	C		–	; 176:	78.8	79.4
AR17	Duntroon	; AR18 1.6 km;	B	2	5.0 km	C		–	; 177:	158.6	159.6
AR18	Crinan Moss	; AR15 3.4 km;	B	3	4.5 km	A		790611;	178:	44.6	45.0
AR18	Crinan Moss	; AR17 1.6 km;	B	2	3.5 km	C		–	; 179:	338.6	339.6
AR28	Dunamuck I	; AR29 0.4 km;	A	2	2.0 km	B	pt	810526;	183:	159.4	160.0
AR28	Dunamuck I	; AR30 0.6 km;	A	2	2.0 km	B	pt	810526;	184:	164.0	164.6
AR29	Dunamuck II	; AR28 0.4 km;	A	2	2.0 km	C		–	; 187:	339.4	340.4
AR30	Dunamuck III	; AR28 0.6 km;	A	2	5.0 km	C		–	; 188:	344.0	344.6

roughly parallel to the first two, is situated some 20m away, perpendicular to the alignment. It is surrounded by three small erect slabs, each about 0.6m tall x 0.5m x 0.2m, forming the central parts of three sides of a rectangle roughly 4.5m x 3.0m. Site plans: Patrick (1979: S80); Thom, Thom & Burl (1984). Arch. status = A; type = 1.

AR6 - Salachary, Argyll. NM 8405 0403. Three menhirs which appear to have formed an alignment about 4m long. Two are about 2.5m tall, one standing and one leaning at about 20° to the horizontal. The third is prostrate, about 3m long. Arch. status = A; type = 2.

AR7 - Torran, Argyll. NM 8788 0488. A menhir some 3m tall x 0.9m x 0.5m. A cross has been incised on the W face (OSAR: NM 80 SE, 37). Arch. status = A; type = 7.

AR8 - Ford, Argyll. NM 8668 0333. A menhir about 3m tall x 0.5m x 0.4m. A second stone 1.9m long is now lying some 650m away at 8653 0268, but is thought originally to have come from near the first (OSAR: NM 80 SE, 42). Arch. status = A; type = 7.

AR9 - Glennan N (Creagantairbh), Argyll. NM 8595 0157. The 2m-high stump of a slab 1.4m x 0.6m. The top part of the stone, which still lay adjacent to the stump in 1979, is some 4m long, and the original height appears to have been almost 5m. There are two cairns in the vicinity, some 150m to the E and 300m to the ENE (Campbell & Sandeman 1961: nos. 80 & 77). Arch. status = A; type = 5.

AR10 - Glennan S, Argyll. NM 8573 0113. A slab 2.0m tall x 1.0m x 0.4m. There are two cairns (Campbell & Sandeman 1961: nos. 106 & 106a) some 100m to the WNW. Arch. status = A; type = 5.

AR12 - Carnasserie, Argyll. NM 8345 0080. An alignment of two slabs, respectively about 2.4m tall x 1.2m x 0.4m and 2.3m tall x 1.5m x 0.4m, some 3m apart. There is a cairn (Campbell & Sandeman 1961: no. 70) some 150m to the SSW. Site plan: Thom, Thom & Burl (1984). Arch. status = A; type = 1.

AR13 - Kilmartin (Slockavullin; Temple Wood), Argyll. NR 8263 9783 (A), 8279 9774 (B), 8282 9760 (C), 8283 9761 (D), 8252 9761 (E). At (A) is the Temple Wood stone circle, a ring 13m in diameter excavated over recent years by Scott (1975; 1976; 1977; 1978; 1979; 1980). Scott (1979) has also uncovered the remains of a second, previously unsuspected circle of earlier date some 20m to the NE of the first. Some 200m to the NE is the Nether Largie round cairn (Henshall 1963: no. ARG23). Some 300m to the SE of the circles, at (C) & (D), is a group of five standing stones as planned by Thom (1971: 46). The SW pair (Thom's S_4 & S_5) are aligned slabs, both about 2.5m tall x 0.8m x 0.3m. The central stone (Thom's S_1) is a slab 2.5m tall x 0.9m x 0.2m, flanked by four small erect slabs, each some 0.5m tall x 0.5m x 0.2m, forming the central parts of the sides of a rectangle some 3m x 2m. Between the SW pair and the central stone are a similar group of three small slabs (Thom's Q) forming the central parts of three sides of a rectangle about 5m x 3m, but without a central monolith. The NE pair of stones (Thom's S_2 & S_3) are an alignment

of slabs both about 2.5m tall x 1.1m x 0.3m. Also in this alignment, but some 150m to the NNW at (B), is a smaller standing
stone (Thom's S$_6$) 1.5m tall x 0.8m x 0.3m. The buried stump of
a further standing stone has been reported by Hawkins (1973).
Its position (E) and a description have been given in a recent
publication (Hawkins 1983: 98, 101-102). Site plans: Thom
(1971: 46); Patrick (1979: S80); Thom, Thom & Burl (1980: 144 &
146; 1984). Arch. status = A; type = 1.

AR15 - Duncracaig (Ballymeanoch), Argyll. NR 8337 9641. A 15m-long
alignment of four slabs up to 4m high; an adjacent and roughly
parallel alignment of two slabs 4m apart; and the site of a
holed stone, recently excavated (Barber 1978). There are two
cairns nearby (Campbell & Sandeman 1961: nos. 64 & 95). Site
plans: Thom (1971: 52); Barber (1978: 105); Thom, Thom & Burl
(1984). Arch. status = A; type = 1.

AR16 - Rowanfield (Poltalloch), Argyll. NR 8205 9585. A slab 2.5m
tall x 1.0m x 0.4m. Arch. status = A; type = 5.

AR17 - Duntroon, Argyll. NR 8034 9561. A small rectangular standing
stone 1.3m tall x 0.5m x 0.3m. Arch. status = A; type = 7.

AR18 - Crinan Moss, Argyll. NR 8083 9410. A setting of four tiny
erect stones, the largest about 1m tall. About 20m to the SE is
another erect stone 0.5m tall, and a second stone listed by
Campbell & Sandeman (1961: no. 173) appears now to be recumbent
and can be detected below the peat surface by prodding. The
sites of other stones listed by Campbell & Sandeman are not
apparent, and there does not seem to be any reason to suppose,
as they suggest, that the site represents the remains of an
alignment. Arch. status = B; type = 8.

AR19 - Inverary, Argyll. NN 0947 0905. A standing stone 2.8m tall x
1.2m x 0.4m, and irregular in cross-section (Campbell & Sandeman
1961: no. 169). Arch. status = A; type = 5.

AR23 - Lechuary (An Car), Argyll. NR 8757 9550. A slab some 3.0m
tall x 0.8m x 0.2m. Arch. status = A; type = 5.

AR24 - Loch na Torrnalaich, Argyll. NR 856 952. A prostrate slab
2.5m long, fitting the description given by Campbell & Sandeman
(1961: no. 186) but now fallen, is situated at the foot of a
line of crags some 30m NE of a narrow pass through them. The
Ordnance Survey (OSAR: NR 89 NE, 10) dismiss it as a fragment of
fractured rock similar to others in the area, which has fallen
from the rock face above and embedded itself in the ground.
However the fact that Campbell & Sandeman described it in 1961
as leaning rather than fallen, and that it is situated 2m beyond
the line of other boulders at the foot of the crags, suggest
otherwise. Since the Ordnance Survey give the Grid Reference of
the site as 8548 9509 rather than that above, and it is marked
on the 1" O.S. map in, rather than to the NE of, the narrow
pass, it is possible that they misidentified the site. Arch.
status = B; type = 8.

(ctd. on page 161

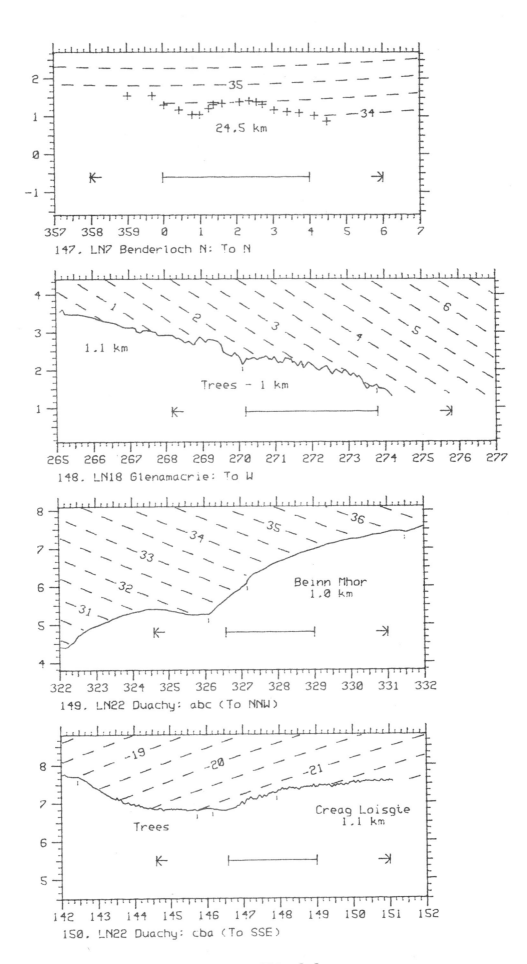

147. LN7 Benderloch N: To N

148. LN18 Glenamacrie: To W

149. LN22 Duachy: abc (To NNW)

150. LN22 Duachy: cba (To SSE)

FIG. 8.2.

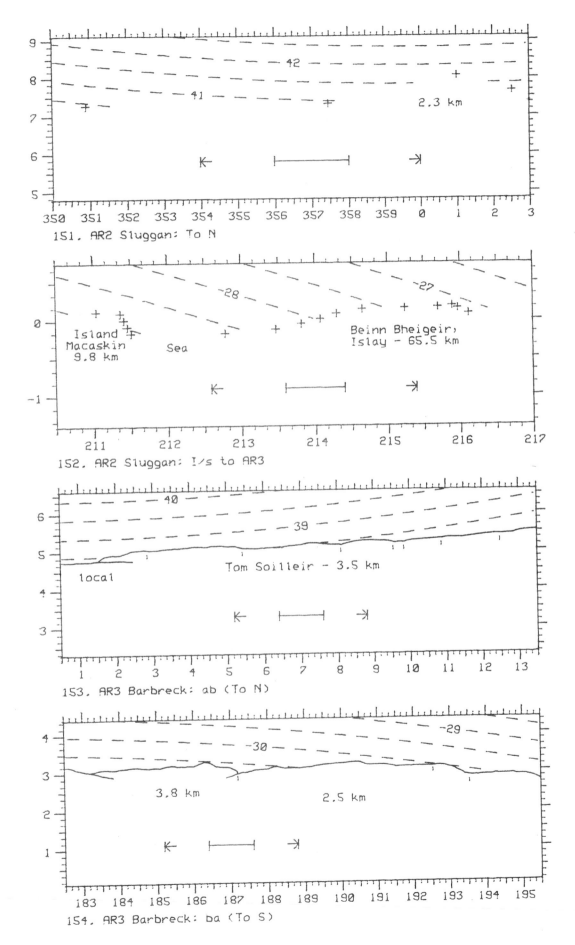

151. AR2 Sluggan: To N

152. AR2 Sluggan: I/s to AR3

153. AR3 Barbreck: ab (To N)

154. AR3 Barbreck: ba (To S)

FIG. 8.3.

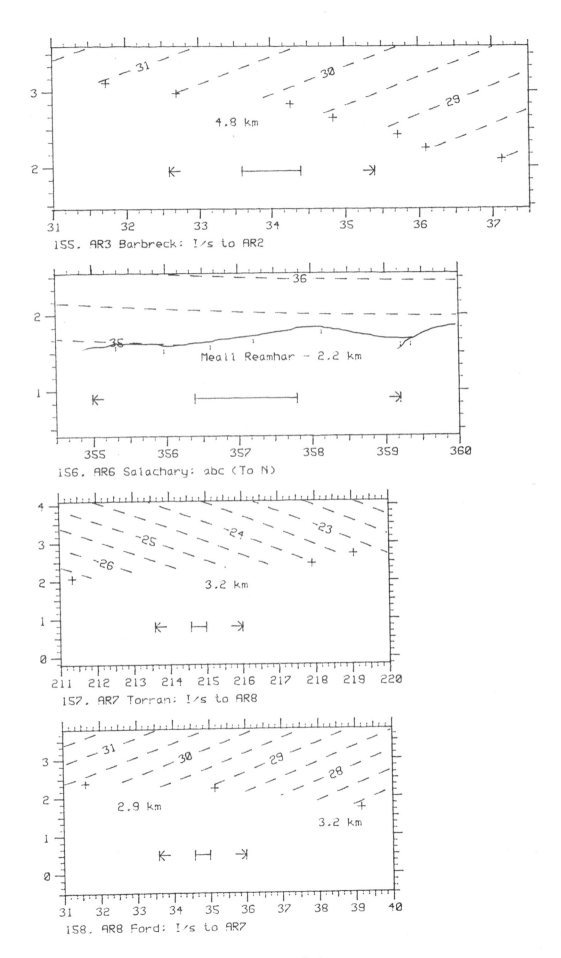

155. AR3 Barbreck: l/s to AR2

156. AR6 Salachary: abc (To N)

157. AR7 Torran: l/s to AR8

158. AR8 Ford: l/s to AR7

FIG. 8.4.

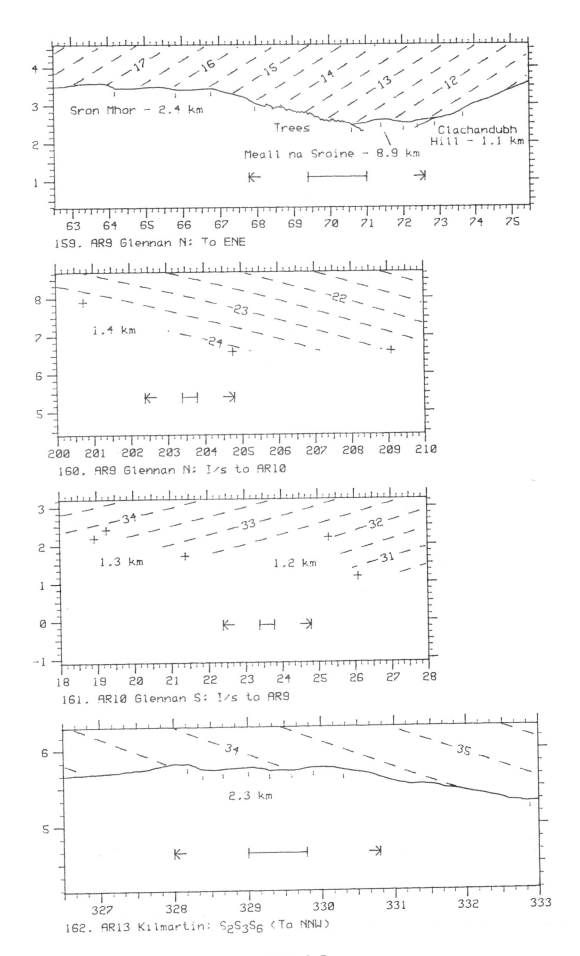

159. AR9 Glennan N: To ENE

160. AR9 Glennan N: I/s to AR10

161. AR10 Glennan S: I/s to AR9

162. AR13 Kilmartin: $S_2S_3S_6$ (To NNW)

FIG. 8.5.

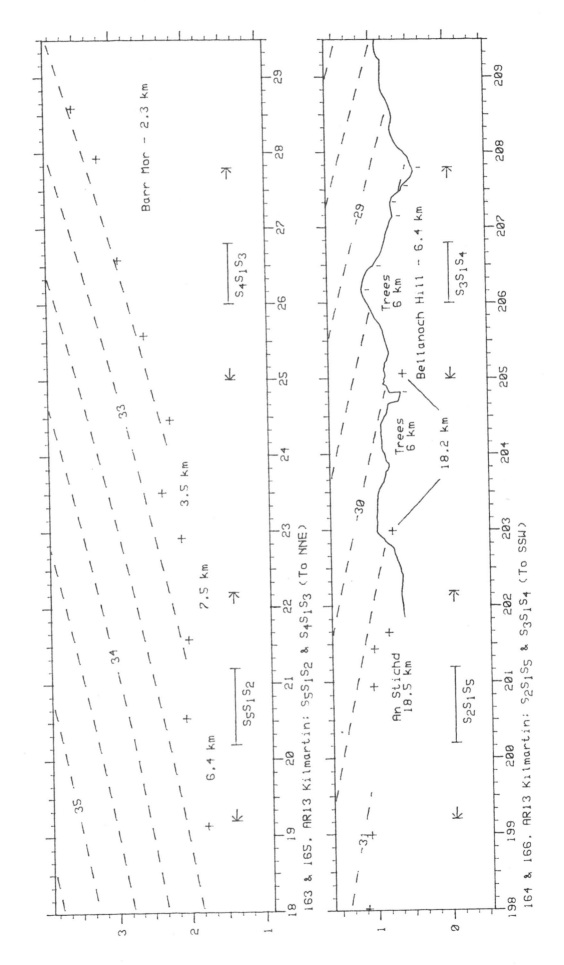

163 & 165. AR13 Kilmartin: $S_5S_1S_2$ & $S_4S_1S_3$ (To NNE)

164 & 166. AR13 Kilmartin: $S_2S_1S_5$ & $S_3S_1S_4$ (To SSW)

FIG. 8.6.

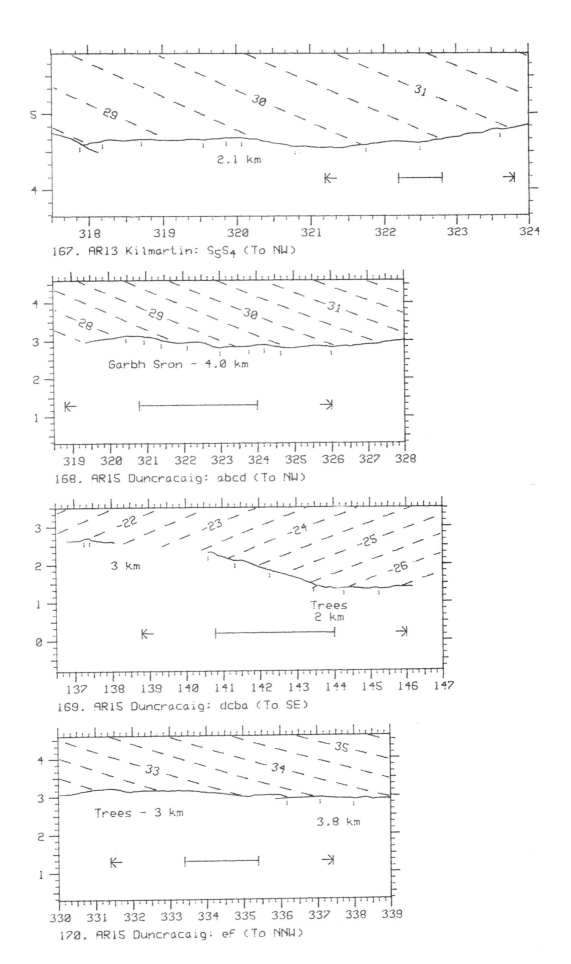

167. AR13 Kilmartin: S_5S_4 (To NW)

168. AR15 Duncracaig: abcd (To NW)

169. AR15 Duncracaig: dcba (To SE)

170. AR15 Duncracaig: ef (To NNW)

FIG. 8.7.

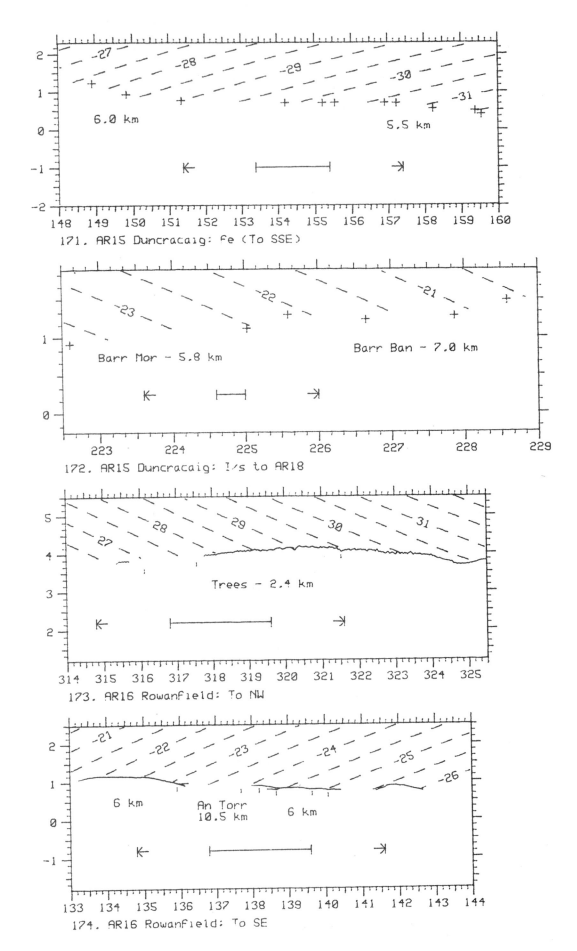

171. AR15 Duncracaig: Fe (To SSE)

172. AR15 Duncracaig: l/s to AR18

173. AR16 Rowanfield: To NW

174. AR16 Rowanfield: To SE

FIG. 8.8.

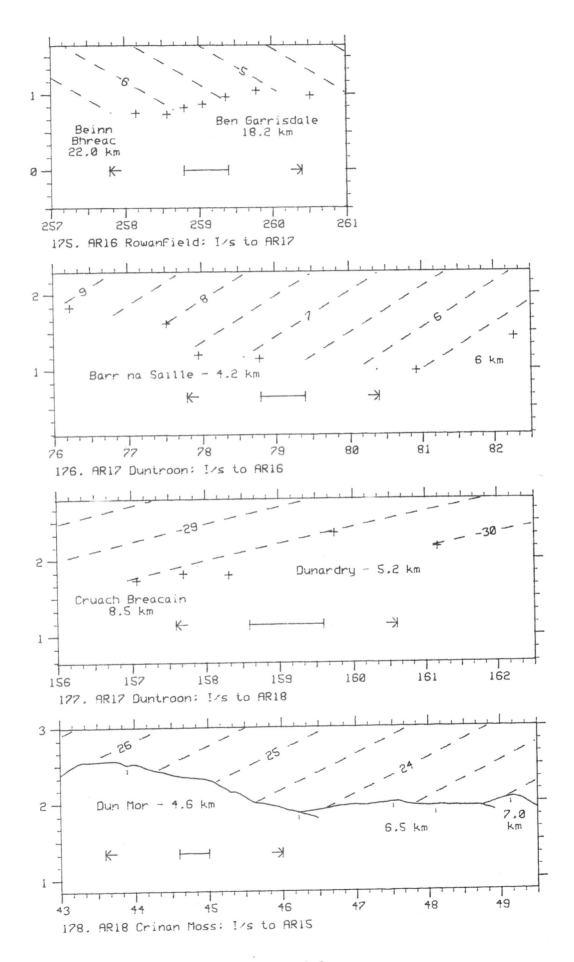

175. AR16 Rowanfield: I/s to AR17

176. AR17 Duntroon: I/s to AR16

177. AR17 Duntroon: I/s to AR18

178. AR18 Crinan Moss: I/s to AR15

FIG. 8.9.

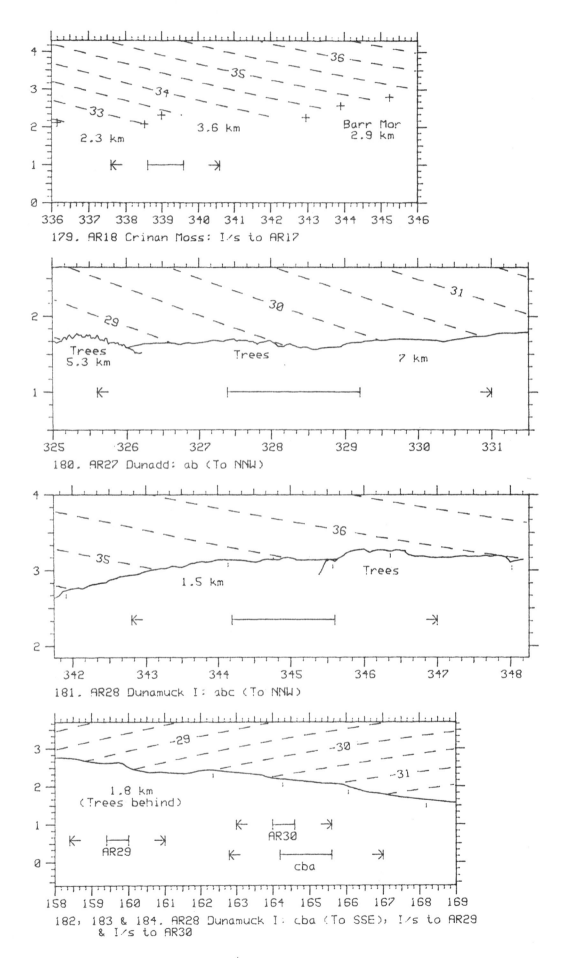

179. AR18 Crinan Moss: l/s to AR17

180. AR27 Dunadd: ab (To NNW)

181. AR28 Dunamuck I: abc (To NNW)

182, 183 & 184. AR28 Dunamuck I: cba (To SSE); l/s to AR29 & l/s to AR30

FIG. 8.10.

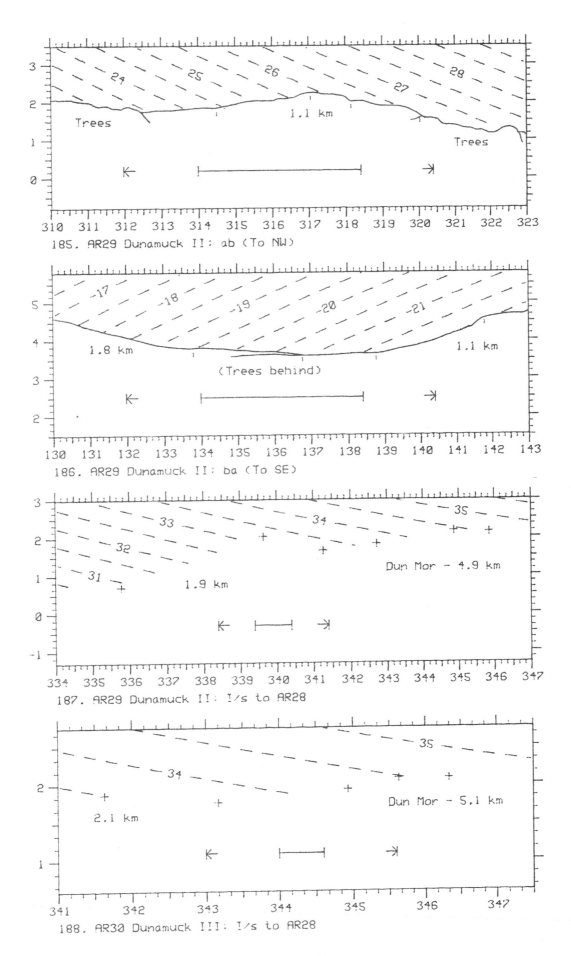

185. AR29 Dunamuck II: ab (To NW)

186. AR29 Dunamuck II: ba (To SE)

187. AR29 Dunamuck II: I/s to AR28

188. AR30 Dunamuck III: I/s to AR28

FIG. 8.11.

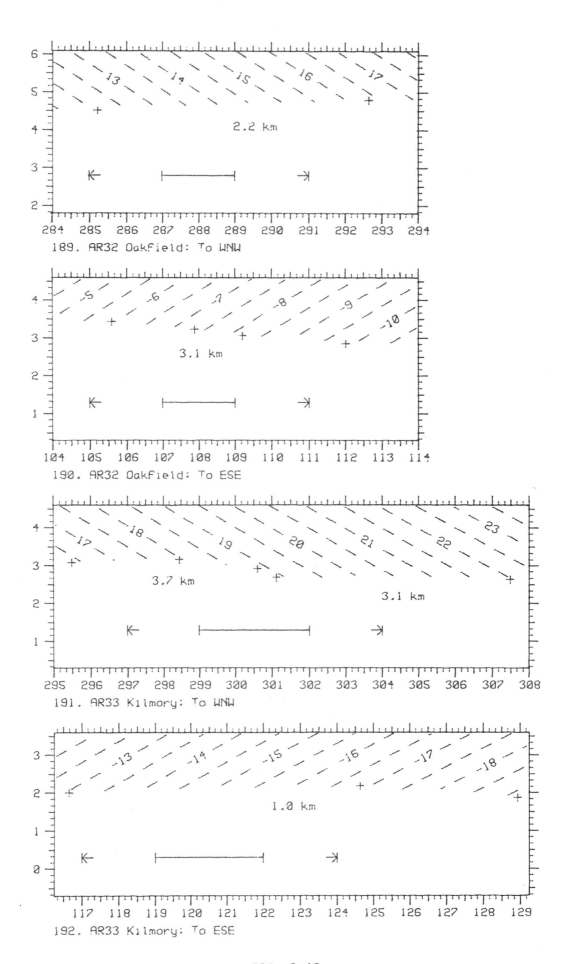

189. AR32 Oakfield: To WNW

190. AR32 Oakfield: To ESE

191. AR33 Kilmory: To WNW

192. AR33 Kilmory: To ESE

FIG. 8.12.

AR25 - Torbhlaran N, Argyll. NR 8639 9449. A slab some 2.0m tall x 1.0m x 0.2m. Arch. status = A; type = 5.

AR27 - Dunadd, Argyll. NR 8386 9362 & 8397 9343. At the first location is a large prostrate slab 4.2m long, which was erect in 1872 and faced ENE (Campbell & Sandeman 1961: no. 175). Some 250m to the NW, at the second location, is a smaller standing stone 1.4m tall x 0.5m x 0.3m. Arch. status = A; type = 4.

AR28 - Dunamuck I, Argyll. NR 8471 9290. A 5m-long three-stone alignment. The end stones are some 2.5m tall, and the central one, which has fallen, is some 3.5m long. Arch. status = A; type = 2.

AR29 - Dunamuck II, Argyll. NR 8484 9248. An alignment of two slabs some 3.5m and 2.5m tall, situated some 6m apart. Site plan: Thom, Thom & Burl (1984). Arch. status = A; type = 1.

AR30 - Dunamuck III, Argyll. NR 8484 9233. Two prostrate slabs, some 4.0m and 3.0m long. Arch. status = A; type = 5.

AR31 - Achnabreck, Argyll. NR 8554 9018 & 8563 8993. At the first location is a prostrate stone some 4.5m long. At the second, about 250m to the SSE, is a slab some 2.5m tall x 1.0m x 0.3m, roughly oriented upon the prostrate stone. Arch. status = A; type = 3.

AR32 - Oakfield (Auchendarroch), Argyll. NR 8572 8852. A slab 1.7m tall x 1.1m at its widest x 0.3m, now standing adjacent to a dairy wall. Two smaller erect stones 130m away at 8559 8855 are probably not prehistoric (OSAR: NR 88 NE, 15). Arch. status = A; type = 5.

AR33 - Kilmory, Argyll. NR 8674 8652. A slab some 2.5m tall x 1.0m x 0.2m, now situated by the side of the approach road to the Argyll and Bute District Council offices at Kilmory castle. Arch. status = A; type = 5.

AR37 - Barnashaig ("Tayvallich"), Knapdale. NR 7298 8640. A standing stone some 3.5m tall x 1.0m x 1.0m, situated at the northern end of a track along a ridge (site AR38 is 320m away at the southern end, but the two sites are not intervisible). A fallen stone referred to by Campbell & Sandeman (1961: no. 160a) could not be located in 1981, but is possibly to be identified with a knocking stone noted by the Ordnance Survey (OSAR: NR 78 NW, 1). Arch. status = A; type = 7.

AR38 - Upper Fernoch ("Tayvallich"), Knapdale. NR 7280 8614 & 7269 8594. At the first location is a slender rectangular standing stone some 2.5m tall x 0.4m x 0.2m, now leaning by about 20° to the E, situated at the southern end of a track along a ridge (site AR37 is at the northern end). At the second location, some 200m to the south, is a group of alleged standing stones at the foot of the steep side of a hillock. They are marked as "Rings A & B" on Thom's plan (1966: fig. 7). While several of these stones appear at first sight to be genuine erect or prostrate menhirs up to some 2.5m long, their situation, added to the presence of several outcrops around them, makes it likely that they are natural (OSAR: NR 78 NW, 7), or at best that the site might have been some sort of quarry. Site plan: Thom (1966: fig. 7); Thom, Thom & Burl (1984). Arch. status = A; type = 7.

AR39 - Lochead, Knapdale. NR 7772 7801. A slab some 2.0m tall x 0.8m x 0.3m. Arch. status = A; type = 5.

8.3   Remarks on the surveys and survey data

The data for the surveys are presented in full in Tables 8.1 and 8.2, for on-site and inter-site lines respectively. Profile diagrams are presented in Figs. 8.2 - 8.12.

Surveys in this area were hampered by trees, and many inter-site lines had to be calculated. In addition, some error is possible in the case of the following surveyed profiles, for the reasons stated.

Line 148 (LN18 Glenamacrie: ab). Trees on the profile itself (1 km).

Line 150 (LN22 Duachy: cba). Trees on the profile itself (1 km).

Line 159 (AR9 Glennan N: To ENE). Trees at 2.5 km obscuring the profile at 9 km.

Line 166 (AR13 Kilmartin: $S_3S_1S_4$). Large parallax correction owing to nearby trees. Measurements have been reduced to the OP from a point some 900m behind it, 200m off line to the left and 57m above it (on a hill slope at 835 984). Calculated points are also shown on the profile diagram. Other profiles to the NNE and SSW at this site were calculated.

Lines 168-170 (AR15 Duncracaig: abcd, dcba & ef). Large parallax corrections owing to intervening trees. Measurements were reduced to the OPs from points 250m behind and 20m off line to the left (Line 168); 250m behind and 30m off line to the right (Line 169) and 250m in front and 225m off line to the right (Line 170).

Lines 173-4 (AR16 Rowanfield: To NW & SE). Trees, on profile itself (2.5 km) (Line 173) & at 6 km obscuring the profile at 10.5 km (Line 174).

Line 180 (AR27 Dunadd: ab). Profile, obscured by nearby trees, was extended by photograph for about 5º in azimuth from the surveyed points.

Lines 181-4 (AR28 Dunamuck I: abc, cba, I/s to AR29 & AR30). Large parallax corrections owing to site being under crop and inaccessible.   Measurements were reduced to the OPs from a point some 100m behind (Line 181) and some 100m in front (Lines 182-4).

Lines 185-6 (AR29 Dunamuck II: ab & ba). As above. Measurements were reduced to the OPs from a point some 200m in front (Line 185) and some 200m behind (Line 186).

9   SITES IN JURA (JU) AND ISLAY (IS)

        C.L.N.Ruggles, J.G.Morgan, R.W.Few, J.A.Cooke, R.P.Norris & P.N.
            Appleton

9.1   Introduction

        Most of the sites in Islay were visited and surveyed by the
authors during 1978. Sites in Jura and the remaining sites in Islay
were covered by CR during 1979, with the assistance of Mary Wilson.
The locations of the sites considered are shown in Fig. 9.1.

9.2   Descriptions and classification of sites

        For general notes on the descriptions that follow, see Section
5.2 (page 75).

JU1 - Tarbert, Jura. NR 6062 8231 & 6089 8221. At the first location
        is a slab some 2.5m tall x 0.6m x 0.3m. At the second, some 290m
        to the ESE, is a smaller slab 1.8m tall x 0.5m x 0.2m, which is
        inside a burial ground and is probably not prehistoric (RCAHMS
        1984: no. 328). Both its faces have an incised cross, but it is
        not out of the question that it is a prehistoric stone and that
        these were added in an attempt to "Christianise" it. Site plan:
        Thom, Thom & Burl (1984). Arch. status = A; type = 4.

JU2 - Knockrome N, Jura. NR 5505 7192. A small erect boulder 0.9m
        tall x about 0.8m x 0.6m. Arch. status = B; type = 8.

JU3 - Ardfernal, Jura. NR 5601 7171. A squat standing stone 1.2m
        tall and triangular in cross-section, with sides 1.3m, 1.3m and
        0.6m. Site plan: Thom (1966: fig. 10). Arch. status = A; type
        = 7.

JU4 - Knockrome, Jura. NR 5503 7148 & 5484 7144. At the first loc-
        ation is a slab 1.4m tall x 0.7m x 0.2m. At the second, some
        200m to the west, is another, 1.5m tall x 1.2m x 0.3m. The first
        is oriented across the line joining them; the second is a few
        degrees out of the line. Together with the menhir at Ardfernal
        (JU3) they form a 900m-long three-stone alignment. Site plans:
        Thom (1966: fig. 10); Thom, Thom & Burl (1984). Arch. status =
        A; type = 3.

JU5 - Leargybreck, Jura. NR 5387 7128. An irregular block of stone
        1.3m tall x about 1.5m x 0.9m. It lies about 1000m west of the
        west end of the Knockrome - Ardfernal alignment, but some 60m
        off the alignment to the north. Arch. status = B; type = 8.

JU6 - Craighouse (Carragh a'Ghlinne), Jura. NR 5128 6648. A rectan-
        gular standing stone 2.4m tall x 0.6m x 0.4m together with three
        prostrate stones 2.8m, 2.4m and 2.4m in length. They appear to
        be the remains of a four-stone alignment about 5m long. The site
        is now in a glade inside a Forestry Commission plantation. Site

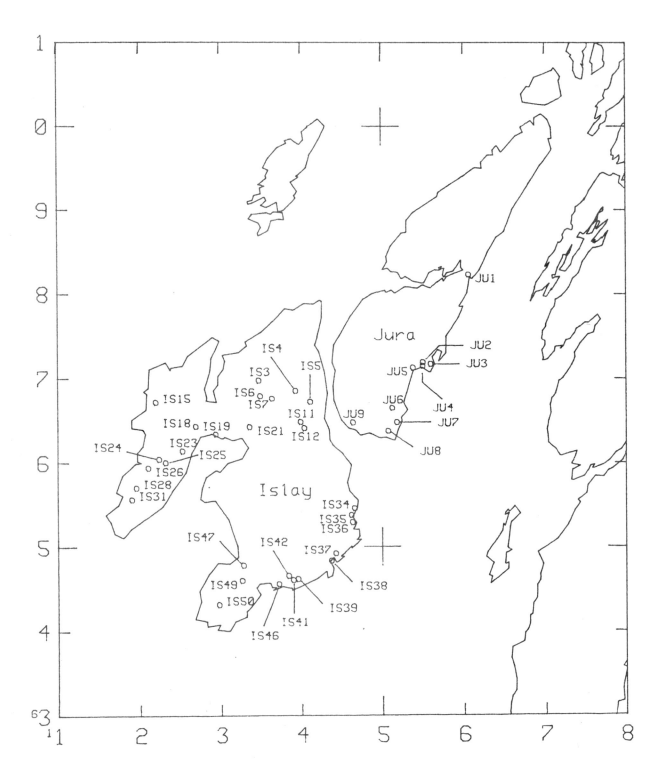

FIG. 9.1. Sites considered in Jura (JU) and Islay (IS).

- 164 -

plans: Thom (1966: fig. 8); RCAHMS (1984: fig. 64D). Arch. status = A; type = 2.

JU7 - Sannaig, Jura. NR 5184 6480. A stone 2.2m tall x 0.5m x 0.3m standing between the 0.3m-high stump of another (a slab 1.2m x 0.7m) and a prostrate stone 2.5m long. A further prostrate stone 1.9m long lying near to the stump may be its upper portion or else a separate fallen stone. The site appears to form the remains of an alignment about 5m long. The RCAHMS (1984: no. 116) also note a further flat slab which may have been a cist-cover, and a small erect stone in a turf wall which is probably not prehistoric. Site plans: RCAHMS (1984: fig. 70E); Thom, Thom & Burl (1984). Arch. status = A; type = 2.

JU8 - Strone, Jura. NR 5078 6375. A standing stone 3.0m tall x 0.5m x 0.3m. Some 2m to its NW is a prostrate stone 2.6m long which appears to have stood at its west end. Site plans: Thom (1966: fig. 8); Thom, Thom & Burl (1984). Arch. status = A; type = 4.

JU9 - Camas an Staca, Jura. NR 4641 6477. A large slab some 3.5m tall x 1.4m x 0.3m. An adjacent reported cairn (D & E 1966: 8) is almost certainly just composed of field clearance stones (OSAR: NR 46 SE, 1; RCAHMS 1984: no. 81). Arch. status = A; type = 5.

IS3 - Beinn a'Chuirn (Clach an Tiampain), Islay. NR 3475 6978. A slab 1.2m tall x 0.9m x 0.3m. Arch. status = A; type = 5.

IS4 - Finlaggan, Islay. NR 3927 6856. A standing stone 2.0m tall x 1.3m x 0.6m. Martin Martin (c. 1695) mentions "two stones .. six feet high" at the site. Arch. status = A; type = 5.

IS5 - Scanistle, Islay. NR 4108 6724. An erect irregular boulder 1.2m tall x 1.0m x 0.4m. Arch. status = A; type = 5.

IS6 - Beinn Cham, Islay. NR 3492 6793. An erect stone 1.1m tall x 0.9m x 0.5m. Adjacent to it lies a loose block of stone about 1.0m x 0.6m x 0.3m which might originally have stood, but has presumably been moved to its present position. Arch. status = A; type = 7.

IS7 - Ballachlavin (Baile Tharbach), Islay. NR 3636 6762. An erect irregularly-shaped stone 1.2m high x 1.2m x 0.5m. Arch. status = A; type = 5.

(ctd. on page 170

- - - - - -

TABLE 9.1. List of on-site indications in Jura (JU) and Islay (IS).

Column headings are as for Table 5.1 (see page 77).

TABLE 9.2. List of inter-site indications in Jura (JU) and Islay (IS).

Column headings are as for Table 5.2 (see page 81).

Table 9.1

Site	Name	Indication	Class	Dist	St	Com	Survey	No.	Az limits
JU1	Tarbert	; ba (To WNW);	4b	5.0 km	A		790617;	193:	285.2 285.6
JU1	Tarbert	; ab (To ESE);	4b	0.4 km	L				
JU4	Knockrome	; ba (To ENE);	3a	1.0 km	B	p	790615;	198:	73.0 73.2
JU4	Knockrome	; ab (To WSW);	3a	5.0 km	A		790615;	199:	253.0 253.2
JU6	Craighouse	; To NE	2c	-	W				
JU6	Craighouse	; To SW	2c	-	W				
JU7	Sannaig	; To NNE	2a	16.5 km	C		- ;	204:	18.0 22.0
JU7	Sannaig	; To SSW	2a	-Sea-	C		- ;	205:	198.0 202.0
JU8	Strone	; ab (To W)	4a	0.3 km	L				
JU8	Strone	; ba (To E)	4a	0.3 km	L				
JU9	Camas an Staca	; To NNW	5a	1.5 km	A		790614;	206:	334.0 334.8
JU9	Camas an Staca	; To SSE	5a	51.0 km	A		790617;	207:	154.0 154.8
IS3	Beinn a'Chuirn	; To ENE	5a	0.3 km	L				
IS3	Beinn a'Chuirn	; To WSW	5a	1.5 km	A		790619;	208:	256.8 257.4
IS4	Finlaggan	; To WNW	5a	4.0 km	A		780723;	209:	296.4 297.2
IS4	Finlaggan	; To ESE	5a	0.9 km	L				
IS5	Scanistle	; To NE	5a	-	W				
IS5	Scanistle	; To SW	5a	-	W				
IS7	Ballachlavin	; To W	5a	0.9 km	L				
IS7	Ballachlavin	; To E	5a	0.3 km	L				
IS11	Knocklearoch	; ab (To ENE);	3a	11.5 km	A		780720;	216:	58.4 61.8
IS11	Knocklearoch	; ba (To WSW);	3a	0.4 km	L				
IS15	Ballinaby	; ab (To NNE);	3a	0.2 km	L				
IS15	Ballinaby	; ba (To SSW);	3a	0.2 km	L				
IS19	Uisgeantsuidhe	; To NNW	5a	0.8 km	L				

Table 9.1 (continued)

Site	Name	Indication	Class	Dist	St	Com	Survey No.	Az limits
IS19	Uisgeantsuidhe	; To SSE	; 5a	17.5 km	A		780721; 221:	168.4 169.6
IS23	Gartacharra	; To W	; 5a	0.4 km	L			
IS23	Gartacharra	; To E	; 5a	17.5 km	A		780726; 223:	92.4 94.0
IS24	Carn Mor	; To NW	; 5a	–	W			
IS24	Carn Mor	; To SE	; 5a	–	W			
IS35	Claggain Bay	; To WNW	; 6	–	W			
IS35	Claggain Bay	; To ESE	; 6	–	W			
IS38	Cnoc Rhaonastil	; ab (To ENE)	; 4b	38.5 km	C	– ;	229:	58.0 59.2
IS38	Cnoc Rhaonastil	; ba (To WSW)	; 4b	3.0 km	C	– ;	230:	238.0 239.2
IS39	Lagavulin N	; To W	; 3b	0.4 km	L			
IS39	Lagavulin N	; To E	; 3b	36.0 km	A		790613; 231:	82.4 86.6
IS41	Laphroaig	; To N	; 2a	0.8 km	L			
IS41	Laphroaig	; To S	; 2a	>70 km	C	– ;	233:	168.4 169.8
IS42	Kilbride	; To ENE	; 3b	–	W			
IS42	Kilbride	; To WSW	; 3b	–	W			
IS47	Kintra	; To NE	; 5a	–	W			
IS47	Kintra	; To SW	; 5a	–	W			

Table 9.2

Site	Name	F/s & dist	St CL	Dist	St Com	Survey	No.	Az limits	
JU2	Knockrome N	; JU3 1.0 km;	B 2	1.0 km	A	790615;	194:	98.6	99.0
JU2	Knockrome N	; JU4 0.4 km;	B 2	-Sea-	W	- ;	- :	178.4	200.4
JU2	Ardfernal	; JU2 1.0 km;	B 2	7.5 km	C	-	195:	278.6	279.0
JU3	Ardfernal	; JU4 1.0 km;	A 2	6.0 km	B p	790615;	196:	253.4	254.0
JU3	Ardfernal	; JU5 2.2 km;	B 2	6.0 km	B p	790615;	197:	255.8	256.2
JU4	Knockrome	; JU2 0.4 km;	B 2	0.7 km	L	- ;	- :	358.4	20.4
JU4	Knockrome	; JU3 1.0 km;	A 1	1.0 km	B p	790615;	200:	73.4	74.0
JU4	Knockrome	; JU5 1.2 km;	B 2	5.0 km	A	790615;	201:	257.0	257.4
JU5	Leargybreck	; JU3 2.2 km;	B 2	2.5 km	B p	790615;	202:	75.8	76.2
JU5	Leargybreck	; JU4 1.2 km;	B 2	2.5 km	B p	790615;	203:	77.0	77.4
IS5	Scanistle	; IS12 3.2 km;	A 3	11.5 km	C	- ;	210:	189.2	189.4
IS6	Beinn Cham	; IS7 1.5 km;	A 2	12.5 km	A	790619;	211:	98.8	99.0
IS6	Beinn Cham	; IS11 5.9 km;	A 3	8.5 km	A	790619;	212:	118.4	118.6
IS7	Ballachlavin	; IS6 1.5 km;	A 1	1.5 km	A	790619;	213:	278.8	279.0
IS7	Ballachlavin	; IS11 4.5 km;	A 3	9.0 km	A	790619;	214:	124.6	124.8
IS7	Ballachlavin	; IS12 5.3 km;	A 3	11.5 km	A	790619;	215:	127.6	128.0
IS11	Knocklearoch	; IS6 5.9 km;	A 3	6.0 km	C	- ;	217:	298.4	298.6
IS11	Knocklearoch	; IS7 4.5 km;	A 3	5.0 km	A	780720;	218:	304.6	304.8
IS12	Mullach Dubh	; IS5 3.2 km;	A 3	-Sea-	C	- ;	219:	9.2	9.4
IS12	Mullach Dubh	; IS7 5.3 km;	A 3	6.0 km	C	- ;	220:	307.6	308.0
IS19	Uisgeantsuidhe	; IS23 4.6 km;	A 3	6.5 km	A	780726;	222:	240.6	241.0
IS23	Gartacharra	; IS19 4.6 km;	A 3	29.5 km	A	780726;	224:	60.6	61.0
IS28	Cultoon	; IS31 1.5 km;	B 2	>55 km	C	- ;	225:	198.0	198.4
IS31	Kelsay	; IS28 1.5 km;	B 1	1.5 km	A	780724;	226:	17.6	18.8
IS35	Claggain Bay	; IS36 0.8 km;	B 2	3.5 km	A	780730;	227:	168.2	168.6

Table 9.2 (continued)

Site	Name	F/s & dist	St CL	Dist	St Com	Survey No.	Az limits
IS36	Trudernish	; IS35 0.8 km; B 2		3.0 km	A	780730; 228:	348.2 348.6
IS39	Lagavulin N	; IS41 0.6 km; A 2		6.0 km	A	780730; 232:	252.4 253.0
IS41	Laphroaig	; IS39 0.6 km; A 1		0.6 km	L	- ; - :	72.4 73.0

IS11 - Knocklearoch, Islay. NR 3989 6483. Two stones 1.7m and 1.5m tall but both leaning to the south, some 2.5m apart. Arch. status = A; type = 3.

IS12 - Mullach Dubh, Islay. NR 4037 6410. An erect stone 1.2m high x 0.8m x 0.5m. Arch. status = A; type = 7.

IS15 - Ballinaby, Islay. NR 2210 6738 (A) & 2200 6719 (B). At (B) is a fine slab 5m tall x 1.1m x 0.3m at the base. Some 200m to the NNE, at (A), is the 2m-high stump of a second menhir. Pennant (1772) refers to "three upright stones, of a stupendous size, placed nearly equidistant". The third stone has now disappeared, but Pennant's description would put its position at about 222 676 if, as seems likely, the three formed an alignment. A stone at 2217 6751 noted by MacKie (1975: 41) and identified with the missing stone is, according to the Ordnance Survey (OSAR: NR 26 NW, 15), merely an isolated exposed part of the nearby rock outcrops. Site plan: Thom, Thom & Burl (1984). Arch. status = A; type = 3.

IS18 - Foreland House, Islay. NR 2692 6429. A standing stone 2m high and trapezoidal in cross-section. Arch. status = A; type = 7.

IS19 - Uisgeantsuidhe, Islay. NR 2938 6335. A slab 2.5m tall x 1.4m x 0.5m. Arch. status = A; type = 5.

IS21 - Knockdon, Islay. NR 3360 6423. A standing stone 1.5m tall x 1.0m x 0.6m. Arch. status = A; type = 7.

IS23 - Gartacharra, Islay. NR 2527 6137. A standing stone 2.7m tall x 0.8m x 0.4m. Arch. status = A; type = 5.

IS24 - Carn Mor (Cnoc nan Guaillean), Islay. NR 2241 6041. A slab some 3m tall x 0.7m x 0.3m, with its longer sides curved. Arch. status = A; type = 5.

IS25 - Cnoc Thornasaig (Cnoc a''Charraigh), Islay. NR 2317 6000. A prostrate slab about 4m long, which probably represents a fallen standing stone. Arch. status = B; type = 8.

IS26 - Droighneach, Islay. NR 2106 5938. A standing stone some 2.5m tall x 1.2m x 0.8m. Arch. status = A; type = 7.

IS28 - Cultoon, Islay. NR 1956 5697. A 40m-diameter stone ring recently excavated by MacKie (1981: 116-28). Site plan: MacKie (1981: 118). Arch. status = A; type = 7.

IS31 - Kelsay, Islay. NR 1901 5561. An erect boulder 1.2m high x 1.0m x 0.8m which is possibly a standing stone, but it stands on the edge of an old lazy-bed enclosure, and may have been set in its present position as a result of clearance for the adjacent cultivation (OSAR: NR 15 NE, 8). Arch. status = B; type = 8.

IS34 - Ardtalla, Islay. NR 4658 5457. An erect stone 1.3m high x 0.5m x 0.4m which is listed as a standing stone by the RCAHMS

(ctd. on page 180

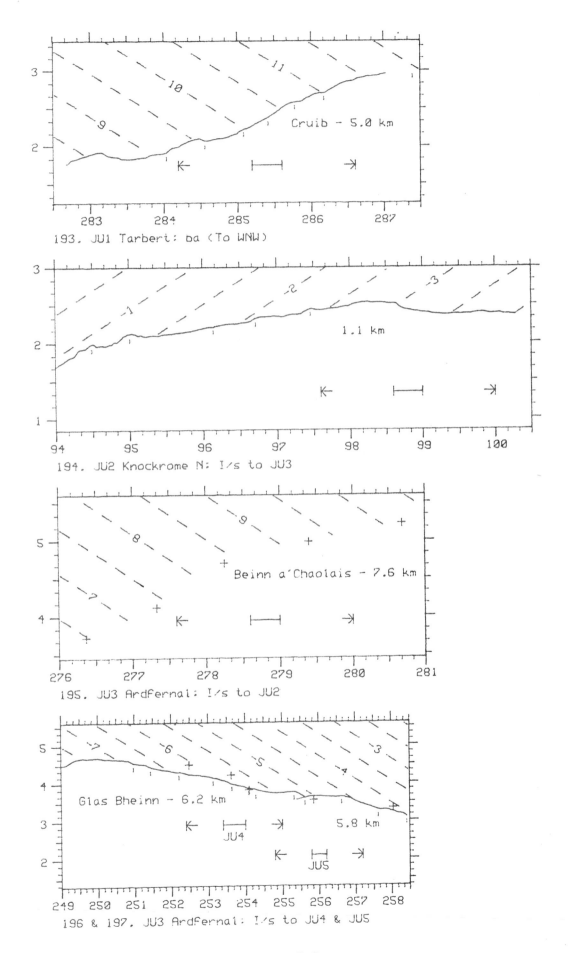

193. JU1 Tarbert: ba (To WNW)

194. JU2 Knockrome N: I/s to JU3

195. JU3 Ardfernal: I/s to JU2

196 & 197. JU3 Ardfernal: I/s to JU4 & JU5

FIG. 9.2.

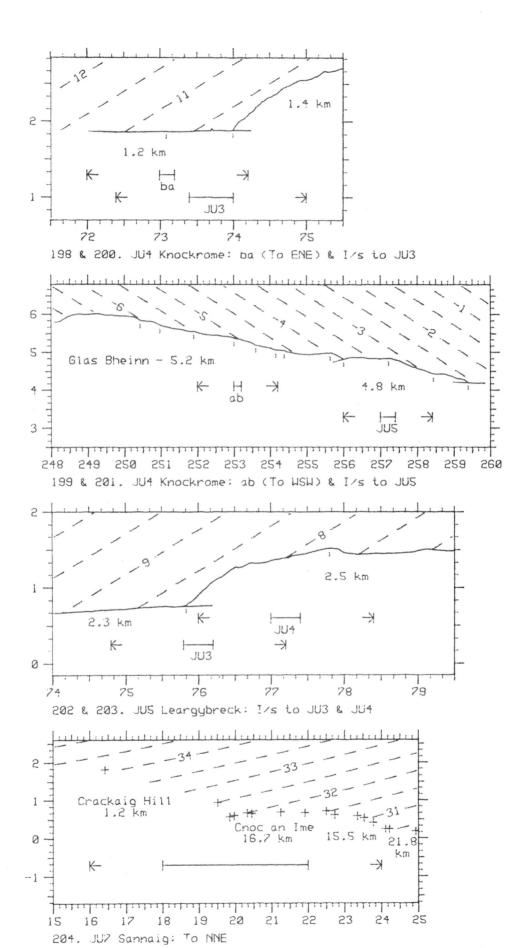

198 & 200. JU4 Knockrome: ba (To ENE) & I/s to JU3

199 & 201. JU4 Knockrome: ab (To WSW) & I/s to JU5

202 & 203. JU5 Leargybreck: I/s to JU3 & JU4

204. JU7 Sannaig: To NNE

FIG. 9.3.

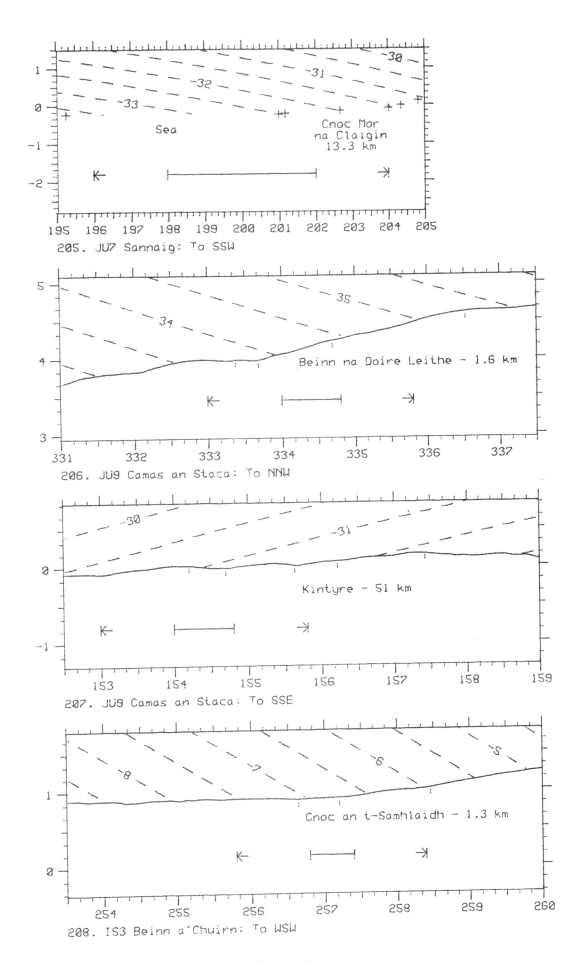

205. JU7 Sannaig: To SSW

206. JU9 Camas an Staca: To NNW

207. JU9 Camas an Staca: To SSE

208. IS3 Beinn a'Chuirn: To WSW

FIG. 9.4.

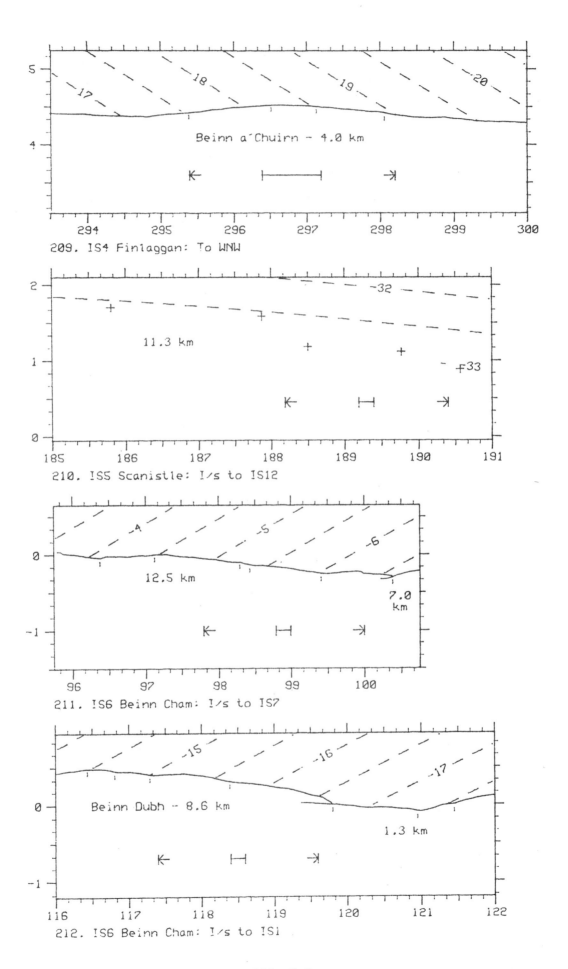

209. IS4 Finlaggan: To WNW

Beinn a'Chuirn - 4.0 km

210. IS5 Scanistle: I/s to IS12

11.3 km

211. IS6 Beinn Cham: I/s to IS7

12.5 km

7.0 km

212. IS6 Beinn Cham: I/s to IS1

Beinn Dubh - 8.6 km

1.3 km

FIG. 9.5.

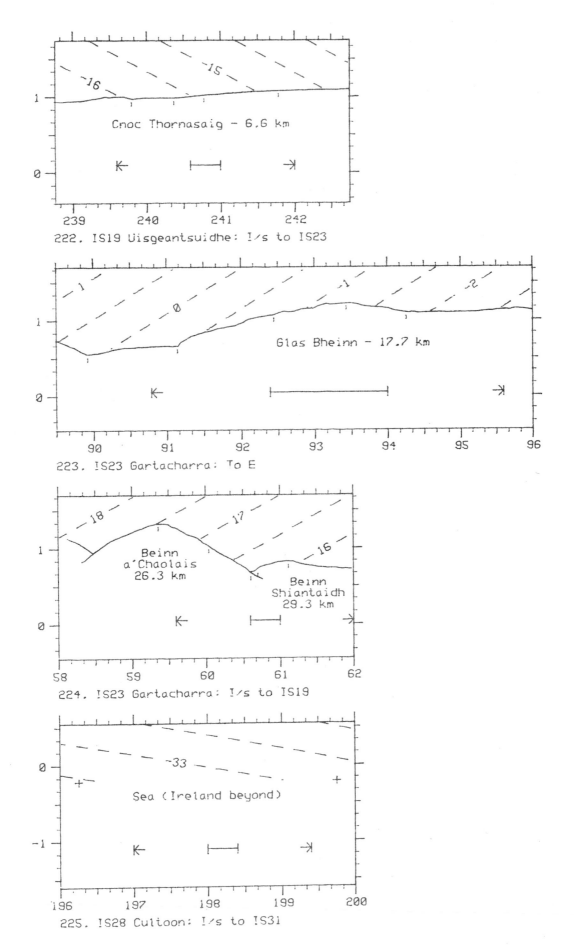

222. IS19 Uisgeantsuidhe: l/s to IS23

Cnoc Thornasaig – 6.6 km

223. IS23 Gartacharra: To E

Glas Bheinn – 17.7 km

224. IS23 Gartacharra: l/s to IS19

Beinn
a'Chaolais
26.3 km

Beinn
Shiantaidh
29.3 km

225. IS28 Cultoon: l/s to IS31

Sea (Ireland beyond)

FIG. 9.8.

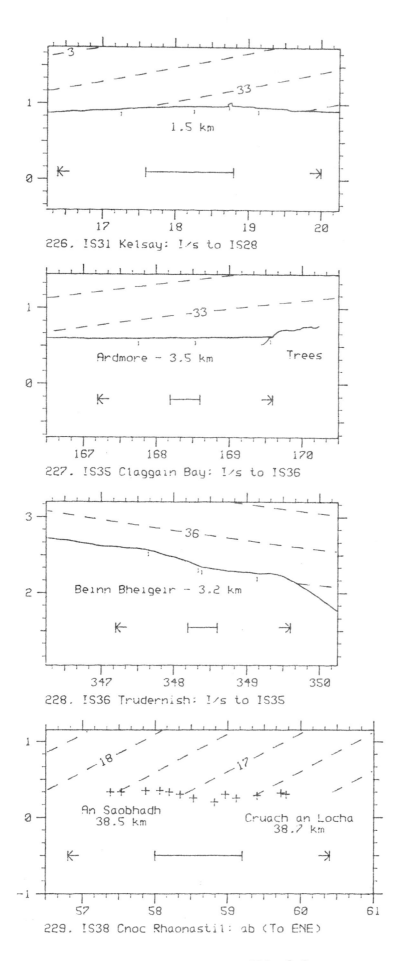

226. IS31 Kelsay: I/s to IS28

227. IS35 Claggain Bay: I/s to IS36

228. IS36 Trudernish: I/s to IS35

229. IS38 Cnoc Rhaonastil: ab (To ENE)

FIG. 9.9.

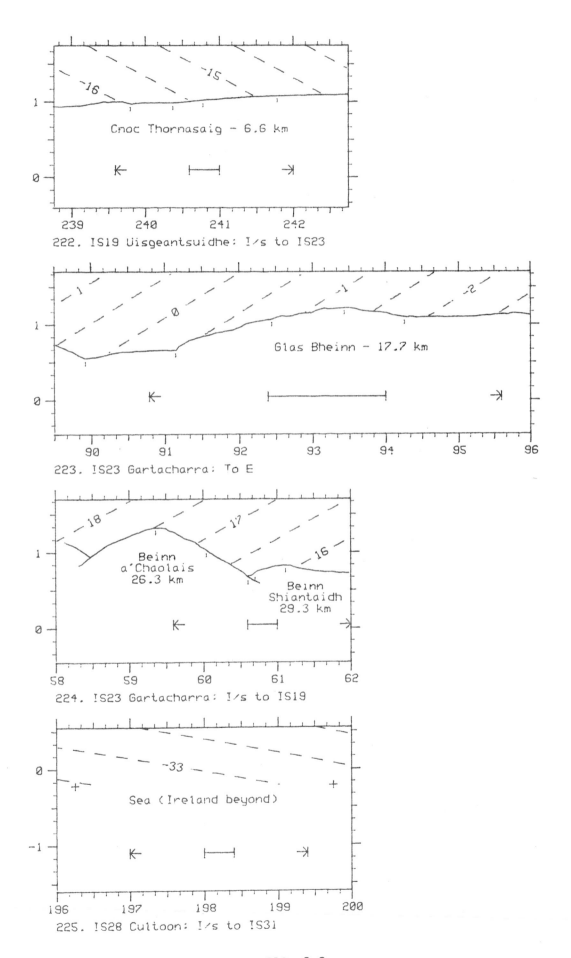

222. IS19 Uisgeantsuidhe: I/s to IS23

Cnoc Thornasaig - 6.6 km

223. IS23 Gartacharra: To E

Glas Bheinn - 17.7 km

224. IS23 Gartacharra: I/s to IS19

Beinn
a'Chaolais
26.3 km

Beinn
Shiantaidh
29.3 km

225. IS28 Cultoon: I/s to IS31

Sea (Ireland beyond)

FIG. 9.8.

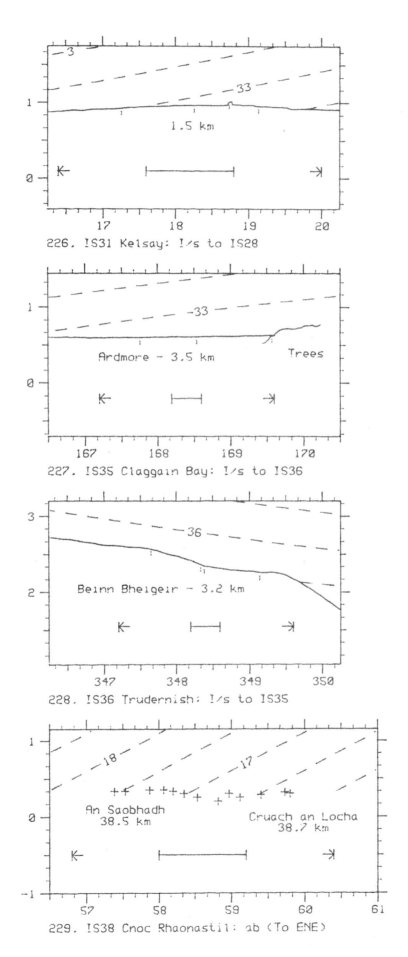

226. IS31 Kelsay: l/s to IS28

227. IS35 Claggain Bay: l/s to IS36

228. IS36 Trudernish: l/s to IS35

229. IS38 Cnoc Rhaonastil: ab (To ENE)

FIG. 9.9.

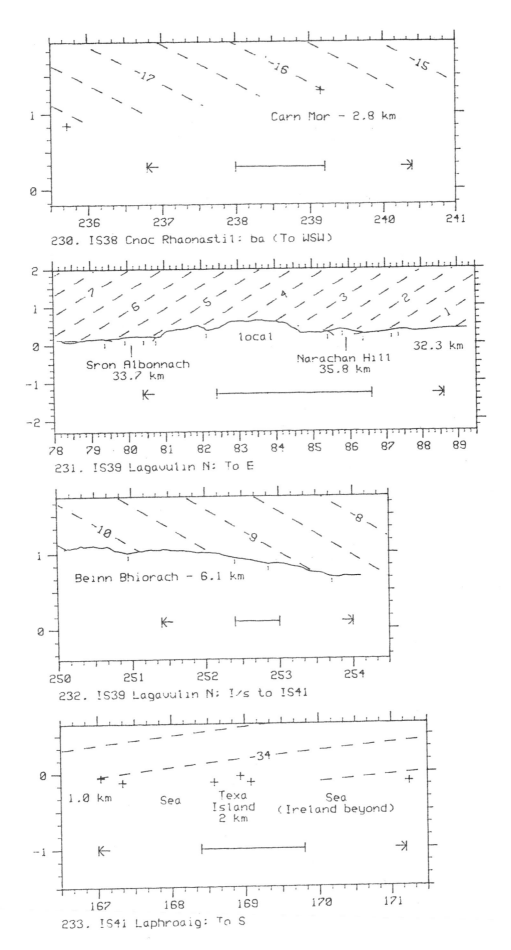

230. IS38 Cnoc Rhaonastil: ba (To WSW)

231. IS39 Lagavulin N: To E

232. IS39 Lagavulin N: l/s to IS41

233. IS41 Laphroaig: To S

FIG. 9.10.

(1984: no. 77). However it is situated by the side of some out-cropping blocks of rock, and may in fact be a natural feature (OSAR: NR 45 SE, 16). Arch. status = B; type = 8.

IS35 - Claggain Bay, Islay. NR 4618 5372. A massive boulder some 1.7m high x 1.8m x 0.8m which may have been erected in anti-quity, but may just be a glacial erratic. Arch. status = B; type = 6.

IS36 - Trudernish, Islay. NR 4630 5290. A standing stone 1.8m tall x 0.6m x 0.35m. Arch. status = A; type = 7.

IS37 - Ardilistry, Islay. NR 4426 4919. A stone ring of the "four-poster" type (Burl 1976: 190-95) consisting of four stones no more than about 0.5m high (RCAHMS 1984: no. 76). Site plan: RCAHMS (1984: fig. 63D). Arch. status = A; type = 7.

IS38 - Cnoc Rhaonastil (Clachan Ceann Ile), Islay. NR 4369 4832. Two erect stones, 1.5m tall x 0.8m x 0.3m and 0.7m high x 0.7m x 0.3m, some 10m apart. Although the first seems reasonable as a prehistoric standing stone, the second is of doubtful status. Arch. status = A; type = 4.

IS39 - Lagavulin N, Islay. NR 3954 4621. A fine slab some 3.5m tall x 1.2m x 0.4m. Some 2m away lies one end (apparently the base) of a fallen slab some 3.5m long and up to 1.0m wide. When this stood, the two stones apparently formed an alignment. Arch. status = A; type = 3.

IS41 - Laphroaig (Achnancarranan), Islay. NR 3895 4607. A 6m-long three-stone alignment. The end stones are between 2.5m and 3.0m tall; the central one is fallen and about 3.0m long. Site plan: RCAHMS (1984: fig. 63A). Arch. status = A; type = 2.

IS42 - Kilbride, Islay. NR 3838 4657. A slab some 2.5m tall x 0.9m x 0.4m. Some 3m to its SW is a sunken stone at least about 2.5m long, which may represent a further fallen stone, although both the Ordnance Survey (OSAR: NR 34 NE, 5) and the RCAHMS (priv. comm. 1980) feel there is insufficient exposed for certainty. If it was a standing stone, it could have stood in line with the orientation of the other. Arch. status = A; type = 3.

IS46 - Port Ellen I, Islay. NR 3715 4559. A fine standing stone some 4.5m tall x 0.9m x 0.5m. Arch. status = A; type = 7.

IS47 - Kintra (Druim an Stuin; Carragh Bhan), Islay. NR 3283 4781. A slab some 2.0m tall x 2.0m x 0.5m, but with irregular longer faces. Arch. status = A; type = 5.

IS49 - Cornabus (Cnoc Ard), Islay. NR 3264 4600. A standing stone 1.5m tall x 1.2m x 0.9m. Arch. status = A; type = 7.

IS50 - Kinnabus (Glac a'Charraigh), Islay. NR 2975 4315. Although listed by the RCAHMS (1984: no. 101) as a standing stone 1.9m high x 0.7m x 0.4m, between their visit in 1977 and ours in 1979 the top had broken off, and in 1979 it lay beside the stump. Arch. status = A; type = 7.

9.3 Remarks on the surveys and survey data

The data for the surveys are presented in full in Tables 9.1 and 9.2, for on-site and inter-site lines respectively. Profile diagrams are presented in Figs. 9.2 - 9.10.

Three indicated profiles in this area are in Ireland, and could not be surveyed owing to poor visibility during both expeditions here. Unfortunately they could not be calculated either, at least without introducing the complication of having to relate the Irish and British Ordnance Survey grids. A flat sea horizon has been assumed in each of the three cases.   Some error is possible in consequence at Line 225 (IS28 Cultoon: I/s to IS31) and Line 233 (IS41 Laphroaig: To S). However at Line 205 (JU7 Sannaig: To SSW) the Ireland profile is sufficiently distant that it is doubtful whether it would show above the sea even in perfect visibility. In this case the declination obtained by assuming a flat sea horizon can safely be assumed correct to the level of accuracy required in this analysis.

Some error is possible in the case of the following surveyed profiles, for the reasons stated.

Lines 196-7 (JU3 Ardfernal: I/s to JU4 & JU5). Large parallax correc-
    tion. Measurements were reduced to the OP from a point 1005m in
    front of it and 39m below it (by menhir a at site JU4).

Line 198 (JU4 Knockrome: ba). Large parallax correction. Measurements
    were reduced to the OP (by menhir b) from a point 190m in front
    of it (by menhir a).

Line 200 (JU4 Knockrome: I/s to JU3). Large parallax correction. Meas-
    urements were reduced to the OP (taken between the two menhirs)
    from a point 95m in front of it (by menhir a).

Lines 202-3 (JU5 Leargybreck: I/s to JU3 & JU4). Large parallax cor-
    rections.   Measurements were reduced to the OP from a point
    1120m in front of it and 15m below it (by menhir a at site JU4).

10   SITES IN KINTYRE (KT)

10.1   Introduction

        Sites in Kintyre were visited and surveyed by the author during
1979, with the assistance of Mari Williams, Chris Jennings and Mary
Wilson, and during 1981 with the assistance of Sal Brown. The site at
Ballochroy (KT10) had been surveyed during 1973 by the author and his
colleagues Guy Morgan, Roger Few, John Cooke and Mark Bailey (Bailey
et al. 1975).   By 1979, forestry commission trees had obscured the
relevant horizon profile at Ballochroy (Cara Island), making direct
resurvey impossible; for this reason the 1973 survey data has been
used in this analysis.   The locations of the sites considered are
shown in Fig. 10.1.

10.2   Descriptions and classification of sites

        For general notes on the descriptions that follow, see Section
5.2 (page 75).

KT1 - Cretshengan, Knapdale. NR 7072 6689. A standing stone 1.6m tall
        x 0.3m x 0.2m, leaning by some 15° out of the vertical. It has
        been wedged into a small rock cleft, which suggests that it may
        not be prehistoric (OSAR: NR 76 NW, 3). Arch. status = B; type
        = 8.

KT2 - Carse (Loch Stornoway), Knapdale. NR 7414 6166 & 7425 6163. Two
        standing stones some 2m apart in a roughly N-S line. One is
        some 3.0m tall x 0.7m x 0.5m, the other a slab some 2.5m tall x
        1.2m x 0.4m.   Both have their longer faces oriented along the
        line.   Some 100m away to the W is a further stone 2.2m tall x
        0.5m x 0.4m. Arch. status = A; type = 3.

KT3   -   Ardpatrick (Achadh-Chaorun), Knapdale. NR 7573 6014. A slab
        2.2m tall x 1.4m x 0.3m. Arch. status = A; type = 5.

KT4 - Avinagillan, Knapdale. NR 8391 6746. A slab 1.9m tall x 1.0m x
        0.2m. Arch. status = A; type = 5.

KT5   -   Escart, Kintyre. NR 8464 6678. A 15m-long five-stone align-
        ment.   The stones are up to 3.3m tall, and the line is rather
        sinuous.   There is some evidence to suggest that there may
        originally have been more menhirs at the site (RCAHMS 1971: no.
        143).   Site plans: Thom (1971: 60); RCAHMS (1971: fig. 34).
        Arch. status = A; type = 1.

KT8   -   Dunskeig, Kintyre. NR 7624 5704. This site is unrecorded on
        any ancient monuments lists. It consists of two stones some 6m
        apart, the SE of which is 1.0m high and leans by 30° or so from
        the vertical, while the NW stone is rounded, 0.4m high, and
        earthfast.   Atkinson has noted (1981: 207-8, Site 38) that they
        could be the surviving grounders of a former field wall, and the
        fact that the line joining them is parallel to an existing wall

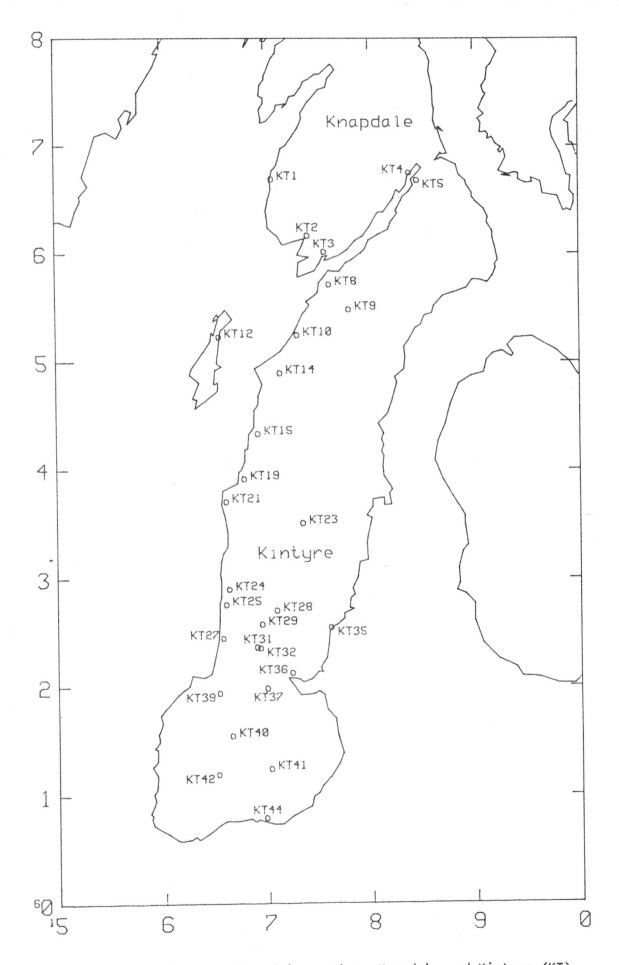

FIG. 10.1. Sites considered in southern Knapdale and Kintyre (KT).

some 10m away to the NE would seem to back up this hypothesis. Arch. status = B; type = 5.

KT9 - Loch Ciaran, Kintyre. NR 7802 5479. A standing stone 1.8m tall x 0.7m x 0.4m. According to the Ordnance Survey (OSAR: NR 75 SE, 1) it is possible that it was only a drove road marker. Arch. status = B; type = 8.

KT10 - Ballochroy I, Kintyre. NR 7309 5241. A 5m-long three-stone alignment. The stones are some 3.5m, 3.0m and 2.0m in height, the last of the three appearing to have been broken off at the top. The second and third stones are slabs oriented across the alignment. Some 35m away, in the alignment, is a cist. A sketch by Edward Lhuyd in about 1700, copied by Stukeley (1776) and re-produced by Burl (1979: 66; 1983: 8) shows this cist covered by a cairn, and also shows a further cairn and standing stone in the alignment. Site plan: Thom (1971: 37). Arch. status = A; type = 1.

KT12 - Tarbert, Gigha. NR 6555 5227. A slab 2.3m tall x 0.9m x 0.4m, leaning by about 20° to the E. Arch. status = A; type = 5.

KT14 - Rhunahaorine, Kintyre. NR 7141 4893. An erect stone 1.1m high x 0.9m x 0.7m, possibly a boundary marker (OSAR: NR 74 NW, 1). Arch. status = A; type = 7.

KT15 - Beacharr I, Kintyre. NR 6926 4330. A huge standing stone some 5.0m tall x 1.5m x 0.8m, situated some 30m from the Beacharra long cairn (Henshall 1963: no. ARG27). Arch. status = A; type = 7.

KT19 - South Muasdale (Carragh Muasdale), Kintyre. NR 6792 3914. A slab some 3.0m tall x 1.1m x 0.5m, oriented roughly N-S. Since our visit in 1979, R.J.C. Atkinson (priv. comm.) has pointed out the existence of the possible stump of a second stone some 12m to the WSW of the first, measuring about 1.1m high x 1.8m x 0.6m, now built into a field wall. Arch. status = A; type = 4.

KT21 - Barlea, Kintyre. NR 6616 3707. A slab 1.8m tall x 1.2m x 0.3m, leaning by about 15° to the W. Arch. status = A; type = 5.

(ctd. on page 189

- - - - - -

TABLE 10.1. List of on-site indications in southern Knapdale and Kintyre (KT).

Column headings are as for Table 5.1 (see page 77).

TABLE 10.2. List of inter-site indications in southern Knapdale and Kintyre (KT).

Column headings are as for Table 5.2 (see page 81).

Table 10.1

Site	Name	Indication	Class	Dist	St	Com	Survey	No.	Az limits
KT2	Carse	ab (To N)	3a	0.5 km	L		-	234:	177.4 177.8
KT2	Carse	ba (To S)	3a	1.5 km	C		-	235:	284.0 284.6
KT2	Carse	ac (To WNW)	3a	2.5 km	A		790606	236:	104.0 104.6
KT2	Carse	ca (To ESE)	3a	8.0 km	B	p	790606	236:	104.0 104.6
KT2	Carse	bc (To WNW)	3a	2.5 km	A		790606	237:	281.8 283.2
KT2	Carse	cb (To ESE)	3a	8.0 km	C		-	238:	101.8 103.2
KT3	Ardpatrick	To NW	5a	8.0 km	A		790606	239:	316.6 317.0
KT3	Ardpatrick	To SE	5a	3.0 km	A		790608	240:	136.6 137.0
KT4	Avinagillan	To N	5a	0.2 km	L		-		
KT4	Avinagillan	To S	5a	4.5 km	C		-	242:	170.4 171.6
KT5	Escart	To NNE	1a	3.0 km	C		-	243:	27.4 28.6
KT5	Escart	To SSW	1a	9.5 km	C		-	244:	207.4 208.6
KT8	Dunskeig	ab (To NW)	5b	0.1 km	L				
KT8	Dunskeig	ba (To SE)	5b	19.0 km	A		790609	245:	128.4 129.2
KT10	Ballochroy	abc (To NE)	1a	0.3 km	L				
KT10	Ballochroy	cba (To SW)	1a	12.0 km	B	t	730903	247:	222.0 224.0
KT12	Tarbert	To N	5a	1.3 km	C		-	248:	4.8 6.4
KT12	Tarbert	To S	5a	0.9 km	L				
KT19	South Muasdale	ba (To ENE)	4b	0.5 km	L				
KT19	South Muasdale	ab (To WSW)	4b	-Sea-	C		-	249:	250.0 250.6
KT21	Barlea	To N	5a	0.6 km	L				
KT21	Barlea	To S	5a	0.2 km	L				
KT23	Beinn an Tuirc	To NE	5a	0.2 km	L				
KT23	Beinn an Tuirc	To SW	5a	5.0 km	A		810519	250:	221.6 225.4
KT27	Clochkeil	abc (To NE)	2a	3.0 km	A		790627	251:	47.4 49.4

Table 10.1 (continued)

Site	Name	Indication	Class	Dist		St Com	Survey	No.	Az limits	
KT27	Clochkeil	; cba (To SW);	2a	>45	km	B V	790627;	252:	227.4	229.4
KT28	Skeroblingarry	; To ENE ;	5a	4.5	km	A	790626;	254:	67.0	72.0
KT28	Skeroblingarry	; To WSW ;	5a	0.8	km	L				
KT29	High Park	; To ENE ;	5a	5.5	km	A	790626;	255:	56.8	59.6
KT29	High Park	; To WSW ;	5a	0.5	km	L				
KT31	Craigs	; To WNW ;	5a	2.5	km	A	790627;	256:	296.4	298.0
KT31	Craigs	; To ESE ;	5a	0.4	km	L				
KT32	Glencraigs S	; To NW ;	5a	0.8	km	L				
KT32	Glencraigs S	; To SE ;	5a	-		W				
KT35	Glenlussa Lodge	; To WNW ;	5a	3.0	km	C	-	; 261:	288.4	289.8
KT35	Glenlussa Lodge	; To ESE ;	5a	63.0	km	C	-	; 262:	108.4	109.8
KT36	Campbeltown	; To W ;	5a	0.1	km	L				
KT36	Campbeltown	; To E ;	5a	0.4	km	L				
KT39	Mingary	; To NW ;	5a	40.0	km	A	790624;	267:	313.4	315.6
KT39	Mingary	; To SE ;	5a	2.5	km	A	790624;	268:	133.4	135.6
KT40	Lochorodale	; To N ;	6	0.3	km	L				
KT40	Lochorodale	; To S ;	6	0.5	km	L				
KT41	Knockstapple	; To NW ;	5a	6.0	km	A	790624;	273:	320.0	324.0
KT41	Knockstapple	; To SE ;	5a	1.5	km	A	790624;	274:	140.0	144.0
KT44	Southend	; To N ;	5a	2.5	km	A	790625;	275:	8.4	9.8
KT44	Southend	; To S ;	5a	>70	km	A	790625;	276:	188.4	189.8

Table 10.2

Site	Name	F/s & dist	St	CL	Dist	St	Com	Survey	No.	Az limits	
KT3	Ardpatrick	; KT8 3.1 km;	B	1	3.0 km	A		790608;	241:	167.4	167.6
KT8	Dunskeig	; KT3 3.1 km;	B	2	9.0 km	A		790609;	246:	347.4	347.6
KT27	Clochkeil	; KT39 5.1 km;	A	3	7.0 km	A		790627;	253:	181.8	182.0
KT31	Craigs	; KT32 0.3 km;	A	2	0.5 km	L		- ;	- :	113.8	114.2
KT31	Craigs	; KT37 3.9 km;	A	3	5.5 km	A		790627;	257:	163.2	163.4
KT31	Craigs	; KT39 5.6 km;	A	3	9.0 km	C		- ;	258:	218.0	218.2
KT32	Glencraigs S	; KT31 0.3 km;	A	2	2.5 km	A		790626;	259:	283.8	284.2
KT32	Glencraigs S	; KT39 5.7 km;	A	3	11.5 km	A		790626;	260:	220.8	221.0
KT36	Campbeltown	; KT37 2.8 km;	A	2	10.0 km	B	p	790625;	263:	236.6	236.8
KT37	Stewarton	; KT31 3.9 km;	A	3	5.5 km	A		790625;	264:	343.2	343.4
KT37	Stewarton	; KT36 2.8 km;	A	2	3.5 km	A		790625;	265:	56.6	56.8
KT37	Stewarton	; KT39 4.6 km;	A	3	5.5 km	A		790625;	266:	261.6	261.8
KT39	Mingary	; KT27 5.1 km;	A	3	12.5 km	A		790624;	269:	1.8	2.0
KT39	Mingary	; KT31 5.6 km;	A	3	13.0 km	C		- ;	270:	38.0	38.2
KT39	Mingary	; KT32 5.7 km;	A	3	13.5 km	A		790624;	271:	40.8	41.0
KT39	Mingary	; KT37 4.6 km;	A	3	33.0 km	A		790624;	272:	81.6	81.8

KT23 - Beinn an Tuirc (Arnicle; Crois Mhic-Aoida), Kintyre. NR 7349 3506. A slab 1.8m tall x 1.4m x 0.3m, now leaning by about 20° from the vertical. Several other stones in the vicinity planned by Thom as possible fallen and sunken menhirs (1971: 56-7) can be seen, following recent Forestry Commission furrowing, to be no more than stray boulders and outcrops (Ruggles 1982: S32-3, Line 36). Arch. status = A; type = 5.

KT24 - Tighnamoile, Kintyre. NR 6641 2898. A small erect stone some 0.8m high x 0.8m x 0.5m, listed by the Ordnance Survey (OSAR: NR 62 NE, 3) as a possible standing stone. It is unimpressive and may, as the O.S. remark, have been set up as a cattle-rubbing stone. Arch. status = B; type = 8.

KT25 - Drumalea, Kintyre. NR 6609 2756. A fallen standing stone 1.8m long, which was standing in 1900 (RCAHMS 1971: no. 142). Arch. status = A; type = 8.

KT27 - Clochkeil, Kintyre. NR 6577 2445. Three stones, two standing and one fallen, which appear to have formed an alignment about 5m long. The standing stones are 1.9m and 1.4m in height and the fallen stone is some 2.0m long. Arch. status = A; type = 2.

KT28 - Skeroblingarry (Skeroblin Cruach), Kintyre. NR 7094 2701. A slab 1.5m high x 0.9m x 0.2m. A circle also noted by Thom (FSL: A4/11) was not located. Arch. status = A; type = 5.

KT29 - High Park, Kintyre. NR 6950 2572. A standing stone some 3.0m tall x 1.3m x 0.6m. Arch. status = A; type = 5.

KT31 - Craigs, Kintyre. NR 6902 2362. A slab some 2.5m tall x 1.7m x 0.3m. Arch. status = A; type = 5.

KT32 - Glencraigs S, Kintyre. NR 6932 2354. A slab some 2.0m tall x 1.1m x 0.4m, but with rounded faces. Arch. status = A; type = 5.

KT35 - Glenlussa Lodge (Peninver), Kintyre. NR 7614 2541. A slab 2.3m tall x 1.2m x 0.5m, now set into a stone wall. Arch. status = A; type = 5.

KT36 - Campbeltown (Balegreggan), Kintyre. NR 7238 2123. A slab some 4.0m tall x 1.4m x 0.5m. Arch. status = A; type = 5.

KT37 - Stewarton, Kintyre. NR 6995 1982. A stone which stood 1.8m tall in 1930 (RCAHMS 1971: no. 147) but is now fallen and broken into two pieces. Arch. status = A; type = 8.

KT39 - Mingary, Kintyre. NR 6533 1940. A standing stone 1.4m tall x 1.0m x 0.4m, standing at the foot of the remains of the outer of two banks surrounding a cairn (RCAHMS 1971: no. 34). Site plan: RCAHMS (1971: fig. 23). Arch. status = A; type = 5.

KT40 - Lochorodale, Kintyre. NR 6657 1546. A small slab some 1.5m tall x 1.3m x 0.2m, now leaning by about 50° from the vertical.

(ctd. on page 201

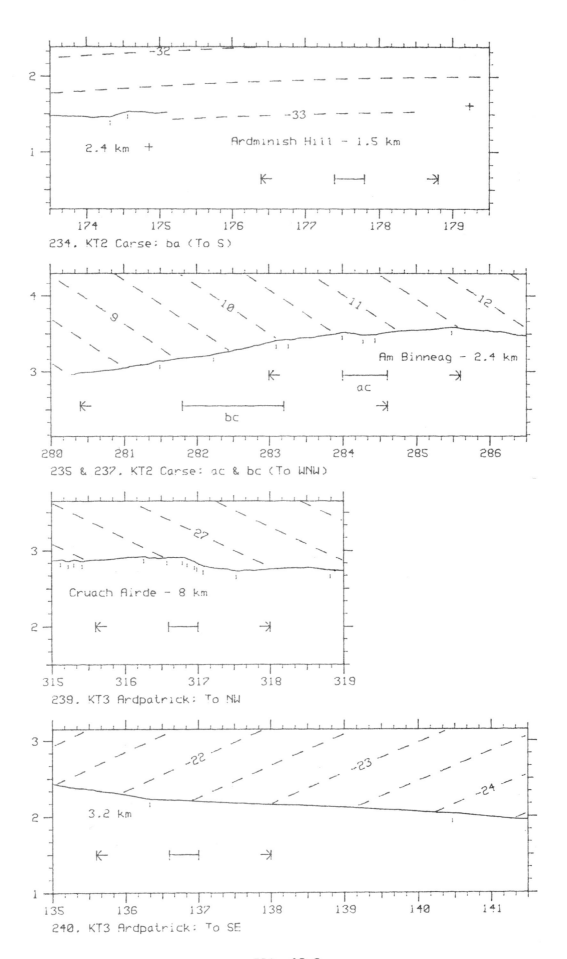

234. KT2 Carse; ba (To S)

235 & 237. KT2 Carse: ac & bc (To WNW)

239. KT3 Ardpatrick: To NW

240. KT3 Ardpatrick: To SE

FIG. 10.2.

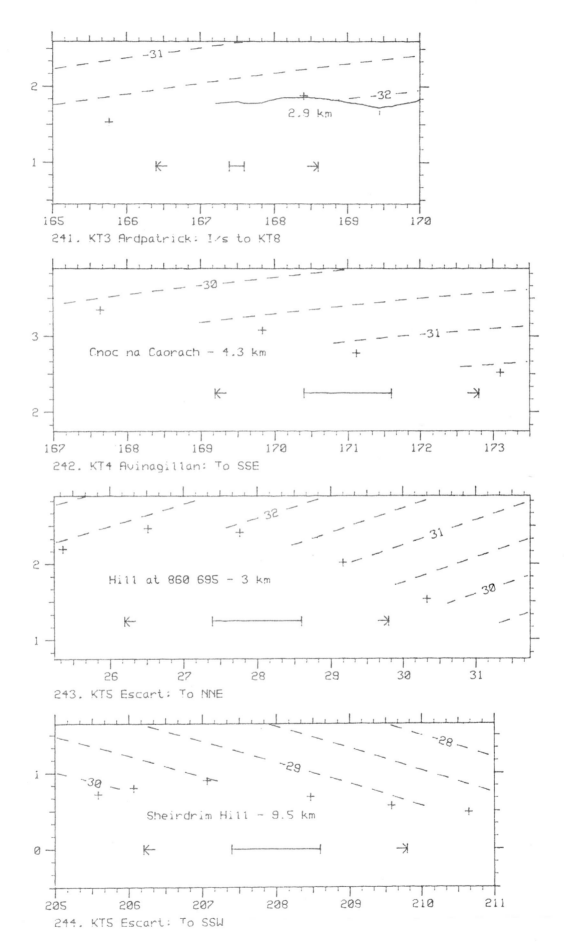

241. KT3 Ardpatrick: l/s to KT8

242. KT4 Avinagillan: To SSE

243. KT5 Escart: To NNE

244. KT5 Escart: To SSW

FIG. 10.3.

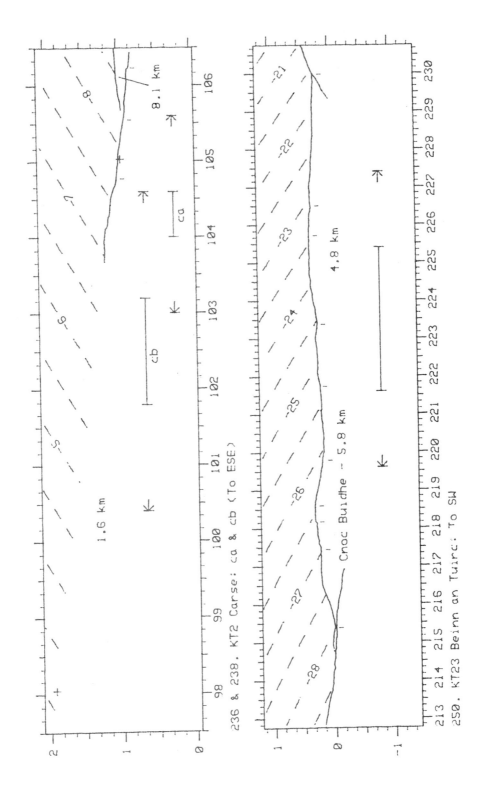

236 & 238. KT2 Carse: ca & cb (To ESE)

250. KT23 Beinn an Tuirc: To SW

FIG. 10.4.

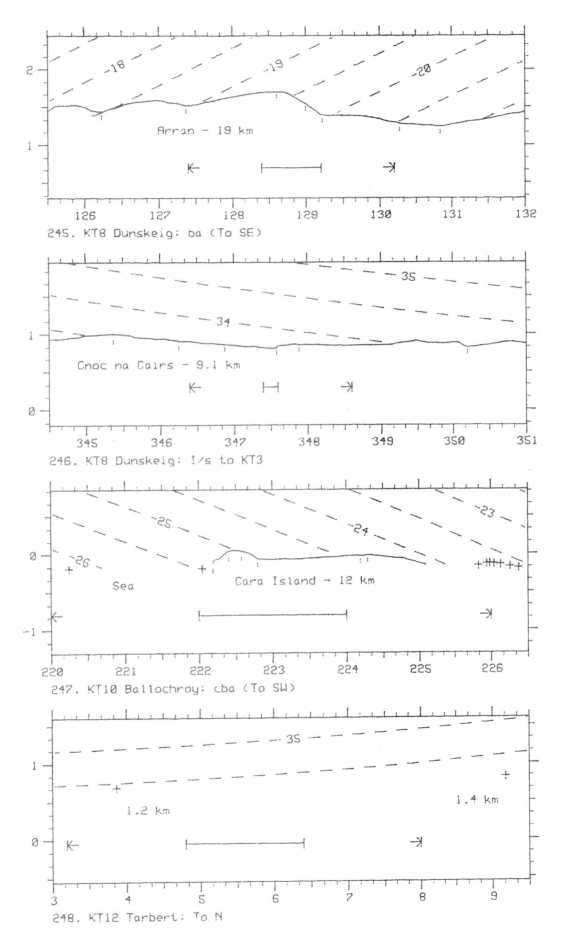

245. KT8 Dunskeig: ba (To SE)

246. KT8 Dunskeig: l/s to KT3

247. KT10 Ballochroy: cba (To SW)

248. KT12 Tarbert: To N

FIG. 10.5.

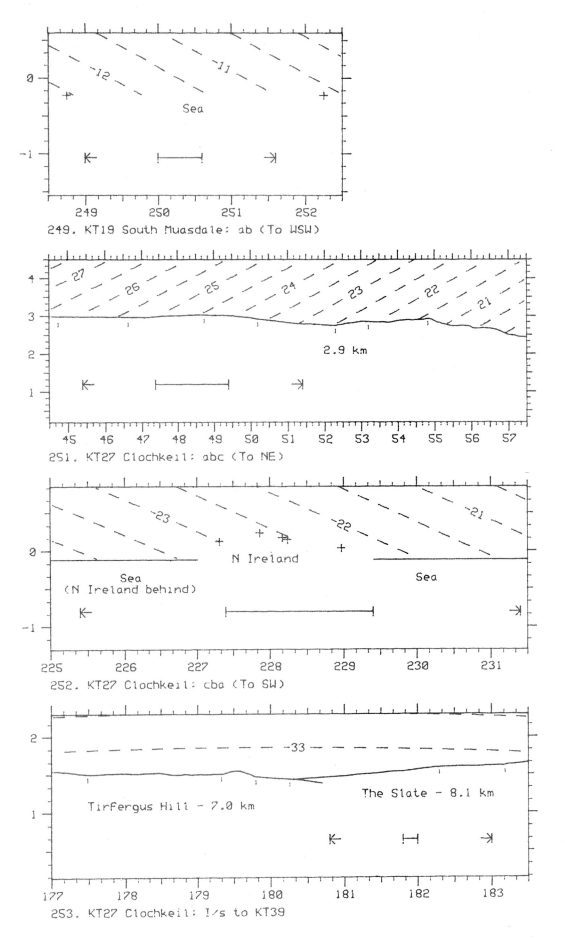

249. KT19 South Muasdale: ab (To WSW)

251. KT27 Clochkeil: abc (To NE)

252. KT27 Clochkeil: cba (To SW)

253. KT27 Clochkeil: I/s to KT39

FIG. 10.6.

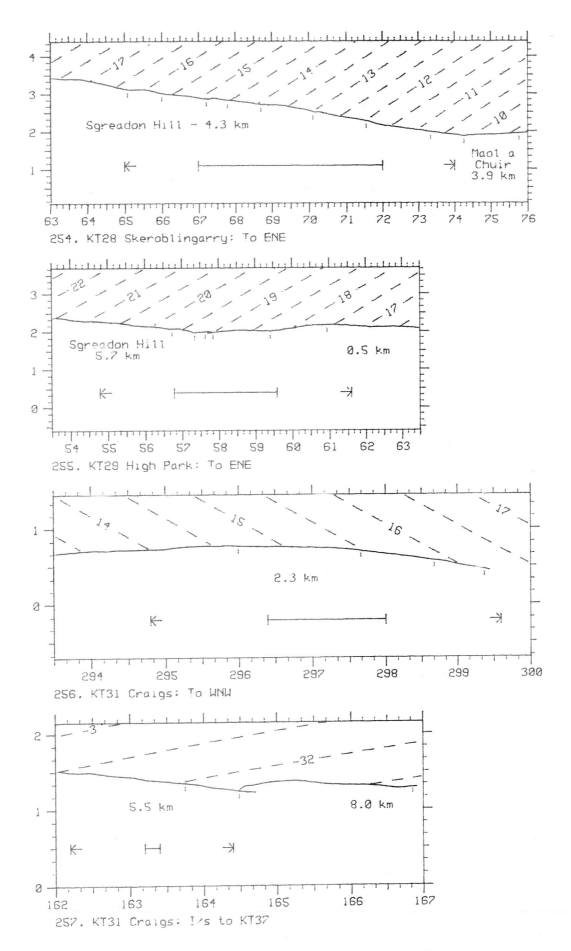

254. KT28 Skeroblingarry: To ENE

255. KT29 High Park: To ENE

256. KT31 Craigs: To WNW

257. KT31 Craigs: I's to KT37

FIG. 10.7.

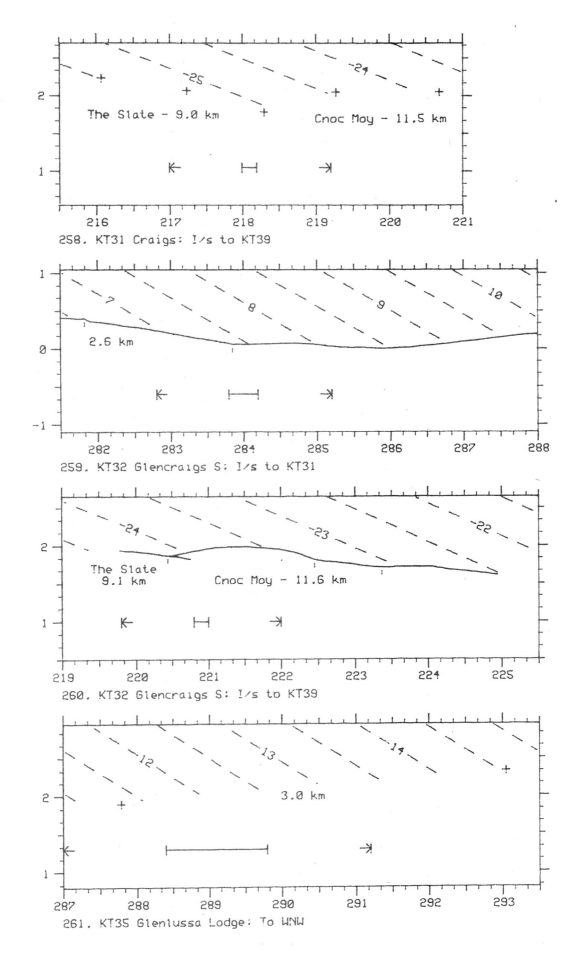

258. KT31 Craigs: I/s to KT39

259. KT32 Glencraigs S: I/s to KT31

260. KT32 Glencraigs S: I/s to KT39

261. KT35 Glenlussa Lodge: To WNW

FIG. 10.8.

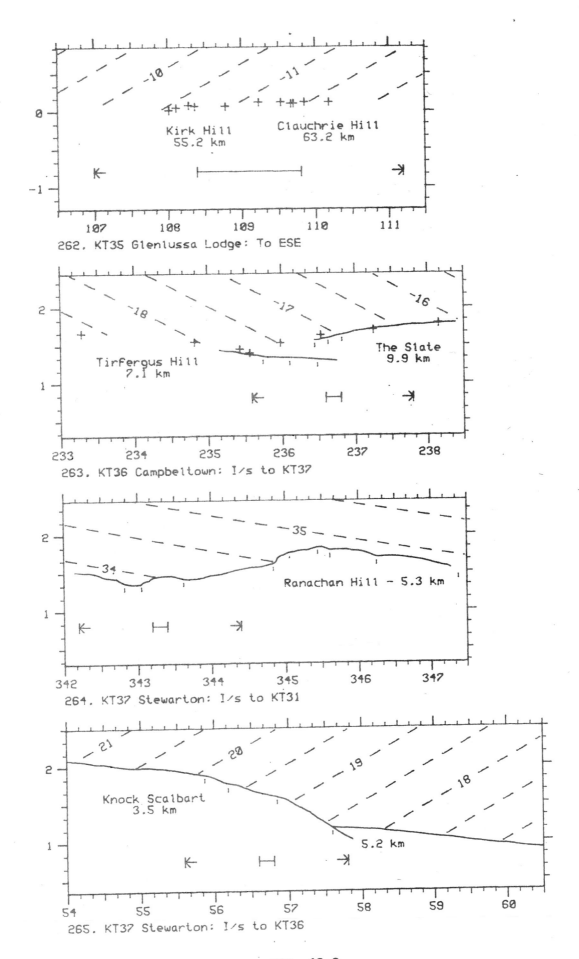

262. KT35 Glenlussa Lodge: To ESE

Kirk Hill
55.2 km

Clauchrie Hill
63.2 km

263. KT36 Campbeltown: l/s to KT37

Tirfergus Hill
7.1 km

The Slate
9.9 km

264. KT37 Stewarton: l/s to KT31

Ranachan Hill - 5.3 km

265. KT37 Stewarton: l/s to KT36

Knock Scalbart
3.5 km

5.2 km

FIG. 10.9.

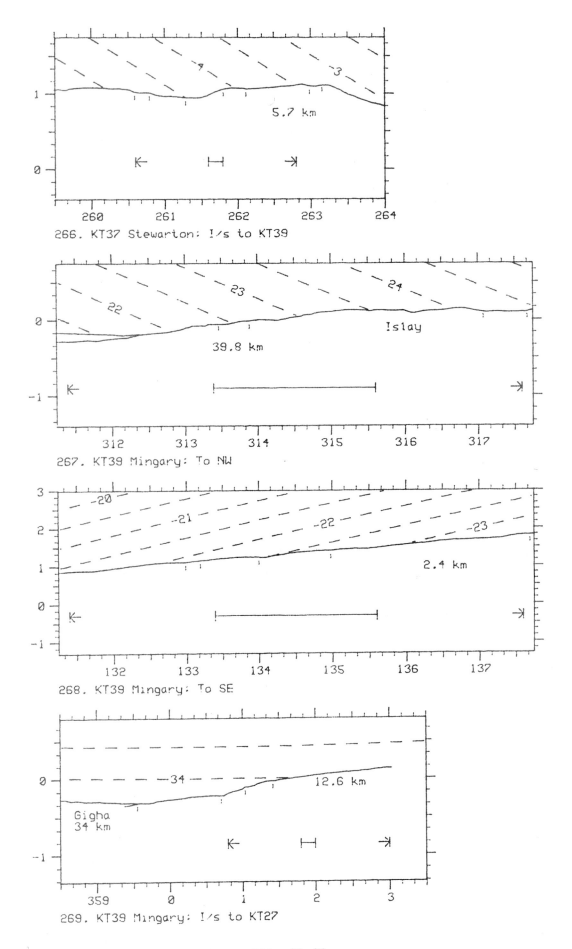

266. KT37 Stewarton: I/s to KT39

267. KT39 Mingary: To NW

268. KT39 Mingary: To SE

269. KT39 Mingary: I/s to KT27

FIG. 10.10.

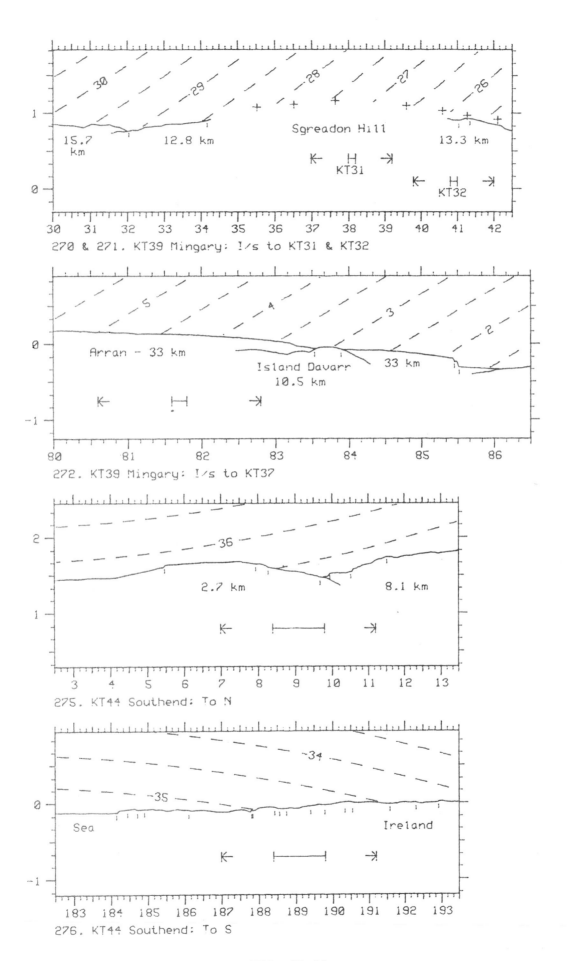

270 & 271. KT39 Mingary: l/s to KT31 & KT32

272. KT39 Mingary: l/s to KT37

275. KT44 Southend: To N

276. KT44 Southend: To S

FIG. 10.11.

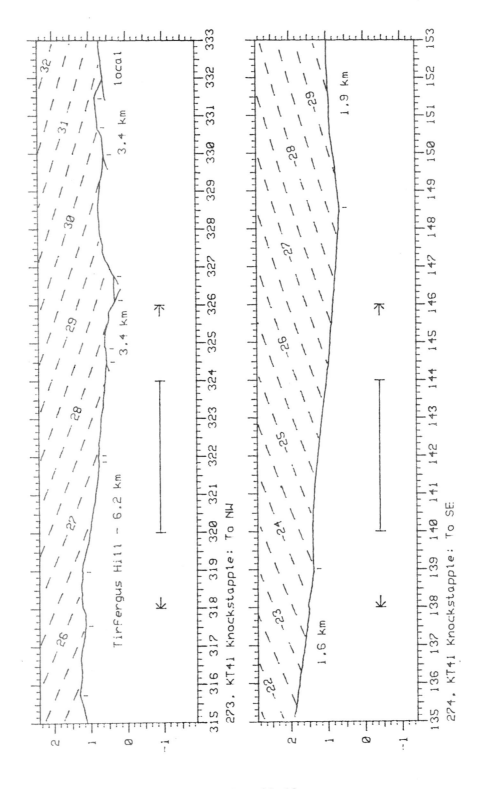

273. KT41 Knockstapple: To NW

274. KT41 Knockstapple: To SE

FIG. 10.12.

- 200 -

The RCAHMS (1971: no. 151) note that it has possibly been moved to its present position. Arch. status = B; type = 6.

KT41 - Knockstapple, Kintyre. NR 7026 1240. A large slab some 3.2m tall x 1.8m x 0.6m. Arch. status = A; type = 5.

KT42 - Culinlongart, Kintyre. NR 6517 1192. A standing stone some 2.0m tall x 1.3m x 0.9m. Arch. status = A; type = 7.

KT44 - Southend (Brunerican), Kintyre. NR 6976 0787. A slab 2.7m tall x 1.5m at its widest x 0.3m. Arch. status = A; type = 5.

10.3   Remarks on the surveys and survey data

The data for the surveys are presented in full in Tables 10.1 and 10.2, for on-site and inter-site lines respectively. Profile diagrams are presented in Figs. 10.2 - 10.12.

Two indicated profiles in this area are in Ireland. In one case (Line 252, KT27 Clochkeil: cba) some survey measurements were taken, though with considerable uncertainty owing to the bad conditions. No photographs were obtained with which to fill in the horizon profile between the surveyed points. In the other case (Line 276, KT44 Southend: To S) no survey was possible. Unfortunately the profiles could not be calculated either, at least without introducing the complication of having to relate the Irish and British Ordnance Survey grids. At Line 252 the isolated surveyed points have been treated as calculated points, and at Line 276 a flat sea horizon has been assumed. Some error is possible in both cases as a result.

Some error is also possible in the cases of the following surveyed profiles, for the reasons stated.

Line 236 (KT2 Carse: ca). Large parallax correction. Measurements were reduced to the OP from a point 115m in front of it (by menhirs a and b).

Line 247 (KT10 Ballochroy: cba). Forestry commission trees some 500m away obscure the profile. This was not the case in 1973, when the site was surveyed by Bailey et al. (1975), and their survey measurements have been used in this analysis.

Line 263 (KT36 Campbeltown: I/s to KT37). Large parallax correction. Measurements were reduced to the OP from a point 2815m in front of it and 10m above it (by site KT37). Because of the very large parallax correction applied, this profile has been calculated as well, and both surveyed and calculated points are shown on the profile diagram.

11   THE DATA FOR ANALYSIS

In this chapter we merely gather together the data presented in the area-by-area chapters into two source lists, one for sites (Table 11.1) and one for indications (Table 11.2). The aim is to make readily accessible the data used in the analyses that follow.

Table 11.1 is a source list of 189 sites selected for analysis out of the original sample of over 300. Table 11.2 lists the 276 indications selected for analysis according to the criteria of Chapter 3.

(ctd. on page 212

- - - - - -

TABLE 11.1. Source list of sites with brief descriptions, classification and survey details.

Column headings

1	Site reference number
2	Site name and location
3	Archaeological status of the site (see Section 3.1)
4	Site description
5	Site type (see Section 3.3)
6	On-site lines in the following categories:
	A Reliably surveyed
	B Less reliably surveyed
	C Calculated
	L Dismissed because horizon is local (see Section 3.4)
	W Dismissed because IAR is too wide (see Section 3.4)
7	Inter-site lines in the same categories
8	Latest year of visit by the author
9	Year(s) when surveys were undertaken

Key to Column 4 (Site Description)

B	Boulder
C	Stone circle or ring
G	Setting of small stones
M	Menhir or earthfast stump
T	Chambered tomb, cairn or mound
FM	Fallen (or recumbent) menhir
ZM	Re-erected menhir
P..	Possible..
X..	Several..
Y..	Site of..
../..	..surrounding..
A(..)	Alignment consisting of.. (N.B. Two menhirs are considered an alignment only if either they are BOTH slabs oriented along the line of centres or there exists documentary evidence of a third which has disappeared)

Table 11.1

Site	Name and location	St	Description	Type	O-S lines					I-S lines					Vis Survey
					A	B	C	L	W	A	B	C	L	W	
LH1	Port of Ness	,Lewis; A;	2M,Y2M	7:	-	-	-	-	-:	0	0	0	0	0:	79: - -
LH5	Ballantrushal	,Lewis; A;	M	5:	0	0	0	2:		0	0	0	0	0:	81: - -
LH6	Carloway	,Lewis; A;	PA(M,2FM)	2:	0	0	0	2:		0	0	0	0	0:	81: - -
LH7	Kirkibost	,Gt Bernera; A;	FM	8:	-	-	-	-:		1	0	0	0	0:	81: 81
LH8	Bernera Bridge	,Gt Bernera; A;	2M,PM,FM	3:	1	0	0	1	0:	1	0	0	0	0:	81: 81
LH10	Beinn Bheag	,Lewis; A;	M,FM	4:	0	1	0	1	0:	5	1	0	0	0:	81: 75
LH16	Callanish	,Lewis; A;	C/T,5A(XM)	1:	5	0	2	3	0:	6	0	0	0	0:	80: 79 75
LH18	Cnoc Fillibhir Bheag	,Lewis; A;	C/C	7:	-	-	-	-	-:	5	0	0	0	0:	80: 79 75
LH19	Cnoc Ceann a Gharaidh	,Lewis; A;	C/T	7:	-	-	-	-	-:	3	0	0	1	1:	80: 79 75
LH21	Ceann Hulavig	,Lewis; A;	C	7:	-	-	-	-	-:	4	0	1	0	0:	80: 75
LH22	Cul a' Chleit	,Lewis; A;	2M	3:	1	0	1	0	0:	4	0	1	0	0:	75: 75
LH24	Airigh nam Bidearan	,Lewis; B;	A(3PM),2PM	3:	2	0	0	0	0:	5	0	1	0	0:	81: 81 75
LH27	Newmarket	,Lewis; B;	PC(3PM)	8:	-	-	-	-:		0	0	0	1	0:	81: - -
LH28	Priests Glen	,Lewis; A;	PC(4FM)	8:	-	-	-	-:		0	0	0	0	1:	81: - -
LH29	Dursainean NE	,Lewis; B;	PM	6:	1	0	0	1	0:	0	0	0	0	0:	81: 81
LH31	Lower Bayble	,Lewis; A;	FM	8:	-	-	-	-:		0	0	0	0	0:	79: - -
LH33	Sideval	,Lewis; A;	C	7:	-	-	-	-:		0	0	0	0	0:	79: - -
LH36	Horgabost	,Harris; A;	M,PT	5:	1	0	0	1	0:	1	0	0	0	0:	79: 79
LH37	Scarista	,Harris; A;	M,2FM,Y2FM,PT	3:	0	0	1	1	0:	1	0	0	0	0:	79: 79
UI6	Borve	,Berneray; A;	M	5:	2	0	0	0	0:	1	0	0	0	0:	81: 81
UI9	Newtonferry	,N Uist; A;	2M	3:	1	0	0	1	0:	1	0	0	0	0:	81: 81 79 77
UI15	Maari	,N Uist; A;	M	7:	-	-	-	-:		0	0	1	0	0:	81: - -
UI19	Blashaval	,N Uist; A;	A(3M)	1:	1	0	0	1	0:	0	0	1	0	0:	81: 77
UI22	South Clettraval	,N Uist; A;	M,2T	7:	-	-	-	-:		2	0	0	0	0:	77: 77
UI23	Toroghas	,N Uist; A;	2M	3:	1	0	0	1	0:	3	0	0	0	0:	81: 81 77

Table 11.1 (continued)

Site	Name and location	St	Description	Type	O-S lines A B C L W	I-S lines A B C L W	Vis	Survey
UI24	Marrogh ,N Uist;	B;	PM,T	8:	- - - - -:	0 0 0 0 0:	79:	--
UI26	Beinn a'Charra ,N Uist;	A;	M	7:	- - - - -:	4 0 0 0 0:	81:	77
UI28	Unival ,N Uist;	A;	M,T	5:	1 0 0 1 0:	3 0 2 0 0:	79:	79 77
UI29	L na Buaile Iochdrach ,N Uist;	B;	PM	6:	0 0 0 2 0:	0 0 0 0 0:	79:	--
UI31	Claddach Kyles ,N Uist;	A;	M,T	5:	1 0 0 1 0:	2 0 2 0 0:	79:	79 77
UI33	Ben Langass ,N Uist;	A;	C	7:	- - - - -:	2 0 0 0 0:	81:	81 77
UI35	Cringraval W ,N Uist;	B;	PC(PM,5PFM)	8:	- - - - -:	3 0 1 0 0:	81:	81
UI37	Loch a'Phobuill ,N Uist;	A;	C	7:	- - - - -:	2 0 1 0 0:	81:	77
UI40	Carinish ,N Uist;	A;	C	7:	- - - - -:	1 0 0 0 0:	81:	81
UI44	Hacklett ,Benbecula;	A;	FM	8:	- - - - -:	0 0 0 0 0:	--:	--
UI46	Stiaraval ,Benbecula;	B;	PM	6:	2 0 0 0 0:	0 0 0 0 0:	81:	77
UI48	Stoneybridge ,S Uist;	A;	M	7:	- - - - -:	1 0 1 0 0:	81:	81 79
UI49	Beinn a'Charra ,S Uist;	A;	M	5:	1 0 1 0 0:	0 0 2 0 0:	81:	81 79
UI50	Ru Ardvule ,S Uist;	A;	M,Y2PFM	7:	- - - - -:	0 0 2 0 0:	81:	--
UI57	Borve ,Barra;	A;	M,FM	3:	2 0 0 0 0:	0 0 0 0 0:	81:	79
UI58	Beul a Bhealaich ,Barra;	B;	PFM	8:	- - - - -:	0 0 0 0 0:	81:	--
UI59	Brevig ,Barra;	A;	M,FM	4:	2 0 0 0 0:	0 0 0 0 0:	79:	79
UI60	Ben Rulibreck ,Vatersay;	A;	M	7:	- - - - -:	0 0 0 0 0:	81:	--
NA1	Branault ,Ardnamurchan;	A;	M,PM	4:	1 1 0 0 0:	0 0 0 0 0:	81:	81
NA3	Camas nan Geall ,Ardnamurchan;	A;	M	5:	1 0 0 1 0:	0 0 0 0 0:	81:	81
NA7	Beinn Bhan ,Morvern;	A;	M	7:	- - - - -:	0 0 0 0 0:	81:	--
CT1	Acha ,Coll;	A;	M,2PT	5:	0 0 1 1 0:	0 0 0 0 0:	79:	--
CT2	Totronald ,Coll;	A;	2M	3:	2 0 0 0 0:	1 0 0 0 0:	79:	79
CT3	Breachacha ,Coll;	A;	M	7:	- - - - -:	1 0 0 0 0:	79:	79
CT4	Caolas ,Coll;	B;	PM	8:	- - - - -:	0 0 0 0 0:	79:	--

Table 11.1 (continued)

Site	Name and location	St	Description	Type	O-S lines A B C L W	I-S lines A B C L W	Vis Survey
CT5	Caoles	,Tiree; A;	M	7:	- - - - -:	0 0 0 0 0:	79: --
CT7	Hough	,Tiree; A;	2C,T	7:	- - - - -:	0 1 0 0 0:	79: 79
CT8	Barrapoll	,Tiree; A;	M	7:	- - - - -:	0 0 1 0 0:	79: --
CT9	Balinoe	,Tiree; A;	M	5:	1 0 0 1 0:	0 0 0 0 0:	79: 79
ML1	Glengorm	,Mull; A;	M,2ZM	7:	- - - - -:	0 0 1 0 0:	76: --
ML2	Quinish	,Mull; A;	A(M,3FM),YM	2:	1 0 0 1 0:	0 0 1 0 0:	79: 76
ML4	Balliscate	,Mull; A;	A(2M,FM)	2:	1 0 1 0 0:	0 0 0 0 0:	76: 76
ML6	Lag	,Mull; A;	M,FM	4:	0 0 0 2 0:	0 0 0 0 0:	79: --
ML7	Cillchriosd	,Mull; A;	M	5:	1 0 0 1 0:	1 0 0 0 0:	79: 79
ML8	Calgary	,Mull; B;	2PFM	5:	0 0 0 2 0:	0 0 0 0 0:	79: --
ML9	Maol Mor	,Mull; A;	A(3M,FM)	1:	0 0 1 1 0:	0 0 1 0 0:	76: --
ML10	Dervaig N	,Mull; A;	A(2M,3FM,PM)	2:	0 1 0 1 0:	0 0 0 0 0:	76: 76
ML11	Dervaig S	,Mull; A;	A(3M),PZM	1:	1 0 0 1 0:	0 0 0 0 0:	79: 76
ML12	Ardnacross	,Mull; A;	A(M,2FM),3T,A(3FM)	2:	2 0 0 0 0:	0 0 0 0 0:	76: 76
ML13	Tenga	,Mull; A;	PC(4M)	7:	- - - - -:	0 0 0 0 0:	76: --
ML14	Tostarie	,Mull; A;	M	7:	- - - - -:	0 0 0 0 0:	76: --
ML15	Killichronan	,Mull; A;	M	7:	- - - - -:	0 0 1 0 0:	76: --
ML16	Gruline	,Mull; A;	2M	3:	0 2 0 0 0:	0 0 1 0 0:	76: 76
ML17	Ormaig	,Ulva; A;	FM	8:	- - - - -:	0 0 0 0 0:	79: --
ML18	Cragaig	,Ulva; A;	2M	3:	1 0 0 1 0:	0 0 0 0 0:	79: 79
ML19	Dishig	,Mull; B;	PM	8:	- - - - -:	0 0 0 0 0:	76: --
ML21	Scallastle	,Mull; A;	A(M,2FM)	2:	0 0 0 2 0:	0 0 0 0 0:	76: --
ML23	Duart	,Mull; A;	M	7:	- - - - -:	0 0 0 0 0:	76: --
ML24	Port Donain	,Mull; B;	PFM,2T	8:	- - - - -:	0 0 0 0 0:	76: --
ML25	Uluvalt I	,Mull; B;	A(3PFM,B),PM,PFM	3:	2 0 0 0 0:	1 0 0 0 0:	79: 79

Table 11.1 (continued)

Site	Name and Location	St	Description	Type	O-S lines A B C L W	I-S lines A B C L W	Vis	Survey
ML27	Rossal	,Mull; B;	PM	8:	- - - - - :	0 0 1 0 0 :	76:	--
ML28	Loch Buie	,Mull; A;	C,4M,T	8:	- - - - - :	0 0 0 0 0 :	76:	--
ML30	Taoslin	,Mull; B;	PM	6:	1 0 0 1 0 :	0 0 0 0 0 :	79:	76
ML31	Uisken	,Mull; A;	M	5:	2 0 0 0 0 :	0 0 0 0 0 :	76:	76
ML33	Ardalanish	,Mull; A;	M,FM	3:	1 0 0 1 0 :	0 0 0 0 0 :	76:	76
ML34	Suie	,Mull; A;	2M,T	3:	0 0 0 0 2 :	0 0 0 0 0 :	76:	--
ML35	Tirghoil	,Mull; B;	PM	8:	- - - - - :	0 0 0 0 0 :	79:	--
ML37	Poit na h-I	,Mull; A;	M	7:	- - - - - :	0 0 0 0 0 :	76:	--
ML39	Achaban House	,Mull; B;	PM	8:	- - - - - :	0 0 0 0 0 :	76:	--
LN1	Acharra	,Appin; A;	M	7:	- - - - - :	0 0 0 0 0 :	81:	--
LN2	Inverfolla	,Appin; A;	FM	8:	- - - - - :	0 0 0 0 0 :	81:	--
LN3	Barcaldine	,Benderloch; A;	M,ZM	7:	- - - - - :	0 0 0 0 0 :	81:	--
LN5	Achacha	,Benderloch; A;	M,T	7:	- - - - - :	0 0 0 0 0 :	81:	--
LN7	Benderloch N	,Benderloch; A;	M,PYC	5:	0 0 1 1 0 :	0 0 0 0 0 :	81:	--
LN8	Benderloch S	,Benderloch; A;	M,PYXM	7:	- - - - - :	0 0 0 0 0 :	81:	--
LN14	Taynuilt	,Lorn; A;	M	7:	- - - - - :	0 0 0 0 0 :	81:	--
LN15	Black Lochs	,Lorn; B;	PM	8:	- - - - - :	0 0 0 0 0 :	81:	--
LN17	Strontoiller	,Lorn; A;	C,M,T	7:	- - - - - :	0 0 0 0 0 :	81:	--
LN18	Glenamacrie	,Lorn; A;	M,B	4:	0 1 0 1 0 :	0 0 0 0 0 :	81:	81
LN22	Duachy	,Lorn; A;	A(3M),M	1:	1 1 0 0 0 :	0 0 0 0 0 :	81:	73
AR2	Sluggan	,Argyll; A;	M,PFM	5:	0 0 1 1 0 :	0 0 1 0 0 :	79:	--
AR3	Barbreck	,Argyll; A;	A(2M),G/M	1:	2 0 0 0 0 :	0 0 1 0 0 :	81:	81
AR6	Salachary	,Argyll; A;	A(2M,FM)	2:	1 0 0 1 0 :	0 0 0 0 0 :	79:	79
AR7	Torran	,Argyll; A;	M	7:	- - - - - :	0 0 1 0 0 :	79:	--
AR8	Ford	,Argyll; A;	M,YM	7:	- - - - - :	0 0 1 0 0 :	79:	--

Table 11.1 (continued)

Site	Name and Location	St	Description	Type	O-S lines A	B	C	L	W	I-S lines A	B	C	L	W	Vis	Survey
AR9	Glennan N	,Argyll;	A; M,2T	;5:	0	1	0	1	0:	0	0	1	0	0:	79:	79
AR10	Glennan S	,Argyll;	A; M	;5:	0	0	0	2	0:	0	0	1	0	0:	79:	--
AR12	Carnasserie	,Argyll;	A; A(2M)	;1:	0	0	0	2	0:	0	0	0	0	0:	79:	--
AR13	Kilmartin	,Argyll;	A; C,YC,G/M,2A(2M),M,G;	1:	2	1	3	2	0:	0	0	0	0	1:	81:	81 79
AR15	Duncracaig	,Argyll;	A; A(4M),A(2M),YM,2T	;1:	0	3	1	0	0:	0	0	1	0	0:	79:	79
AR16	Rowanfield	,Argyll;	A; M	;5:	0	2	0	0	0:	0	1	0	1	0:	81:	81
AR17	Duntroon	,Argyll;	A; M	;7:	-	-	-	-	-:	0	0	2	0	0:	79:	--
AR18	Crinan Moss	,Argyll;	B; XPM	;8:	-	-	-	1	0:	1	0	1	0	0:	79:	79
AR19	Inverary	,Argyll;	A; M	;5:	0	0	0	2	0:	0	0	0	0	0:	--:	--
AR23	Lechuary	,Argyll;	A; M	;5:	0	0	0	2	0:	0	0	0	0	0:	79:	--
AR24	Loch na Torrnalaich	,Argyll;	B; PFM	;8:	-	-	-	-	-:	0	0	0	0	0:	81:	--
AR25	Torbhlaran N	,Argyll;	A; M	;5:	0	0	0	2	0:	0	0	0	0	0:	79:	--
AR27	Dunadd	,Argyll;	A; FM,M	;4:	0	1	0	1	0:	0	0	0	0	0:	81:	81
AR28	Dunamuck I	,Argyll;	A; A(2M,FM)	;2:	2	0	2	0	0:	0	2	0	0	0:	81:	81
AR29	Dunamuck II	,Argyll;	A; A(2M)	;1:	0	2	0	0	0:	0	0	1	0	0:	81:	81
AR30	Dunamuck III	,Argyll;	A; 2FM	;5:	0	0	0	2	0:	0	0	1	0	0:	81:	--
AR31	Achnabreck	,Argyll;	A; M,FM	;4:	0	0	0	2	0:	0	0	0	0	0:	79:	--
AR32	Oakfield	,Argyll;	A; M	;5:	0	0	2	0	0:	0	0	0	0	0:	79:	--
AR33	Kilmory	,Argyll;	A; M	;5:	0	0	2	0	0:	0	0	0	0	0:	79:	--
AR37	Barnashaig	,Knapdale;	A; M	;7:	-	-	-	-	-:	0	0	0	0	0:	81:	--
AR38	Upper Fernoch	,Knapdale;	A; M	;7:	-	-	-	-	-:	0	0	0	0	0:	81:	--
AR39	Lochead	,Knapdale;	A; M	;5:	0	0	0	2	0:	0	0	0	0	0:	79:	--
JU1	Tarbert	,Jura;	A; M,PM	;4:	1	0	0	1	0:	0	0	0	0	0:	79:	79
JU2	Knockrome N	,Jura;	B; PM	;8:	-	-	-	-	-:	1	0	0	1	0:	79:	79
JU3	Ardfernal	,Jura;	A; M	;7:	-	-	-	-	-:	0	2	1	0	0:	79:	79

Table 11.1 (continued)

Site	Name and location	St	Description	Type	O-S lines					I-S lines					Vis	Survey
					A	B	C	L	W	A	B	C	L	W		
JU4	Knockrome	,Jura; A;	2M	3:	1	1	0	0	0:	1	1	0	1	0:	79:	79
JU5	Leargybreck	,Jura; B;	PM	8:	-	-	-	-	-:	0	2	0	0	0:	79:	79
JU6	Craighouse	,Jura; A;	A(M,3FM)	2:	0	0	0	0	2:	0	0	0	0	0:	79:	--
JU7	Sannaig	,Jura; A;	A(2M,FM),PFM,PM	2:	0	0	2	0	0:	0	0	0	0	0:	79:	--
JU8	Strone	,Jura; A;	M,FM	4:	0	0	0	2	0:	0	0	0	2	0:	79:	--
JU9	Camas an Staca	,Jura; A;	M	5:	2	0	0	0	0:	0	0	0	0	0:	79:	79
IS3	Beinn a Chuirn	,Islay; A;	M	5:	1	0	0	1	0:	0	0	0	0	0:	79:	79
IS4	Finlaggan	,Islay; A;	M,YM	5:	1	0	0	1	0:	0	0	0	0	0:	78:	78
IS5	Scanistle	,Islay; A;	M	5:	0	-	-	0	2:	0	0	1	0	0:	78:	--
IS6	Beinn Cham	,Islay; A;	M,PYM	7:	-	-	2	-	-:	2	0	0	0	0:	79:	79
IS7	Ballachlavin	,Islay; A;	M	5:	0	0	0	2	0:	3	0	0	0	0:	79:	79
IS11	Knocklearoch	,Islay; A;	2M	3:	1	0	0	1	0:	1	0	1	0	0:	78:	78
IS12	Mullach Dubh	,Islay; A;	M	7:	-	0	-	-	-:	0	0	2	0	0:	79:	--
IS15	Ballinaby	,Islay; A;	PA(2M,YM)	3:	0	0	0	2	0:	0	0	0	0	0:	79:	--
IS18	Foreland House	,Islay; A;	M	7:	-	-	0	-	-:	0	0	0	0	0:	78:	--
IS19	Uisgeantsuidhe	,Islay; A;	M	5:	1	0	0	1	0:	1	0	0	0	0:	78:	78
IS21	Knockdon	,Islay; A;	M	7:	-	0	-	-	-:	0	0	0	0	0:	78:	--
IS23	Gartacharra	,Islay; A;	M	5:	1	0	0	1	0:	1	0	0	0	0:	78:	78
IS24	Carn Mor	,Islay; A;	M	5:	0	-	-	0	2:	0	0	0	0	0:	78:	--
IS25	Cnoc Thornasaig	,Islay; B;	PFM	8:	-	-	-	-	-:	0	0	0	0	0:	78:	--
IS26	Droigneach	,Islay; A;	M	7:	-	-	-	-	-:	0	0	0	0	0:	78:	--
IS28	Cultoon	,Islay; A;	C	7:	-	-	-	-	-:	0	0	1	0	0:	78:	--
IS31	Kelsay	,Islay; B;	PM	8:	-	-	1	-	-:	1	0	0	0	0:	78:	78
IS34	Ardtalla	,Islay; B;	PM	8:	-	-	0	-	-:	0	0	0	0	0:	78:	--
IS35	Claggain Bay	,Islay; B;	PM	6:	0	0	0	2	1:	1	0	0	0	0:	79:	78

Table 11.1 (continued)

Site	Name and location	St	Description	Type	O-S lines A B C L W					I-S lines A B C L W					Vis	Survey
IS36	Trudernish	,Islay;	A; M	;7:	–	–	–	–	–:	1	0	0	0	0:	79:	78
IS37	Ardilistry	,Islay;	A; C	;7:	–	–	–	–	–:	0	0	0	0	0:	–:	––
IS38	Cnoc Rhaonastil	,Islay;	A; M,PM	;4:	0	0	2	0	0:	0	0	0	0	0:	79:	––
IS39	Lagavulin N	,Islay;	A; M,FM	;3:	1	0	0	0	0:	1	0	0	0	0:	79:	79 78
IS41	Laphroaig	,Islay;	A; A(2M,FM)	;2:	0	0	1	1	0:	0	0	0	1	0:	78:	––
IS42	Kilbride	,Islay;	A; M,PFM	;3:	0	0	0	0	2:	0	0	0	0	0:	78:	––
IS46	Port Ellen I	,Islay;	A; M	;7:	–	–	–	–	–:	0	0	0	0	0:	78:	––
IS47	Kintra	,Islay;	A; M	;5:	0	0	0	0	2:	0	0	0	0	0:	78:	––
IS49	Cornabus	,Islay;	A; M	;7:	–	–	–	–	–:	0	0	0	0	0:	78:	––
IS50	Kinnabus	,Islay;	A; M	;7:	–	–	–	–	–:	0	0	0	0	0:	78:	––
KT1	Cretshengan	,Knapdale;	B; PM	;8:	–	–	–	–	–:	0	0	0	0	0:	79:	––
KT2	Carse	,Knapdale;	A; A(2M),M or 3M	;3:	2	1	2	1	0:	0	0	0	0	0:	79:	79
KT3	Ardpatrick	,Knapdale;	A; M	;5:	2	0	0	0	0:	1	0	0	0	0:	79:	79
KT4	Avinagillan	,Knapdale;	A; M	;5:	0	0	1	1	0:	0	0	0	0	0:	79:	––
KT5	Escart	,Kintyre;	A; A(5M),PYXM	;1:	0	0	2	0	0:	0	0	0	0	0:	79:	––
KT8	Dunskeig	,Kintyre;	B; PM,B	;5:	1	0	0	1	0:	1	0	0	0	0:	79:	79
KT9	Loch Ciaran	,Kintyre;	B; PM	;8:	–	–	–	–	–:	0	0	0	0	0:	79:	––
KT10	Ballochroy I	,Kintyre;	A; A(3M,T,YM,YT)	;1:	0	1	0	1	0:	0	0	0	0	0:	81:	73
KT12	Tarbert	,Gigha;	A; M	;5:	0	0	1	1	0:	0	0	0	0	0:	81:	––
KT14	Rhunahaorine	,Kintyre;	B; PM	;7:	–	–	–	–	–:	0	0	0	0	0:	81:	––
KT15	Beacharr I	,Kintyre;	A; M,T	;7:	–	–	–	–	–:	0	0	0	0	0:	79:	––
KT19	South Muasdale	,Kintyre;	A; M,PM	;4:	0	0	1	1	0:	0	0	0	0	0:	81:	79
KT21	Barlea	,Kintyre;	A; M	;5:	0	0	0	2	0:	0	0	0	0	0:	79:	––
KT23	Beinn an Tuirc	,Kintyre;	A; M	;5:	1	0	0	1	0:	0	0	0	0	0:	81:	81 79
KT24	Tighnamoile	,Kintyre;	B; PM	;8:	–	–	–	–	–:	0	0	0	0	0:	81:	––

Table 11.1 (continued)

Site	Name and location	St	Description	Type	O-S lines A B C L W	I-S lines A B C L W	Vis	Survey
KT25	Drumalea	,Kintyre; A;	FM	; 8:	- - - -:	0 0 0 0 0:	79:	--
KT27	Clochkeil	,Kintyre; A;	A(2M,FM)	; 2:	- 1 0 0 0:	1 0 0 0 0:	79:	79
KT28	Skeroblingarry	,Kintyre; A;	M	; 5:	1 0 0 1 0:	0 0 0 0 0:	79:	79
KT29	High Park	,Kintyre; A;	M	; 5:	1 0 0 1 0:	0 0 0 0 0:	79:	79
KT31	Craigs	,Kintyre; A;	M	; 5:	1 0 0 1 0:	1 0 1 1 0:	79:	79
KT32	Glencraigs S	,Kintyre; A;	M	; 5:	0 0 0 1 1:	2 0 0 0 0:	79:	79
KT35	Glenlussa Lodge	,Kintyre; A;	M	; 5:	0 0 2 0 0:	0 0 0 0 0:	81:	--
KT36	Campbeltown	,Kintyre; A;	M	; 5:	0 0 0 2 0:	0 1 0 0 0:	79:	79
KT37	Stewarton	,Kintyre; A;	FM	; 8:	- - - -:	3 0 0 0 0:	79:	79
KT39	Mingary	,Kintyre; A;	M,T	; 5:	2 0 0 0 0:	3 0 1 0 0:	79:	79
KT40	Lochorodale	,Kintyre; B;	PM	; 5:	0 0 0 2 0:	0 0 0 0 0:	79:	--
KT41	Knockstapple	,Kintyre; A;	M	; 5:	2 0 0 0 0:	0 0 0 0 0:	79:	79
KT42	Culinlongart	,Kintyre; A;	M	; 7:	- - - -:	0 0 0 0 0:	79:	--
KT44	Southend	,Kintyre; A;	M	; 5:	2 0 0 0 0:	0 0 0 0 0:	79:	79

The information presented about sites and indications in the two tables is similar to that given by Thom in his source list (Thom 1967: Table 8.1).   Our selection of data for analysis, however, has been undertaken entirely independently.   We have been at pains to present in preceding chapters both the archaeological details of the sites concerned and the various selection decisions which have resulted in this particular accumulation of source material.

- - - - - -

TABLE 11.2.   Source list of indications, with classification details and indicated azimuths and declinations.

Column_headings

1	Indication reference number
2	Site reference number and indication details
3	Azimuth limits within the IAR (inner values) and AAR (outer values)
4	Declination limits within the IAR (inner values) and AAR (outer values)
5	Classification details, whether on-site or inter-site (see Sections 3.3 and 3.5)
6	Distance of the horizon profile
7	Survey status (see Section 4.3): A Reliably surveyed B Less reliably surveyed C Calculated

Table 11.2

No.	Site and indication	Azimuth limits AAR	IAR	IAR	AAR	Declination limits AAR	IAR	IAR	AAR	Class O-S	I-S	Hor dist	St
1:	LH7 – LH8	; 250.6	251.6	251.8	252.8;	-10.1	-9.5	-9.3	-8.9:	B 1,		8.0 km	A
2:	LH8 ba (To SW)	; 217.4	219.4	223.6	225.6;	-23.8	-23.1	-21.6	-20.6:		3a,	14.5 km	A
3:	LH8 – LH7	; 70.6	71.6	71.8	72.8;	9.5	10.0	10.1	10.7:	B 1,		1.5 km	A
4:	LH10 ab (To SE)	; 145.0	146.0	147.0	148.0;	-27.1	-26.7	-26.5	-26.1:		4a,	10.0 km	B
5:	LH10 – LH16	; 193.8	194.8	195.0	196.0;	-30.9	-30.7	-30.5	-29.7:	A 2,		29.0 km	A
6:	LH10 – LH18	; 169.4	170.4	170.6	171.6;	-31.2	-31.1	-31.0	-30.6:	A 1,		27.0 km	A
7:	LH10 – LH19	; 175.0	176.0	176.2	177.2;	-32.1	-31.9	-31.9	-31.9:	A 1,		16.0 km	A
8:	LH10 – LH21	; 166.6	167.6	167.8	168.8;	-30.8	-30.8	-30.7	-30.6:	A 3,		27.0 km	A
9:	LH10 – LH22	; 150.4	151.4	151.6	152.6;	-28.2	-28.0	-27.9	-27.6:	A 3,		22.5 km	B
10:	LH10 – LH24	; 163.2	164.2	164.4	165.4;	-30.4	-30.3	-30.2	-30.0:	B 3,		22.0 km	A
11:	LH16 av W to N	; 5.6	7.6	10.8	12.8;	32.1	32.1	32.5	32.5:		1a,	3.5 km	A
12:	LH16 av E to N	; 7.8	9.8	12.0	14.0;	31.9	32.3	32.5	32.5:		1a,	3.5 km	A
13:	LH16 S row to N	; 358.4	359.4	0.0	1.0;	32.3	32.4	32.4	32.5:		1a,	3.0 km	A
14:	LH16 W row to W	; 264.0	266.0	268.6	270.6;	-2.8	-1.8	-0.6	0.3:		1a,	1.5 km	A
15:	LH16 W row to E	; 84.0	86.0	88.6	90.6;	-0.1	0.9	2.3	3.3:		1a,	6.0 km	C
16:	LH16 E row to W	; 257.8	258.8	259.6	260.6;	-5.5	-5.2	-5.0	-4.6:		1a,	1.5 km	C
17:	LH16 E row to E	; 77.8	78.8	79.6	80.6;	5.3	5.9	6.3	6.7:		1a,	9.0 km	A
18:	LH16 – LH10	; 13.8	14.8	15.0	16.0;	31.3	31.6	31.7	31.9:	A 2,		3.0 km	A
19:	LH16 – LH18	; 98.8	99.8	100.8	101.8;	-5.6	-5.1	-4.6	-4.1:	A 1,		10.5 km	A
20:	LH16 – LH19	; 107.8	109.6	111.4	113.2;	-12.1	-11.1	-10.2	-9.3:	A 1,		2.5 km	A
21:	LH16 – LH21	; 142.0	143.0	143.2	144.2;	-25.3	-24.9	-24.8	-24.6:	A 3,		6.5 km	A
22:	LH16 – LH22	; 123.0	124.0	124.6	125.6;	-18.1	-17.7	-17.4	-16.9:	A 1,		4.5 km	A
23:	LH16 – LH24	; 140.6	141.6	141.8	142.8;	-24.8	-24.5	-24.5	-24.0:	B 3,		6.5 km	A
24:	LH18 – LH10	; 349.2	350.2	350.4	351.4;	32.3	32.5	32.5	32.5:	A 2,		3.5 km	A
25:	LH18 – LH16	; 276.8	278.8	283.6	285.6;	3.6	4.5	7.0	8.0:	A 1,		12.0 km	A

Table 11.2 (continued)

No.	Site and indication	Azimuth limits AAR	IAR	IAR	AAR	Declination limits AAR	IAR	IAR	AAR	Class O-S	I-S	Hor dist	St
26:	LH18 - LH19 ;	245.2	247.2	251.0	253.0;	-11.9	-10.9	-9.1	-8.0:		A 1,	6.0 km	A
27:	LH18 - LH21 ;	163.2	164.2	164.4	165.4;	-30.1	-29.9	-29.9	-29.8:		A 1,	19.5 km	A
28:	LH18 - LH24 ;	156.8	157.8	158.2	159.2;	-29.3	-29.3	-29.2	-28.9:		B 2,	21.0 km	A
29:	LH19 - LH10 ;	355.0	356.0	356.2	357.2;	32.8	32.9	33.0	33.0:		A 3,	3.5 km	A
30:	LH19 - LH22 ;	127.8	128.8	129.2	130.2;	-20.0	-19.6	-19.4	-18.9:		A 1,	8.5 km	A
31:	LH19 - LH24 ;	151.0	152.0	152.2	153.2;	-27.8	-27.4	-27.4	-27.2:		B 2,	19.5 km	A
32:	LH21 - LH10 ;	346.6	347.6	347.8	348.8;	31.1	31.3	31.4	31.5:		A 3,	5.5 km	C
33:	LH21 - LH16 ;	321.2	322.6	324.0	325.4;	23.8	24.4	24.8	25.4:		A 1,	4.0 km	A
34:	LH21 - LH18 ;	343.0	344.0	344.4	345.4;	30.2	30.5	30.6	30.8:		A 2,	3.5 km	A
35:	LH21 - LH22 ;	87.6	88.6	89.0	90.0;	0.3	1.0	1.3	2.0:		A 2,	7.5 km	A
36:	LH21 - LH24 ;	133.8	134.8	135.4	136.4;	-21.7	-21.2	-21.0	-20.5:		B 2,	3.0 km	A
37:	LH22 ba (To NNE);	31.0	33.0	35.8	37.8;	25.3	25.8	26.5	27.3:	3a,		9.5 km	C
38:	LH22 ab (To SSW);	211.0	213.0	215.8	217.8;	-26.6	-25.8	-24.5	-24.0:	3a,		14.0 km	A
39:	LH22 - LH10 ;	330.4	331.4	331.6	332.6;	27.2	27.7	27.8	28.2:		A 3,	6.0 km	C
40:	LH22 - LH16 ;	303.2	304.2	304.8	305.8;	16.4	16.8	17.1	17.5:		A 1,	8.0 km	A
41:	LH22 - LH19 ;	307.8	308.8	309.2	310.2;	18.4	18.8	19.0	19.5:		A 3,	13.5 km	A
42:	LH22 - LH21 ;	267.0	268.0	268.4	269.4;	-1.0	-0.3	-0.2	0.1:		A 2,	17.0 km	A
43:	LH22 - LH24 ;	241.8	243.8	247.8	249.8;	-13.9	-13.1	-11.0	-10.0:		B 2,	25.0 km	A
44:	LH24 bcd(To NNW);	340.0	342.0	344.0	346.0;	29.5	29.9	30.5	30.9:	3c,		8.0 km	C
45:	LH24 dcb(To SSE);	160.0	162.0	164.0	166.0;	-29.6	-29.6	-29.2	-29.2:	3c,		16.5 km	A
46:	LH24 - LH10 ;	343.2	344.2	344.4	345.4;	30.3	30.5	30.6	30.8:		B 3,	8.0 km	C
47:	LH24 - LH16 ;	320.4	321.4	322.0	323.0;	23.3	23.7	24.0	24.4:		B 3,	4.5 km	A
48:	LH24 - LH18 ;	336.8	337.8	338.2	339.2;	28.8	29.0	29.2	29.3:		B 2,	7.5 km	A
49:	LH24 - LH19 ;	331.0	332.0	332.2	333.2;	26.9	27.3	27.4	27.7:		B 2,	14.0 km	A
50:	LH24 - LH21 ;	312.0	313.4	314.8	316.2;	20.3	20.8	21.4	21.8:		B 2,	8.0 km	A

Table 11.2 (continued)

No.	Site and indication	Azimuth limits				Declination limits				Class		Hor	St
		AAR	IAR	IAR	AAR	AAR	IAR	IAR	AAR	O-S	I-S	dist	
51:	LH24 - LH22 ;	64.2	65.2	65.6	66.6;	12.3	12.8	13.0	13.4:		B 2,	14.0 km	A
52:	LH29 To NW ;	303.6	305.4	307.2	309.0;	16.5	17.4	18.3	19.0:	6,		12.5 km	A
53:	LH36 To WNW ;	282.4	284.4	289.0	291.0;	5.8	6.9	9.6	10.9:	5a,		5.0 km	A
54:	LH36 - LH37 ;	206.6	207.6	207.8	208.8;	-27.4	-27.3	-27.2	-26.8:		A 3,	8.0 km	A
55:	LH37 ba (To WNW);	300.0	302.0	305.0	307.0;	14.8	15.8	17.0	18.1:	3b,		-Sea-	C
56:	LH37 - LH36 ;	26.6	27.6	27.8	28.8;	29.3	29.3	29.4	29.5:		A 3,	17.5 km	A
57:	UI6 To WNW ;	292.0	293.0	294.0	295.0;	10.8	11.3	11.8	12.3:	5a,		-Sea-	A
58:	UI6 To ESE ;	112.0	113.0	114.0	115.0;	-13.3	-12.8	-12.3	-11.8:	5a,		63.5 km	A
59:	UI6 - UI9 ;	211.0	212.0	212.4	213.4;	-27.2	-27.0	-26.8	-26.4:		A 3,	13.5 km	A
60:	UI9 ba (To SW) ;	227.0	227.0	232.4	234.4;	-21.1	-20.6	-18.9	-18.0:	3a,		8.0 km	A
61:	UI9 - UI6 ;	31.0	32.0	32.4	33.4;	26.9	27.4	27.6	27.9:		A 3,	6.0 km	A
62:	UI15 - UI19 ;	110.8	111.8	112.8	113.8;	-13.1	-12.6	-12.2	-11.9:		A 2,	3.0 km	C
63:	UI19 abc(To WNW);	287.0	288.8	290.6	292.4;	10.7	11.7	12.5	12.9:	1a,		2.5 km	A
64:	UI19 - UI15 ;	291.0	292.0	292.6	293.6;	12.6	12.9	13.0	13.3:		A 2,	2.5 km	C
65:	UI22 - UI26 ;	114.2	115.2	115.6	116.6;	-14.3	-13.8	-13.5	-13.2:		A 3,	83	km A
66:	UI22 - UI31 ;	152.4	153.4	153.8	154.8;	-30.0	-29.6	-29.3	-28.8:		A 3,	19.5 km	A
67:	UI23 ba (To E) ;	92.0	94.0	96.0	98.0;	-4.1	-2.8	-1.2	0.3:	3a,		4.0 km	A
68:	UI23 - UI26 ;	119.4	120.4	120.8	121.8;	-16.3	-16.1	-15.9	-15.5:		A 1,	80	km A
69:	UI23 - UI28 ;	132.6	133.6	133.8	134.8;	-22.7	-22.3	-22.2	-21.5:		A 1,	4.5 km	A
70:	UI23 - UI31 ;	174.2	175.2	175.4	176.4;	-33.0	-33.0	-32.9	-32.7:		A 3,	55.0 km	A
71:	UI26 - UI22 ;	294.2	295.2	295.6	296.6;	12.2	12.9	13.1	13.7:		A 1,	4.0 km	A
72:	UI26 - UI23 ;	299.4	300.4	300.8	301.8;	15.5	16.0	16.2	16.7:		A 2,	4.5 km	A
73:	UI26 - UI28 ;	142.8	143.8	144.2	145.2;	-26.6	-26.1	-25.9	-25.3:		A 1,	2.5 km	A
74:	UI26 - UI31 ;	203.8	204.8	205.2	206.2;	-30.6	-30.4	-30.3	-30.0:		A 3,	-Sea-	A
75:	UI28 To SSE ;	153.2	154.8	156.4	158.0;	-30.6	-30.0	-29.8	-29.4:	5a,		22.0 km	A

Table 11.2 (continued)

No.	Site and indication	Azimuth limits AAR	IAR	IAR	AAR	Declination limits AAR	IAR	IAR	AAR	Class O-S	I-S	Hor dist	St
76:	UI28 – UI23 ;	312.6	313.6	313.8	314.8;	21.0	21.5	21.6	22.0:	A	3,	5.0 km	A
77:	UI28 – UI26 ;	322.8	323.8	324.2	325.2;	25.1	25.4	25.6	25.9:	A	2,	4.5 km	A
78:	UI28 – UI33 ;	107.8	108.8	109.2	110.2;	-11.1	-10.5	-10.2	-9.9:	A	3,	12.0 km	A
79:	UI28 – UI35 ;	149.0	150.0	150.2	151.2;	-28.9	-28.6	-28.5	-28.3:	B	2,	14.5 km	C
80:	UI28 – UI37 ;	137.4	138.4	138.8	139.8;	-25.1	-24.5	-24.3	-24.0:	A	3,	6.5 km	C
81:	UI31 To ESE ;	106.0	107.4	108.8	110.2;	-9.9	-9.3	-9.1	-8.6:	5a,		14.5 km	A
82:	UI31 – UI22 ;	332.4	333.4	333.8	334.8;	29.1	29.4	29.6	29.9:	A	3,	6.0 km	C
83:	UI31 – UI23 ;	354.2	355.2	355.4	356.4;	33.0	33.1	33.1	33.1:	A	3,	4.5 km	A
84:	UI31 – UI26 ;	23.8	24.8	25.2	26.2;	29.8	29.9	30.0	30.2:	A	3,	5.5 km	A
85:	UI31 – UI35 ;	106.6	107.6	108.2	109.2;	-9.3	-9.2	-9.1	-8.9:	B	3,	14.0 km	C
86:	UI33 – UI28 ;	287.8	288.8	289.2	290.2;	9.4	10.1	10.4	11.2:	A	1,	4.5 km	A
87:	UI33 – UI37 ;	209.0	210.0	211.0	212.0;	-28.7	-28.4	-28.0	-27.7:	A	2,	3.5 km	A
88:	UI35 – UI28 ;	329.0	330.0	330.2	331.2;	27.8	28.2	28.3	28.8:	B	1,	2.5 km	A
89:	UI35 – UI31 ;	286.6	287.6	288.2	289.2;	8.1	8.7	9.0	9.5:	B	3,	8.0 km	A
90:	UI35 – UI37 ;	124.0	125.0	126.0	127.0;	-19.3	-18.7	-18.2	-17.7:	B	2,	2.5 km	A
91:	UI35 – UI40 ;	148.2	149.2	149.6	150.6;	-28.6	-28.3	-28.1	-27.8:	B	3,	5.0 km	C
92:	UI37 – UI28 ;	317.4	318.4	318.8	319.8;	23.3	23.9	24.1	24.7:	A	1,	5.0 km	A
93:	UI37 – UI33 ;	29.0	30.0	31.0	32.0;	27.9	28.3	28.7	29.0:	A	2,	3.0 km	A
94:	UI37 – UI35 ;	304.0	305.0	306.0	307.0;	17.4	17.8	18.3	18.7:	B	2,	2.5 km	C
95:	UI40 – UI35 ;	328.2	329.2	329.6	330.6;	27.0	27.4	27.5	28.0:	B	3,	7.5 km	A
96:	UI46 To NW ;	302.6	303.6	304.4	305.4;	16.1	16.6	17.0	17.4:	6 ,		84 km	A
97:	UI46 To SE ;	122.6	123.6	124.4	125.4;	-18.8	-18.2	-18.0	-17.5:	6 ,		120 km	A
98:	UI48 – UI49 ;	107.4	108.4	108.6	109.6;	-8.3	-7.5	-7.4	-6.4:	A	3,	9.0 km	A
99:	UI48 – UI50 ;	181.8	182.8	183.2	184.2;	-33.4	-33.3	-33.3	-33.3:	A	3,	-Sea-	C
100:	UI49 To NE ;	50.2	51.2	52.0	53.0;	22.1	22.4	22.4	22.6:	5a,		5.5 km	A

Table 11.2 (continued)

No.	Site and indication	Azimuth limits AAR	IAR	IAR	AAR	Declination limits AAR	IAR	IAR	AAR	Class O-S	I-S	Hor dist	St
101:	UI49 To SW ;	230.2	231.2	232.0	233.0;	-21.0	-20.6	-20.2	-19.7:	5a,		-Sea-	C
102:	UI49 - UI48 ;	287.4	288.4	288.6	289.6;	8.6	9.1	9.2	9.7:		A 1,	-Sea-	C
103:	UI49 - UI50 ;	225.0	226.0	226.4	227.4;	-23.2	-22.8	-22.6	-22.2:		A 3,	-Sea-	C
104:	UI50 - UI48 ;	1.8	2.8	3.2	4.2;	32.2	32.3	32.3	32.3:		A 1,	5.0 km	C
105:	UI50 - UI49 ;	45.0	46.0	46.4	47.4;	21.8	22.1	22.2	22.6:		A 3,	5.5 km	C
106:	UI57 ab (To NE) ;	31.4	33.4	37.6	39.6;	29.8	30.0	30.9	31.4:	3b,		1.5 km	A
107:	UI57 ba (To SW) ;	211.4	213.4	217.6	219.6;	-21.7	-21.4	-21.0	-20.8:	3b,		3.0 km	A
108:	UI59 ab (To WNW);	296.6	298.6	300.6	302.6;	23.3	23.8	24.7	25.9:	4a,		1.0 km	A
109:	UI59 ba (To ESE);	116.6	118.6	120.6	122.6;	-17.6	-16.8	-15.8	-14.8:	4a,		110 km	A
110:	NA1 ab (To NNW);	326.4	328.0	329.6	331.2;	27.2	28.1	28.4	29.1:	4a,		29.0 km	B
111:	NA1 ba (To SSE);	146.4	148.0	149.6	151.2;	-26.4	-25.8	-25.5	-25.4:	4a,		2.5 km	A
112:	NA3 To NNW ;	326.0	328.0	331.0	333.0;	33.1	33.3	34.9	35.5:	5a,		1.0 km	A
113:	CT1 To S ;	176.0	178.0	181.4	183.4;	-34.1	-34.1	-34.1	-34.0:	5a,		-Sea-	C
114:	CT2 ab (To NNE);	16.6	17.8	19.0	20.2;	30.7	31.2	31.5	31.8:	3a,		3.0 km	A
115:	CT2 ba (To SSW);	196.6	197.8	199.0	200.2;	-32.6	-32.5	-32.1	-31.9:	3a,		4.0 km	A
116:	CT2 - CT3 ;	203.6	204.6	205.0	206.0;	-31.0	-30.7	-30.6	-30.4:		A 2,	-Sea-	A
117:	CT3 - CT2 ;	23.6	24.6	25.0	26.0;	29.7	29.8	29.9	30.2:		A 1,	5.5 km	A
118:	CT7 - CT8 ;	202.8	204.0	205.2	206.4;	-30.3	-30.0	-29.7	-29.6:		A 2,	5.0 km	B
119:	CT8 - CT7 ;	22.8	24.0	25.2	26.4;	29.3	29.7	29.9	30.3:		A 2,	2.5 km	C
120:	CT9 To SSW ;	193.4	195.0	196.6	198.2;	-31.1	-31.1	-31.0	-30.6:	5a,		2.5 km	A
121:	ML1 - ML9 ;	174.0	175.0	175.6	176.6;	-32.3	-32.2	-32.1	-32.0:		A 3,	12.0 km	C
122:	ML2 To SSE ;	164.0	166.0	170.0	172.0;	-31.5	-31.5	-30.8	-30.5:	2c,		8.0 km	A
123:	ML2 - ML7 ;	239.0	240.0	241.0	242.0;	-15.9	-15.4	-14.9	-14.5:		A 3,	6.0 km	C
124:	ML4 abc (To N) ;	2.6	4.4	6.2	8.0;	32.8	33.2	34.0	34.2:	2a,		13.5 km	C
125:	ML4 cba (To S) ;	182.6	184.4	186.2	188.0;	-28.7	-28.6	-28.4	-28.2:	2a,		1.5 km	A

Table 11.2 (continued)

No.	Site and indication	Azimuth limits				Declination limits				Class		Hor dist	St
		AAR	IAR	IAR	AAR	AAR	IAR	IAR	AAR	O-S	I-S		
126:	ML7 To SE ;	131.6	132.6	133.4	134.4;	-20.9	-20.5	-20.2	-19.6:	5a,		5.5 km	A
127:	ML7 − ML2 ;	59.0	60.0	61.0	62.0;	15.5	15.8	16.3	16.8:		A 3,	9.5 km	A
128:	ML9 To NNW ;	339.0	341.0	343.0	345.0;	30.2	30.9	31.6	31.9:	1a,		47.0 km	C
129:	ML9 − ML1 ;	354.0	355.0	355.6	356.6;	31.7	32.0	32.3	32.3:		A 3,	10.5 km	C
130:	ML10 To NNW ;	326.6	328.6	331.0	333.0;	26.7	27.5	28.7	29.8:	2a,		3.0 km	B
131:	ML11 abc(To SSE);	155.0	156.4	157.8	159.2;	-29.3	-29.0	-28.9	-28.5:	1a,		8.0 km	A
132:	ML12 abc(To NNE);	24.0	26.0	29.2	31.2;	29.8	30.4	31.3	31.8:	2c,		8.0 km	A
133:	ML12 cba(To SSW);	204.0	206.0	209.2	211.2;	-23.5	-23.2	-22.2	-21.6:	2c,		2.0 km	A
134:	ML15 − ML16 ;	161.4	163.4	167.2	169.2;	-27.0	-27.0	-27.0	-26.8:		A 2,	5.0 km	C
135:	ML16 ba (To NW) ;	306.6	307.6	308.6	309.6;	21.8	22.3	23.0	23.7:	3a,		4.0 km	B
136:	ML16 ab (To SE) ;	126.6	127.6	128.6	129.6;	-18.6	-18.3	-17.7	-17.1:	3a,		10.5 km	B
137:	ML16 − ML15 ;	341.4	343.4	347.2	349.2;	34.9	35.3	35.9	36.2:		A 2,	3.0 km	C
138:	ML18 ba (To ENE);	65.6	66.6	67.6	68.6;	16.9	17.5	18.0	18.8:	3a,		9.0 km	A
139:	ML25 abc (To NW);	315.2	316.4	317.6	318.8;	35.8	36.8	37.3	37.4:	3c,		3.5 km	A
140:	ML25 cba (To SE);	135.2	136.4	137.6	138.8;	-18.9	-18.5	-17.9	-17.4:	3c,		4.0 km	A
141:	ML25 − ML27 ;	190.6	191.6	192.0	193.0;	-30.1	-30.0	-29.9	-29.8:		B 2,	4.5 km	A
142:	ML27 − ML25 ;	10.6	11.6	12.0	13.0;	37.7	38.0	38.1	38.3:		B 2,	3.0 km	C
143:	ML30 To NNW ;	326.2	328.2	330.4	332.4;	27.0	27.5	28.5	28.9:	6,		2.5 km	A
144:	ML31 To NE ;	48.4	49.4	50.2	51.2;	22.2	22.6	23.0	23.4:	5a,		6.5 km	A
145:	ML31 To SW ;	228.4	229.4	230.2	231.2;	-22.0	-21.3	-21.0	-20.7:	5a,		4.0 km	A
146:	ML33 ba (To WNW);	280.0	281.6	283.2	284.8;	7.9	8.8	9.5	10.8:	3b,		1.0 km	A
147:	LN7 To N ;	358.0	0.0	4.0	6.0;	33.7	34.0	34.5	34.8:	5a,		24.5 km	C
148:	LN18 ab (To W);	268.2	270.2	273.8	275.8;	1.2	1.7	3.1	4.0:	4a,		1.0 km	B
149:	LN22 abc(To NNW);	324.6	326.6	329.0	331.0;	31.7	32.7	34.8	35.9:	1a,		1.0 km	A
150:	LN22 cba(To SSE);	144.6	146.6	149.0	151.0;	-21.8	-21.5	-21.2	-20.6:	1a,		1.0 km	B

Table 11.2 (continued)

No.	Site and indication	Azimuth limits				Declination limits				Class		Hor dist	St
		AAR	IAR	IAR	AAR	AAR	IAR	IAR	AAR	O-S	I-S		
151:	AR2 To N	354.0	356.0	358.0	0.0;	40.7	40.9	41.0	41.6:	5a,		2.5 km	C
152:	AR2 – AR3	212.6	213.6	214.4	215.4;	−28.7	−28.2	−27.7	−27.3:		A 2,	65.5 km	C
153:	AR3 ab (To N)	5.2	6.4	7.6	8.8;	38.4	38.5	38.6	38.7:	1b,		3.5 km	A
154:	AR3 ba (To S)	185.2	186.4	187.6	188.8;	−30.7	−30.7	−30.5	−30.5:	1b,		4.0 km	A
155:	AR3 – AR2	32.6	33.6	34.4	35.4;	29.1	29.7	30.1	30.6:		A 2,	5.0 km	C
156:	AR6 abc (To N)	355.0	356.4	357.8	359.2;	34.9	35.0	35.3	35.3:	2a,		2.0 km	A
157:	AR7 – AR8	213.6	214.6	215.0	216.0;	−25.8	−25.4	−25.2	−24.8:		A 2,	3.0 km	C
158:	AR8 – AR7	33.6	34.6	35.0	36.0;	28.5	29.0	29.2	29.5:		A 2,	3.0 km	C
159:	AR9 To ENE	67.8	69.4	71.0	72.6;	11.6	12.4	13.9	14.6:	5a,		9.0 km	B
160:	AR9 – AR10	202.4	203.4	203.8	204.8;	−24.1	−24.0	−24.0	−23.9:		A 2,	1.5 km	C
161:	AR10 – AR9	22.4	23.4	23.8	24.8;	32.2	32.3	32.4	32.5:		A 2,	1.0 km	C
162:	AR13 S2-S3-S6	328.0	329.0	329.8	330.8;	33.5	33.8	34.2	34.3:	1a,		2.5 km	A
163:	AR13 S5-S1-S2	19.2	20.2	21.2	22.2;	32.8	33.0	33.2	33.2:	1a,		6.5 km	C
164:	AR13 S2-S1-S5	199.2	200.2	201.2	202.2;	−31.1	−30.9	−30.7	−30.6:	1a,		18.5 km	C
165:	AR13 S4-S1-S3	25.0	26.0	26.8	27.8;	32.3	32.4	32.5	32.5:	1a,		2.5 km	C
166:	AR13 S3-S1-S4	205.0	206.0	206.8	207.8;	−29.9	−29.5	−29.3	−29.3:	1a,		6.5 km	B
167:	AR13 S5-S4	321.2	322.2	322.8	323.8;	29.8	30.3	30.5	31.0:	1b,		2.0 km	A
168:	AR15 abcd(To NW)	318.8	320.8	324.0	326.0;	27.3	28.3	29.3	29.9:	1a,		4.0 km	B
169:	AR15 dcba(To SE)	138.8	140.8	144.0	146.0;	−26.5	−25.8	−23.7	−22.7:	1a,		3.0 km	B
170:	AR15 ef (To NNW)	331.4	333.4	335.4	337.4;	32.2	32.7	33.2	33.6:	1b,		4.0 km	B
171:	AR15 fe (To SSE)	151.4	153.4	155.4	157.4;	−30.8	−30.2	−29.6	−29.0:	1b,		5.5 km	C
172:	AR15 – AR18	223.6	224.6	225.0	226.0;	−23.3	−22.8	−22.6	−22.0:		B 3,	6.0 km	C
173:	AR16 To NW	314.8	316.8	319.6	321.6;	26.3	27.2	28.8	29.5:	5a,		2.5 km	B
174:	AR16 To SE	134.8	136.8	139.6	141.6;	−25.5	−24.7	−23.5	−22.4:	5a,		10.5 km	B
175:	AR16 – AR17	257.8	258.8	259.4	260.4;	−6.5	−5.9	−5.4	−4.8:		A 2,	18.0 km	C

Table 11.2 (continued)

No.	Site and indication	Azimuth Limits				Declination limits				Class		Hor dist	St
		AAR	IAR	IAR	AAR	AAR	IAR	IAR	AAR	O-S	I-S		
176:	AR17 – AR16 ;	77.8	78.8	79.4	80.4;	5.9	6.5	6.9	7.6:		A 2,	4.0 km	C
177:	AR17 – AR18 ;	157.6	158.6	159.6	160.6;	-29.8	-29.7	-29.5	-29.5:		B 2,	5.0 km	C
178:	AR18 – AR15 ;	43.6	44.6	45.0	46.0:	24.8	25.1	25.3	25.9:		B 3,	4.5 km	A
179:	AR18 – AR17 ;	337.6	338.6	339.6	340.6:	32.8	33.1	33.5	33.7:		B 2,	3.5 km	C
180:	AR27 ab (To NNW);	325.6	327.4	329.2	331.0;	28.7	29.3	29.9	30.6:	4a,		7.0 km	B
181:	AR28 abc(To NNW);	342.8	344.2	345.6	347.0;	34.9	35.3	35.6	35.9:	2a,		1.5 km	B
182:	AR28 cba(To SSE);	162.8	164.2	165.6	167.0;	-31.5	-31.0	-30.6	-30.1:	2a,		2.0 km	B
183:	AR28 – AR29 ;	158.4	159.4	160.0	161.0;	-29.8	-29.4	-29.2	-28.8:		A 2,	2.0 km	B
184:	AR28 – AR30 ;	163.0	164.0	164.6	165.6:	-31.0	-30.8	-30.5	-30.2:		A 2,	2.0 km	B
185:	AR29 ab (To NW) ;	312.0	314.0	318.4	320.4;	23.3	24.2	26.3	26.6:	1b,		1.0 km	B
186:	AR29 ba (To SE) ;	132.0	134.0	138.4	140.4;	-21.9	-21.5	-19.5	-18.4:	1b,		2.0 km	B
187:	AR29 – AR28 ;	338.4	339.4	340.4	341.4;	32.5	33.1	33.3	33.3:		A 2,	2.0 km	C
188:	AR30 – AR28 ;	343.0	344.0	344.6	345.6;	33.7	34.0	34.1	34.5:		A 2,	5.0 km	C
189:	AR32 To WNW ;	285.0	287.0	289.0	291.0;	11.9	13.1	14.3	15.4:	5a,		2.0 km	C
190:	AR32 To ESE ;	105.0	107.0	109.0	111.0;	-9.2	-8.1	-6.8	-5.6:	5a,		3.0 km	C
191:	AR33 To WNW ;	297.0	299.0	302.0	304.0;	17.2	18.2	19.3	20.3:	5a,		3.5 km	C
192:	AR33 To ESE ;	117.0	119.0	122.0	124.0;	-16.5	-15.6	-14.2	-13.2:	5a,		1.0 km	C
193:	JU1 ba (To WNW);	284.2	285.2	285.6	286.6;	9.3	10.1	10.5	11.4:	4b,		5.0 km	A
194:	JU2 – JU3 ;	97.6	98.6	99.0	100.0;	-3.8	-3.3	-2.9	-2.4:		B 2,	1.0 km	A
195:	JU3 – JU2 ;	277.6	278.6	279.0	280.0;	7.6	8.6	8.9	9.7:		B 2,	7.5 km	C
196:	JU3 – JU4 ;	252.4	253.4	254.0	255.0;	-6.3	-6.0	-5.8	-5.3:		A 2,	6.0 km	B
197:	JU3 – JU5 ;	254.8	255.8	256.2	257.2;	-5.5	-5.1	-4.8	-4.5:		B 2,	6.0 km	B
198:	JU4 ba (To ENE);	72.0	73.0	73.2	74.2;	10.2	10.6	10.8	11.3:	3a,		1.0 km	B
199:	JU4 ab (To WSW);	252.0	253.0	253.2	254.2;	-5.4	-5.1	-5.0	-4.7:	3a,		5.0 km	A
200:	JU4 – JU3 ;	72.4	73.4	74.0	75.0;	10.2	10.2	10.5	11.1:		A 1,	1.0 km	B

Table 11.2 (continued)

No.	Site and indication	Azimuth limits				Declination limits				Class		Hor dist	St
		AAR	IAR	IAR	AAR	AAR	IAR	IAR	AAR	O-S	I-S		
201:	JU4 - JU5	256.0	257.0	257.4	258.4;	-3.9	-3.3	-3.1	-2.9:		B 2,	5.0 km	A
202:	JU5 - JU3	74.8	75.8	76.2	77.2;	8.0	8.2	8.3	8.7:		B 2,	2.5 km	B
203:	JU5 - JU4	76.0	77.0	77.4	78.4;	7.4	7.9	8.1	8.3:		B 2,	2.5 km	B
204:	JU7 To NNE	16.0	18.0	22.0	24.0;	30.7	31.6	33.3	34.2:	2a,		16.5 km	C
205:	JU7 To SSW	196.0	198.0	202.0	204.0;	-33.5	-33.1	-32.2	-31.5:	2a,		-Sea-	C
206:	JU9 To NNW	333.0	334.0	334.8	335.8;	33.7	34.0	34.5	35.0:	5a,		1.5 km	A
207:	JU9 To SSE	153.0	154.0	154.8	155.8;	-31.3	-31.1	-30.8	-30.7:	5a,		51.0 km	A
208:	IS3 To WSW	255.8	256.8	257.4	258.4;	-7.5	-7.0	-6.6	-6.0:	5a,		1.5 km	A
209:	IS4 To WNW	295.4	296.4	297.2	298.2;	17.5	18.2	18.6	19.0:	5a,		4.0 km	A
210:	IS5 - IS12	188.2	189.2	189.4	190.4;	-33.0	-32.9	-32.9	-32.7:		A 3,	11.5 km	C
211:	IS6 - IS7	97.8	98.8	99.0	100.0;	-6.3	-5.7	-5.6	-4.9:		A 2,	12.5 km	A
212:	IS6 - IS11	117.4	118.4	118.6	119.6;	-16.5	-15.8	-15.7	-15.0:		A 3,	8.5 km	A
213:	IS7 - IS6	277.8	278.8	279.0	280.0;	6.3	6.8	6.9	7.3:		A 1,	1.5 km	A
214:	IS7 - IS11	123.6	124.6	124.8	125.8;	-19.1	-18.7	-18.6	-17.8:		A 3,	9.0 km	A
215:	IS7 - IS12	126.6	127.6	128.0	129.0;	-20.2	-19.8	-19.6	-19.3:		A 3,	11.5 km	A
216:	IS11 ab (To ENE)	56.4	58.4	61.8	63.8;	16.0	16.6	18.6	19.9:	3a,		11.5 km	A
217:	IS11 - IS6	297.4	298.4	298.6	299.6;	15.0	15.5	15.6	16.1:		A 3,	6.0 km	C
218:	IS11 - IS7	303.6	304.6	304.8	305.8;	18.2	18.4	18.5	19.0:		A 3,	5.0 km	A
219:	IS12 - IS5	8.2	9.2	9.4	10.4;	32.7	32.7	32.8	33.0:		A 3,	-Sea-	C
220:	IS12 - IS7	306.6	307.6	308.0	309.0;	19.2	19.7	19.9	20.4:		A 3,	6.0 km	C
221:	IS19 To SSE	167.2	168.4	169.6	170.8;	-33.8	-33.7	-33.6	-33.5:	5a,		17.5 km	A
222:	IS19 - IS23	239.6	240.6	241.0	242.0;	-16.0	-15.5	-15.3	-14.7:		A 3,	6.5 km	A
223:	IS23 To E	90.8	92.4	94.0	95.6;	-2.5	-1.6	-0.8	-0.3:	5a,		17.5 km	A
224:	IS23 - IS19	59.6	60.6	61.0	62.0;	15.5	16.2	16.3	17.3:		A 3,	29.5 km	A
225:	IS28 - IS31	197.0	198.0	198.4	199.4;	-33.4	-33.2	-33.1	-32.9:		B 2,	>55 km	C

Table 11.2 (continued)

No.	Site and indication	Azimuth limits AAR	IAR	IAR	AAR	Declination limits AAR	IAR	IAR	AAR	Class O-S	I-S	Hor dist	St
226:	IS31 – IS28	; 16.4	17.6	18.8	20.0;	32.5	32.8	33.0	33.2:		B 1,	1.5 km	A
227:	IS35 – IS36	; 167.2	168.2	168.6	169.6;	-33.5	-33.4	-33.3	-33.2:		B 2,	3.5 km	A
228:	IS36 – IS35	; 347.2	348.2	348.6	349.6;	35.5	35.5	35.6	35.7:		B 2,	3.0 km	A
229:	IS38 ab (To ENE)	; 56.8	58.0	59.2	60.4;	16.0	16.6	17.3	17.8:	4b,		38.5 km	C
230:	IS38 ba (To WSW)	; 236.8	238.0	239.2	240.4;	-17.5	-16.7	-16.0	-15.4:	4b,		3.0 km	C
231:	IS39 To E	; 80.4	82.4	86.6	88.6;	0.7	1.8	4.3	5.2:	3b,		36.0 km	A
232:	IS39 – IS41	; 251.4	252.4	253.0	254.0;	-9.8	-9.4	-9.1	-8.7:		A 2,	6.0 km	A
233:	IS41 To S	; 167.0	168.4	169.8	171.2;	-34.6	-34.5	-34.3	-34.0:	2a,		>70 km	C
234:	KT2 ba (To S)	; 176.4	177.4	177.8	178.8;	-32.9	-32.9	-32.9	-32.9:	3a,		1.5 km	C
235:	KT2 ac (To WNW)	; 283.0	284.0	284.6	285.6;	9.9	10.6	10.9	11.5:	3a,		2.5 km	A
236:	KT2 ca (To ESE)	; 103.0	104.0	104.6	105.6;	-8.3	-7.5	-7.1	-6.5:	3a,		8.0 km	B
237:	KT2 bc (To WNW)	; 280.4	281.8	283.2	284.6;	8.1	9.0	10.0	10.9:	3a,		2.5 km	A
238:	KT2 cb (To ESE)	; 100.4	101.8	103.2	104.6;	-7.5	-6.6	-5.7	-4.7:	3a,		8.0 km	C
239:	KT3 To NW	; 315.6	316.6	317.0	318.0;	26.0	26.5	26.6	27.0:	5a,		8.0 km	A
240:	KT3 To SE	; 135.6	136.6	137.0	138.0;	-23.0	-22.5	-22.3	-21.8:	5a,		3.0 km	A
241:	KT3 – KT8	; 166.4	167.4	167.6	168.6;	-31.9	-31.8	-31.8	-31.8:		B 1,	3.0 km	A
242:	KT4 To S	; 169.2	170.4	171.6	172.8;	-31.5	-31.3	-30.9	-30.5:	5a,		4.5 km	C
243:	KT5 To NNE	; 26.2	27.4	28.6	29.8;	30.6	31.4	32.0	32.4:	1a,		3.0 km	C
244:	KT5 To SSW	; 206.2	207.4	208.6	209.8;	-29.9	-29.5	-29.3	-29.1:	1a,		9.5 km	C
245:	KT8 ba (To SE)	; 127.4	128.4	129.2	130.2;	-20.5	-19.9	-19.3	-18.9:	5b,		19.0 km	A
246:	KT8 – KT3	; 346.4	347.4	347.6	348.6;	33.7	33.7	33.7	33.9:		B 2,	9.0 km	A
247:	KT10 cba (To SW)	; 220.0	222.0	224.0	226.0;	-26.3	-25.5	-24.5	-23.7:	1a,		12.0 km	B
248:	KT12 To N	; 3.2	4.8	6.4	8.0;	34.3	34.4	34.4	34.5:	5a,		1.3 km	C
249:	KT19 ab (To WSW)	; 249.0	250.0	250.6	251.6;	-12.4	-11.8	-11.3	-10.7:	4b,		-Sea-	C
250:	KT23 To SW	; 219.6	221.6	225.4	227.4;	-26.1	-25.3	-23.5	-22.7:	5a,		5.0 km	A

Table 11.2 (continued)

No.	Site and indication	Azimuth limits AAR	IAR	IAR	AAR	Declination limits AAR	IAR	IAR	AAR	Class O-S	I-S	Hor dist	St
251:	KT27 abc (To NE);	45.4	47.4	49.4	51.4;	23.0	24.1	25.0	25.9:	2a,		3.0 km	A
252:	KT27 cba (To SW);	225.4	227.4	229.4	231.4;	-24.1	-22.9	-22.2	-21.3:	2a,		>45 km	B
253:	KT27 - KT39 ;	180.8	181.8	182.0	183.0;	-33.4	-33.3	-33.3	-33.2:		A 3,	7.0 km	A
254:	KT28 To ENE ;	65.0	67.0	72.0	74.0;	10.4	11.7	15.0	16.4:	5a,		4.5 km	A
255:	KT29 To ENE ;	54.8	56.8	59.6	61.6;	17.3	18.2	19.7	20.9:	5a,		5.5 km	A
256:	KT31 To WNW ;	294.8	296.4	298.0	299.6;	14.0	14.9	15.7	16.2:	5a,		2.5 km	A
257:	KT31 - KT37 ;	162.2	163.2	163.4	164.4;	-32.2	-31.9	-31.8	-31.5:		A 3,	5.5 km	A
258:	KT31 - KT39 ;	217.0	218.0	218.2	219.2;	-25.2	-25.1	-25.1	-24.5:		A 3,	9.0 km	C
259:	KT32 - KT31 ;	282.8	283.8	284.2	285.2;	7.0	7.4	7.6	8.1:		A 2,	2.5 km	A
260:	KT32 - KT39 ;	219.8	220.8	221.0	222.0;	-24.3	-24.0	-23.8	-23.4:		A 3,	11.5 km	A
261:	KT35 To WNW ;	287.0	288.4	289.8	291.2;	10.9	11.7	12.5	13.4:	5a,		3.0 km	C
262:	KT35 To ESE ;	107.0	108.4	109.8	111.2;	-12.2	-11.4	-10.7	-10.0:	5a,		63.0 km	C
263:	KT36 - KT37 ;	235.6	236.6	236.8	237.8;	-17.8	-17.1	-17.0	-16.3:		A 2,	10.0 km	B
264:	KT37 - KT31 ;	342.2	343.2	343.4	344.4;	33.8	34.0	34.0	34.3:		A 3,	5.5 km	A
265:	KT37 - KT36 ;	55.6	56.6	56.8	57.8;	18.3	19.2	19.4	20.1:		A 2,	3.5 km	A
266:	KT37 - KT39 ;	260.6	261.6	261.8	262.8;	-4.8	-4.3	-4.1	-3.5:		A 3,	5.5 km	A
267:	KT39 To NW ;	311.4	313.4	315.6	317.6;	21.3	22.4	23.5	24.4:	5a,		40.0 km	A
268:	KT39 To SE ;	131.4	133.4	135.6	137.6;	-23.4	-22.9	-22.2	-21.6:	5a,		2.5 km	A
269:	KT39 - KT27 ;	0.8	1.8	2.0	3.0;	33.8	34.0	34.0	34.1:		A 3,	12.5 km	A
270:	KT39 - KT31 ;	37.0	38.0	38.2	39.2;	26.8	27.2	27.3	27.7:		A 3,	13.0 km	C
271:	KT39 - KT32 ;	39.8	40.8	41.0	42.0;	25.4	25.8	25.9	26.5:		A 3,	13.5 km	A
272:	KT39 - KT37 ;	80.6	81.6	81.8	82.8;	3.7	4.3	4.4	5.0:		A 3,	33.0 km	A
273:	KT41 To NW ;	318.0	320.0	324.0	326.0;	25.8	26.4	27.5	28.0:	5a,		6.0 km	A
274:	KT41 To SE ;	138.0	140.0	144.0	146.0;	-27.7	-26.8	-24.8	-23.9:	5a,		1.5 km	A
275:	KT44 To N ;	7.0	8.4	9.8	11.2;	35.2	35.2	35.5	35.7:	5a,		2.5 km	A
276:	KT44 To S ;	187.0	188.4	189.8	191.2;	-35.1	-34.9	-34.7	-34.5:	5a,		>70 km	A

12   ANALYSIS AND RESULTS

12.1 Introduction

In this chapter we analyse the indicated azimuths and declinations in our source data. As explained in the introductory chapter
(Section 1.3), the aim of our statistical tests will be to compare the
observed distribution of indicated azimuths and declinations with that
expected given random structure orientations. If the two differ
significantly, we must investigate possible causes. One of the causes
to be investigated is that astronomical considerations affected the
orientations of some of the structures in the sample.

Even if no single factor (or simple combination of factors) did
substantially affect the structure orientations in our sample, so that
they are effectively random, the resulting scatter of azimuths and
declinations will not correspond exactly to that expected under the
null (random) hypothesis. The expected distribution is merely an aver-
age over the many different formations a random scatter of data could
produce. As an example consider points scattered at random within a
given area. The expected distribution may be uniform, by which we
mean that the probability of a point falling in one place is as great
as that of it falling at any other. However a random scatter of points
will very rarely end up evenly spaced over the area. Instead they will
almost always exhibit clusterings, gaps, alignments, and other recog-
nisable patterns. This phenomenon is evident from the pattern of
bright stars in the night sky, and is all too familiar to those who
find themselves having to refute the arguments of ley line enthusiasts
on statistical grounds (see Williamson & Bellamy 1983). In fact, too
regular a scatter is itself a very special sort of pattern and is very
unlikely to occur by chance. Our statistical tests must tell us
whether the observed deviations from the expected distribution (such
as, in the example above, clusterings of points at certain places
within the area) are in fact sufficiently marked that they represent
evidence that should force us to reject the null hypothesis.

If the distinction is confusing between the expected distribution of random points and the actual formations that scatters of such
points tend to produce, it only serves to emphasize the importance of
actually performing a rigorous statistical test to establish whether
the null hypothesis should be rejected. Visual representations, while
often providing a valuable illustration of the statistical results,
can, if taken on their own account, be very misleading indeed.

Using our statistical tests, then, we wish to determine whether
the deviations from the expected distribution are significant. A particular statistical test will be geared towards detecting a particular
type of deviation from the expected distribution, such as clustering.
The results are expressed in terms of a significance level, which is
an estimate of the percentage of cases in which random data would have
resulted in a distribution deviating from the expected one by as much
as that observed. Conventionally, if the significance level is below
5%, it is taken to indicate that the null hypothesis is inadequate to
explain the observed data. A significance level of 1% or better constitutes strong evidence against the null hypothesis.

Unfortunately we must be wary whenever we have not just one but the choice of many different hypotheses to test. This situation arises in our analyses of both azimuths and declinations, though for different reasons, and is in fact symptomatic of the nature of data retrieval and hypothesis testing in archaeology as a whole (a fuller discussion of this point follows in Chapter 13). In brief, the hypothesis that "indicated declinations at all sites show evidence of clustering at a precision of $0°.2$" is different from the hypothesis that "indicated declinations at sites in Mull show evidence of clustering at a precision of $0°.2$" and different again from the hypothesis that "indicated declinations at sites in Mull show evidence of clustering at a precision of $1°.0$". Considering many different hypotheses and testing them separately clearly increases the probability that a low significance level will occur somewhere amongst our tests merely by chance; indeed, a significance level of 5% or better will be expected to occur purely fortuitously in one test out of every twenty or so. Thus we should lower the significance level at which we are prepared to reject the null hypothesis in favour of any particular alternative.

The analysis of indicated azimuths is simpler than that of declinations because under the null (random) hypothesis the expected distribution of azimuths is uniform: with declinations this is not the case. The expected distribution of declinations under the null hypothesis is illustrated in Fig. 12.1. It has been calculated there for a particular precision, but the general form is always the same. A glance at a selection of the profile diagrams in Chapters 5 - 10 will illustrate why. Declination lines are nearly horizontal around due north and south, so that large variations in azimuth produce only small variations in declination. Thus a relatively large number of randomly-placed structures, those oriented within a wide margin of north and south, will indicate declinations within only a small range. The most probable declinations are close to the colatitude in the north and minus the colatitude in the south. (The colatitude varies from $31°$ to $35°$ in the region under consideration.) Declination lines rise and set more steeply elsewhere on the horizon, so that fewer randomly-placed structures will indicate any particular declination range between plus and minus the colatitude than will indicate a range of equal width in the vicinity of these values. Declination values much above the colatitude represent circumpolar objects which never set; similarly, large negative declinations represent southern sky objects which never rise above the horizon. These declinations can never be indicated. Further details are given in Section 12.4.

- - - - - -

FIG. 12.1. Example histogram showing observed declinations falling within various target bins $1°.5$ wide, compared with the distribution which would have been expected by chance.

Values shown represent the declination of the centre of the bin, so that (e.g.) the bin marked "-30" represents the declination interval from $-30°.75$ to $-29°.25$. Each star indicates that one IAR in the source list "hits" the target, i.e. that at least part of that IAR falls within the target interval. The single line indicates the number of hits that would have been expected by chance.

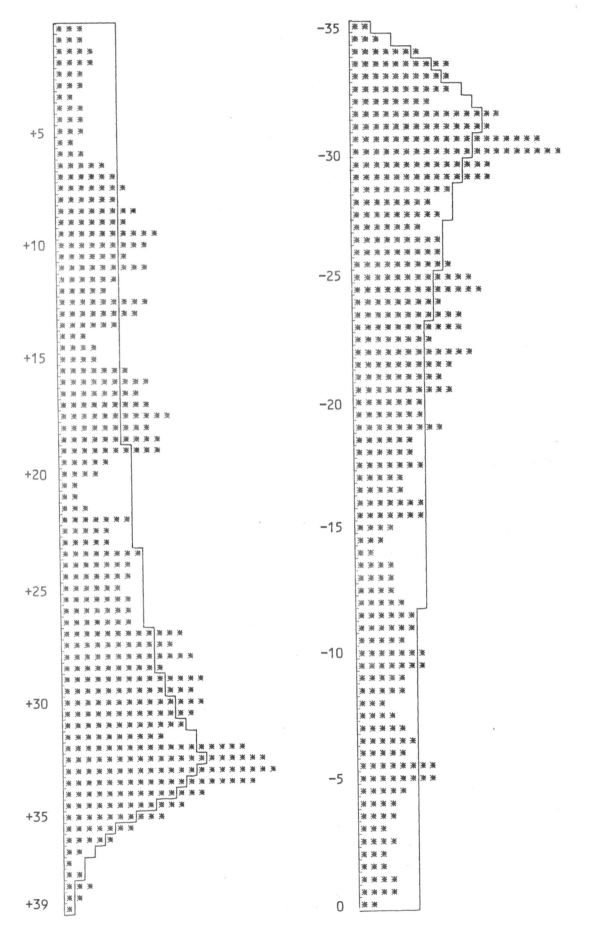

FIG. 12.1.

A final consideration in implementing statistical tests is that each item of data (indicated azimuth or declination) should be independent of all the rest. By this we mean that no particular indicated azimuth or declination should, purely as a consequence of how we have selected our data, bear direct relation to any other: in other words there should be no direct relation between two items of data in our list which holds regardless of whether or not the structure orientations are random. Clearly there is one direct violation of this rule amongst our data. Wherever we have considered both directions along a structure orientation or inter-site line, we obtain indications with azimuths exactly 180° apart and declinations near to minus each other (although this will depend upon the altitudes of the horizon profiles concerned). Fortunately this inadequacy in our data, once recognised, is easily allowed for when implementing statistical tests.

A different way in which non-independent data would arise, and one rather more difficult to deal with, would be if too many alignments had been considered between the same stones. Fortunately this possibility has been avoided by the careful choice of selection criteria in Chapter 3. An example would be if we had extended site types 3 - 5 to include up to 12 lines of the relevant class. The three lines joining any two of three stones are mutually independent, making a total of six indications when considered in both directions. However only five of the six possible lines between any two of four stones are independent, the sixth direction being deducable from the other five. The non-independence of items of data is a fundamental flaw in many statistical arguments about the astronomical significance of single complex sites, notably Stonehenge (Hawkins 1963; Hawkins & White 1966; but see Heggie 1981b: 145-151, 195-202).

12.2 Analysis of indicated azimuths: a nearest-neighbour method

In this section we investigate whether the indicated azimuths in our source data are consistent with random structure orientations. Clearly the expected distribution of azimuths under the null (random) hypothesis is uniform.

12.2.1 The method

We use a statistical test proposed by Neave and Selkirk (1983). Their method considers a set of points distributed on a circle, and tests the hypothesis that they are distributed uniformly randomly against the alternative hypothesis of clustering or over-regularity. If the null hypothesis is rejected, the test tells us whether this is because of clustering or over-regularity, but gives us no further details about the nature of either.

The statistic used (t) is the sum of nearest-neighbour distances, defined as follows. For each data point in turn on the circle, the distance is measured (along the circumference) to whichever other point is the nearest. These n distances are summed, and the statistic t is obtained by dividing this sum by the circumference of the circle. The expected value of t under the random hypothesis is 0.5, but t may take any value between 0 and 1. Small values of t indicate clustering, whereas large values indicate an unnatural degree of regularity.

To the central azimuth of each IAR we assign the appropriate point on the circle, so that for example an IAR of $|274.0, 276.0|$* will be represented by a point on the circle oriented at $275°.0$ from the centre. This test assigns exactly the same statistical weight to each IAR centre, regardless of the width of the IAR or the reliability of the line. Alternative tests which could take these factors into account are described in Section 12.3 below.

As it stands, Neave and Selkirk's test assumes that each item of data is independent of all the others. We now have to consider ways of allowing for the fact that our data contain a large number of opposite pairs of azimuths. Two different ways are considered below.

Firstly, where opposite pairs of azimuths occur we can select one of the two for inclusion in the analysis. One method would be to make the selection randomly: this would not bias the result, but it would introduce unneccesary chance variation into the behaviour of the statistic and might obscure any significant trends in the data. Instead, we have omitted that member of a pair which has the nearer horizon. In the few cases where the horizons were at equal distances, one azimuth of the pair has been selected at random. This is unlikely to obscure significant trends in the data if they are the result of astronomical considerations influencing structure orientations, given that these would tend to favour more distant horizons. Consequently this selection procedure should emphasize rather than obscure any evidence for deliberate astronomical orientations.

The second method is deliberately to consider opposite pairs of points, and to amend the statistical test accordingly. Fortunately, this can be done very simply. It can be shown (Appendix II) that when the points to be considered form n opposite pairs rather than $2n$ single independent values, we need simply to calculate the same test statistic t but to treat it in the analysis as if we had n single independent points. Thus we only need to restore the opposite direction in those cases where it was omitted because of a nearby horizon, and to rerun the statistical test.

Having applied this test to the data as a whole, we repeated it on various subsets of the data. These were obtained by separating on-site and inter-site lines, by concentrating on particular geographical locations, and by progressively eliminating those indications with the lowest classifications in our classification system. Wherever results of apparent significance were obtained, we investigated further subsets of the data in an attempt to isolate those particular ones for which the significance levels were lowest. Since the statistical test tells us no more than that any particular set of data _is_ significantly clustered, this is our only way of investigating whether certain subsets of that data are predominently causing the clustering observed. The price that we must pay for tracking down the "most favourable hypothesis" in this way is that we need to lower dramatically the significance level at which we are prepared to reject the null hypothesis in favour of any particular alternative.

- - - - - -

* We use the interval notation $|a, b|$ to represent the range of values
  of a variable n for which $a <= n <= b$.

The results of the statistical tests are tabulated in Table 12.1. Values of the test statistic t are given in columns 5 and 9 respectively for single independent lines (obtained by selecting more distant horizons from opposite pairs) and for opposite pairs. In the following columns we note the corresponding percentage point of the standard normal distribution, a figure which is reliable when n is 30 or greater, but only provides an increasingly crude indication for smaller n. If there is evidence for clustering or unnatural regularity, then a significance level is quoted in the remaining columns. This is taken from Neave and Selkirk's own table (1983: Table 1) where $n < 30$, and from tables of the standard normal distribution otherwise. Neave & Selkirk tabulate t-values for a discrete set of significance levels, namely 10%, 5%, 2.5%, 1% and 0.5%. Thus we only consider these levels in Table 12.1, even in cases where n is greater than 30 and more precise significance levels could have been estimated from tables of the standard normal distribution.

(ctd. on page 235

- - - - - -

TABLE 12.1. Analysis of the azimuth data.

Column headings

Sites included in a particular subset of the azimuth data:

1   On-site lines only, inter-site lines only, or both
2   Geographical areas included
3   Classes of indication included
4   Total number n of independent items of data or opposite pairs

Information from the analysis of single independent lines (obtained by selecting more distant horizons from opposite pairs):

5   Value of test statistic t
6   Corresponding percentage point of the standard normal distribution (when n is less than 30 this value is unreliable and is enclosed in brackets)
7   Significance level at which the null (random) hypothesis should be rejected in favour of clustering
8   Significance level at which the null (random) hypothesis should be rejected in favour of unnatural regularity

Information from the analysis of opposite pairs:

9   As column 5
10   As column 6
11   As column 7
12   As column 8

Table 12.1

OS/IS	Area(s)	Class(es)	n	MORE DISTANT				PAIRS			
				t	% pt	SL(clus)	SL(unif)	t	% pt	SL(clus)	SL(unif)
Both	ALL	ALL	165	0.518	+0.57	-	-	0.513	+0.42	-	-
Both	LH	ALL	33	0.478	-0.31	-	-	0.549	+0.70	-	-
Both	UI	ALL	29	0.504	(+0.06)	-	-	0.437	(-0.84)	-	-
Both	ML	ALL	24	0.443	(-0.70)	-	-	0.578	(+0.96)	-	-
Both	AR	ALL	27	0.631	(+1.69)	-	5 %	0.553	(+0.68)	-	-
Both	IS	ALL	25	0.372	(-1.60)	10 %	-	0.345	(-1.94)	5 %	-
Both	KT	ALL	27	0.522	(+0.29)	-	-	0.520	(+0.26)	-	-
OS	ALL	ALL	90	0.474	-0.61	-	-	0.443	-1.32	10 %	-
OS	LH	ALL	12	0.274	(-1.99)	5 %	-	0.548	(+0.43)	-	-
OS	UI	ALL	10	0.548	(+0.39)	-	-	0.431	(-0.56)	-	-
OS	ML	ALL	18	0.529	(+0.31)	-	-	0.643	(+1.53)	-	10 %
OS	AR	ALL	19	0.491	(-0.10)	-	-	0.589	(+0.98)	-	-
OS	IS	ALL	12	0.291	(-1.85)	5 %	-	0.531	(+0.27)	-	-
OS	KT	ALL	19	0.525	(+0.27)	-	-	0.469	(-0.33)	-	-
OS	ALL	1 - 4	54	0.505	+0.09	-	-	0.497	-0.06	-	-
OS	LH	1 - 4	10	0.368	(-1.07)	-	-	0.552	(+0.42)	-	-
OS	UI	1 - 4	5	0.385	(-0.69)	-	-	0.361	(-0.84)	-	2.5%
OS	ML	1 - 4	12	0.596	(+0.85)	-	-	0.712	(+1.87)	-	-
OS	AR	1 - 4	13	0.391	(-1.00)	-	-	0.552	(+0.48)	-	-
OS	IS	1 - 4	7	0.596	(+0.67)	-	-	0.603	(+0.71)	-	-
OS	KT	1 - 4	7	0.227	(-1.89)	5 %	-	0.454	(-0.32)	-	-

Table 12.1 (continued)

OS/IS	Area(s)	Class(es)	MORE DISTANT						PAIRS			
			n	t	% pt	SL(clus)	SL(unif)	:	t	% pt	SL(clus)	SL(unif)
OS	ALL	1 – 3	46	0.530	+0.51	–	–	:	0.524	+0.40	–	–
OS	LH	1 – 3	9	0.419	(–0.63)	–	–	:	0.534	(+0.27)	–	–
OS	UI	1 – 3	4	0.583	(+0.45)	–	–	:	0.332	(–0.92)	–	–
OS	ML	1 – 3	11	0.628	(+1.08)	–	–	:	0.741	(+2.05)	–	2.5%
OS	AR	1 – 3	11	0.264	(–2.00)	5 %	–	:	0.313	(–1.59)	10 %	–
OS	IS	1 – 3	5	0.714	(+1.28)	–	–	:	0.542	(+0.25)	–	–
OS	KT	1 – 3	6	0.167	(–2.16)	2.5%	–	:	0.332	(–1.09)	–	–
OS	ALL	1 – 2	28	0.423	(–1.02)	–	–	:	0.483	(–0.22)	–	–
OS	LH	1 – 2	5	0.081	(–2.52)	0.5%	–	:	0.162	(–2.03)	5 %	–
OS	ML	1 – 2	6	0.252	(–1.61)	10 %	–	:	0.348	(–0.99)	–	–
OS	AR	1 – 2	11	0.264	(–2.00)	5 %	–	:	0.313	(–1.59)	10 %	–
OS	ALL	1 only	19	0.396	(–1.14)	–	–	:	0.529	(+0.32)	–	–
OS	LH	1 only	5	0.081	(–2.52)	0.5%	–	:	0.162	(–2.03)	5 %	–
OS	AR	1 only	9	0.158	(–2.65)	0.5%	–	:	0.221	(–2.16)	2.5%	–
OS	ALL	1 – 2	28	0.423	(–1.02)	–	–	:	0.483	(–0.22)	–	–
OS	UI,ML,AR,IS,KT	1 – 2	23	0.388	(–1.34)	10 %	–	:	0.413	(–1.05)	–	–
OS	ML,AR,IS,KT	1 – 2	22	0.298	(–2.38)	1 %	–	:	0.266	(–2.75)	0.5%	–
OS	ML,AR,IS	1 – 2	19	0.274	(–2.47)	1 %	–	:	0.208	(–3.20)	(0.1%)	–
OS	ML,AR	1 – 2	17	0.297	(–2.11)	2.5%	–	:	0.238	(–2.73)	0.5%	–
OS	ML	1 – 2	6	0.252	(–1.61)	10 %	–	:	0.348	(–0.99)	–	–
OS	AR	1 – 2	11	0.264	(–2.00)	5 %	–	:	0.313	(–1.59)	10 %	–

Table 12.1 (continued)

OS/IS	Area(s)	Class(es)	n		MORE DISTANT				PAIRS			
					t	% pt	SL(clus)	SL(unif)	t	% pt	SL(clus)	SL(unif)
OS	ALL	1 only	19	:	0.396	(-1.14)	-	-	0.529	(+0.32)	-	-
OS	UI,ML,AR,IS,KT	1 only	14	:	0.316	(-1.75)	5 %	-	0.467	(-0.32)	-	-
OS	ML,AR,IS,KT	1 only	13	:	0.225	(-2.52)	1 %	-	0.319	(-1.65)	10 %	-
OS	ML,AR	1 only	11	:	0.190	(-2.63)	0.5%	-	0.250	(-2.12)	2.5%	-
OS	AR	1 only	9	:	0.158	(-2.65)	0.5%	-	0.221	(-2.16)	2.5%	-
OS	ALL	5 - 6	36	:	0.496	-0.06	-	-	0.515	+0.22	-	-
OS	UI,ML,AR,IS,KT	5 - 6	34	:	0.463	-0.54	-	-	0.518	+0.27	-	-
OS	ML,AR,IS,KT	5 - 6	29	:	0.493	(-0.10)	-	-	0.525	(+0.34)	-	-
OS	AR,IS,KT	5 - 6	23	:	0.496	(-0.05)	-	-	0.567	(+0.80)	-	-
OS	IS,KT	5 - 6	17	:	0.645	(+1.51)	-	10 %	0.581	(+0.84)	-	-
OS	KT	5 - 6	12	:	0.565	(+0.57)	-	-	0.503	(+0.03)	-	-
IS	ALL	ALL	75	:	0.494	-0.13	-	-	0.558	+1.23	-	-
IS	LH	ALL	21	:	0.535	(+0.40)	-	-	0.569	(+0.79)	-	-
IS	UI	ALL	19	:	0.412	(-0.97)	-	-	0.422	(-0.85)	-	-
IS	ML	ALL	6	:	0.325	(-1.13)	-	-	0.383	(-0.76)	-	-
IS	AR	ALL	8	:	0.472	(-0.21)	-	-	0.346	(-1.13)	-	-
IS	IS	ALL	13	:	0.374	(-1.15)	-	-	0.376	(-1.14)	-	-
IS	KT	ALL	8	:	0.455	(-0.33)	-	-	0.493	(-0.05)	-	-

Table 12.1 (continued)

OS/IS	Area(s)	Class(es)	n	t	MORE DISTANT % pt	SL(clus)	SL(unif)	:	t	PAIRS % pt	SL(clus)	SL(unif)
IS	ALL	1 – 2	43	0.461	−0.63	–	–	::				
IS	LH	1 – 2	14	0.398	(−0.97)	–	–	::				
IS	UI	1 – 2	7	0.507	(+0.05)	–	–	::				
IS	ML	1 – 2	4	0.535	(+0.19)	–	–	::				
IS	AR	1 – 2	7	0.472	(−0.19)	–	–	::				
IS	IS	1 – 2	8	0.431	(−0.51)	–	–	::				
IS	ALL	1 only	11	0.372	(−1.09)	–	–	::				
IS	LH	1 only	8	0.344	(−1.15)	–	–	::				
IS	ALL	A 1 – A 3	55	0.483	−0.32	–	–	::				
IS	LH	A 1 – A 3	14	0.596	(+0.91)	–	–	::				
IS	UI	A 1 – A 3	15	0.424	(−0.75)	–	–	::				
IS	ML	A 1 – A 3	5	0.335	(−0.99)	–	–	::				
IS	AR	A 1 – A 3	6	0.348	(−0.98)	–	–	::				
IS	IS	A 1 – A 3	8	0.371	(−0.95)	–	–	::				
IS	KT	A 1 – A 3	7	0.495	(−0.03)	–	–	::				
IS	ALL	A 1 – A 2	28	0.491	(−0.12)	–	–	::				
IS	LH	A 1 – A 2	9	0.438	(−0.48)	–	–	::				
IS	UI	A 1 – A 2	5	0.513	(+0.08)	–	–	::				
IS	AR	A 1 – A 2	6	0.348	(−0.98)	–	–	::				
IS	ALL	A 1 only	10	0.445	(−0.44)	–	–	::				
IS	LH	A 1 only	7	0.417	(−0.57)	–	–	::				

12.2.2 The results

When the azimuth data from the entire source list were analysed, values were obtained for t of 0.518 and 0.513 in the case of single and paired data respectively. These values are very close to the value of 0.5 expected under the null (random) hypothesis. Thus the tests provide no evidence for clustering or over-regularity in our azimuth data taken as a whole.

The data were then divided into the six geographical areas LH, UI, ML, AR, IS & KT, and sites from each area were considered separately. In addition, on-site and inter-site lines were considered separately as well as together. This provided a total of twenty additional tests on both single and paired data. In none of these cases was a significance level obtained lower than 5%.

On-site and inter-site indications were then considered in turn, progressively eliminating those with the lowest classifications in our classification system. At each stage in the elimination process the data were considered as a whole and also separated into the six geographical regions.

In the case of inter-site lines, those of class 3 were removed first, then those of class 2 as well. Lines of archaeological status B were then removed and the whole process repeated. Results have been quoted wherever the number of points n remains above 3, although as the sample size drops to small values the test becomes increasingly unreliable. Data from opposite pairs of indications could not be considered here, since their classifications often differ from each other. A total of 21 tests were nonetheless carried out on subsets of the inter-site data. In not a single case was a significance level obtained as low as 10%, let alone one lower than 5%.

In the case of on-site lines, those of classes 5 & 6 were removed first, then those of class 4 as well, and so on. Significance levels of 0.5% in favour of clustering were obtained in two cases, both with single directional data. The data subsets involved were

   (i) indications of class 1 only in area LH; and
   (ii) indications of class 1 only in area AR.

The set of indications of classes 1 and 2 in area LH also shows a 0.5% significance level, but in fact there are no class 2 indications in this area, and this result merely repeats (i) above.

When class 1 and 2 indications are considered in isolation, low significance levels in favour of clustering result in a high proportion of cases, in addition to the very low figures noted above. This fact encouraged us to investigate further both indications of classes 1 and 2 together and those of class 1 alone, grouping them in different ways by geographical location. Starting from the full data set in each case, we progressively eliminated peripheral geographical areas. This produced further evidence of clustering at very low significance levels. There were a total of eight different cases where significance levels of 1% or lower were encountered, as follows.

(i) Lines of classes 1 & 2 in areas ML, AR, IS & KT taken together,
       single directions ($\underline{n}$ = 22, SL = 1%).
  (ii) Lines of classes 1 & 2 in areas ML, AR & IS taken together,
       single directions ($\underline{n}$ = 19, SL = 1%).
 (iii) Lines of classes 1 & 2 in areas ML, AR, IS & KT taken together,
       opposite pairs ($\underline{n}$ = 22, SL = 0.5%).
  (iv) Lines of classes 1 & 2 in areas ML, AR & IS taken together,
       opposite pairs ($\underline{n}$ = 19, SL = 0.1%).
   (v) Lines of classes 1 & 2 in areas ML & AR taken together,
       opposite pairs ($\underline{n}$ = 17, SL = 0.5%).
  (vi) Lines of class 1 only in areas ML, AR, (IS) & KT taken
       together, single directions ($\underline{n}$ = 13, SL = 1%).
 (vii) Lines of class 1 only in areas ML & AR taken together, single
       directions ($\underline{n}$ = 11, SL = 0.5%).
(viii) Lines of class 1 only in area AR, single directions ($\underline{n}$ = 9, SL
       = 0.5%).
  (ix) Lines of class 1 only in area LH, single directions ($\underline{n}$ = 5, SL
       = 0.5%).

A very low value indeed was obtained for the test statistic in case
(iv), and a significance level could not be obtained from Neave & Selkirk's table. A value of 0.1% has been listed, but this estimate is
probably conservative. Such a low significance level should certainly
lead us to reject the null hypothesis, despite the many alternatives
proposed in Table 12.1. The values of 0.5% and 1% obtained elsewhere
might also lead us to do so, but with less confidence.

     The data sets which are significantly clustered are illustrated
in Figs. 12.2 - 12.9, with the exception of case (v) which can be
obtained from case (iv) by simply extracting two pairs of lines. In
Figs. 12.2 - 12.3 and 12.6 - 12.9, indication numbers are shown by the
azimuths to which they refer. In Figs. 12.4 & 12.5 the indication numbers can be deduced from the corresponding single-direction diagrams.

     In each of the nine cases above, further sub-samples of the data
were investigated to see if the significance levels obtained could be
decreased still further. We considered

  (i) lines of survey status A or B, and A only;
 (ii) lines where the IAR width was 1° or less, and 0°.8 or less; and
(iii) lines where the horizon distance was at least 2.5 km, and at
      least 5 km.

In no case could the significance level be improved in this way, although it should be noted that the number of points in the starting
samples was at most 22, so that the size of each sub-sample was now
very small indeed.

     Finally, it might be argued that we have been blinkered by our
own classification system into assuming that only the highest classification lines might be significant if considered on their own. In
order to counter this, we have also examined on-site lines of classes
5 & 6 in isolation. The results are included in Table 12.1. No significance levels lower than 10% emerged.

(ctd. on page 241

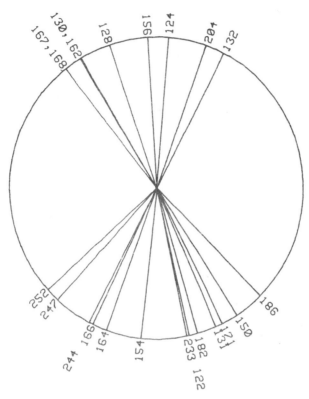

FIG. 12.2. Central azimuths of indications, omitting those members of
opposite pairs which have the nearer horizon. ML, AR, IS & KT, on-site
lines of classes 1 & 2 (total 22 indications).

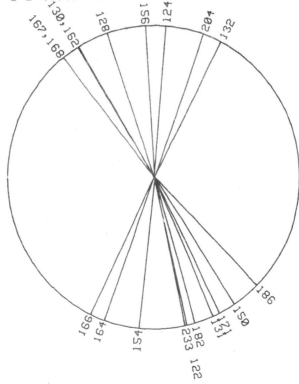

FIG. 12.3. As Fig. 12.2. ML, AR & IS, on-site lines of classes 1 & 2
(total 19 indications).

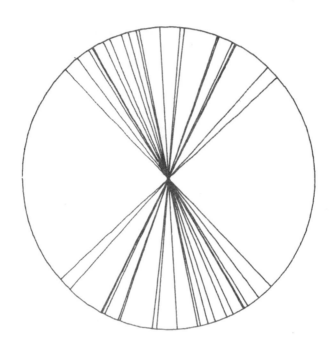

FIG. 12.4. Central azimuths of indications, considered in both directions
(even when one horizon is local). ML, AR, IS & KT, on-site lines of
classes 1 & 2 (total 22 pairs).

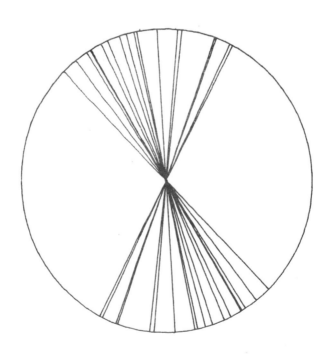

FIG. 12.5. As Fig. 12.4. ML, AR & IS, on-site lines of classes 1 & 2
(total 19 pairs).

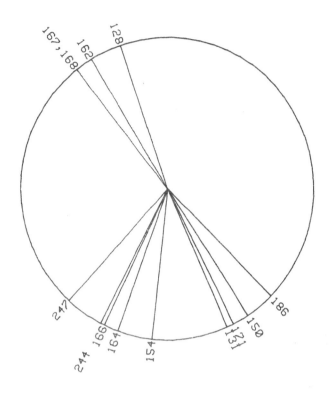

FIG. 12.6. Central azimuths of indications, omitting those members of opposite pairs which have the nearer horizon. ML, AR & KT, on-site lines of class 1 only (total 13 indications).

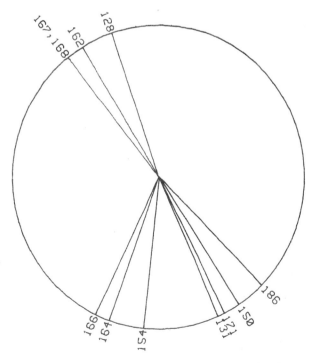

FIG. 12.7. As Fig. 12.6. ML & AR, on-site lines of class 1 only (total 11 indications).

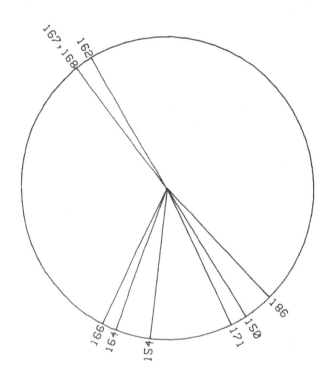

FIG. 12.8. As Fig. 12.6. AR, on-site lines of class 1 only (total
9 indications).

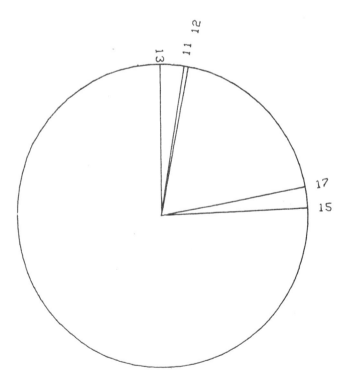

FIG. 12.9. As Fig. 12.6. LH, on-site lines of class 1 only (total
5 indications).

12.2.3 Interpretation

Nowhere amongst any subsets of the azimuth data is there any clear indication of significant unnatural regularity. This is perhaps reassuring, since it is difficult to conceive of any causal factors that could bring this about.

Evidence for clustering amongst the azimuth data emerges in nine instances, as listed above (p. 236). All involve indications of class 1 only, i.e. alignments of standing menhirs, or of classes 1 and 2, i.e. alignments and possible alignments of standing or fallen stones. With a single exception, all nine cases involve only geographical areas ML, AR, IS & KT, i.e. the Inner Hebrides and mainland Argyll.

The exception is case (ix). In fact, the data constituting this case (Fig. 12.9) consist only of 5 lines, which are all from the same site: Callanish (LH16). The five directions are those formed by the five radial rows of stones, and are clearly inter-related through the cruciform design of the site. The clustering is a simple consequence of this. We can say no more about the motivation for this site design, since it is unique in western Scotland, and so case (ix) will concern us no further.

Although data in the remaining cases come from a variety of sites, the low significance levels obtained could still derive in some measure from the particular design of certain sites in the sample. This will happen if
  (i) more than one pair of indications have been included from the same site, and
  (ii) the design of that site is such that the structures giving rise to the indications are near-parallel.
Near-parallel structures will lead to two (or more) similar azimuths being included in the same sample. Where this happens, the nearest-neighbour distance for each indication concerned will be small, and the value of the test statistic t could be substantially lower than if we had included only one of the indications. In cases (i) – (viii) there are two sites where multiple indications occur: Kilmartin (AR13) and Duncracaig (AR15). We should check, then, whether the designs of these sites will affect the overall t-values.

Lines 168 – 171 represent opposite directions along the two adjacent alignments of slabs (abcd and ef) at Duncracaig (AR15). The orientations of abcd and ef are about 12° apart, which is sufficient to ensure that the relevant indications do not form neighbouring data in any of the samples. (Furthermore the more distant horizons in the two cases are in opposite directions, so that the two north-westerly and the two south-easterly azimuths each only appear together when opposite pairs are considered.) We conclude that the design of the Duncracaig site itself has not contributed noticeably to the low t-values.

Lines 162 – 167 represent six indications from four alignments at Kilmartin (AR13). Lines 164 & 166 (or, in the opposite direction, 163 & 165) represent the diagonals ($S_2 S_1 S_5$ & $S_3 S_1 S_4$) of the five-stone arrangement and indicate azimuths only 6° apart. These fall adjacent in all the data samples and will have contributed to the low t-value.

Lines 162 & 167 ($S_2S_3S_6$ & S_5S_4) represent the two aligned pairs of slabs (the extra stone S_6 falling in one of these alignments), and indicate azimuths $7°$ apart. If each of the azimuth pairs from lines 162 & 167 and 164 & 166 is replaced by a single data point whose azimuth is the mean of the two indications, then the corrected test results in cases (i) - (viii) are as follows:

$$
\begin{array}{llll}
\text{(i)} & n = 20, & t = 0.333, & SL = 5\ \% \ ; \\
\text{(ii)} & n = 17, & t = 0.324, & SL = 5\ \% \ ; \\
\text{(iii)} & n = 20, & t = 0.328, & SL = 5\ \% \ ; \\
\text{(iv)} & n = 17, & t = 0.286, & SL = 2.5\% \ ; \\
\text{(v)} & n = 15, & t = 0.275, & SL = 2.5\% \ ; \\
\text{(vi)} & n = 11, & t = 0.242, & SL = 2.5\% \ ; \\
\text{(vii)} & n = 9, & t = 0.222, & SL = 2.5\% \ ; \\
\text{(viii)} & n = 7, & t = 0.181, & SL = 2.5\% \ .
\end{array}
$$

Remarkably, eliminating the multiple indications at Kilmartin has, at a stroke, reduced the significance levels to values where our rejection of the null hypothesis is not automatic. Our conclusion must be that an essential factor in the significant clustering detected in cases (i) - (viii) is the particular layout of the Kilmartin site and the fact that we chose to include four inter-related indications from that same site in our data set. It may however be premature to cease our examination of the data at this point, as in case (ix), since it is possible that each of the near- but not exactly parallel alignments at Kilmartin and Duncracaig may have a deliberate separate significance, one which could be relevant to all the other structures and sites in the sample. Thus we should continue to examine the causes of the low significance levels in cases (i) - (viii), bearing in mind that the design of the Kilmartin site is an essential (though possibly impenetrable) factor to be taken into account.

The other main contributory factor to the low significance levels in cases (i) - (viii) is evident from Figs. 12.2 - 12.8. It is that azimuths are confined to the northern and southern quarters of the compass. It may be found surprising that when lines 162 & 167 and 164 & 166 are merged the data are no longer sufficient to support the clustering hypothesis at a low significance level, whereas the N-S trend is still evident in the figures. However this merely serves to emphasize the points made in Section 12.1. Our statistical method tests whether there is clustering, but does not elaborate on the nature of that clustering. If we now devised a method to test whether the azimuths were significantly clustered about N and S, we would doubtless get a much more conclusive rejection of the null (random) hypothesis. But the alternative hypothesis would be a special one formulated in hindsight on the basis of the data available: the very data upon which the hypothesis was subsequently tested. A significance level obtained in this way, just like a conclusion based purely on visual representations of the data, can be very misleading. The reader is again referred to Chapter 13 for a fuller discussion.

The N-S trend has been isolated by our statistical test, however, and we must now ask whether it can be explained by ground-based factors such as local topography. Eighteen stone alignments constitute the data in cases (i) & (iii), the most extensive data set arising in this discussion. Six are located in Mull, one in Lorn, six in the Kilmartin area of Argyll, and the remainder in Jura, Islay and Kintyre.

Four the six sites in Mull - Quinish (ML2), Maol Mor (ML9), Dervaig N (ML10) and Dervaig S (ML11) - are located within 5 km of one another on the western side of the Mishnish peninsula of northern Mull. Here a NNW-SSE ridge slopes down to the sea, to an inlet (Loch a'Chumbainn) and to the valley of the River Bellart. All four stone alignments are oriented NNW-SSE and thus reflect the local topography. The remaining Mull sites - Balliscate (ML4) and Ardnacross (ML12) - are situated on the eastern coast of Mull overlooking E-W valleys. Balliscate however is oriented N-S and Ardnacross NNE-SSW.

Four of the Argyll sites - Kilmartin (AR13), Duncracaig (AR15), Dunamuck I (AR28) and Dunamuck II (AR29) - lie within 6 km of one another in the Kilmartin valley. Salachary (AR6) is some 7 km to the north, Barbreck (AR3) some 9 km to the north, and Duachy (LN22) some 25 km to the north. The Kilmartin area is one of the largest and most fertile low-lying areas in western Scotland, and features extensive material remains from different periods of prehistory. In the vicinity of Kilmartin village the valley is about 400m wide and runs NNE-SSW. About 1.5 km to the south it opens out into a large low-lying plain sharply bounded in the east by foothills running NNW-SSE. The Duncracaig alignments and the two Dunamuck sites, which all lie on the east of the plain, are all oriented NNW-SSE, following this line. The Kilmartin site itself stands at the mouth of the narrower valley running NNE-SSW. The longer axis of the five-stone formation follows this valley, but the individual slabs making up the formation are oriented NNW-SSE, in line with the sites to the south. We note in passing that the orientation of slabs $S_5 S_4$ at Kilmartin is almost exactly the same as that of alignment abcd at Duncracaig.

The Barbreck site consists of three large slabs whose architectural similarity to the Kilmartin site has been noted in the literature (Patrick 1979). It lies in a NE-SW valley, but in contrast to the case at Kilmartin its orientation seems unrelated to this. The longer axis of the formation (ac & bc) is WNW-ESE and the individual slabs are oriented N-S. The Duachy site is situated adjacent to a valley running NE-SW, but the orientation of the three-stone alignment is NNW-SSE.

Although the orientations of the stone alignments often follow the local topography, the sites at Balliscate, Ardnacross, Duachy and Barbreck provide clear counter-examples. The N-S orientation trend demands a different explanation. However the particular orientations of sites within the desired range may well have been influenced by the local topography, or by other factors such as the practice at nearby sites. The orientational consistency of the sites in north-western Mull, and in the Kilmartin valley, would certainly support this idea.

Thus in brief:
(i) The analysis of indicated azimuths focuses our attention upon stone alignments in the Inner Hebrides and mainland Argyll.
(ii) Although a preference is evident amongst these sites for orientations in the northern and southern quarters of the compass, only when the multiple indications from Kilmartin are included in the analysis is the trend sufficiently marked to constitute conclusive statistical evidence against the hypothesis of random orientations.
(iii) The orientation trend can not adequately be explained by local topography alone.

12.3   Other statistical tests on the azimuth data

In this section we outline some other statistical tests that might be used upon our azimuth data, and mention some of the problems involved.   We also give a visual presentation of the data in a manner used extensively in the past by Thom. This, it is hoped, will aid discussion and also, for those interested, facilitate comparison with Thom's results.   However our warnings about basing conclusions upon visual data alone (Section 12.1) are emphasized.

12.3.1 A vector sum method

In this method we consider the central azimuth of each IAR and represent it by a vector whose argument is that value (i.e. by a vector pointing in the appropriate direction).

The statistical test used in Section 12.2 made no allowance for the fact that we might wish to assign different statistical weights to different indications, depending upon the width of the IAR or the reliability of the line. We may now do so by assigning an appropriate length to the vector concerned. Longer vectors will carry the greater statistical weight.   We can, for example, take the width of the IAR into account in a natural way by thinking of it as an uncertainty in the central azimuth. The required length of a given vector will then be inversely proportional to the square of the IAR width.

We now sum the various vectors representing our data. The test statistic R is the length of this sum vector. If azimuths are dist- ributed uniformly randomly, the vectors will tend when added to cancel one another out, so that the length of the sum vector will be small. Thus large values of R will indicate a significant departure from the distribution expected under the null hypothesis. The probability den- sity function of R is given in analytical form by Mardia (1972: 94). However the formula involves the integration of products of Bessel functions, and requires numerical integration for its solution.

This test is good at detecting certain deviations from uniform- ity, such as a tendency for all the data to fall in one half of the circle. However data clustered about two opposite points, such as the data shown in Figs. 12.2 - 12.8, would produce vectors in opposite directions which would tend to cancel out, and the clustering would not be detected. This is a serious shortcoming of the method.

12.3.2 A cumulative probability method

Another way of taking into account the widths of IARs is to assign a fixed statistical weight to each indication, but to spread that weight over the entire IAR in some predetermined way. Thus for sharply-defined indications (narrow IARs) the weight will be concen- trated in a narrow range of azimuths, whereas for poorly defined indications it will be more diffused. The weights from all the data are then added together. The result is a cumulative value for each azimuth which will be high if that azimuth is "preferred" and low if it is avoided. The distribution of the cumulative values can then be compared statistically with that which would have been expected under the null (random) hypothesis.

The statistical weight could be spread over individual IARs in a variety of ways. One is simply to spread it uniformly over the IAR. However it is more likely that the intended orientation of a structure was near to the centre of the IAR than to its limits. This suggests that we should assign the greatest weight to the central azimuth and a progressively smaller weight as we approach the IAR limits. A natural way to do this is to use the normal distribution, selecting a standard deviation (SD) proportional to the width of the IAR. For example, an SD of half the IAR width will assign approximately 70% of the statistical weight within the IAR and the remainder just outside its limits.

Various types of deviation from the expected cumulative distribution could be investigated. For example, we might wish to test whether the highest cumulative values obtained (i.e. the apparently preferred azimuths) are actually significant. Where the probability is spread evenly over each IAR and the expected distribution is uniform, it is possible to devise appropriate statistical tests, although problems do arise. However when individual IARs are represented by more complicated distributions the problem becomes more formidable and may only be soluble by simulation methods. Detailed discussion is anticipated in forthcoming work by C.L.N. Ruggles and P.R. Freeman.

Although rigorous statistical methods are lacking at present, the cumulative probability approach lends itself easily to visual representation. Statistical weights assigned to IARs according to the normal distribution can be displayed graphically as gaussian areas. As these are added together, gaussian humps are plotted cumulatively so as to produce a sort of histogram showing the preferred azimuths. Indeed, this method of displaying data has been used by Thom ever since his earliest publications (Thom 1955; 1967; 1971). The word "curvigram" has been coined (Ruggles 1981) to describe such graphs.

Curvigrams are an exceedingly good way of visualising data of this sort, but they do have to be approached with caution and can be considerably misleading for two reasons. The first (recalling Section 12.1) is simply the tendency for the human brain to spot particular patterns which are not as significant as they might appear. The second is that while only the final (top) line in a curvigram is in fact indicative of anything, the shape of individual constituent humps (which are usually included for completeness) tends to draw the eye away from the final curve and to emphasize certain peaks in a misleading way. A different plotting order will change the appearance of these humps completely, although the final curve will of course be unaltered.

We present four different curvigrams to illustrate aspects of the azimuth data. In the first (Fig. 12.10) all data are included. The area under each gaussian hump is 1 unit, and the scale of the vertical axis is 5 units. Hump centres correspond to IAR centres and their SDs are half the relevant IAR width. This diagram looks very different from the curvigrams of Thom, largely because of the variety of IAR widths included. It would be difficult however even for the eye of faith to pick out anything but random noise from this diagram.

(ctd. on page 254

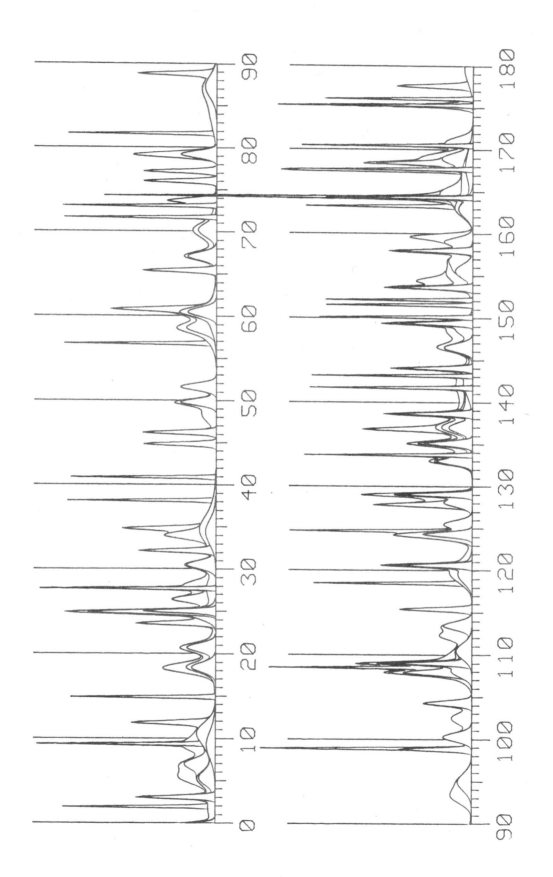

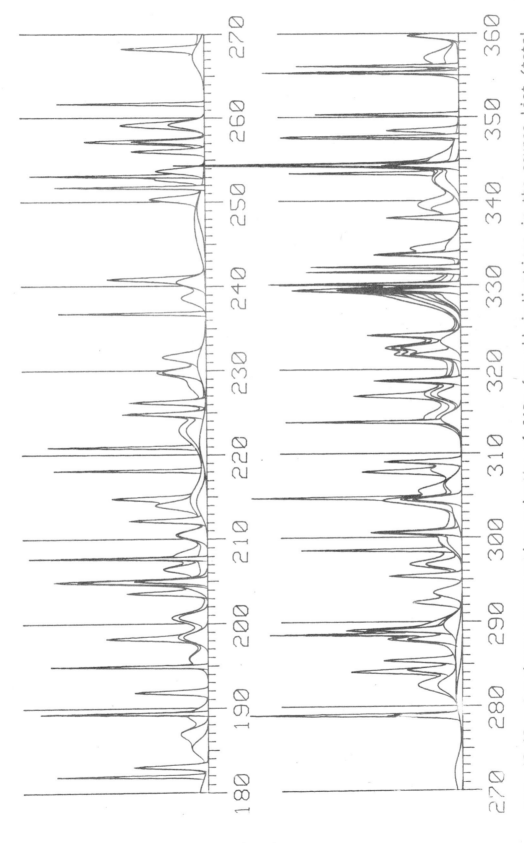

FIG. 12.10. Curvigram representing azimuths of IARs for all indications in the source list (total 276 indications). The scale of the vertical axis is 5 units.

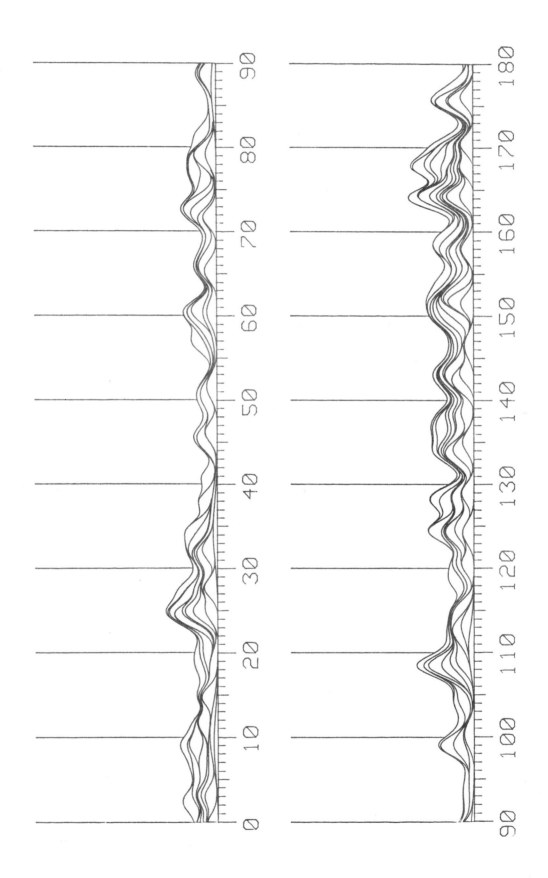

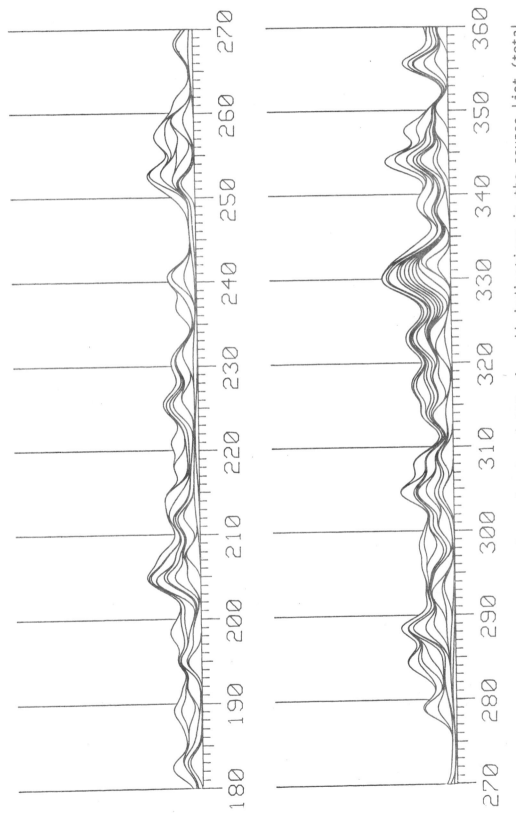

FIG. 12.11. Curvigram representing azimuths of AARs for all indications in the source list (total 276 indications). The scale of the vertical axis is 5 units.

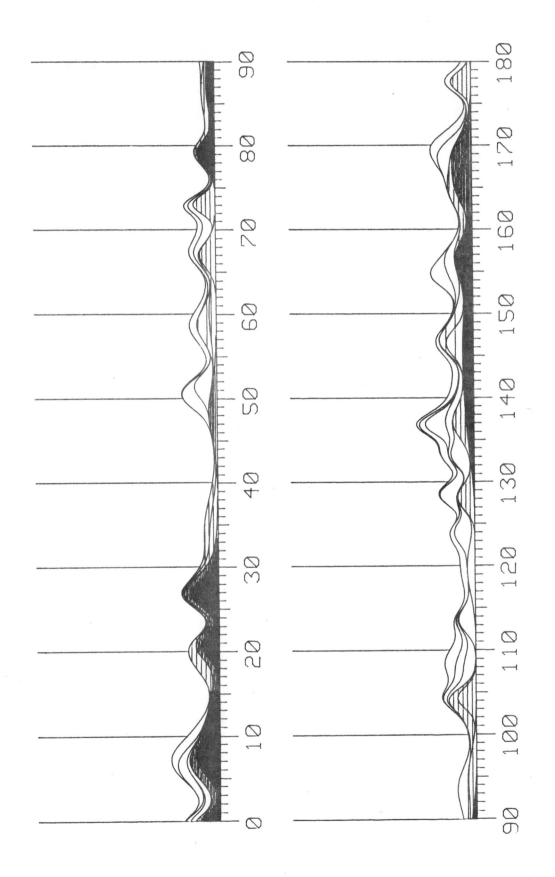

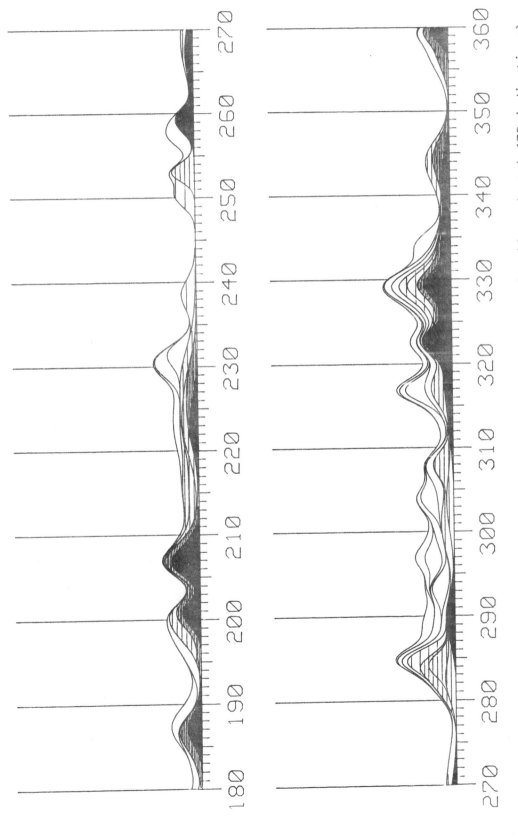

FIG. 12.12. Curvigram representing azimuths of AARs for all on-site lines (total 130 indications). Lines of classes 1, 2, 3, 4 & 5/6 are indicated by differential shading, class 1 being the darkest. The scale of the vertical axis is 3 units.

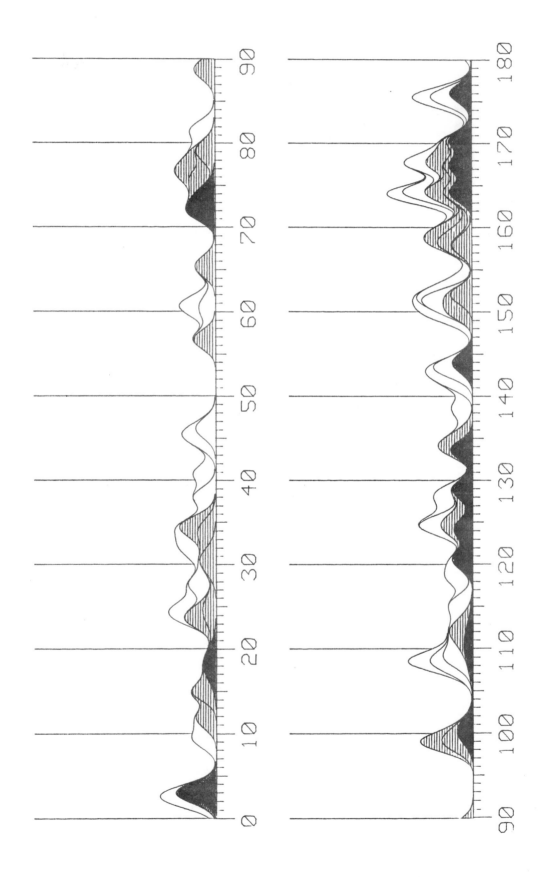

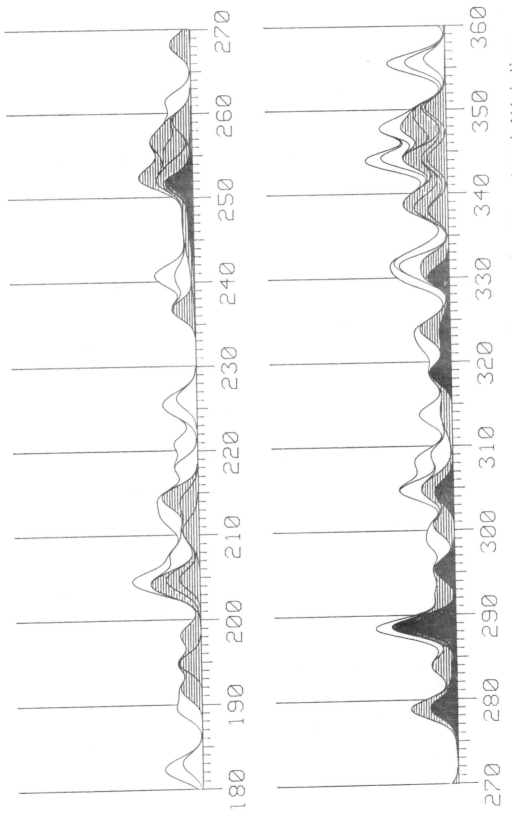

FIG. 12.13. Curvigram representing azimuths of AARs for all inter-site lines (total 146 indications). Lines of classes 1, 2 & 3 are indicated by differential shading, class 1 being the darkest. The scale of the vertical axis is 3 units.

In Fig. 12.11 we have replaced IARs by AARs, so that the SDs are more similar and the high spikes have disappeared. This has the effect of concentrating our attention on features of lower precision, say 1° or 2° at most. The diagram much more closely resembles a curvigram of Thom's. But the general appearance is still one of random data.

Finally in Figs. 12.12 and 12.13 we have separated the data into on-site and inter-site indications. In each case the classifications of the indications are indicated by differential shading, lines of the highest classification being shaded darkest and plotted first. Thus by concentrating upon only the darkest humps we can picture just the class 1 data, and so on. The avoidance of azimuths around east and west by class 1 and 2 on-site data from areas ML, AR, IS & KT is obscured in Fig. 12.12 by the inclusion of class 1 and 2 data from Lewis and the Uists.

12.4 Analysis of indicated declinations using Monte-Carlo simulations

In this section we investigate whether the indicated declinations in our source data are consistent with random structure orientations. Because the expected distribution under the null (random) hypothesis is non-uniform, no simple test is available and we have resorted to computer simulations in order to assess significance levels.

Problems immediately arise because we lack a method of testing for clustering as a whole: instead we must test whether particular declination ranges are significantly favoured or avoided. Since we do not wish to prejudge the issue by concentrating only upon certain declinations, and since we do not know how precisely any given orientation was (or might have been intended to be) set up, we must test for clustering within a comprehensive range of declination "windows" of varying centres and widths. Thus we must effectively consider some hundreds of different hypotheses, and lower accordingly the significance level at which we are prepared to reject the null hypothesis in favour of any one of them.

12.4.1 The method

The point of a Monte-Carlo simulation is to determine by sheer computer power how random data would behave. By running simulations over and over again and averaging their results we eventually build up a picture of the expected behaviour of the random data against which the behaviour of the observed data can be compared.

The property we wish to randomise is a structure orientation, and the property we wish to investigate is the indicated declination. We immediately hit a problem here, though, because the indicated declination depends not only upon the indicated azimuth, but also upon the latitude of the site and upon the altitude of the indicated horizon (Appendix I). Furthermore we are actually interested in an indication of finite width which will include a range of declinations. Thus the width of the IAR is relevant, and also the shape of the horizon. Each of these other properties needs to be distributed in exactly the same way amongst the simulated data as it is amongst the observed data.

Each of our 276 indications has an associated latitude, altitude, IAR width and horizon profile. We shall make one simplification, however, and assume that all horizon profiles are flat, taking their altitude to be the mean of the actual altitude range within the IAR. Thus we have 276 sets of associated values for latitude, altitude and IAR width. When combined with the azimuth of any indication, these data are sufficient for us to calculate the declination at both ends of the IAR (since we are now assuming that the horizons are flat). These declinations will represent the limiting indicated declinations except in those cases where the IAR includes due north or south (in which case one of the limiting declinations must be calculated at the north or south point).

In order to generate a set of simulated declinations we now do the following. First we produce three lists, respectively containing the 276 values of the latitude, altitude and IAR width for the observed data. We now shuffle two of the lists randomly and recombine the first entry from each, and so on, so as to produce 276 new latitude-altitude-width triplets. To each triplet we now assign an azimuth selected at random, and calculate the limiting declinations of the simulated indication. A set of 276 declination intervals produced in this way will satisfy the requirement that orientations have been randomised, but that all other properties reflect exactly those present in the observed data. This constitutes a single simulation. To generate further simulations we merely reshuffle two of the three lists and repeat the process.

As mentioned above, we shall consider a range of declination "target" windows of various centres and widths. We wish to calculate the number of "hits" on any particular target scored by our observed data and to compare it with the number scored by the simulated data. For this purpose we stipulate that a declination interval |d1, d2| scores a hit upon the target window |t1, t2| if

$$d1 <= t2$$
$$\text{and} \quad d2 >= t1,$$

in other words if there is any overlap between the two ranges. (If the two intervals just touch, we also count a hit.)

(ctd. on page 261

TABLE 12.2. Analysis of the declination data.

Row headings indicate target window centres
Column headings indicate target window widths

Table entries indicate significance levels where these are below 5%
    <.> indicates preference
    >.< indicates avoidance

Table 12.2

```
        :0.2 0.4 0.6 0.8 1.0 1.5 2.0 2.5 3.0 4.0 5.0 6.0 7.0 8.0 10. 12. 15. 20.
-35.0 : ..   ..   ..   ..   ..   ..   ..
-34.5 : ..   ..   ..   ..   ..   ..   ..
-34.0 : ..   ..   ..   ..   ..   ..   ..
-33.5 : ..   ..   ..   ..   ..   ..   ..
-33.0 : ..   ..   ..   ..   ..   ..   ..
-32.5 : ..   ..   ..   ..   ..   ..   ..
-32.0 : ..   ..   ..   ..   ..   ..   ..
-31.5 :      >5<  ..   ..   ..   ..   ..
-31.0 : <4>: ..   ..   ..   ..   ..   ..
-30.5 : <1>: :<0>:<0>:<2>:<2>: ..        :<5>
-------------------------------------------------------------
-30.0 :      ..   :<2>:<0>:<0>:<3>: ..
-29.5 : <4>: :<5>:<4>:      :<2>:<0>: ..
-29.0 : ..   ..   ..        :<0>:      ..
-28.5 : ..   ..   ..   :<5>:       ..
-28.0 :      ..   :<2>:<4>:<4>: ..            :<5>
-27.5 : >5<  ..        :<1>: :<4>: ..
-27.0 : ..   ..   ..        :<2>:<5>: ..       :<5>
-26.5 : ..   ..   ..        :<2>:<4>:<4>:
-26.0 : ..   ..   ..             :<1>:
-25.5 : ..   ..   ..        :<4>:<0>:
-------------------------------------------------------------
-25.0 : :<5>:     :<3>:       ..   ..              :<0>:
-24.5 : <1>: :<2>::<3>:       ..   ..              :<3>:
-24.0 : ..   ..        :<3>:  ..   ..
-23.5 : ..   ..   ..   ..   ..   ..
-23.0 : ..   ..        :<5>: ..        :<5>:
-22.5 : <0>: ..   :<5>:     ..        :<3>:
-22.0 : ..   ..   ..   ..   ..   ..
-21.5 : ..   ..   ..   ..   ..   ..
-21.0 : ..   ..   ..   ..   ..   ..
-20.5 : ..   ..   ..   ..   ..   ..
-------------------------------------------------------------
```

Table 12.2 (continued)

	0.2	0.4	0.6	0.8	1.0	1.5	2.0	2.5	3.0	4.0	5.0	6.0	7.0	8.0	10.	12.	15.	20.
-20.0	..	..	..	..	..	..	..	..	..	..	..	..	..	..	..	..	..	..
-19.5	..	..	..	..	..	..	..	..	..	..	..	..	..	..	..	..	..	..
-19.0	..	..	..	..	..	..	..	..	..	..	..	..	..	..	..	..	..	..
-18.5	..	..	..	..	..	..	..	..	..	..	..	..	..	..	..	..	..	..
-18.0	..	..	..	..	..	..	..	..	..	..	..	..	..	..	..	..	..	..
-17.5	..	..	..	..	..	..	..	..	..	..	..	..	..	..	..	..	..	..
-17.0	..	..	..	..	..	..	..	..	..	..	..	..	..	..	..	..	..	..
-16.5	..	..	..	..	..	..	..	..	..	..	..	..	..	..	..	..	..	..
-16.0	..	..	..	..	..	..	..	..	..	..	..	..	..	..	..	..	..	..
-15.5	..	..	..	..	..	..	..	..	..	..	..	..	..	..	..	..	..	..
-15.0	..	..	..	..	..	..	..	..	..	..	..	..	..	..	..	..	..	..
-14.5	..	..	..	..	..	..	..	..	..	..	..	..	..	..	..	..	..	..
-14.0	..	..	..	..	>3<	..	..	..	..	..	..	..	..	..	..	..	..	..
-13.5	..	..	..	..	..	..	..	..	>5<	..	..	..	..	..	..	..	..	..
-13.0	..	..	..	..	..	..	..	..	..	..	..	..	..	..	..	..	..	..
-12.5	..	..	..	..	..	..	..	..	..	>3<	..	..	..	..	..	..	..	..
-12.0	..	..	..	..	..	..	..	..	..	..	..	..	..	..	..	..	..	..
-11.5	..	..	..	..	..	..	..	..	..	..	..	>4<	..	..	..	..	..	..
-11.0	..	..	..	..	..	..	..	..	..	..	>5<	..	..	..	..	..	..	..
-10.5	..	..	..	..	..	..	..	..	..	..	..	>5<	..	..	..	..	..	..
-10.0	..	..	..	..	..	..	..	..	..	..	..	..	..	..	..	..	..	..
-9.5	..	..	..	..	..	..	..	..	..	..	..	..	..	..	..	..	..	>5<
-9.0	..	>4<	>3<	>3<	>1<	..	..	..	..	..	..	..	..	..	..	..	..	>4<
-8.5	..	..	..	>5<	..	..	..	..	..	..	..	..	..	..	..	..	..	>1<
-8.0	..	..	..	..	..	..	..	..	..	..	..	..	..	..	..	..	>3<	>2<
-7.5	..	..	..	..	..	..	..	..	..	..	..	..	..	..	..	..	>2<	>2<
-7.0	..	..	..	..	..	..	..	..	..	..	..	..	..	..	..	..	>2<	>1<
-6.5	..	..	..	..	..	..	..	..	..	..	..	..	..	..	..	..	>2<	>1<
-6.0	..	..	..	..	..	..	..	..	..	..	..	..	..	..	..	..	>2<	>1<
-5.5	..	..	..	<2>	..	..	..	..	..	..	..	..	..	..	..	..	>3<	>1<

Table 12.2 (continued)

:0.2 0.4 0.6 0.8 1.0 1.5 2.0 2.5 3.0 4.0 5.0 6.0 7.0 8.0 10. 12. 15. 20.

Table 12.2 (continued)

```
    :0.2 0.4 0.6 0.8 1.0 1.5 2.0 2.5 3.0 4.0 5.0 6.0 7.0 8.0 10. 12. 15. 20.
10.0 :..  ..  ..  ..  ..  ..  ..  ..  ..  ..  ..  ..  ..  ..  ..  ..  ..  ..
10.5 :..  ..  ..  ..  ..  ..  ..  ..  ..  ..  ..  ..  ..  ..  ..  ..  ..  ..
11.0 :..  ..  ..  ..  ..  ..  ..  ..  ..  ..  ..  ..  ..  ..  ..  ..  ..  ..
11.5 :..  ..  ..  ..  ..  ..  ..  ..  ..  ..  ..  ..  ..  ..  ..  ..  ..  ..
12.0 :..  ..  ..  ..  ..  ..  ..  ..  ..  ..  ..  ..  ..  ..  ..  ..  ..  ..
12.5 :..  ..  ..  ..  ..  ..  ..  ..  ..  ..  ..  ..  ..  ..  ..  ..  ..  ..
13.0 :<5> ..  ..  ..  ..  ..  ..  ..  ..  ..  ..  ..  ..  ..  ..  ..  ..  ..
13.5 :..  ..  ..  ..  ..  ..  ..  ..  ..  ..  ..  ..  ..  ..  ..  ..  ..  ..
14.0 :..  ..  ..  ..  ..  ..  ..  ..  ..  ..  ..  ..  ..  ..  ..  ..  ..  ..
14.5 :..  ..  ..  ..  ..  ..  ..  ..  <4> ..  ..  ..  ..  ..  ..  ..  ..  ..
-------------------------------------------------------------------------------
15.0 :..  ..  ..  ..  ..  ..  ..  ..  ..  ..  ..  ..  ..  ..  ..  ..  ..  ..
15.5 :..  ..  ..  ..  ..  ..  ..  ..  ..  ..  ..  ..  ..  ..  ..  ..  ..  ..
16.0 :..  ..  ..  ..  ..  ..  ..  ..  ..  ..  ..  ..  ..  ..  ..  ..  ..  ..
16.5 :..  ..  ..  ..  ..  ..  ..  ..  ..  ..  ..  ..  ..  ..  ..  ..  ..  ..
17.0 :..  ..  ..  ..  ..  ..  ..  ..  ..  ..  ..  ..  ..  ..  ..  ..  ..  ..
17.5 :..  ..  ..  ..  ..  ..  ..  ..  ..  ..  ..  ..  ..  ..  ..  ..  ..  ..
18.0 :<1>:<5>:<5>:..  ..  ..  ..  ..  ..  ..  ..  ..  ..  ..  ..  ..  ..  ..
18.5 :<2>:<4>:<5>:..  ..  ..  ..  ..  ..  ..  ..  ..  ..  ..  ..  ..  ..  ..
19.0 :..  ..  ..  ..  ..  ..  ..  ..  ..  ..  ..  ..  ..  ..  ..  ..  ..  ..
19.5 :..  ..  ..  ..  ..  ..  ..  ..  ..  ..  ..  ..  ..  ..  ..  ..  ..  ..
-------------------------------------------------------------------------------
20.0 :<5>:..  ..  ..  ..  ..  ..  ..  ..  ..  ..  ..  ..  ..  ..  ..  ..  ..
20.5 :..  :>3<:>2<:>2<:..  ..  ..  ..  ..  ..  ..  ..  ..  ..  ..  ..  ..  ..
21.0 :..  :>5<: :>3<:>0<:..  ..  ..  ..  ..  ..  ..  ..  ..  ..  ..  ..  ..
21.5 :..  ..  ..  ..  ..  ..  ..  :>3<:..  ..  ..  ..  ..  ..  ..  ..  ..  ..
22.0 :..  ..  ..  ..  ..  ..  ..  ..  ..  ..  ..  ..  ..  ..  ..  ..  ..  ..
22.5 :..  ..  ..  ..  ..  ..  ..  ..  ..  ..  ..  ..  ..  ..  ..  ..  ..  ..
23.0 :..  ..  ..  ..  ..  ..  ..  ..  ..  ..  ..  ..  ..  ..  ..  ..  ..  ..
23.5 :..  ..  ..  ..  ..  ..  ..  ..  ..  ..  ..  ..  >3<:..  ..  ..  ..  ..
24.0 :..  ..  ..  ..  ..  ..  ..  ..  ..  ..  ..  ..  ..  ..  ..  ..  ..  ..
24.5 :..  ..  ..  ..  ..  ..  ..  ..  ..  ..  ..  ..  ..  ..  ..  ..  ..  ..
-------------------------------------------------------------------------------
```

Table 12.2 (continued)

	:0.2	0.4	0.6	0.8	1.0	1.5	2.0	2.5	3.0	4.0	5.0	6.0	7.0	8.0	10.	12.	15.	20.
25.0																		
25.5																		
26.0																		
26.5																		
27.0				<3>														
27.5		<0>	<1>	<1>	<4>						<5>	<5>						
28.0				<5>							<2>					<2>		
28.5		<4>								<3>	<3>							
29.0				<4>	<5>	<2>			<2>						<3>	<5>		
29.5				<2>	<2>	<5>					<5>		<3>		<3>	<4>	<5>	
30.0										<1>	<1>	<2>	<1>		<5>			
30.5										<2>	<0>	<1>	<1>					
31.0									<4>	<0>	<2>	<2>	<2>	<4>				
31.5									<1>	<1>	<1>	<2>	<3>					
32.0									<0>	<3>	<1>	<1>						
32.5	<5>	<0>	<0>	<3>	<4>		<5>			<4>	<2>	<1>	<0>					
33.0	<1>		<1>	<3>	<1>						<5>	<3>	<1>					
33.5			<0>	<1>	<2>		<5>				<1>	<1>						
34.0	<0>	<3>					<3>	<4>			<3>	<3>	<5>					
34.5	<3>						<3>		<4>			<1>	<5>					
35.0			<3>			<3>					<5>	<4>	<4>		<2>			
35.5	<2>	<5>									<5>	<5>	<4>	<5>				
36.0											<2>	<4>	<4>	<4>				
36.5								<4>			<4>	<4>	<4>	<4>		<5>		
37.0							<5>				<3>	<2>	<4>			<5>		
37.5								<4>				<3>	<5>					
38.0												<3>	<4>	<2>	<3>	<4>	<2>	<5>
38.5															<3>			<4>
39.0														<4>	<4>			

We ran 100 simulations as described above. For each target window, we calculated the number of hits scored by the observed data upon that target. We then asked the following questions:

(i) In how many of the 100 simulations were there as many or more hits upon this target?
(ii) In how many of the 100 simulations were there as many or fewer hits upon this target?

The answer to question (i), expressed as a percentage, then gives the significance level at which the null hypothesis can be rejected in favour of this target being preferred; similarly question (ii) expresses the significance level in favour of avoidance.

The answers to questions (i) and (ii) for the various target windows are tabulated in Table 12.2. Wherever answers of 5 or less were obtained to either question, they are shown in the table. Numbers enclosed thus <.> indicate preference; >.< indicates avoidance. The centres of target windows are spaced at intervals of $0^{o}.5$, and widths from $0^{o}.2$ up to 20° are considered. At the highest precision concerned ($0^{o}.2$), the spacing of target window centres is too coarse and could fail to reveal features of interest. For this reason target windows of width $0^{o}.2$ are listed separately in Table 12.3, with their centres spaced at $0^{o}.1$ intervals.

In view of the large number of hypotheses effectively being considered, we need to lower the significance level at which we are prepared to reject the null hypothesis in favour of any one of them. The precise amount by which we should do this, however, is uncertain. Freeman & Elmore (1979) have noted the problem, but we still lack the theoretical framework to deal with it in a rigorous way. In what follows we shall only take an interest in significance levels less than about 1%, i.e. figures of 1 or 0 occurring in the tables. However in the absence of a developed statistical theory on this point, the only formal statement we can make is that if we can confidently reject the null (random) hypothesis in favour of any of the alternatives presented, it is in favour of those we shall now pick out. We note also that the expected distribution upon which we base our results is itself only an estimate obtained from 100 simulations, and will as a result itself be subject to uncertainties.

(ctd. on page 264

- - - - - -

TABLE 12.3. Analysis of the declination data for target window widths of $0^{o}.2$.

Column and row headings, when combined, indicate the target window centre

Table entries indicate significance levels where these are below 5%
  <.> indicates preference
  >.< indicates avoidance

Table 12.3

minus..	-30	-25	-20	-15	-10	-5	0	::	0	5	10	15	20	25	30	35	..plus
-5.0																	0.0
-4.9			<5>										>5<				0.1
-4.8			<1>					>5<									0.2
-4.7			<3>														0.3
-4.6			<2>													<4>	0.4
-4.5			<1>													<2>	0.5
-4.4																<1>	0.6
-4.3		<4>															0.7
-4.2																	0.8
-4.1																	0.9
-4.0																	1.0
-3.9																	1.1
-3.8							>5<										1.2
-3.7																	1.3
-3.6																	1.4
-3.5			>5<														1.5
-3.4																	1.6
-3.3																	1.7
-3.2																	1.8
-3.1																	1.9
-3.0																	2.0
-2.9																	2.1
-2.8															<2>		2.2
-2.7			<4>														2.3
-2.6			<1>														2.4

Table 12.3 (continued)

minus..	:-30	-25	-20	-15	-10	-5	0 :: 0	5	10	15	20	25	30	35:	..plus
-2.5		>5<	<0>				::					<0>	<5>		2.5
-2.4							::						<5>		2.6
-2.3			<1>				::								2.7
-2.2							::								2.8
-2.1							::								2.9
-2.0							::	<5>							3.0
-1.9							::					<0>			3.1
-1.8				>4<			::					<2>			3.2
-1.7							::				<3>	<0>			3.3
-1.6							::				<1>	<5>			3.4
-1.5							::								3.5
-1.4							::								3.6
-1.3							::								3.7
-1.2							::								3.8
-1.1							::								3.9
-1.0							::					<0>			4.0
-0.9		<5>					::					<0>			4.1
-0.8		<0>					::					<2>			4.2
-0.7		<0>					::					<4>			4.3
-0.6							::								4.4
-0.5							::					<3>			4.5
-0.4							::								4.6
-0.3							::								4.7
-0.2							::								4.8
-0.1		<1>					::								4.9

12.4.2 Evidence of avoidance

In this and the following section we locate the particular declination target windows for which we obtain evidence for avoidance or preference, and examine the data that constitute that evidence.

Strong evidence of avoidance occurs with target windows over 4° in width in the vicinity of declination 0°. It is strongest when very wide windows are considered. The lowest number of hits was obtained in the case of declination interval |-14.0, +6.0|. The number of hits upon this interval was 39 as opposed to the 65 expected by chance. The 39 lines in question are listed below. Capital letters are used to distinguish on-site indications from inter-site ones.

|-14.0, +6.0|. Total hits 39, expected 65.

Line 1:	LH7 – LH8	B 1	Kirkibost – Bernera Bridge
Line 14:	LH16 W row to W	1a	CALLANISH (ALIGNMENT)
Line 15:	LH16 W row to E	1a	CALLANISH (ALIGNMENT)
Line 16:	LH16 E row to W	1a	CALLANISH (ALIGNMENT)
Line 17:	LH16 E row to E	1a	CALLANISH (ALIGNMENT)
Line 19:	LH16 – LH18	A 1	Callanish – Cnoc Fillibhir Bheag
Line 20:	LH16 – LH19	A 1	Callanish – Cnoc Ceann a'Gharaidh
Line 25:	LH18 – LH16	A 1	Cnoc Fillibhir Bheag – Callanish
Line 26:	LH18 – LH19	A 1	Cnoc Fillibhir Bheag – Cnoc Ceann a'G
Line 35:	LH21 – LH22	A 2	Ceann Hulavig – Cul a'Chleit
Line 42:	LH22 – LH21	A 2	Cul a'Chleit – Ceann Hulavig
Line 43:	LH22 – LH24	B 2	Cul a'Chleit – Airigh nam Bidearan
Line 58:	UI6 To ESE	5a	BORVE, BERNERAY (SLAB)
Line 62:	UI15 – UI19	A 2	Maari – Blashaval
Line 65:	UI22 – UI26	A 3	South Clettraval – Beinn a'Charra(NU)
Line 67:	UI23 ba (To E)	3a	TOROGHAS (PAIR)
Line 78:	UI28 – UI33	A 3	Unival – Ben Langass
Line 81:	UI31 To ESE	5a	CLADDACH KYLES (SLAB)
Line 85:	UI31 – UI35	B 3	Claddach Kyles – Cringraval W
Line 98:	UI48 – UI49	A 3	Stoneybridge – Beinn a'Charra (SU)
Line 148:	LN18 ab (To W)	4a	GLENAMACRIE (POSSIBLE PAIR)
Line 175:	AR16 – AR17	A 2	Rowanfield – Duntroon
Line 190:	AR32 To ESE	5a	OAKFIELD (SLAB)
Line 194:	JU2 – JU3	B 2	Knockrome W – Ardfernal
Line 196:	JU3 – JU4	A 2	Ardfernal – Knockrome
Line 197:	JU3 – JU5	B 2	Ardfernal – Leargybreck
Line 199:	JU4 ab (To WSW)	3a	KNOCKROME (PAIR)
Line 201:	JU4 – JU5	B 2	Knockrome – Leargybreck
Line 208:	IS3 To WSW	5a	BEINN A'CHUIRN (SLAB)
Line 211:	IS6 – IS7	A 2	Beinn Cham – Ballachlavin
Line 223:	IS23 To E	5a	GARTACHARRA (SLAB)
Line 231:	IS39 To E	3b	LAGAVULIN N (SLAB, FALLEN SLAB)
Line 232:	IS39 – IS41	A 2	Lagavulin N – Laphroaig
Line 236:	KT2 ca (To ESE)	3a	CARSE (OUTLIER TO ALIGNED SLABS)
Line 238:	KT2 cb (To ESE)	3a	CARSE (OUTLIER TO ALIGNED SLABS)
Line 249:	KT19 ab (To WSW)	4b	SOUTH MUASDALE (MENHIR, POSS. MENHIR)
Line 262:	KT35 To ESE	5a	GLENLUSSA LODGE (SLAB)
Line 266:	KT37 – KT39	A 3	Stewarton – Mingary
Line 272:	KT39 – KT37	A 3	Mingary – Stewarton

The data which do hit this declination interval consist of 17 on-site and 22 inter-site indications. This proportion is not significantly different from 130:146, the value in the data set as a whole, and consequently that which would have been expected by chance. Thus it appears that both on-site and inter-site indications contribute to the evidence of avoidance of declinations between -14° and $+6^\circ$.

The 22 inter-site indications consist of 8 in Lewis (7 in the vicinity of Callanish), 5 in the Uists, 1 in mid-Argyll, 4 in Jura, 2 in Islay and 2 in Kintyre. This again is roughly in the proportions expected by chance, although the absence of data from Mull might be noteworthy. The data from Jura consist entirely of alignments between sites in the vicinity of Knockrome.

Of the 17 on-site indications, only 4 involve alignments and none involves intact aligned slabs. This is only a little less than the number expected by chance, since 43 out of the total 130 on-site alignments fall into classes 1 & 2. Nonetheless it is of interest that the four alignments are simply the east and west rows at Callanish (LH16), each viewed in both directions. The radial alignments there are unique, and Callanish is the only example where no single class 1 or 2 indication can be regarded as reflecting the general orientation of the site as a whole. The remaining class 1 & 2 indications (stone alignments) completely avoid declinations within about 10° of 0°.

Five indications involve the line joining pairs of menhirs. Two - those at Toroghas, North Uist (UI23) and Knockrome, Jura (JU4) - are intact, and a third - at Lagavulin N, Islay (IS39) - involves one standing and one fallen slab. However the remaining two indications arise at Carse, Kintyre (KT2). This site consists of an aligned pair of flat menhirs and a third outlying menhir in a direction unrelated to the alignment. The class (3a) indications represent orientations between the outlier and each menhir of the aligned pair in turn: the indication along the aligned pair did not quite qualify as class (1b) because one of the aligned stones failed to meet the "width equals twice thickness" criterion and was not counted as a slab.

The site at Glenamacrie, Lorn (LN18) consists of a menhir and a nearby rounded boulder which might or might not be artificially placed and associated with it. The indication formed by the line joining them hits the declination window |−14.0, +6.0|. So also does one indication formed by the menhir and possible stump of a second at South Muasdale, Kintyre (KT19). The remaining six on-site indications hitting the window are formed by the flat faces of slabs.

Thus although the proportions of lines of particular classifications hitting declination window |−14.0, +6.0| are much as would be expected by chance, a number of the higher-classified on-site lines are either exceptional or unimpressive.

Evidence of avoidance also occurs in three isolated cases at much higher precision. They are as follows.

|−9.0, −8.0|. Total hits 1, expected 5.

Line 190: AR32 To ESE   5a   OAKFIELD (SLAB)

|+4.6, +5.4|. Total hits 1, expected 5.

Line 25:   LH18 - LH16   A 1 Cnoc Fillibhir Bheag - Callanish

|+20.0, +22.0|. Total hits 2, expected 8.

Line 50:   LH24 - LH21   B 2 Airigh nam Bidearan - Ceann Hulavig
Line 76:   UI28 - UI23   A 3 Unival - Toroghas

In these cases, however, it is impssible to draw any meaningful conclusions.

12.4.3 Evidence of preference

There is evidence of preference for certain southern and northern declinations at a variety of precisions. We consider the southern declinations first, beginning at the lowest precision.

There is a marked preference for declinations within about 6° of -25°. Target intervals |-31.5, -19.5| and |-31.0, -19.0| both have zero values, indicating that in no simulation were there as many hits in the window as were attained by the observed data. The significance falls off sharply when the centre of the window is moved by a degree or two. The lines hitting the two windows are in fact exactly the same, but the expected number of hits is slightly smaller (so that the significance is slightly greater) in the case of |-31.0, -19.0|. The lines in question are listed below.

|-31.0, -19.0|. Total hits 72, expected 54.

Line 2:   LH8 ba (To SW)   3a   BERNERA BRIDGE (PAIR OF THREE)
Line 4:   LH10 ab (To SE)   4a   BEINN BHEAG (MENHIR, POSS. MENHIR)
Line 5:   LH10 - LH16   A 2 Beinn Bheag - Callanish
Line 6:   LH10 - LH18   A 1 Beinn Bheag - Cnoc Fillibhir Bheag
Line 8:   LH10 - LH21   A 3 Beinn Bheag - Ceann Hulavig
Line 9:   LH10 - LH22   A 3 Beinn Bheag - Cnoc Ceann a'Gharaidh
Line 10:   LH10 - LH24   B 3 Beinn Bheag - Airigh nam Bidearan
Line 21:   LH16 - LH21   A 3 Callanish - Ceann Hulavig
Line 23:   LH16 - LH24   B 3 Callanish - Airigh nam Bidearan
Line 27:   LH18 - LH21   A 1 Cnoc Fillibhir Bheag - Ceann Hulavig
Line 28:   LH18 - LH24   B 2 Cnoc Fillibhir Bheag - Airigh nam Bid.
Line 30:   LH19 - LH22   A 1 Cnoc Ceann a'Gharaidh - Cul a'Chleit
Line 31:   LH19 - LH24   B 2 Cnoc Ceann a'Gharaidh - Airigh nam B.
Line 36:   LH21 - LH24   B 2 Ceann Hulavig - Airigh nam Bidearan
Line 38:   LH22 ab (To SSW) 3a   CUL A'CHLEIT (PAIR)
Line 45:   LH24 dcb(To SSE) 3c   AIRIGH NAM BIDEARAN (ALIGNMENT, POSS.)
Line 54:   LH36 - LH37   A 3 Horgabost - Scarista
Line 59:   UI6 - UI9   A 3 Borve, Berneray - Newtonferry
Line 60:   UI9 ba (To SW)   3a   NEWTONFERRY (PAIR)
Line 66:   UI22 - UI31   A 3 South Clettraval - Claddach Kyles
Line 69:   UI23 - UI28   A 1 Toroghas - Unival
Line 73:   UI26 - UI28   A 1 Beinn a'Charra (NU) - Unival
Line 74:   UI26 - UI31   A 3 Beinn a'Charra (NU) - Claddach Kyles
Line 75:   UI28 To SSE   5a   UNIVAL (SLAB)

```
Line 79:  UI28  - UI35       B 2  Unival - Cringraval W
Line 80:  UI28  - UI37       A 3  Unival - Loch a'Phobuill
Line 87:  UI33  - UI37       A 2  Ben Langass - Loch a'Phobuill
Line 91:  UI35  - UI40       B 3  Cringraval W - Carinish
Line 101: UI49  To SW        5a   BEINN A'CHARRA (SU) (SLAB)
Line 103: UI49  - UI50       A 3  Beinn a'Charra (SU) - Ru Ardvule
Line 107: UI57 ba (To SW)    3b   BORVE, BARRA (PAIR)
Line 111: NA1  ba (To SSE)   4a   BRANAULT (MENHIR, POSS. MENHIR)
Line 116: CT2   - CT3        A 2  Totronald - Breacacha
Line 118: CT7   - CT8        A 2  Hough - Barrapoll
Line 120: CT9   To SSW       5a   BALINOE (SLAB)
Line 122: ML2   To SSE       2c   QUINISH (ALIGNMENT)
Line 125: ML4  cba (To S)    2a   BALLISCATE (ALIGNMENT)
Line 126: ML7   To SE        5a   CILLCHRIOSD (SLAB)
Line 131: ML11 abc(To SSE)   1a   DERVAIG S (ALIGNMENT)
Line 133: ML12 cba(To SSW)   2c   ARDNACROSS (ALIGNMENT)
Line 134: ML15 - ML16        A 2  Killichronan - Gruline
Line 141: ML25 - ML27        B 2  Uluvalt - Rossal
Line 145: ML31 To SW         5a   UISKEN (SLAB)
Line 150: LN22 cba(To SSE)   1a   DUACHY (ALIGNMENT)
Line 152: AR2   - AR3        A 2  Sluggan - Barbreck
Line 154: AR3  ba (To S)     1b   BARBRECK (TWO ALIGNED SLABS)
Line 157: AR7   - AR8        A 2  Torran - Ford
Line 160: AR9   - AR10       A 2  Glennan N - Glennan S
Line 164: AR13 S2-S1-S5      1a   KILMARTIN (ALIGNMENT)
Line 166: AR13 S3-S1-S4      1a   KILMARTIN (ALIGNMENT)
Line 169: AR15 dcba(To SE)   1a   DUNCRACAIG (ALIGNMENT)
Line 171: AR15 fe (To SSE)   1b   DUNCRACAIG (TWO ALIGNED SLABS)
Line 172: AR15 - AR18        B 3  Duncracaig - Crinan Moss
Line 174: AR16 To SE         5a   ROWANFIELD (SLAB)
Line 177: AR17 - AR18        B 2  Duntroon - Crinan Moss
Line 182: AR28 cba(To SSE)   2a   DUNAMUCK I (ALIGNMENT)
Line 183: AR28 - AR29        A 2  Dunamuck I - Dunamuck II
Line 184: AR28 - AR30        A 2  Dunamuck I - Dunamuck III
Line 186: AR29 ba (To SE)    1b   DUNAMUCK II (TWO ALIGNED SLABS)
Line 207: JU9   To SSE       5a   CAMAS AN STACA (SLAB)
Line 215: IS7   - IS12       A 3  Ballachlavin - Mullach Dubh
Line 240: KT3   To SE        5a   ARDPATRICK (SLAB)
Line 242: KT4   To S         5a   AVINAGILLAN (SLAB)
Line 244: KT5   To SSW       1a   ESCART (ALIGNMENT)
Line 245: KT8  ba (To SE)    5b   DUNSKEIG (POSSIBLE PAIR)
Line 247: KT10 cba (To SW)   1a   BALLOCHROY (ALIGNMENT)
Line 250: KT23 To SW         5a   BEINN AN TUIRC (SLAB)
Line 252: KT27 cba (To SW)   2a   CLOCHKEIL (ALIGNMENT)
Line 258: KT31 - KT39        A 3  Craigs - Mingary
Line 260: KT32 - KT39        A 3  Glencraigs S - Mingary
Line 268: KT39 To SE         5a   MINGARY (SLAB)
Line 274: KT41 To SE         5a   KNOCKSTAPPLE (SLAB)
```

These data comprise 35 on-site and 37 inter-site indications, so that the proportion of one to the other is much as would be expected by chance. The proportions of on-site indications of particular classifications are also much as would be expected by chance, although the number of class 1 & 2 indications is somewhat high (15 as opposed to 11 expected by chance). It is notable, however, that all the class 1 & 2 indications are from sites in the Inner Hebrides and mainland Argyll, whereas some contribution from LH & UI sites (which account for 8 of the 29 class 1 indications) might have been expected. It is even more noticeable that of the nine sites in areas ML, AR, IS & KT which account for the 21 class 1 indications in the data as a whole, all but one are represented in the sample above.

At higher resolutions the indications isolated above split into two distinct groupings, each of which gives rise to low significance levels at higher precisions. The more southerly grouping leads to low significance levels with target intervals of a variety of widths, each of which has $-31^{\circ}.0$ as its lower limit. At a target width of 4° we obtain the following:

|-31.0, -27.0|. Total hits 37, expected 25.

Line 5:	LH10 – LH16	A 2	Beinn Bheag – Callanish
Line 6:	LH10 – LH18	A 1	Beinn Bheag – Cnoc Fillibhir Bheag
Line 8:	LH10 – LH21	A 3	Beinn Bheag – Ceann Hulavig
Line 9:	LH10 – LH22	A 3	Beinn Bheag – Cnoc Ceann a'Gharaidh
Line 10:	LH10 – LH24	B 3	Beinn Bheag – Airigh nam Bidearan
Line 27:	LH18 – LH21	A 1	Cnoc Fillibhir Bheag – Ceann Hulavig
Line 28:	LH18 – LH24	B 2	Cnoc Fillibhir Bheag – Airigh nam Bid.
Line 31:	LH19 – LH24	B 2	Cnoc Ceann a'Gharaidh – Airigh nam B.
Line 45:	LH24 dcb(To SSE)	3c	AIRIGH NAM BIDEARAN (ALIGNMENT, POSS.)
Line 54:	LH36 – LH37	A 3	Horgabost – Scarista
Line 59:	UI6 – UI9	A 3	Borve, Berneray – Newtonferry
Line 66:	UI22 – UI31	A 3	South Clettraval – Claddach Kyles
Line 74:	UI26 – UI31	A 3	Beinn a'Charra (NU) – Claddach Kyles
Line 75:	UI28 To SSE	5a	UNIVAL (SLAB)
Line 79:	UI28 – UI35	B 2	Unival – Cringraval W
Line 87:	UI33 – UI37	A 2	Ben Langass – Loch a'Phobuill
Line 91:	UI35 – UI40	B 3	Cringraval W – Carinish
Line 116:	CT2 – CT3	A 2	Totronald – Breacacha
Line 118:	CT7 – CT8	A 2	Hough – Barrapoll
Line 120:	CT9 To SSW	5a	BALINOE (SLAB)
Line 122:	ML2 To SSE	2c	QUINISH (ALIGNMENT)
Line 125:	ML4 cba (To S)	2a	BALLISCATE (ALIGNMENT)
Line 131:	ML11 abc(To SSE)	1a	DERVAIG S (ALIGNMENT)
Line 134:	ML15 – ML16	A 2	Killichronan – Gruline
Line 141:	ML25 – ML27	B 2	Uluvalt – Rossal
Line 152:	AR2 – AR3	A 2	Sluggan – Barbreck
Line 154:	AR3 ba (To S)	1b	BARBRECK (TWO ALIGNED SLABS)
Line 164:	AR13 S2-S1-S5	1a	KILMARTIN (ALIGNMENT)
Line 166:	AR13 S3-S1-S4	1a	KILMARTIN (ALIGNMENT)
Line 171:	AR15 fe (To SSE)	1b	DUNCRACAIG (TWO ALIGNED SLABS)
Line 177:	AR17 – AR18	B 2	Duntroon – Crinan Moss
Line 182:	AR28 cba(To SSE)	2a	DUNAMUCK I (ALIGNMENT)
Line 183:	AR28 – AR29	A 2	Dunamuck I – Dunamuck II
Line 184:	AR28 – AR30	A 2	Dunamuck I – Dunamuck III
Line 207:	JU9 To SSE	5a	CAMAS AN STACA (SLAB)
Line 242:	KT4 To S	5a	AVINAGILLAN (SLAB)
Line 244:	KT5 To SSW	1a	ESCART (ALIGNMENT)

Again, the overall proportions of indications of particular classifications are much as expected, but a predominance of alignments from Mull and Argyll is beginning to become clear. Three of the six Mull alignments and four of the six Argyll ones feature in this list.

At a target width of 1°.5 we obtain the following:

|-30.75, -29.25|. Total hits 21, expected 12.

Line 5:	LH10 - LH16	A 2	Beinn Bheag - Callanish
Line 8:	LH10 - LH21	A 3	Beinn Bheag - Ceann Hulavig
Line 10:	LH10 - LH24	B 3	Beinn Bheag - Airigh nam Bidearan
Line 27:	LH18 - LH21	A 1	Cnoc Fillibhir Bheag - Ceann Hulavig
Line 28:	LH18 - LH24	B 2	Cnoc Fillibhir Bheag - Airigh nam Bid.
Line 45:	LH24 dcb(To SSE)	3c	AIRIGH NAM BIDEARAN (ALIGNMENT, POSS.)
Line 66:	UI22 - UI31	A 3	South Clettraval - Claddach Kyles
Line 74:	UI26 - UI31	A 3	Beinn a'Charra (NU) - Claddach Kyles
Line 75:	UI28 To SSE	5a	UNIVAL (SLAB)
Line 116:	CT2 - CT3	A 2	Totronald - Breacacha
Line 118:	CT7 - CT8	A 2	Hough - Barrapoll
Line 141:	ML25 - ML27	B 2	Uluvalt - Rossal
Line 154:	AR3 ba (To S)	1b	BARBRECK (TWO ALIGNED SLABS)
Line 164:	AR13 S2-S1-S5	1a	KILMARTIN (ALIGNMENT)
Line 166:	AR13 S3-S1-S4	1a	KILMARTIN (ALIGNMENT)
Line 171:	AR15 fe (To SSE)	1b	DUNCRACAIG (TWO ALIGNED SLABS)
Line 177:	AR17 - AR18	B 2	Duntroon - Crinan Moss
Line 182:	AR28 cba(To SSE)	2a	DUNAMUCK I (ALIGNMENT)
Line 183:	AR28 - AR29	A 2	Dunamuck I - Dunamuck II
Line 184:	AR28 - AR30	A 2	Dunamuck I - Dunamuck III
Line 244:	KT5 To SSW	1a	ESCART (ALIGNMENT)

The proportion of class 1 and 2 indications amongst the on-site lines appearing in this list is six out of eight, far more than would have been expected by chance. One of the two exceptions is in fact the alignment of possible menhirs at Airigh nam Bidearan in Lewis, which only has a low classification because of the uncertain archaeological status of the site. Thus all but one of the on-site lines in this sample represent stone alignments. Furthermore a geographical trend of possible significance has become evident: the four Argyll sites noted above remain in the list, whereas the Mull alignments have now disappeared.

It is worth remembering here that the presence of inter-related indications may produce misleading clumping in our declination data. Three inter-related sets of lines can be recognised amongst those hitting the |-30.75, -29.25| target interval:

(i) Lines 5, 8 & 10 are all from Beinn Bheag to other sites in the vicinity of Callanish.
(ii) Lines 164 & 166 are along adjacent lines of three stones in the formation of five at Kilmartin.
(iii) Lines 182, 183 & 184 are along the alignment at Dunamuck I, and from this site to the two other Dunamuck sites, which are also in the direction of the alignment.

At target widths of 0°.4 and 0°.2 we obtain the following:

|-30.7, -30.3|. Total hits 9, expected 5.

Line 5:   LH10 - LH16   A 2 Beinn Bheag - Callanish

```
Line 8:    LH10 - LH21      A 3  Beinn Bheag - Ceann Hulavig
Line 10:   LH10 - LH24      B 3  Beinn Bheag - Airigh nam Bidearan
Line 74:   UI26 - UI31      A 3  Beinn a'Charra (NU) - Claddach Kyles
Line 116:  CT2  - CT3       A 2  Totronald - Breacacha
Line 154:  AR3  ba (To S)   1b   BARBRECK (TWO ALIGNED SLABS)
Line 164:  AR13 S2-S1-S5    1a   KILMARTIN (ALIGNMENT)
Line 182:  AR28 cba(To SSE) 2a   DUNAMUCK I (ALIGNMENT)
Line 184:  AR28 - AR30      A 2  Dunamuck I - Dunamuck III
```

|-30.9, -30.7|. Total hits 10, expected 4.

```
Line 5:    LH10 - LH16      A 2  Beinn Bheag - Callanish
Line 8:    LH10 - LH21      A 3  Beinn Bheag - Ceann Hulavig
Line 116:  CT2  - CT3       A 2  Totronald - Breacacha
Line 122:  ML2  To SSE      2c   QUINISH (ALIGNMENT)
Line 154:  AR3  ba (To S)   1b   BARBRECK (TWO ALIGNED SLABS)
Line 164:  AR13 S2-S1-S5    1a   KILMARTIN (ALIGNMENT)
Line 182:  AR28 cba(To SSE) 2a   DUNAMUCK I (ALIGNMENT)
Line 184:  AR28 - AR30      A 2  Dunamuck I - Dunamuck III
Line 207:  JU9  To SSE      5a   CAMAS AN STACA (SLAB)
Line 242:  KT4  To S        5a   AVINAGILLAN (SLAB)
```

|-30.8, -30.6|. Total hits 9, expected 4.

As above, but missing Line 242.

It is noteworthy that three of the Argyll alignments remain in these lists.

A grouping is evident in Table 12.2 at declinations in the vicinity of -25°, although low significance levels are only achieved when the target width is reduced to its minimum value of $0^\circ.2$. The relevant cases are the following:

|-25.2, -25.0|. Total hits 7, expected 3.

```
Line 38:   LH22 ab (To SSW) 3a   CUL A'CHLEIT (PAIR)
Line 157:  AR7  - AR8       A 2  Torran - Ford
Line 169:  AR15 dcba(To SE) 1a   DUNCRACAIG (ALIGNMENT)
Line 247:  KT10 cba (To SW) 1a   BALLOCHROY (ALIGNMENT)
Line 250:  KT23 To SW       5a   BEINN AN TUIRC (SLAB)
Line 258:  KT31 - KT39      A 3  Craigs - Mingary
Line 274:  KT41 To SE       5a   KNOCKSTAPPLE (SLAB)
```

|-24.9, -24.7|. Total hits 7, expected 3.

```
Line 21:   LH16 - LH21      A 3  Callanish - Ceann Hulavig
Line 38:   LH22 ab (To SSW) 3a   CUL A'CHLEIT (PAIR)
Line 169:  AR15 dcba(To SE) 1a   DUNCRACAIG (ALIGNMENT)
Line 174:  AR16 To SE       5a   ROWANFIELD (SLAB)
Line 247:  KT10 cba (To SW) 1a   BALLOCHROY (ALIGNMENT)
Line 250:  KT23 To SW       5a   BEINN AN TUIRC (SLAB)
Line 274:  KT41 To SE       5a   KNOCKSTAPPLE (SLAB)
```

|-24.6, -24.4|. Total hits 7, expected 3.

```
Line 23:  LH16 - LH24        B 3   Callanish - Airigh nam Bidearan
Line 38:  LH22 ab (To SSW)   3a    CUL A'CHLEIT (PAIR)
Line 80:  UI28 - UI37        A 3   Unival - Loch a'Phobuill
Line 169: AR15 dcba(To SE)   1a    DUNCRACAIG (ALIGNMENT)
Line 174: AR16 To SE         5a    ROWANFIELD (SLAB)
Line 247: KT10 cba (To SW)   1a    BALLOCHROY (ALIGNMENT)
Line 250: KT23 To SW         5a    BEINN AN TUIRC (SLAB)
```

These data include a high proportion of on-site indications, and show a notable bias towards sites in Kintyre and Argyll.

Low significance levels are evident in Table 12.3 for three target intervals of width $0°.2$ in the vicinity of $-22°.5$. The central one, for which a value of zero is obtained, is the following.

|-22.6, -22.4|. Total hits 7, expected 3.

```
Line 2:   LH8  ba (To SW)    3a    BERNERA BRIDGE (PAIR OF THREE)
Line 103: UI49 - UI50        A 3   Beinn a'Charra (SU) - Ru Ardvule
Line 133: ML12 cba(To SSW)   2c    ARDNACROSS (ALIGNMENT)
Line 172: AR15 - AR18        B 3   Duncracaig - Crinan Moss
Line 240: KT3  To SE         5a    ARDPATRICK (SLAB)
Line 252: KT27 cba (To SW)   2a    CLOCHKEIL (ALIGNMENT)
Line 268: KT39 To SE         5a    MINGARY (SLAB)
```

The proportion of on-site indications in this list is high also, and again it includes three Kintyre sites.

* * * * * *

The main group of preferred northern declinations is between $+27°$ and $+34°$, but there is an isolated grouping around $+18°$ which appears marginally significant at reasonably high precision. A value of one was obtained for the following target interval:

|+17.8, +18.2|. Total hits 7, expected 3.

```
Line 52:  LH29 To NW         6     DURSAINEAN NE (POSSIBLE SLAB)
Line 94:  UI37 - UI35        B 2   Loch a'Phobuill - Cringraval W
Line 138: ML18 ba (To ENE)   3a    CRAGAIG (PAIR)
Line 191: AR33 To WNW        5a    KILMORY (SLAB)
Line 209: IS4  To WNW        5a    FINLAGGAN (SLAB)
Line 216: IS11 ab (To ENE)   3a    KNOCKLEAROCH (PAIR)
Line 255: KT29 To ENE        5a    HIGH PARK (SLAB)
```

As with the previous lists the proportion of on-site lines is high. Here they consist entirely of stone pairs and single slabs, though from a selection of geographical areas.

For northern declinations the situation at low precision is less clear cut than for the southern ones. Nonetheless a general preference is evident for declinations between about $+27°$ and $+34°$. The target interval |+28.0, +34.0| shows the effect most markedly.

|+28.0, +34.0|. Total hits 54, expected 30.

```
Line 11:  LH16 av W to N    1a   CALLANISH (ALIGNMENT)
Line 12:  LH16 av E to N    1a   CALLANISH (ALIGNMENT)
Line 13:  LH16 S row to N   1a   CALLANISH (ALIGNMENT)
Line 18:  LH16 - LH10       A 2  Callanish - Beinn Bheag
Line 24:  LH18 - LH10       A 2  Cnoc Fillibhir Bheag - Beinn Bheag
Line 29:  LH19 - LH10       A 3  Cnoc Ceann a'Gharaidh - Beinn Bheag
Line 32:  LH21 - LH10       A 3  Ceann Hulavig - Beinn Bheag
Line 34:  LH21 - LH18       A 2  Ceann Hulavig - Cnoc Fillibhir Bheag
Line 44:  LH24 bcd(To NNW)  3c   AIRIGH NAM BIDEARAN (ALIGNMENT, POSS.)
Line 46:  LH24 - LH10       B 3  Airigh nam Bidearan - Beinn Bheag
Line 48:  LH24 - LH18       B 2  Airigh nam Bidearan - Cnoc Fillibhir B
Line 56:  LH37 - LH36       A 3  Scarista - Horgabost
Line 82:  UI31 - UI22       A 3  Claddach Kyles - South Clettraval
Line 83:  UI31 - UI23       A 3  Claddach Kyles - Toroghas
Line 84:  UI31 - UI26       A 3  Claddach Kyles - Beinn a'Charra (NU)
Line 88:  UI35 - UI28       B 1  Cringraval W - Unival
Line 93:  UI37 - UI33       A 2  Loch a'Phobuill - Ben Langass
Line 104: UI50 - UI48       A 1  Ru Ardvule - Stoneybridge
Line 106: UI57 ab (To NE)   3b   BORVE, BARRA (PAIR)
Line 110: NA1  ab (To NNW)  4a   BRANAULT (MENHIR, POSS. MENHIR)
Line 112: NA3  To NNW       5a   CAMAS NAN GEALL (SLAB)
Line 114: CT2  ab (To NNE)  3a   TOTRONALD (PAIR)
Line 117: CT3  - CT2        A 1  Breacacha - Totronald
Line 119: CT8  - CT7        A 2  Barrapoll - Hough
Line 124: ML4  abc (To N)   2a   BALLISCATE (ALIGNMENT)
Line 128: ML9  To NNW       1a   MAOL MOR (ALIGNMENT)
Line 129: ML9  - ML1        A 3  Maol Mor - Glengorm
Line 130: ML10 To NNW       2a   DERVAIG N (ALIGNMENT)
Line 132: ML12 abc(To NNE)  2c   ARDNACROSS (ALIGNMENT)
Line 143: ML30 To NNW       6    TAOSLIN (SLAB)
Line 147: LN7  To N         5a   BENDERLOCH N (SLAB)
Line 149: LN22 abc(To NNW)  1a   DUACHY (ALIGNMENT)
Line 155: AR3  - AR2        A 2  Barbreck - Sluggan
Line 158: AR8  - AR7        A 2  Ford - Torran
Line 161: AR10 - AR9        A 2  Glennan S - Glennan N
Line 162: AR13 S2-S3-S6     1a   KILMARTIN (ALIGNMENT)
Line 163: AR13 S5-S1-S2     1a   KILMARTIN (ALIGNMENT)
Line 165: AR13 S4-S1-S3     1a   KILMARTIN (ALIGNMENT)
Line 167: AR13 S5-S4        1b   KILMARTIN (TWO ALIGNED SLABS)
Line 168: AR15 abcd(To NW)  1a   DUNCRACAIG (ALIGNMENT)
Line 170: AR15 ef (To NNW)  1b   DUNCRACAIG (TWO ALIGNED SLABS)
Line 173: AR16 To NW        5a   ROWANFIELD (SLAB)
Line 179: AR18 - AR17       B 2  Crinan Moss - Duntroon
Line 180: AR27 ab (To NNW)  4a   DUNADD (PAIR)
Line 187: AR29 - AR28       A 2  Dunamuck II - Dunamuck I
Line 188: AR30 - AR28       A 2  Dunamuck III - Dunamuck I
Line 204: JU7  To NNE       2a   SANNAIG (ALIGNMENT)
Line 206: JU9  To NNW       5a   CAMAS AN STACA (SLAB)
Line 219: IS12 - IS5        A 3  Mullach Dubh - Scanistle
Line 226: IS31 - IS28       B 1  Kelsay - Cultoon
Line 243: KT5  To NNE       1a   ESCART (ALIGNMENT)
Line 246: KT8  - KT3        B 2  Dunskeig - Ardpatrick
Line 264: KT37 - KT31       A 3  Stewarton - Craigs
Line 269: KT39 - KT27       A 3  Mingary - Clochkeil
```

The proportion of on-site to inter-site indications in this list is much as expected by chance, but 12 of the 26 on-site lines are of class 1, which is unexpectedly high. The list features four of the six Mull alignments together with two from Argyll and one each from Lorn, Jura and Kintyre. It also includes the alignment of possible menhirs at Airigh nam Bidearan in Lewis and three of the five radial alignments at Callanish.

At higher resolutions the indications isolated above split into two distinct groupings, each of which gives rise to low significance levels at higher precisions. The more southerly grouping is in the vicinity of +28°. At a target width of 0°.2 we obtain zero values for two target intervals 1° apart:

|+27.4, +27.6|. Total hits 7, expected 3.

```
Line 49:   LH24 - LH19        B 2   Airigh nam Bidearan - Cnoc Ceann a'G.
Line 61:   UI9  - UI6         A 3   Newtonferry - Borve, Berneray
Line 95:   UI40 - UI35        B 3   Carinish - Cringraval W
Line 130:  ML10 To NNW        2a    DERVAIG N (ALIGNMENT)
Line 143:  ML30 To NNW        6     TAOSLIN (SLAB)
Line 173:  AR16 To NW         5a    ROWANFIELD (SLAB)
Line 273:  KT41 To NW         5a    KNOCKSTAPPLE (SLAB)
```

|+28.3, +28.5|. Total hits 7, expected 3.

```
Line 88:   UI35 - UI28        B 1   Cringraval W - Unival
Line 93:   UI37 - UI33        A 2   Loch a'Phobuill - Ben Langass
Line 110:  NA1  ab (To NNW)   4a    BRANAULT (MENHIR, POSS. MENHIR)
Line 130:  ML10 To NNW        2a    DERVAIG N (ALIGNMENT)
Line 143:  ML30 To NNW        6     TAOSLIN (SLAB)
Line 168:  AR15 abcd(To NW)   1a    DUNCRACAIG (ALIGNMENT)
Line 173:  AR16 To NW         5a    ROWANFIELD (SLAB)
```

Although the proportion of on-site indications is a little high, no noticeable tendency is evident amongst the on-site lines concerned.

The more northerly grouping occurs at declinations between 32° and 34°. The following target intervals, both of which attain zero values in Table 12.2, straddle this range.

|+32.2, +32.8|. Total hits 13, expected 7.

```
Line 11:   LH16 av W to N     1a    CALLANISH (ALIGNMENT)
Line 12:   LH16 av E to N     1a    CALLANISH (ALIGNMENT)
Line 13:   LH16 S row to N    1a    CALLANISH (ALIGNMENT)
Line 24:   LH18 - LH10        A 2   Cnoc Fillibhir Bheag - Beinn Bheag
Line 104:  UI50 - UI48        A 1   Ru Ardvule - Stoneybridge
Line 129:  ML9  - ML1         A 3   Maol Mor - Glengorm
Line 149:  LN22 abc(To NNW)   1a    DUACHY (ALIGNMENT)
Line 161:  AR10 - AR9         A 2   Glennan S - Glennan N
Line 165:  AR13 S4-S1-S3      1a    KILMARTIN (ALIGNMENT)
Line 170:  AR15 ef (To NNW)   1b    DUNCRACAIG (TWO ALIGNED SLABS)
Line 204:  JU7  To NNE        2a    SANNAIG (ALIGNMENT)
```

Line 219: IS12 - IS5   A 3 Mullach Dubh - Scanistle
Line 226: IS31 - IS28   B 1 Kelsay - Cultoon

|+33.0, +34.0|. Total hits 18, expected 11.

Line 29:   LH19 - LH10   A 3 Cnoc Ceann a'Gharaidh - Beinn Bheag
Line 83:   UI31 - UI23   A 3 Claddach Kyles - Toroghas
Line 112: NA3 To NNW   5a   CAMAS NAN GEALL (SLAB)
Line 124: ML4 abc (To N) 2a   BALLISCATE (ALIGNMENT)
Line 147: LN7 To N   5a   BENDERLOCH N (SLAB)
Line 149: LN22 abc(To NNW) 1a   DUACHY (ALIGNMENT)
Line 162: AR13 S2-S3-S6   1a   KILMARTIN (ALIGNMENT)
Line 163: AR13 S5-S1-S2   1a   KILMARTIN (ALIGNMENT)
Line 170: AR15 ef (To NNW) 1b   DUNCRACAIG (TWO ALIGNED SLABS)
Line 179: AR18 - AR17   B 2 Crinan Moss - Duntroon
Line 187: AR29 - AR28   A 2 Dunamuck II - Dunamuck I
Line 188: AR30 - AR28   A 2 Dunamuck III - Dunamuck I
Line 204: JU7 To NNE   2a   SANNAIG (ALIGNMENT)
Line 206: JU9 To NNW   5a   CAMAS AN STACA (SLAB)
Line 226: IS31 - IS28   B 1 Kelsay - Cultoon
Line 246: KT8 - KT3   B 2 Dunskeig - Ardpatrick
Line 264: KT37 - KT31   A 3 Stewarton - Craigs
Line 269: KT39 - KT27   A 3 Mingary - Clochkeil

     Although the proportion of on-site lines in the first list above
is much as expected by chance, it consists entirely of class 1 and 2
indications.   However three of these are the architecturally related
alignments at the Callanish site. Of the nine on-site indications in
the second list, several alignments appear also. They represent sites
in Mull, Lorn, Argyll and Jura.

     At target widths of $0°.2$ we obtain the following:

|+33.0, +33.2|. Total hits 10, expected 3.

Line 29:   LH19 - LH10   A 3 Cnoc Ceann a'Gharaidh - Beinn Bheag
Line 83:   UI31 - UI23   A 3 Claddach Kyles - Toroghas
Line 124: ML4 abc (To N) 2a   BALLISCATE (ALIGNMENT)
Line 149: LN22 abc(To NNW) 1a   DUACHY (ALIGNMENT)
Line 163: AR13 S5-S1-S2   1a   KILMARTIN (ALIGNMENT)
Line 170: AR15 ef (To NNW) 1b   DUNCRACAIG (TWO ALIGNED SLABS)
Line 179: AR18 - AR17   B 2 Crinan Moss - Duntroon
Line 187: AR29 - AR28   A 2 Dunamuck II - Dunamuck I
Line 204: JU7 To NNE   2a   SANNAIG (ALIGNMENT)
Line 226: IS31 - IS28   B 1 Kelsay - Cultoon

|+33.2, +33.4|. Total hits 8, expected 3.

Line 112: NA3 To NNW   5a   CAMAS NAN GEALL (SLAB)
Line 124: ML4 abc (To N) 2a   BALLISCATE (ALIGNMENT)
Line 149: LN22 abc(To NNW) 1a   DUACHY (ALIGNMENT)
Line 163: AR13 S5-S1-S2   1a   KILMARTIN (ALIGNMENT)
Line 170: AR15 ef (To NNW) 1b   DUNCRACAIG (TWO ALIGNED SLABS)
Line 179: AR18 - AR17   B 2 Crinan Moss - Duntroon

```
Line 187: AR29 - AR28      A 2   Dunamuck II - Dunamuck I
Line 204: JU7  To NNE       2a    SANNAIG (ALIGNMENT)
```

|+33.9, +34.1|. Total hits 9, expected 3.

```
Line 112: NA3  To NNW       5a    CAMAS NAN GEALL (SLAB)
Line 124: ML4  abc (To N)   2a    BALLISCATE (ALIGNMENT)
Line 147: LN7  To N         5a    BENDERLOCH N (SLAB)
Line 149: LN22 abc(To NNW)  1a    DUACHY (ALIGNMENT)
Line 162: AR13 S2-S3-S6     1a    KILMARTIN (ALIGNMENT)
Line 188: AR30 - AR28       A 2   Dunamuck III - Dunamuck I
Line 206: JU9  To NNW       5a    CAMAS AN STACA (SLAB)
Line 264: KT37 - KT31       A 3   Stewarton - Craigs
Line 269: KT39 - KT27       A 3   Mingary - Clochkeil
```

|+34.0, +34.2|. Total hits 9, expected 3.

As above.

The general pattern that emerges here is that the proportion of on-site alignments is high, but that they represent a variety of sites from a variety of geographical areas.

An isolated instance of a low significance level occurs for an even more northerly target window:

|+35.5, +35.7|. Total hits 4, expected 1.

```
Line 137: ML16 - ML15       A 2   Gruline - Killichronan
Line 181: AR28 abc(To NNW)  2a    DUNAMUCK I (ALIGNMENT)
Line 228: IS36 - IS35       B 2   Trudernish - Claggain Bay
Line 275: KT44 To N         5a    SOUTHEND (SLAB)
```

Here, however, the list is so short that it is impossible to draw any meaningful conclusions.

12.4.4 Possible astronomical significance of preferred declinations

Until now the consideration of particular astronomical objects has not entered our discussion. We shall now examine possible astronomical interpretations of the declination trends isolated in the previous section.

To summarise our conclusions so far:

(i) At the roughest level, there is strong evidence of an avoidance of declinations between about -15° and $+15^{\circ}$.

(ii) There is a marked preference for declinations between -31° and -19°. This resolves at higher precisions into a grouping between -31° and about -29°, one around -25°, and a third around $-22^{\circ}.5$.

(iii) There is a marginally significant grouping within about 1° of $+18^{\circ}$.

(iv) There is a preference for declinations between $+27^o$ and $+34^o$. This resolves at higher precisions into a grouping around $+28^o$ and another between $+32^o$ and $+34^o$.

The limiting annual declinations of the sun in the third and second millennia BC were near to $\pm24^o$ (Appendix I). Thus the grouping of indications around declination -25° may relate to the winter solstice. However because the most significant grouping occurs at a declination 1° beyond the maximum southerly rising or setting track of the sun, we have no evidence that the precision of any solstially oriented structures was greater than a degree or two (i.e. within one or two solar diameters of the true solstitial position). There is no evidence whatsoever of preferential orientation towards the summer solstice, and there is actually strong evidence of _avoidance_ of declinations in the vicinity of the equinoctial rising or setting sun.

The limiting monthly declinations of the moon vary over a nineteen year cycle (Appendix I). In the third and second millennia BC its southern limiting monthly declination varied between about $-30^o.0$ and $-19^o.5$. This coincides to within 1° with the declination range for which a marked preference has been observed in our data. This grouping could well have resulted from sites being preferentially oriented towards the southern monthly limit of the moon's motions. This practice being undertaken at arbitrary points in the nineteen-year cycle in the case of different sites would result in structure orientations being scattered within the declination interval $|-30.0, -19.5|$, exactly as is observed. Orienting structures upon the (monthly) maximum southerly moonrise or set need not have involved nightly observations of the moon in a given month. It could have been achieved simply by observing the rising or setting of the full moon nearest to the summer solstice.

There is evidence of a finer structure of preferred declinations within the -31° to -19° declination interval. The grouping around -25° may be solstitial, but the remaining groupings around -30° and $-22^o.5$ demand an explanation. At first sight the grouping at -30° looks like clear evidence that structures were preferentially oriented towards the extreme southern limit of the moon's motions, or "major standstill" (Appendix I). This would have involved co-ordinated lunar observations lasting at least for the extent of one nineteen-year cycle. However orientations towards the monthly limiting moonrise or set, set up at arbitrary points in the nineteen-year cycle, would actually result in a distribution of indicated declinations within the interval $|-30.0, -19.5|$ quite similar to that observed. The reason is that the motion of the moon's monthly limit within this interval over the course of the nineteen year cycle is sinusoidal, so that it spends more of its time near the ends of the range than in the middle. Limiting monthly moonrise or set will in fact occur within $2^o.5$ of one or other limit (i.e. within the outer quarters of the interval) for two-thirds of the time.

Some aspects of the preferred declinations in the north seem to corroborate the idea that the monthly, and perhaps even the nineteen-year, limits of the moon's motions were preferentially indicated by structure orientations. In the third and second millennia BC its northern limiting monthly declinations varied between about $+18^o.0$ and $+28^o.0$. Marginally significant groupings are observed within 1° of both values.

However the main evidence from the northern declinations is of a preference for values between +27° and +34°. Since declinations above +28° can not be related to the rising or setting of the sun or moon, this might temper our initial enthusiasm that a solar or lunar interpretation can adequately account for all the declination preferences observed. We must remember here, though, that while archaeo-astronomers have concentrated almost exclusively upon the hypothesis that horizon astronomical events were of importance (a rare exception being provided by Burl 1980), the significance of events occurring above the horizon, or to one side of a structure orientation, is also a possibility. The preference for indicated declinations above +27° (we note here that the northern bound of the declination range is in fact formed by the limits of physical possibility) may provide evidence that sites were preferentially oriented so as to point farther to the north than the sun or moon ever rose or set. This would imply that co-ordinated lunar observations were made over several years.

We should recall at this point that the majority of our data are pairs of indications in opposite directions formed by a single structure orientation. It is likely (though not of course inevitable) that in the majority of cases only one direction (if any) was of particular significance. A comparison of the lists of indications hitting the southern declination interval |-31, -19| with those hitting the northern interval |+28, +34| (Section 12.4.3) shows that a great many which appear in one list have their opposite number appearing in the other. Thus we must consider whether the apparent preference for either of these intervals might have come about simply because it is formed by structure orientations whose actual significance was related to the opposite direction.

Finally, we should consider astronomical objects other than the sun and moon. Planets for example, especially Venus, might well have influenced orientations. Unfortunately, however, the motions of the planets are complex. Furthermore their paths are confined to the part of the celestial sphere in which the sun and moon also move, making planetary orientations difficult to distinguish from solar or lunar ones.

Stellar orientations present two problems. Firstly, stellar risings and settings on all but the most elevated horizons are extremely difficult to observe because of extinction (Thom 1967: 15). Thus if structures were oriented upon stars, it is likely that the stars were at a considerable altitude above the horizon profile rather than rising or setting behind it. The value of the altitude difference in any particular case would be unknown to us. Secondly, the declination of any particular star changes significantly on a timescale of centuries (Appendix I). We do not know the dates of construction and use of most megalithic sites to within a millennium, let alone to within a century. These two uncertainties mean that it is possible to fit a first magnitude star (i.e. one of the fifteen or so brightest) together with a date and an altitude to almost any indication. It is possible to conceive of statistical tests which would determine the stars, dates and altitudes that would best explain the declination preferences in our data. However if a solar and/or lunar explanation can account for all the observed declination preferences, then resort to stellar explanations seems unwarranted (cf. Thom 1955; see also Heggie 1981b: 162-68).

Given the declination trends isolated in Section 12.4.3, we may summarise the astronomical possibilities as follows:

(1) The grouping of declinations in the vicinity of -25° may relate to the winter solstice.

(2A) The marked preference for declinations between -31° and -19° may reflect the orientation of structures upon the (monthly) maximum southerly moonrise or set.

(2B) The preference for declinations above $+27^{\circ}$ may indicate that structures were oriented to point farther along the horizon to the north than the sun or moon ever reached.

(3) Groupings around declinations -30°, $+18^{\circ}$ and $+27^{\circ}$ may indicate a specific interest in the lunar standstills, so that co-ordinated lunar observations must have been made over at least one nine-teen-year cycle. On the other hand these groupings may have arisen fortuitously.

(4) Groupings around declinations $-22^{\circ}.5$ and $+33^{\circ}$ may indicate a specific interest in astronomical bodies other than the sun or moon, but may just have arisen fortuitously.

If either (2A) or (2B) is accepted, the other may simply follow as a consequence of our having included in our data many opposite pairs of indications formed by the same structures.

It is clearly of very great interest whether some megalithic structures were deliberately oriented towards lunar rising or setting positions at the extremes of its nineteen-year cycle. If so, this implies that co-ordinated lunar observations were made over a period of several years. As it stands, our evidence does not point conclu- sively one way or the other. In the following section we shall look more closely at the coherence of the sites which constitute the dif- ferent declination groupings, in the hope that this may go further towards resolving the issue.

12.4.5 Coherent groups of sites and possible astronomical motivations in their design

In Section 12.4.3 we found that certain coherent groups of sites seemed to feature predominantly amongst the indications which fell in particular "preferred" declination intervals. We can now attempt to link together this evidence with the astronomical possibilities dis- cussed in Section 12.4.4.

At several stages during Section 12.4.3 we noted a preponderance of stone alignments amongst the lists of indications. We also noted that the radial alignments at Callanish (LH16) were exceptional, this site being the only example where no single alignment can be regarded as reflecting the general orientation of the site as a whole. We list below all indications involving stone alignments or two aligned slabs, including two - at Airigh nam Bidearan, Lewis (LH24) and Uluvalt, Mull (ML25) - where the alignment is of uncertain archaeological status, but excluding the alignments at Callanish. In each case we show the declination interval indicated and whether the indication points east (to rising celestial bodies) or west (setting).

```
Line 233: IS41 To S        2a -34.5 -34.3  Rise Laphroaig, Islay
Line 205: JU7  To SSW      2a -33.1 -32.2  Set  Sannaig, Jura
Line 122: ML2  To SSE      2c -31.5 -30.8  Rise Quinish, Mull
Line 182: AR28 cba(To SSE) 2a -31.0 -30.6  Rise Dunamuck I, Argyll
Line 164: AR13 S2-S1-S5    1a -30.9 -30.7  Set  Kilmartin, Argyll
Line 154: AR3  ba  (To S)  1b -30.7 -30.5  Set  Barbreck, Argyll
Line 171: AR15 fe (To SSE) 1b -30.2 -29.6  Rise Duncracaig, Argyll
Line 45:  LH24 dcb(To SSE) 3c -29.6 -29.2  Rise Airigh nam Bid., Lewis
Line 244: KT5  To SSW      1a -29.5 -29.3  Set  Escart, Kintyre
Line 166: AR13 S3-S1-S4    1a -29.5 -29.3  Set  Kilmartin, Argyll
Line 131: ML11 abc(To SSE) 1a -29.0 -28.9  Rise Dervaig S, Mull
Line 125: ML4  cba (To S)  2a -28.6 -28.4  Set  Balliscate, Mull
Line 169: AR15 dcba(To SE) 1a -25.8 -23.7  Rise Duncracaig, Argyll
Line 247: KT10 cba (To SW) 1a -25.5 -24.5  Set  Ballochroy, Kintyre
Line 133: ML12 cba(To SSW) 2c -23.2 -22.2  Set  Ardnacross, Mull
Line 252: KT27 cba (To SW) 2a -22.9 -22.2  Set  Clochkeil, Kintyre
Line 150: LN22 cba(To SSE) 1a -21.5 -21.2  Rise Duachy, Lorn
Line 186: AR29 ba (To SE)  1b -21.5 -19.5  Rise Dunamuck II, Argyll
Line 140: ML25 cba (To SE) 3c -18.5 -17.9  Rise Uluvalt, Mull
Line 63:  UI19 abc(To WNW) 1a  11.7  12.5  Set  Blashaval, N Uist
Line 251: KT27 abc (To NE) 2a  24.1  25.0  Rise Clochkeil, Kintyre
Line 185: AR29 ab (To NW)  1b  24.2  26.3  Set  Dunamuck II, Argyll
Line 130: ML10 To NNW      2a  27.5  28.7  Set  Dervaig N, Mull
Line 168: AR15 abcd(To NW) 1a  28.3  29.3  Set  Duncracaig, Argyll
Line 44:  LH24 bcd(To NNW) 3c  29.9  30.5  Set  Airigh nam Bid., Lewis
Line 167: AR13 S5-S4       1b  30.3  30.5  Set  Kilmartin, Argyll
Line 132: ML12 abc(To NNE) 2c  30.4  31.3  Rise Ardnacross, Mull
Line 128: ML9  To NNW      1a  30.9  31.6  Set  Maol Mor, Mull
Line 243: KT5  To NNE      1a  31.4  32.0  Rise Escart, Kintyre
Line 204: JU7  To NNE      2a  31.6  33.3  Rise Sannaig, Jura
Line 165: AR13 S4-S1-S3    1a  32.4  32.5  Rise Kilmartin, Argyll
Line 170: AR15 ef (To NNW) 1b  32.7  33.2  Set  Duncracaig, Argyll
Line 149: LN22 abc(To NNW) 1a  32.7  34.8  Set  Duachy, Lorn
Line 124: ML4  abc (To N)  2a  33.2  34.0  Rise Balliscate, Mull
Line 163: AR13 S5-S1-S2    1a  33.0  33.2  Rise Kilmartin, Argyll
Line 162: AR13 S2-S3-S6    1a  33.8  34.2  Set  Kilmartin, Argyll
Line 156: AR6  abc (To N)  2a  35.0  35.3  Set  Salachary, Argyll
Line 181: AR28 abc(To NNW) 2a  35.3  35.6  Set  Dunamuck I, Argyll
Line 139: ML25 abc (To NW) 3c  36.8  37.3  Set  Uluvalt, Mull
Line 153: AR3  ab  (To N)  1b  38.5  38.6  Rise Barbreck, Argyll
```

With the exception of Sannaig, Jura (JU7) and Laphroaig, Islay
(IS41), all indicated declinations in the south fall within $1°.5$ of
the interval $|-30.0, -19.5|$ which represents the range of values where
the moon's southern limiting monthly declination can fall. The line
from Blashaval, North Uist (UI19) is also clearly anomalous. Sannaig,
Laphroaig and Blashaval represent three of four geographically isolated stone alignments appearing in the above list: the fourth is the
alignment of uncertain archaeological status at Airigh nam Bidearan,
Lewis (LH24). If we remove these sites from consideration, we are left
solely with stone alignments from Mull and mainland Argyll.

The sixteen remaining southern indications are the following:

```
Line 122: ML2  To SSE      2c -31.5 -30.8  Rise Quinish, Mull
Line 182: AR28 cba(To SSE) 2a -31.0 -30.6  Rise Dunamuck I, Argyll
Line 164: AR13 S2-S1-S5    1a -30.9 -30.7  Set  Kilmartin, Argyll
```

```
Line 154: AR3   ba   (To S)    1b -30.7 -30.5   Set  Barbreck, Argyll
Line 171: AR15  fe (To SSE)    1b -30.2 -29.6   Rise Duncracaig, Argyll
Line 244: KT5   To SSW         1a -29.5 -29.3   Set  Escart, Kintyre
Line 166: AR13  S3-S1-S4       1a -29.5 -29.3   Set  Kilmartin, Argyll
Line 131: ML11  abc(To SSE)    1a -29.0 -28.9   Rise Dervaig S, Mull
Line 125: ML4   cba  (To S)    2a -28.6 -28.4   Set  Balliscate, Mull
Line 169: AR15  dcba(To SE)    1a -25.8 -23.7   Rise Duncracaig, Argyll
Line 247: KT10  cba  (To SW)   1a -25.5 -24.5   Set  Ballochroy, Kintyre
Line 133: ML12  cba(To SSW)    2c -23.2 -22.2   Set  Ardnacross, Mull
Line 252: KT27  cba  (To SW)   2a -22.9 -22.2   Set  Clochkeil, Kintyre
Line 150: LN22  cba(To SSE)    1a -21.5 -21.2   Rise Duachy, Lorn
Line 186: AR29  ba   (To SE)   1b -21.5 -19.5   Rise Dunamuck II, Argyll
Line 140: ML25  cba  (To SE)   3c -18.5 -17.9   Rise Uluvalt, Mull
```

The extreme entries in this list represent fallen alignments whose original orientation is in some doubt. At Quinish (ML2) only one stone stands, and a further three are recumbent. The site at Uluvalt (ML25) is an alignment of prostrate slabs whose status is uncertain. The directions of the indications at Dunamuck I (AR28) and Dunamuck II (AR29) are in some doubt owing to the fact that both sites were in the middle of fields under crop and neither could actually be approached during the fieldwork: their orientations were deduced from a distance of 100m and 200m respectively. Finally, Lines 164 and 166 represent directions along the diagonals of the five-stone arrangement at Kilmartin (AR13). Our selection criteria had us include both diagonals amongst our indications, but in retrospect it is conceivable that the formation of stones merely represents a local variation on the concept of a single alignment, and that the intended orientation was centrally along the formation. In this case the true indicated declination would lie between the values included in our list.

The uncertainties noted above affect the first three and last two entries in the list. With the exception of Ardnacross (ML12) the remaining indications are all formed by alignments in which at least two stones still stand. It is possible that, following further survey work or excavation to determine the direction of fallen alignments, the southern declinations might be found to fit even more neatly into the lunar range. Clearly such work would be of the greatest interest.

Nine of the sixteen indications give declinations to the south of $-28°$, rather more than would have been expected if orientations upon the (monthly) southern limit of the moon were set up at arbitrary times in the nineteen-year cycle. On the other hand two of these are the related Lines 164 & 166 from Kilmartin. There are also fewer indications at the northern end of the range than would have been expected. Thus there is some evidence (but not it is not conclusive) that the southern extreme of the nineteen-year cycle was observed. The additional work recommended above could help to resolve the issue.

No trends are clarified by separating rising and setting lines in the above list. There is some evidence that Argyll sites are preferentially oriented in the south of the range, but this trend is insufficiently marked to be conclusive. There is no convincing evidence from these data that some of the indications in the vicinity of $-25°$ might actually be solar solstitial.

Three of the sixteen alignments have local horizons (i.e. horizons nearer than 1 km) in the opposite direction. They are Quinish (ML2: Line 122), Dervaig S (ML11: Line 131) and Ballochroy (KT10: Line 247). The corresponding northerly indications in the remaining cases are as follows.

```
Line 251: KT27 abc (To NE)  2a  24.1  25.0  Rise Clochkeil, Kintyre
Line 185: AR29 ab (To NW)   1b  24.2  26.3  Set  Dunamuck II, Argyll
Line 168: AR15 abcd(To NW)  1a  28.3  29.3  Set  Duncracaig, Argyll
Line 132: ML12 abc(To NNE)  2c  30.4  31.3  Rise Ardnacross, Mull
Line 243: KT5  To NNE       1a  31.4  32.0  Rise Escart, Kintyre
Line 165: AR13 S4-S1-S3     1a  32.4  32.5  Rise Kilmartin, Argyll
Line 170: AR15 ef (To NNW)  1b  32.7  33.2  Set  Duncracaig, Argyll
Line 149: LN22 abc(To NNW)  1a  32.7  34.8  Set  Duachy, Lorn
Line 124: ML4  abc (To N)   2a  33.2  34.0  Rise Balliscate, Mull
Line 163: AR13 S5-S1-S2     1a  33.0  33.2  Rise Kilmartin, Argyll
Line 181: AR28 abc(To NNW)  2a  35.3  35.6  Set  Dunamuck I, Argyll
Line 139: ML25 abc (To NW)  3c  36.8  37.3  Set  Uluvalt, Mull
Line 153: AR3  ab  (To N)   1b  38.5  38.6  Rise Barbreck, Argyll
```

Thus many high northern declinations which are indicated but are beyond the northern limits of movement of the sun or moon may simply arise because southern lunar events are indicated in the opposite direction. The remaining northern indications in the list are the following:

```
Line 130: ML10 To NNW      2a  27.5  28.7  Set  Dervaig N, Mull
Line 167: AR13 S5-S4       1b  30.3  30.5  Set  Kilmartin, Argyll
Line 128: ML9  To NNW      1a  30.9  31.6  Set  Maol Mor, Mull
Line 162: AR13 S2-S3-S6    1a  33.8  34.2  Set  Kilmartin, Argyll
Line 156: AR6  abc (To N)  2a  35.0  35.3  Set  Salachary, Argyll
```

In every one of these cases the southern indication at the site was dismissed as local, and not considered further. This exclusion criterion must now be called seriously into question. The horizon distance in the opposite directions are approximately 700m (AR6), 600m (AR13 S6-S3-S2), 500m (ML10 & AR13 S4-S5) and 300m (ML9), not so close that indications at a precision of a degree or two would be inconceivable. It is easily within the bounds of possibility that the southern declinations at each of these sites fall within the lunar range, and is clearly of the greatest interest to verify by site survey whether this is in fact the case. This would provide very clear evidence that the direction of significance at the sites was always south, and that this direction was of lunar significance.

There is no conclusive evidence that more distant horizons were preferred, contrary to the expectation expressed during our azimuthal analysis (see page 229). Although most of the sixteen southern declinations listed above represent a horizon more distant than that in the opposite direction, there are four notable exceptions: Line 169 at Duncracaig (3.0 km; other way 4.0 km), Line 133 at Ardnacross (2.0 km; other way 8.0 km), Line 124 at Balliscate (1.5 km; other way 13.5 km), and Line 150 at Duachy (1.0 km both ways). Furthermore the five local horizons listed above, if shown to fall in the same lunar range, will destroy completely any idea that even moderately distant horizons were a prerequisite to lunar orientation.

It was also found in Section 12.4.3 that on-site indications of all types from Mull and mainland Argyll were featured predominantly amongst the indications which fell in certain preferred declination intervals. There are 51 on-site structures in our source list from Mull (including Ulva) and mainland Argyll (including Gigha), excluding only lines ac and bc at Carse (see page 265 above).

The southern indications, where these are non-local, are listed below. Those indications falling outside the vicinity of the lunar range are separated from the bulk of the data. A star appearing after the declination limits indicates that the opposite (northern) indication also falls within the range of monthly limiting lunar values. An "L" in this position indicates that the opposite horizon is local.

```
Line 276: KT44 To S          5a -34.9 -34.7   Set  Southend, Kintyre
Line 234: KT2  ba (To S)     3a -32.9 -32.9 L Rise Carse, Knapdale

Line 122: ML2  To SSE        2c -31.5 -30.8 L Rise Quinish, Mull
Line 242: KT4  To S          5a -31.3 -30.9 L Rise Avinagillan, Knapdale
Line 182: AR28 cba(To SSE)   2a -31.0 -30.6   Rise Dunamuck I, Argyll
Line 164: AR13 S2-S1-S5      1a -30.9 -30.7   Set  Kilmartin, Argyll
Line 154: AR3  ba  (To S)    1b -30.7 -30.5   Set  Barbreck, Argyll
Line 171: AR15 fe (To SSE)   1b -30.2 -29.6   Rise Duncracaig, Argyll
Line 166: AR13 S3-S1-S4      1a -29.5 -29.3   Set  Kilmartin, Argyll
Line 244: KT5  To SSW        1a -29.5 -29.3   Set  Escart, Kintyre
Line 131: ML11 abc(To SSE)   1a -29.0 -28.9 L Rise Dervaig S, Mull
Line 125: ML4  cba (To S)    2a -28.6 -28.4   Set  Balliscate, Mull
Line 274: KT41 To SE         5a -26.8 -24.8 * Rise Knockstapple, Kintyre
Line 111: NA1  ba (To SSE)   4a -25.8 -25.5 * Rise Branault,Ardnamurchan
Line 247: KT10 cba (To SW)   1a -25.5 -24.5 L Set  Ballochroy, Kintyre
Line 169: AR15 dcba(To SE)   1a -25.8 -23.7 * Rise Duncracaig, Argyll
Line 250: KT23 To SW         5a -25.3 -23.5 L Set  Beinn an Tuirc, Kint.
Line 174: AR16 To SE         5a -24.7 -23.5 * Rise Rowanfield, Argyll
Line 133: ML12 cba(To SSW)   2c -23.2 -22.2   Set  Ardnacross, Mull
Line 252: KT27 cba (To SW)   2a -22.9 -22.2 * Set  Clochkeil, Kintyre
Line 268: KT39 To SE         5a -22.9 -22.2 * Rise Mingary, Kintyre
Line 240: KT3  To SE         5a -22.5 -22.3 * Rise Ardpatrick, Knapdale
Line 150: LN22 cba(To SSE)   1a -21.5 -21.2   Rise Duachy, Lorn
Line 145: ML31 To SW         5a -21.3 -21.0 * Set  Uisken, Mull
Line 186: AR29 ba (To SE)    1b -21.5 -19.5 * Rise Dunamuck II, Argyll
Line 126: ML7  To SE         5a -20.5 -20.2 L Rise Cillchriosd, Mull
Line 245: KT8  ba (To SE)    5b -19.9 -19.3 L Rise Dunskeig, Kintyre
Line 140: ML25 cba (To SE)   3c -18.5 -17.9   Rise Uluvalt, Mull
Line 136: ML16 ab (To SE)    3a -18.3 -17.7 * Rise Gruline, Mull

Line 192: AR33 To ESE        5a -15.6 -14.2 * Rise Kilmory, Argyll
Line 249: KT19 ab (To WSW)   4b -11.8 -11.3 L Set  S Muasdale, Kintyre
Line 262: KT35 To ESE        5a -11.4 -10.7   Rise Glenlussa Lodge,Kint.
Line 190: AR32 To ESE        5a  -8.1  -6.8   Rise Oakfield, Argyll
```

Only six sites manifest southern declinations which fall substantially outside the range of monthly lunar limiting values. It is notable that five of these are in situations where it is especially possible that movement or re-erection has taken place: the menhir at Southend (KT44) is in a golf course; that at Kilmory (AR33) is beside the approach road to the offices of the Argyll & Bute District Council in Lochgilphead; one of those at South Muasdale (KT19) is a possible stump set into a field wall; that at Glenlussa Lodge (KT35) is built into the garden wall of a house; and that at Oakfield (AR32) is situated in the grounds of an estate next to the wall of a dairy. None of the sites in the bulk of the list is subject to comparable uncertainty.

Structures where the southern indication is lunar but the northern is not will concern us no further. We can however divide the remaining structures into three categories:

(1) those indicating limiting lunar declinations to the north;
(2) those not indicating limiting lunar declinations to the north, but where the southern indication is local and possibly lunar; and
(3) those not indicating limiting lunar declinations in either direction.

The three categories are listed in full below. Stars and "L"s following the declination limits in an entry have the same meaning as above.

(1) Structures indicating limiting lunar declinations to the north

Line 138:	ML18	ba (To ENE)	3a	17.5	18.0 L	Rise	Cragaig, Ulva
Line 191:	AR33	To WNW	5a	18.2	19.3	Set	Kilmory, Argyll
Line 255:	KT29	To ENE	5a	18.2	19.7 L	Rise	High Park, Kintyre
Line 135:	ML16	ba (To NW)	3a	22.3	23.0 *	Set	Gruline, Mull
Line 144:	ML31	To NE	5a	22.6	23.0 *	Rise	Uisken, Mull
Line 267:	KT39	To NW	5a	22.4	23.5 *	Set	Mingary, Kintyre
Line 251:	KT27	abc (To NE)	2a	24.1	25.0 *	Rise	Clochkeil, Kintyre
Line 185:	AR29	ab (To NW)	1b	24.2	26.3 *	Set	Dunamuck II, Argyll
Line 239:	KT3	To NW	5a	26.5	26.6 *	Set	Ardpatrick, Knapdale
Line 273:	KT41	To NW	5a	26.4	27.5 *	Set	Knockstapple, Kintyre
Line 143:	ML30	To NNW	6	27.5	28.5 L	Set	Taoslin, Mull
Line 173:	AR16	To NW	5a	27.2	28.8 *	Set	Rowanfield, Argyll
Line 130:	ML10	To NNW	2a	27.5	28.7 L	Set	Dervaig N, Mull
Line 110:	NA1	ab (To NNW)	4a	28.1	28.4 *	Set	Branault,Ardnamurchan
Line 168:	AR15	abcd(To NW)	1a	28.3	29.3 *	Set	Duncracaig, Argyll
Line 180:	AR27	ab (To NNW)	4a	29.3	29.9 L	Set	Dunadd, Argyll

(2) Structures not indicating limiting lunar declinations to the north, but local (and possibly lunar) to the south

Line 256:	KT31	To WNW	5a	14.9	15.7 L	Set	Craigs, Kintyre
Line 167:	AR13	S5-S4	1b	30.3	30.5 L	Set	Kilmartin, Argyll
Line 128:	ML9	To NNW	1a	30.9	31.6 L	Set	Maol Mor, Mull
Line 162:	AR13	S2-S3-S6	1a	33.8	34.2 L	Set	Kilmartin, Argyll
Line 112:	NA3	To NNW	5a	33.3	34.9 L	Set	Camas nan Geall,Ardn.
Line 147:	LN7	To N	5a	34.0	34.5 L	Rise	Benderloch N,Benderl.
Line 248:	KT12	To N	5a	34.4	34.4 L	Rise	Tarbert, Gigha
Line 156:	AR6	abc (To N)	2a	35.0	35.3 L	Set	Salachary, Argyll
Line 151:	AR2	To N	5a	40.9	41.0 L	Set	Sluggan, Argyll

(3) Structures not indicating limiting lunar declinations in either direction

```
Line 148: LN18 ab (To W)    4a  1.7   3.1 L Set  Glenamacrie, Lorn
Line 146: ML33 ba (To WNW)  3b  8.8   9.5 L Set  Ardalanish, Mull
Line 261: KT35 To WNW       5a 11.7  12.5   Set  Glenlussa Lodge,Kint.
Line 159: AR9  To ENE       5a 12.4  13.9 L Rise Glennan N, Argyll
Line 254: KT28 To ENE       5a 11.7  15.0 L Rise Skeroblingarry, Kint.
Line 189: AR32 To WNW       5a 13.1  14.3   Set  Oakfield, Argyll
Line 275: KT44 To N         5a 35.2  35.5   Rise Southend, Kintyre
```

Although many structures indicate limiting lunar declinations in the northern range, all but six of these also indicate limiting lunar declinations to the south. Five of the six remaining indications are local to the south and might well indicate southern declinations in the lunar range. The only exception is Kilmory (AR33), which has been commented upon above.

Nine of the remaining sixteen indications are local to the south and may well be lunar. Only seven indications remain which are non-local and non-lunar in both directions. Of these, Glenlussa Lodge (KT35), Oakfield (AR32) and Southend (KT44) have been mentioned above. One of the stones at Glenamacrie (LN18) is a rounded, and possibly natural, boulder, and the indication may be spurious. In the remaining three cases, however, there is no particular reason to think that movement or re-erection might have occurred. One of the stones at Ardalanish (ML33) is prostrate and partially buried, but there is no apparent reason why it should have been moved; the menhir at Glennan N (AR9) is the stump of a higher slab, but the top survives and the orientation of the stump appears representative; and the slab at Skeroblingarry (KT28) appears intact.

As was the case with alignments alone, the distribution of indications within the southern limiting lunar range is not quite as would be expected if orientations were set up at arbitrary points during the nineteen-year cycle. However the deviations from the distribution expected under this hypothesis are not sufficient to constitute conclusive evidence that more specific orientations were intentional. A concentration of indications is evident between -31° and $-28^o.5$, which includes four Argyll alignments (Barbreck, Kilmartin, Duncracaig and Dunamuck I), three Mull alignments (Quinish, Dervaig S and Balliscate) and the alignment at Escart, Kintyre.

An interesting distribution is obtained if the Kintyre and southern Knapdale sites are studied in isolation. The southern indications are:

```
Line 242: KT4  To S        5a -31.3 -30.9 L Rise Avinagillan, Knapdale
Line 244: KT5  To SSW      1a -29.5 -29.3   Set  Escart, Kintyre
Line 274: KT41 To SE       5a -26.8 -24.8 * Rise Knockstapple, Kintyre
Line 247: KT10 cba (To SW) 1a -25.5 -24.5 L Set  Ballochroy, Kintyre
Line 250: KT23 To SW       5a -25.3 -23.5 L Set  Beinn an Tuirc, Kint.
Line 252: KT27 cba (To SW) 2a -22.9 -22.2 * Set  Clochkeil, Kintyre
Line 268: KT39 To SE       5a -22.9 -22.2 * Rise Mingary, Kintyre
Line 240: KT3  To SE       5a -22.5 -22.3 * Rise Ardpatrick, Knapdale
Line 245: KT8  ba (To SE)  5b -19.9 -19.3 L Rise Dunskeig, Kintyre
```

These sites manifest a concentration towards the centre of the
limiting lunar range, quite the opposite of the concentration towards
the edges that would be expected if they were set up at arbitrary
points in the lunar cycle. The distribution may indicate that, in
Kintyre at least, the orientation of some sites was upon the winter
solstice, to within a precision of about 2°. However the number of
sites is too small for this evidence to be conclusive.

We may summarise as follows:

(1) Where we have data (i.e. in all cases where indications were not
dismissed as local), we find that stone alignments, stone pairs
and single flat-faced slabs in Mull and mainland Argyll are,
with very few exceptions, oriented in the south upon (monthly)
lunar limiting declinations. The majority of exceptions to this
rule occur at sites where it is especially possible that the
indication may be in error or spurious.

(2) There are many sites which indicate local horizons (i.e. horizons nearer than 1 km) in the south that might well fall within
the limiting lunar range. Resurvey of these sites would provide
a valuable test for the lunar hypothesis.

(3) There is no conclusive evidence for higher-precision structure
within the southern limiting lunar range, though there are
indications that alignments in Mull and Argyll may be preferentially oriented upon the southerly limit of this range (major
standstill) and that Kintyre alignments and slabs may actually
be oriented upon the winter solstice.

12.5   Curvigrams illustrating the declination data

The statistical method used in Section 12.4 effectively assigns
equal weight to each declination within a particular IAR. We mention
here simply that it is possible to spread the weight in the form of a
gaussian hump, as discussed for azimuths in Section 12.3.2. The problems of devising a statisical test upon such data are the same as were
discussed there, but the curvigram again provides a good way of visualising the data. Accordingly we present a number of different
declination curvigrams to illustrate some of the points raised in the
preceding discussion.

In Fig. 12.14 we present all the declination data together. The
area under each gaussian hump is 1 unit, and the scale of the vertical
axis is 25 units. Hump centres correspond to IAR centres and their
SDs are half the relevant IAR width.

In Fig. 12.15 we have replaced IARs by AARs, so that the SDs are
more similar and the high spikes in the vicinity of the colatitude
have disappeared. However the structure at middling declinations has
become more smoothed out.

In Figs. 12.16 & 12.17 we repeat the first two diagrams in turn,
but with a constraint put on SDs to keep them above a certain value.
This enables us to concentrate our attention upon features of lower
precision. The minimum SD in Fig. 12.16 (IARs) is 0°.1, and in Fig.

(ctd. on page 302

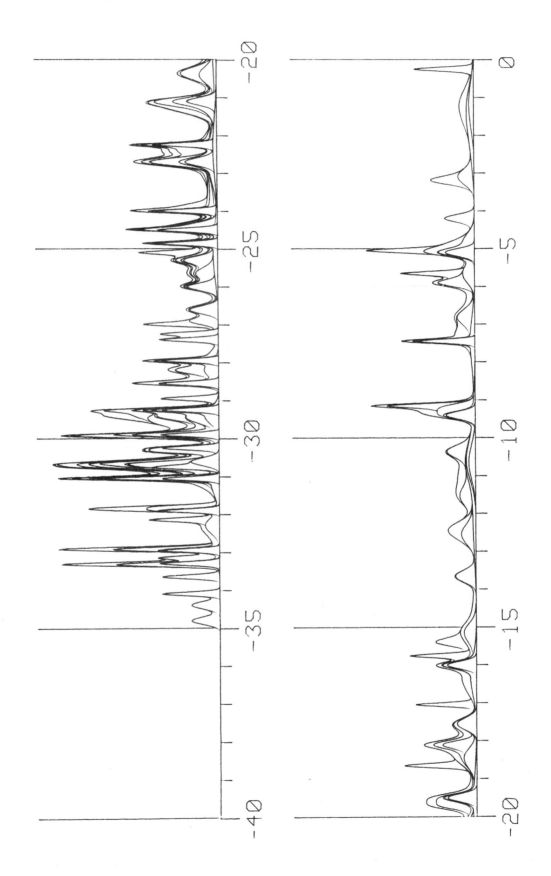

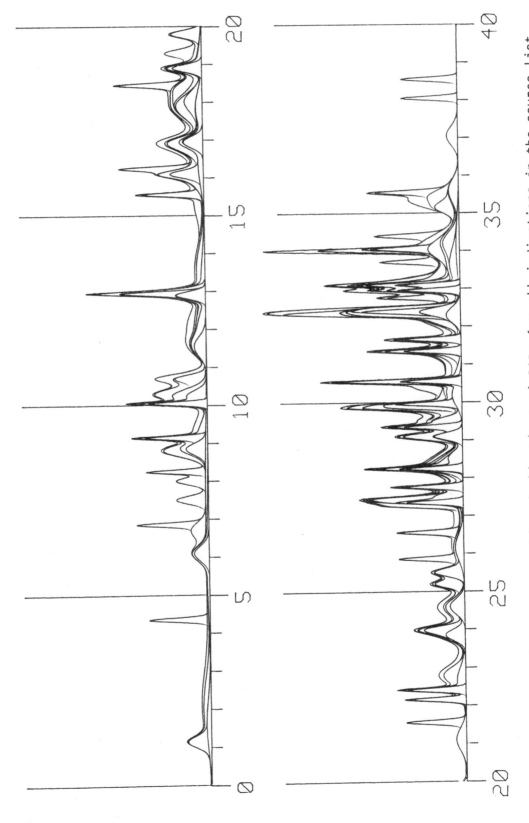

FIG. 12.14. Curvigram representing declinations of IARs for all indications in the source list (total 276 indications). The scale of the vertical axis is 25 units.

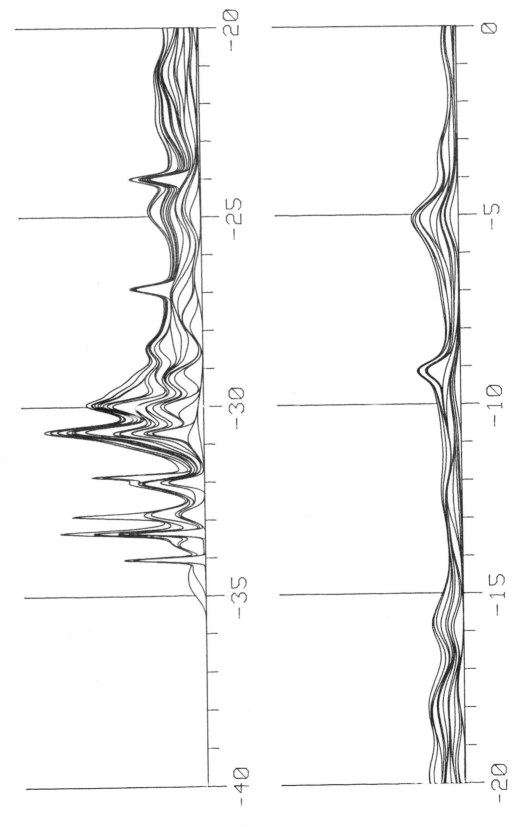

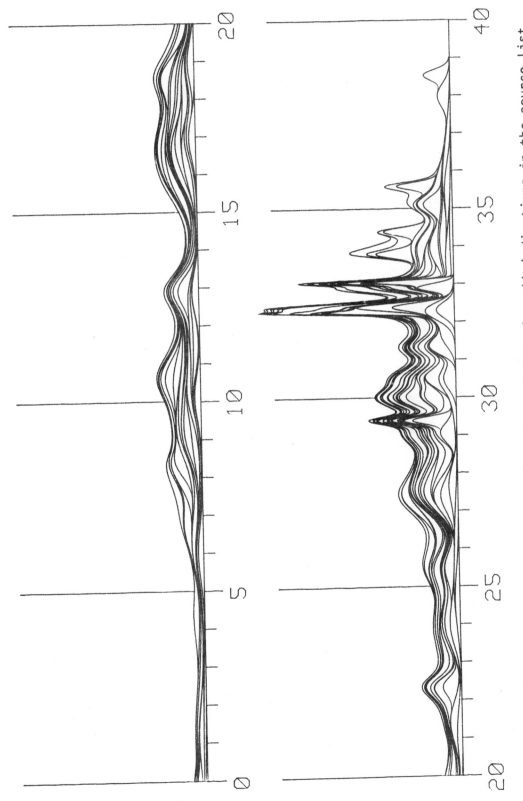

FIG. 12.15. Curvigram representing declinations of AARs for all indications in the source list (total 276 indications). The scale of the vertical axis is 25 units.

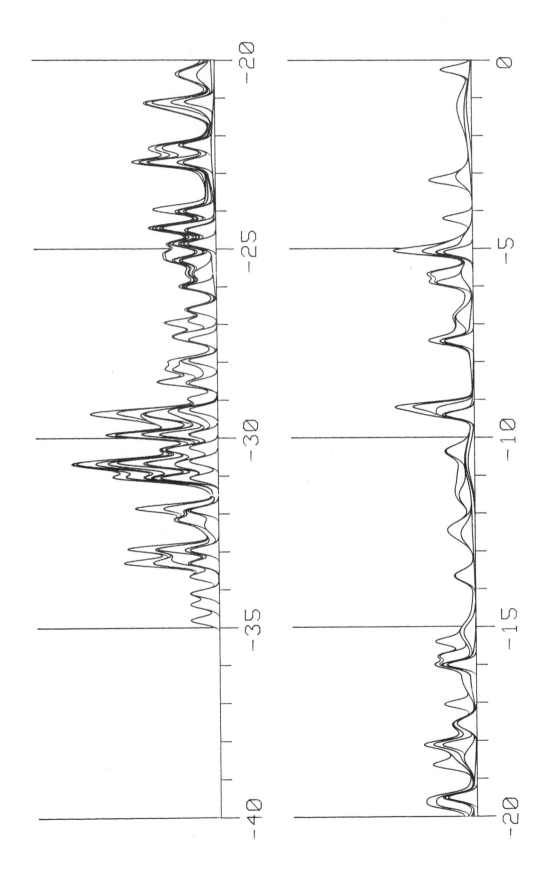

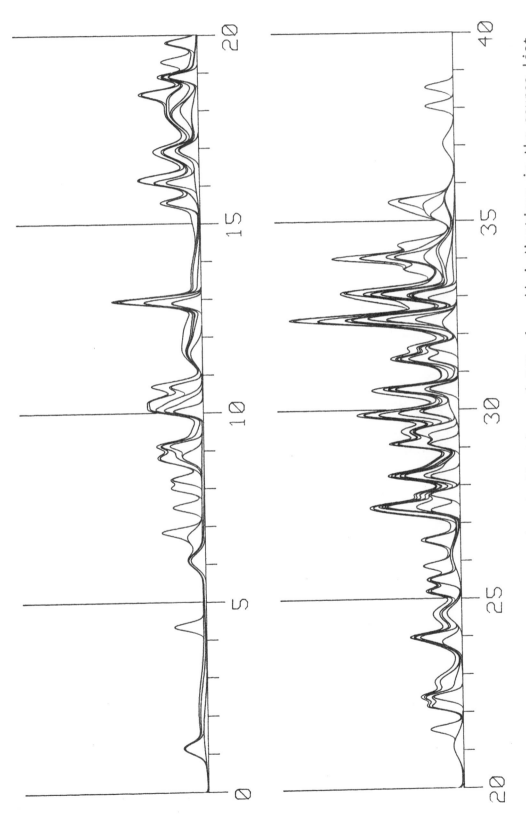

FIG. 12.16. Curvigram representing declinations of IARs for all indications in the source list, as in Fig. 12.14, but with the standard deviation of humps constrained to be at least 0°.1. The scale of the vertical axis is 25 units.

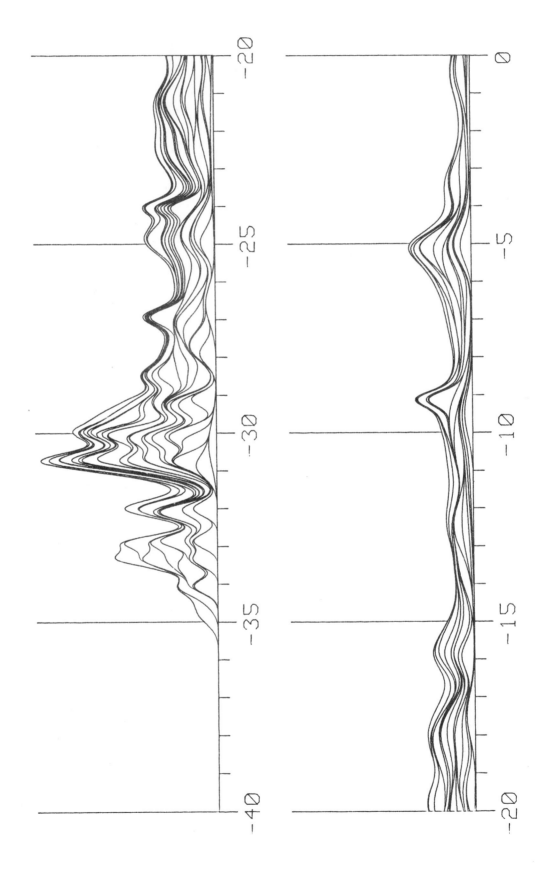

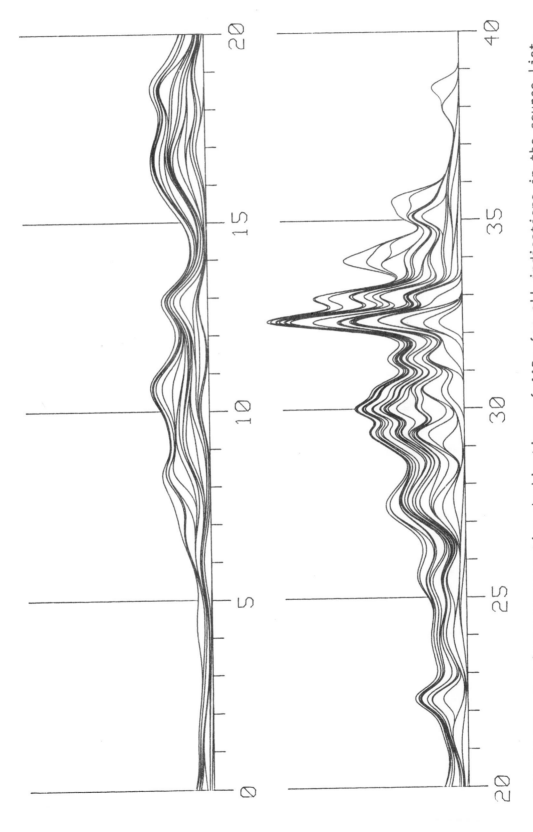

FIG. 12.17. Curvigram representing declinations of AARs for all indications in the source list, as in Fig. 12.15, but with the standard deviation of humps constrained to be at least 0°.2. The scale of the vertical axis is 15 units.

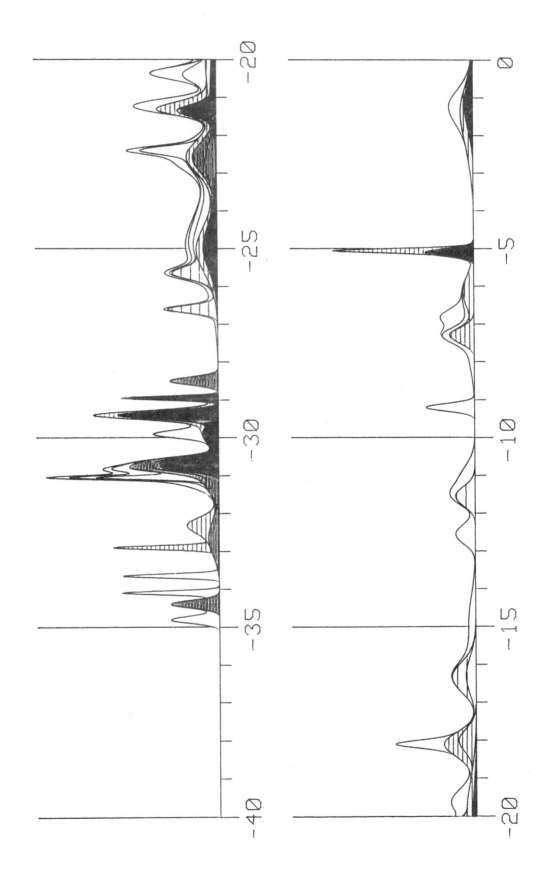

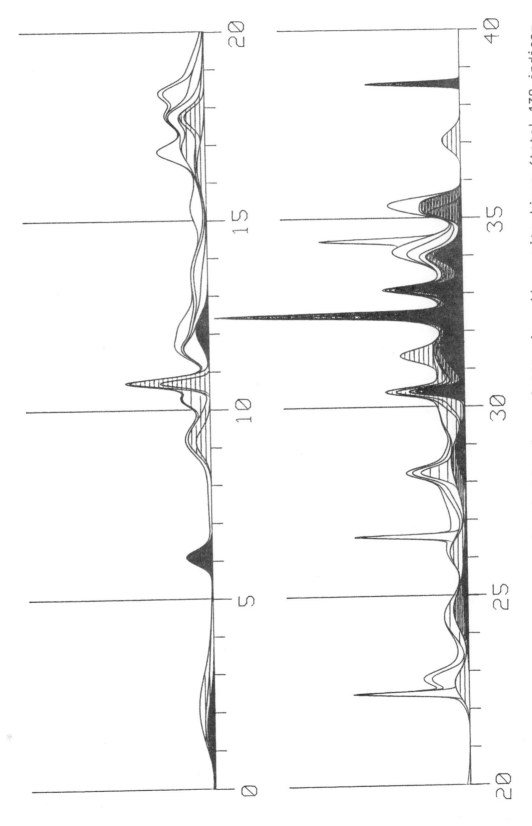

FIG. 12.18. Curvigram representing declinations of IARs for all on-site lines (total 130 indications). Lines of classes 1, 2, 3, 4 & 5/6 are indicated by differential shading, class 1 being
the darkest. The scale of the vertical axis is 15 units.

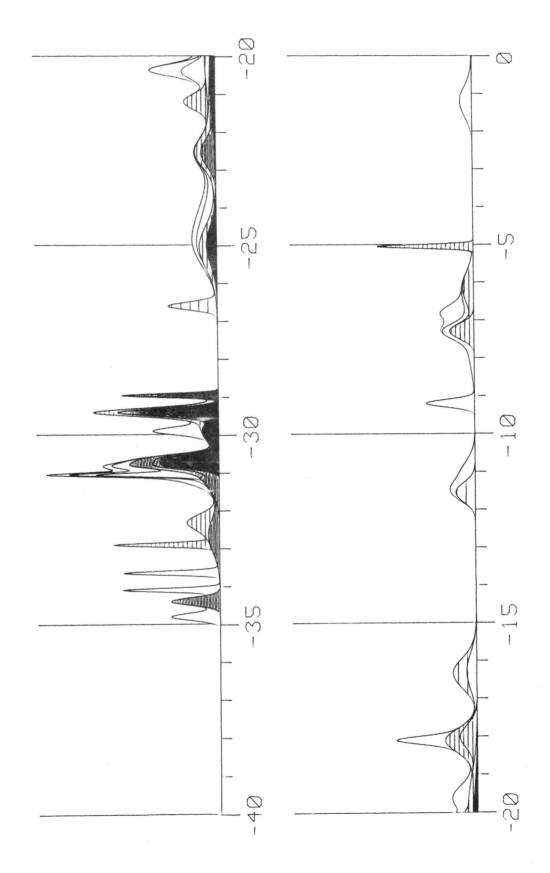

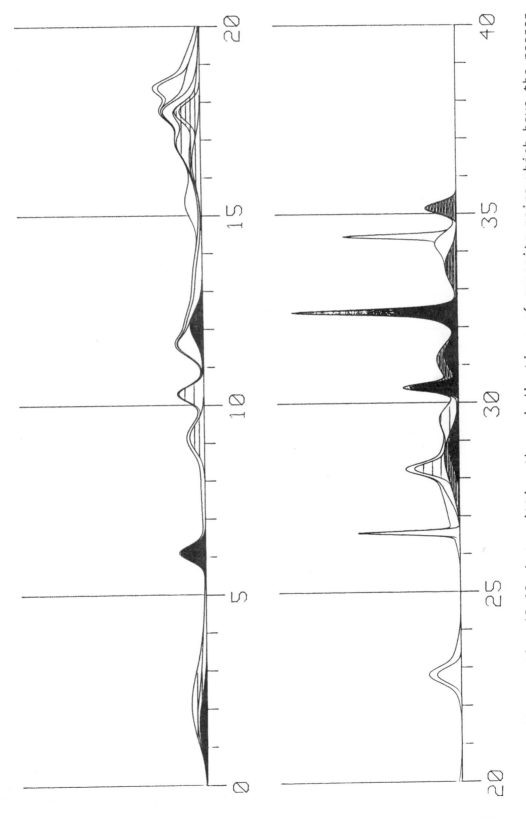

FIG. 12.19. As Fig. 12.18, but omitting those indications of opposite pairs which have the nearer horizon (total 90 indications).

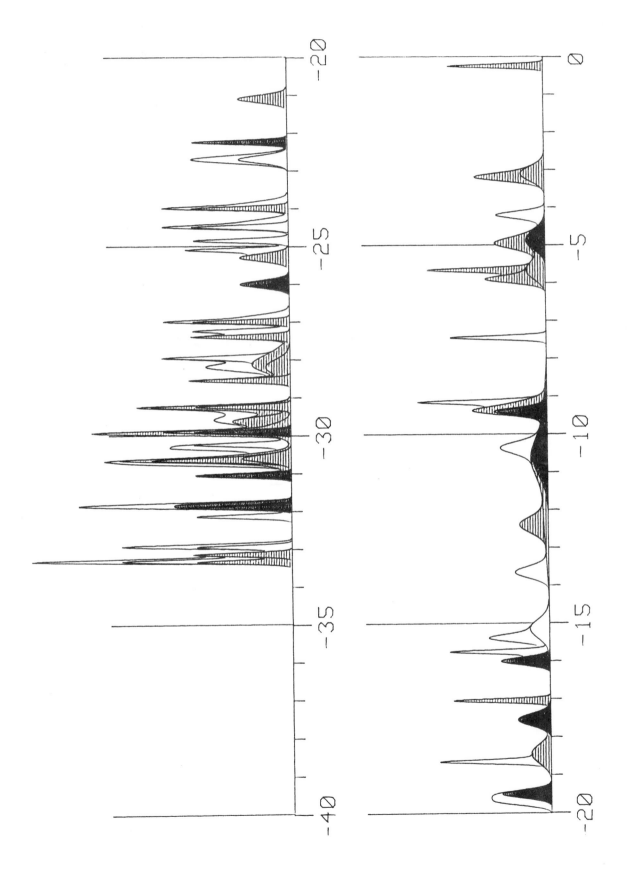

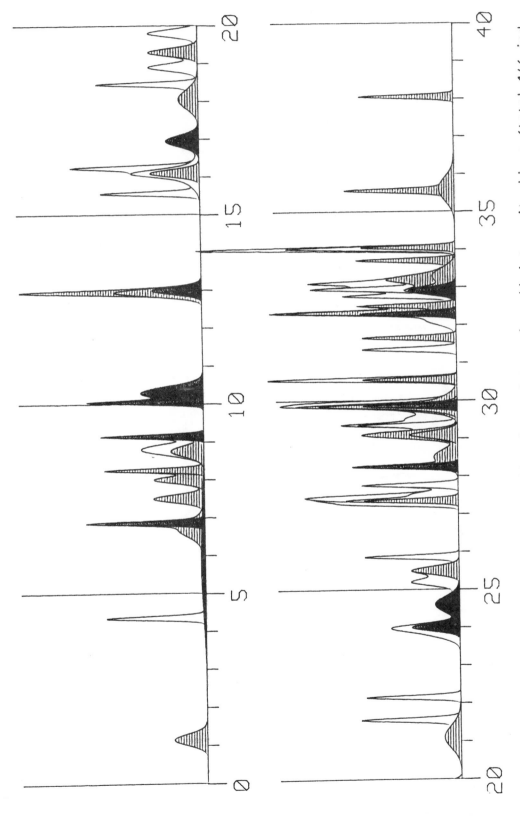

FIG. 12.20. Curvigram representing declinations of IARs for all inter-site lines (total 146 indications). Lines of classes 1, 2 & 3 are indicated by differential shading, class 1 being the darkest. The scale of the vertical axis is 15 units.

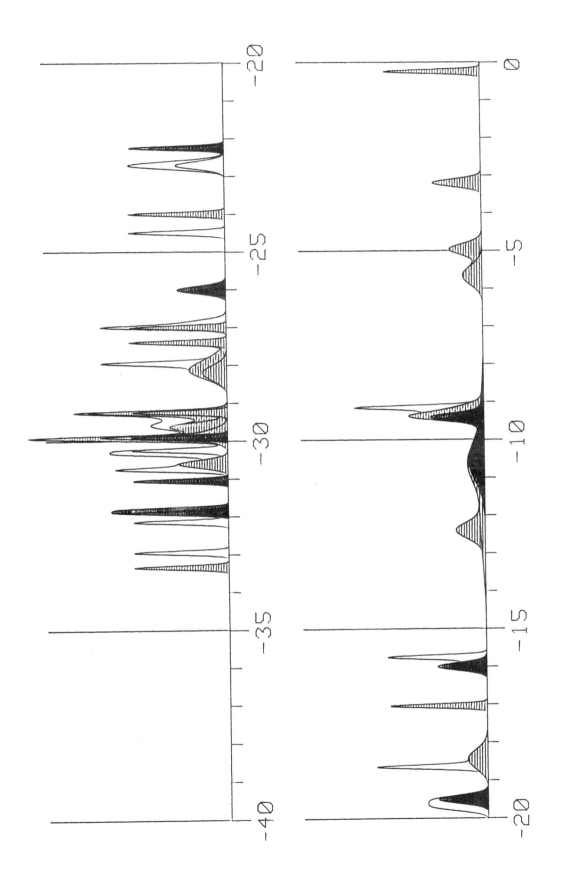

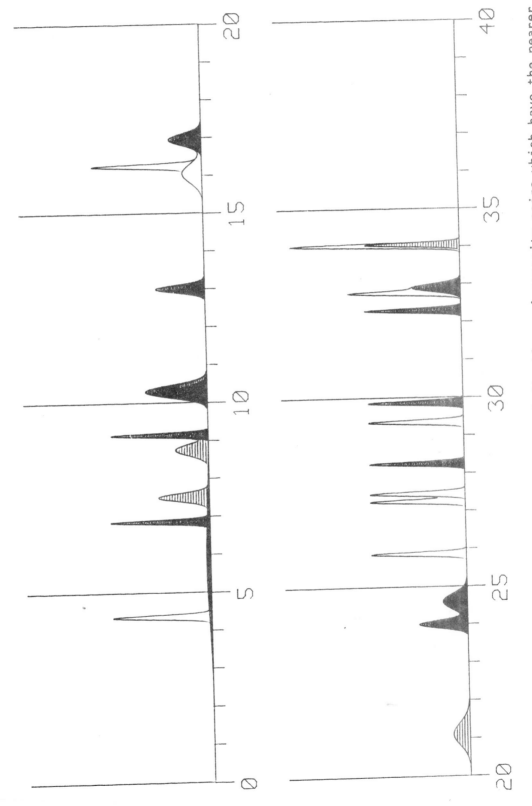

FIG. 12.21. As Fig. 12.20, but omitting those indications of opposite pairs which have the nearer horizon (total 75 indications).

12.17 (AARs) 0°.2. The vertical scale has been exaggerated in Fig. 12.17. Fig. 12.16 is perhaps the diagram most directly comparable with those of Thom (1955; 1967: Fig. 8.1).

In the remaining figures we have separated on-site from inter-site indications. In each case the classifications of the indications are indicated by differential shading, lines of the highest classification being shaded darkest and plotted first. Thus by concentrating upon only the darkest humps we can picture just the class 1 data, and so on.

The on-site data are plotted in Fig. 12.18. The concentration of higher-classification lines between -31° and -19° in the south, and at high northern declinations, is evident. Evident also is the sparsity of indications falling at between about ±15°. In Fig. 12.19 the same data are plotted, but omitting those indications of opposite pairs which have the nearer horizon. Certain features, such as the concentration of indications around -30°, are emphasized, but the temptation to conclude that there is clear evidence of observations of the lunar major standstill should be tempered by the discussions of the previous section.

The inter-site data are plotted in Fig. 12.20. There is apparent evidence of clumping which could be astronomically related, such as the two class 1 lines and a well-defined wider grouping of six lines falling near to +24° (the summer solstice). However the conclusion that they are deliberate is deviod of statistical backing and should be approached with caution. The final diagram, Fig. 12.21, presents the same data but omitting those indications of opposite pairs which have the nearer horizon. A clumping of lines is now evident in the vicinity of -30°, but again any astronomical explanation should be approached with caution.

13   DISCUSSION

13.1   Summary of the conclusions

A list of 322 reported sites of free-standing megaliths in certain areas of western Scotland was compiled from various available sources. After an archaeological reappraisal, 189 were considered for analysis. Various selection criteria were defined in order to determine objectively what constitute structure orientations of possible interest at a site of any particular form. Indications formed by viewing one site from another ("inter-site" indications) were also examined. Horizons closer than 1 km, however, were excluded from consideration. Surveys were undertaken between 1973 and 1981, and the remaining horizon profiles were calculated from Ordnance Survey maps. A total of 130 on-site and 146 inter-site indications were produced for analysis.

The statistical analysis of the 276 indicated declinations manifests trends at three levels of precision. At the lowest level, declinations between about -15° and $+15^{\circ}$ are strongly avoided. This reflects a general preference for structures to be oriented N-S, NW-SE or NE-SW rather than E-W.

At the second level, there is a marked preference for southern declinations between -31° and -19°, and for northern declinations above $+27^{\circ}$. Since the majority of our data represent opposite pairs of indications along the same structures, one of these trends is almost certainly a simple consequence of the other. The southern range very closely matches (i.e. matches to within about a degree at either end) the range of declinations which the moon can reach at the southern limit of its monthly motions. (Its monthly limit at any particular time varies within this range over a nineteen-year cycle.) The northern range corresponds (again to within about a degree) to those declinations to the north of any ever reached by the moon (or sun). If the southern trend represents the cause and the northern one the effect, then this implies that structures were preferentially oriented upon the southerly limit of the moon's motions in a particular month. This need not have involved nightly observations of the moon in a given month, but could have been achieved simply by observing the rising or setting of the full moon nearest to the summer solstice. If on the other hand the northern trend represents the cause and the southern one the effect, then this implies that structures were oriented preferentially to point farther along the horizon to the north than the moon (or consequently the sun) ever rose or set. Statistical analysis of the data as a whole can not formally distinguish between these two possibilities.

At the most precise level, there is marginal evidence of a preference for six particular declination values to within a precision of one or two degrees (i.e. within three or four solar or lunar diameters of a particular "event"). Three of the declinations (-30°, $+18^{\circ}$ and $+27^{\circ}$) may indicate a specific interest in the edges of the lunar limiting bands (the lunar "standstills"), and would imply that organised observations were undertaken over periods of at least twenty years.

However there is no evidence of any interest in the other lunar stand-still declination (-19°.5). The fourth preferred declination is -25°, and may indicate an interest in the winter solstice. The fifth value (-22°.5) has no particular solar or lunar significance and the last (+33°) is well outside those declinations attainable by the sun or moon.

Although there is clear evidence of lunar orientation, and marginal evidence of orientation upon the winter solstice, there is no evidence whatsoever for an interest in the summer solstice or equinoxes (indeed, declinations in the vicinity of the equinoxes are strongly avoided). We find no evidence of astronomical orientations of a precision greater than about one degree.

Certain coherent groups of sites are found to feature predominantly amongst the indications which fall in particular "preferred" declination intervals. These are sites in Mull and mainland Argyll in general, and stone alignments in these areas in particular. No significant azimuth or declination trends were detected amongst sites in the Outer Hebrides or those in Jura and Islay. We find no evidence of any significant trends amongst inter-site indications.

The statistical analysis of indicated azimuths also focuses our attention upon stone alignments in Mull and mainland Argyll. The orientations of these sites are exclusively in the northern and southern quarters of the compass. This trend can not adequately be explained by local topography alone.

When our investigations are confined to stone alignments, pairs and single flat slabs in Mull and mainland Argyll, the declination trends noted above become more marked. Twenty-seven such structures (13 alignments, 3 aligned pairs of slabs, 3 pairs and 8 single slabs) are oriented in the south upon a declination which the moon can reach at the southern limit of its monthly motions. At a further fourteen structures (4 alignments, 1 aligned pair of slabs, 2 pairs and 7 single slabs) the southern indication was excluded from consideration because the horizon was nearer than 1 km. A mere ten structures (4 pairs and 6 single slabs) remain of which six represent cases where there is special reason to believe the "indication" to be spurious. None of the exceptions is a stone alignment.

The exclusion from consideration of horizons closer than 1 km leaves us lacking vital data which bears upon the lunar hypothesis. However it brings unwittingly a considerable bonus: the opportunity to test out that hypothesis at a future date on "fresh" data.

There is no conclusive evidence for higher-precision structure within the southern limiting lunar range: in other words the distribution of the 27 indicated declinations within this range is consistent with that expected if structures were preferentially oriented upon the southerly limit of the moon's motions in a particular month. We repeat that this need not have involved nightly observations of the moon in a given month, but could have been achieved simply by observing the rising or setting of the full moon nearest to the summer solstice.

The distribution of southern declinations does however deviate in noticeable ways from that expected under the hypothesis above, and there is some indication that more precise phenomena might have been observed. Alignments in Mull and mid-Argyll appear to be preferentially oriented upon the southern limit of the range (i.e. upon the "major standstill" moon). The sites involved are Quinish (ML2), Balliscate (ML4), Dervaig S (ML11), Barbreck (AR3), Kilmartin (AR13), Duncracaig (AR15) and Dunamuck I (AR28). Alignments and slabs in Kintyre and southern Knapdale are preferentially oriented in the middle of the range, which may indicate an interest not in the moon but in the winter solstice. The primary candidates are Ardpatrick (KT3), Ballochroy (KT10), Beinn an Tuirc (KT23), Clochkeil (KT27), Mingary (KT39) and Knockstapple (KT41). If it is posited that these preferences are real, then a third preference for declinations in the vicinity of $-22^{\circ}.5$ (for which there is no obvious solar or lunar explanation) also needs elucidation. The acquisition of additional data from sites with local southern horizons may help us to decide whether these higher-precision phenomena are real. A study of the longer axes of single rectangular stones in Kintyre, many of which failed to meet our criterion to qualify as slabs, might also be worthwhile.

13.2 Implications of the results

The idea of a lunar significance in the orientations of certain free-standing megalithic sites in Mull and mainland Argyll, particularly the stone alignments, lends considerable support to the ideas of Burl (1980; 1981; 1983) that astronomical, and particularly lunar, orientations were incorporated in certain megalithic burial and ceremonial sites. However while Burl has presented a number of examples to back up his ideas, and has stressed the importance of considering coherent groups of archaeologically similar sites, his work has lacked the support of rigorous statistical analysis. This study provides such support from an independent group of sites which emerge from a much larger and (geographically and architecturally) diverse starting sample. It should be emphasized though that the lunar orientations for which there is convincing evidence here (as opposed to the more tentative higher-precision trends) require no more than the observation of the full moon nearest to the summer solstice, whereas even Burl's interpretation of the Aberdeenshire Recumbent Stone Circles involved the extreme positions of the moon in its nineteen-year cycle and thus would have required organised lunar observations over a period of at least twenty years. (The RSC work is now being revised in the light of resurveys and more rigorous analysis by the present author - see Ruggles 1984; Ruggles & Burl 1985.)

That the moon, rather than the sun, seems predominantly to have influenced the orientation of certain free-standing megalithic sites comes perhaps as little surprise in view of what is found in the ethnographic record. The cycle of lunar phases is the most obvious cycle in the sky after the daily one; it demarcates time periods of a convenient length; and it closely matches natural cycles such as the human menstrual cycle. Knowledge of the lunar month is almost universal, and many seasonal calendars are lunar-based (Baity 1973; Thorpe 1981; Carlson & von del Chamberlain 1985). On the other hand horizon solar observations, apart from in a few well-known cases such as the Hopi (McCluskey 1977), tend to be of secondary significance (for a poignant example see Turton & Ruggles 1978).

We obtain marginal evidence in favour of orientations upon the southern extreme declination of the moon in its nineteen-year cycle (the "major standstill"). Such orientations would imply that organised observations were made over a period of at least twenty years. Even this, however, could have been easily achieved: occasional observations of the full moon nearest the summer solstice would have sufficed.

It is interesting that we obtain marginal evidence for orientations upon the winter solstice but not for any other solar events. While there are some well-known individual cases of winter solstitial alignments in megalithic tombs – such as the Newgrange roof-box and passage (Patrick 1974) and a possibly similar phenomenon at Maes Howe (Moir 1981: 223-24) – no evidence has emerged before that the winter solstice might have been of particular ceremonial interest. In fact, this also comes as no surprise from the ethnographic record, where winter solstice ceremonies are often of great importance, the sun needing to be turned back from its southward movement (Thorpe 1981; Carlson & von del Chamberlain 1985).

Our conclusions are at variance in several important respects with Thom's earliest work (Thom 1955; 1967: ch. 8). Since this project was originally motivated by the work of Thom, and since our approach has been similar to Thom's in several respects, it is of some interest to compare rather more directly our conclusions with Thom's and to attempt to explain the differences between them. This is done in Section 13.3 below. Here it suffices to say that the results of this project, together with the results of separate reassessments of Thom's later work (Ruggles 1981; 1982b; 1983), strongly suggest that any claimed astronomical sightlines of a precision of $0°.5$ and better can be completely explained away as chance occurrences emphasized purely by the process by which they were selected for analysis in the first place.

Our conclusions are also at variance with those of Patrick (1979), who could find no lunar alignment at Barbreck (see page 20). In his analysis of the site he omitted the one most obvious alignment there, that along the two aligned slabs, dismissing it because "neither direction of the stones' faces can indicate important lunar declinations". In fact the southern indication points within a degree of the major standstill moon (Section 12.4.5; Fig. 8.3). This correction is important, for Patrick used the architectural similarity of the Barbreck and Kilmartin sites, and the lack of lunar alignments at the former, as an argument against the intentionality of the lunar alignments at the latter. His argument is in fact in error and should not be allowed to confuse the conclusions of this volume.

13.3 Comparison with the conclusions of A. Thom

In his earliest work Thom measured the declinations indicated by 72 structures at 39 megalithic sites, and plotted the results in the form of a curvigram (Thom 1955: Fig. 8). This evidence was later extended to 262 structure indications at 145 sites (Thom 1967: Fig. 8.1). On the basis of these curvigrams and associated statistical tests Thom suggested the existence of deliberate solar, lunar and stellar alignments set up to a precision of about half a degree. The solar alignments are concentrated at the solstices, equinoxes and two other declinations which together form the rising and setting position of the sun at intervals of 1/8 year. The lunar alignments are concentrated at the four "standstill" declinations. Although we find marginal evidence that three of the four standstill declinations were preferred, the precision involved is about one degree at most. We also find marginal evidence that the winter solstitial declination was preferred, but again at precision of about one degree at most. We find no evidence whatsoever for preference of the equinoctial, summer solstitial or other calendrical declinations. We note finally that Thom also obtained peaks at declinations of $-22^{o}.5$ and $+33^{o}$, declinations for which we find marginal evidence of preference.

We find no evidence of any significant trends amongst inter-site lines. Although this may come as little surprise in view of the diversity of the sites concerned, it was fair to test this possibility in the light of Thom's work.

The principal reasons for the discrepancy between Thom's results and ours may be the following.

(i) The selection of sites for consideration. However we have found nothing in Thom's selection of sites which would significantly have influenced the results of his astronomical analysis.

(ii) The selection of potential indications at each site. In the 1955 analysis rigid selection criteria were adhered to by Thom. He considered only indications defined by an outlier to a circle, two slabs in line, or a row of three or more stones. In the later analysis, however, there are no such clear-cut selection criteria, and there are a number of instances where astronomical lines may have been preferentially selected. For example, at some sites only the indication one way along an alignment has been included, and not the other. It is possible that such decisions were unwittingly based upon one line being astronomical and not the other.

(iii) Some archaeological misinterpretations are included amongst Thom's indication data.

(iv) The inclusion of sightlines to what are considered to be indicated horizon foresights, such as notches between mountains. Such lines account for about 20% of the 1967 data. In these cases we are not often not told what the claimed method of indication is; we are often not told what the foresight is; and we are never told how wide the indication is, and how many other equally prominent and well-indicated horizon foresights might equally well have been chosen by the investigator.

(v) Thom used fixed widths for his gaussian humps, so that a fixed uncertainty was assigned to each indicated declination regardless of the nature and present state of the indication. Where the direction of the original structure orientation is uncertain within wide bounds, this means that a subjective decision was made as to the original probable indication. This decision might unwittingly have been influenced by astronomical considerations.

Thom considered a geographically more diverse selection of megalithic sites than we did, and a more diverse set of possible structures as putative indications (for example he included lines from the centres of stone rings to outlying stones).

Because of the selection uncertainties listed above, there is little point in revisiting and resurveying the 276 indications listed by Thom in order to reassess them. The only adequate form of reassessment is to carry out an independent survey from scratch, paying attention to rigorous selection procedures. This is precisely what has been attempted in this volume.

In 1967 Thom analysed further those of his 276 indications which fell near the solar solstitial declinations, about 30 of them (Thom 1967: ch. 9), and found evidence that the upper and lower limbs were preferentially observed; the further analysis of the lunar lines (ibid.: ch. 10), of which there are about 40, suggests the same thing. This increased the inferred precision to about 10 minutes of arc.

In our data, declination preferences of possible significance occur at 1° or so from obvious lunar or solar events that would explain them, so that lunar and solar explanations fit the data well at a precision of a degree or two, but break down at higher precisions. Furthermore there are no instances in Table 12.3 of low significance levels occurring $0^\circ.5$ apart, which would be comparable to Thom's double-peak evidence (1967: Fig. 10.1). Thus we obtain no evidence that the separate limbs of the sun or moon were observed at any particular event.

We have not examined our data for very high precision indications using distant horizon features such as notches, on the grounds that there is no motivation from our data at lower precisions to do so. However in case anyone should wish to scrutinise our data for such evidence, all the information is available in this volume, in the form of background information, profile diagrams and tabulated data, to enable them to do so.

Later work by Thom (on his own and together with his son A.S. Thom) concentrates upon lunar sightlines of very high precision (Thom 1971: ch. 7; Thom & Thom 1978a; 1980a; A.S. Thom 1981). This evidence depends upon the precise distribution of indicated declinations in the proximity of a significant astronomical "target" (such as a mean lunar standstill) about that target, and so the question of the selection of sites themselves, and of potential indicating structures at those sites, is of minor importance compared with the selection of horizon features for inclusion. This means that adequate reassessments can be carried out by visiting and resurveying just those sites considered by Thom himself. Such reassessments have been undertaken by the current author and published elsewhere (Ruggles 1981; 1982b; 1983). When questions of selection are tackled, and the data adjusted accordingly, the author finds no evidence to suggest that the Thoms' sightlines of very high precision can not be completely explained away as chance occurrences.

13.4 Methodological implications

In this volume we have tried to establish methodological guidelines by which evidence can be sought from orientations in the surface record which is acceptable both in its statistical rigour and in its archaeological applicability. Too much energy has been expended in the past on efforts demonstrably lacking in one or other respect. Thus there has been a great deal of debate about individual sites such as Ballochroy (Thom 1954: 396-404; 1971: 36-37; Bailey et al. 1975; Burl 1979: 66-67; 1983: 6-11), Kintraw (Heggie 1981a: S29-31 and references therein) and Kilmartin, or Temple Wood (Thom 1971: 45-51; Patrick 1979): these debates which could never satisfactorily be resolved on their own merits. They were deficient on both statistical and archaeo-logical grounds. Some studies of coherent groups of sites, notably those of Burl (1980; 1981), are on archaeologically safer ground but lack statistical rigour. And finally the work of Thom (1955; 1967: ch. 8), which has stood for thirty years as the only serious attempt at a statistically rigorous approach, had serious shortcomings in archaeological terms.

The general guideline we have adopted is that statistical rigour must precede interpretative reasoning. Both stages are essential, and hopefully this study demonstrates that they can be successful. However divorced from cultural reality our selection criteria of Chapter 3 might have seemed, they resulted in an objective set of data upon which meaningful statistical tests could be performed, and meaningful results obtained. Our attention is now focused upon a coherent selec-tion of sites and astronomical possibilities. At this point (but no earlier) a more interpretative approach can - and indeed must - be adopted if the results are to be properly considered in their cultural context.

There is a one serious problem which emerges when using statis-tical testing upon the archaeological record in this way. It is not insurmountable, but must be recognised. It is that we effectively consider a multitude of hypotheses, so that we should lower the sig-nificance level at which we are prepared to reject the null hypothesis in favour of any particular alternative. This is in fact symptomatic of archaeology as a whole. It arises because evidence in the archaeo-logical record is severely limited, and so the data upon which hypoth-eses are based is the only data readily available with which to test them. This is in direct contrast to the whole philosophy of the nat-ural sciences, where a hypothesis based on the available experimental data can be tested by devising and performing new experiments and obtaining new data.

Prehistoric astronomy is both an area of importance and one in which the surface record can give us valuable information in advance of excavation. In archaeology as a whole, it is possible to design investigations (for example an excavation strategy) in order to test particular hypotheses rather than merely to collect data. This becomes increasingly important for the overall progress of the subject as resources become increasingly scarce. If we can use the surface data to set up viable hypotheses in areas of importance, then we have both a working hypothesis in advance of any excavation, and also a strategy which should save resources if ever we are in a position to undertake one. If corroborative evidence on prehistoric astronomy is sought from excavation, then we have isolated a group of sites where such work might preferentially be undertaken, together with hypotheses (solar and lunar association) which might be tested.

Evidence of astronomical orientation can, if produced with sufficent care and rigour, be a reliable factor to be fed into the archaeological equation. Following the groundwork presented in this volume we can now turn to the most promising groups of sites, the alignments, and to the most promising areas, Mull and mainland Argyll, and study them with all the archaeological means at our disposal and in their full archaeological and cultural context. Hopefully this volume has laid a proper and reliable basis for the sort of co-operation involved and for more broad-based work of this nature.

APPENDIX I. Declination

A number of explanations of the concept of <u>declination</u> have
appeared in scholarly and popular books on archaeoastronomy. The
reader is referred to any one of the following: Thom (1967: ch. 3);
Heggie (1981b: ch. 5); Krupp (1977: ch. 1) and Wood (1978: ch. 4).
The account that follows is deliberately simplistic and does not have
the benefit of explanatory diagrams.

We can regard all the heavenly bodies - sun, moon, planets and
stars - as positioned on a "celestial sphere" surrounding the earth.
From any position on the earth at a particular time we can observe the
half of the celestial sphere which is above our horizon, as in a
planetarium. The earth rotates once daily inside the celestial sphere;
thus if we regard the earth as fixed, the celestial sphere rotates
once daily with all the heavenly bodies affixed to it. It has a north
and south pole (the celestial poles), an equator (the celestial
equator) and lines of latitude and longitude, just like the earth.
<u>Declination</u> is simply a synonym for celestial latitude. The celestial
equator is the line where declination = 0°; by convention declinations
north of the celestial equator are positive and those to the south
negative.   The declination of the north celestial pole is $+90^o$ and
that of the south celestial pole -90°. The significance of declination is that all the heavenly bodies move daily around lines of
constant latitude on the celestial sphere, i.e. around lines of
constant declination.   Thus the Pleiades have a declination of about
$+24^o$, and Polaris, which is very near to the north celestial pole, has
a declination of $+89^o$.   By surveying the azimuth and altitude of a
point on the horizon from some observing position, and knowing the
latitude of that position, one can calculate the declination of the
horizon point using a simple formula (Thom 1967: ch. 3). Hence, by
referring to astronomical texts, one knows at a stroke all the
heavenly bodies that will rise or set there at some time during the
daily cycle.

On timescales longer than a single day, life is not as simple.
This is because the sun, moon and planets in fact move slowly about on
the celestial sphere as it rotates. Thus at June solstice the sun is
north of the celestial equator at a declination of about $+23^o.5$, at
the equinoxes it is roughly on the celestial equator, and at December
solstice it is at the southerly declination of about $-23^o.5$. The
moon's declination varies monthly between northerly and southerly
limits, and these limits themselves vary over a period a little under
19 years. Thus at one point in this cycle the moon's declination will
be varying each month between limits of $+17^o.5$ and $-19^o.5$; a little
over nine years later these monthly limits will have expanded to $+28^o$
and $-29^o.5$; and after another nine years they will have contracted
back to $+17^o.5$ and $-19^o.5$. The maximum northerly and southerly limits
of the moon's motions are sometimes known, following Thom (1971: 18),
as the "major standstill" declinations, and this terminology will be
adopted in this volume. However it should be noted that in no sense

does the moon actually stand still; it constantly moves from its
northerly declination limit to its southerly one and back over a
monthly cycle.   Similarly the minimum northerly and southerly limits
of the moon's motion are known as the "minor standstill" declinations.
The motions of the planets are more complicated, but they are confined
to roughly the same ranges of declination as the sun and moon.

On a timescale of centuries the declinations of the stars gradually change.   This is not because the individual stars move slowly
about on the celestial sphere as it rotates: this does happen, of
course, but only on an even longer timescale. It is because, relative
to the distant stars, the earth slowly pivots like a spinning top over
a period of some 26000 years. If we regard the earth as fixed, this
means that over the centuries the entire network of stars on the
celestial sphere gradually shifts position, so that (for example)
different stars are now located near to the celestial poles and
different ones now fall on the celestial equator. This effect is
known as the "precession of the equinoxes".

The limiting annual and monthly declinations of the sun and moon
are not affected by the precession of the equinoxes, but they do
change noticeably over a timescale of millennia. Since 2000 BC they
have changed by about $0°.5$, an amount roughly equal to the width of
the solar or lunar disc. If we specify that we are talking about the
centre of the sun or moon, it becomes meaningful to quote limiting
declinations more accurately, say to $0°.1$.   The solar solstitial
declinations in 2000 BC were $+23°.9$ and $-23°.9$, the lunar major
standstill declinations were $+28°.2$ and $-30°.0$, and the lunar minor
standstill declinations were $+17°.9$ and $-19°.7$. The declinations of
the upper limb of the sun or moon at these limits are obtained by
adding $0°.25$ to these values (whether they are positive or negative),
and that of the lower limb by subtracting $0°.25$.

All these changes with time are well documented. Hence, by
determining the declination of a horizon point one knows at a stroke
not only all the heavenly bodies that will rise or set there today,
but all that would have done so at any specified epoch in the past.

APPENDIX II. <u>An extension of Neave & Selkirk's method to deal with</u>
<u>the distribution of opposite pairs of points on a circle</u>

Instead of considering independent points distributed on the
circle, we wish to consider n pairs of diametrically opposite points.

Had our 2n points been independent of one another, we would have
calculated the test statistic t as follows. Let S be the sum of the
2n nearest-neighbour distances. t is then given by S divided by the
circumference of the circle.

Consider any half of the circle, for example the azimuth inter-
val |0, 180) consisting of those azimuths in the range 0 <= AZ < 180.
Note that the interval must be semi-closed, i.e. one of its bounds (in
this case 0) will be included in the interval, whereas the other (in
this case 180) will be excluded. (The square- and round-bracket
notation expresses this.) Exactly one point from each of our n pairs
will fall in the interval. Under the null (random) hypothesis our n
points will be distributed uniformly on |0, 180).

Each of the extreme points in the range |0, 180) has as its
neighbour in the full circle the opposite number of the other extreme
point in |0, 180). This means that the nearest-neighbour distances of
all n points in |0, 180) assuming wrap-around (so that, say, a point
at 179° is 2° away from one at 1°) are exactly the same as they are on
the full circle. Since the complementary interval |180, 360) contains
an exact image of the distribution of points in |0, 180), the sum of n
nearest-neighbour distances in |0, 180) assuming wrap-around is
exactly half of our previous sum of 2n nearest-neighbour distances,
i.e. S / 2.

Now consider our n selected points in isolation and double their
azimuths. Under the null hypothesis the new points will be distributed
uniformly on the semi-closed interval |0, 360). The sum of their
nearest-neighbour distances assuming wrap-around is twice what we had
before, i.e. S. But the semi-closed interval |0, 360) with wrap-around
is simply another way of describing the circle! Thus under the null
hypothesis our n points are distributed uniformly on the circle and
hence deviations from randomness can be estimated using Neave & Selkirk's statistic t. This is given by S divided by the circumference,
or exactly the same value as we calculated from our 2n points at the
outset.

Hence when our points form n opposite pairs rather than 2n
single independent points, we need simply to calculate the same test
statistic t but to treat it in the analysis as if we had n single
independent points.

REFERENCES

Ashbee, P. (1970). The earthen long barrow in Britain. London.

Atkinson, R.J.C. (1981). Comments on the archaeological status of some of the sites. Appendix 4.2 to Ruggles (1981), op. cit.

Aveni, A.F. (1980). Skywatchers of ancient Mexico. Austin & London.

Bailey, M.E., Cooke, J.A., Few, R.W., Morgan, J.G. & Ruggles, C.L.N. (1975). Survey of three megalithic sites in Argyllshire. Nature, 253, 431-33.

Baity, E.C. (1973). Archaeoastronomy and ethnoastronomy so far. Current anthropology, 14, 389-449.

Barber, J.W. (1978). The excavation of the holed-stone at Ballymeanoch, Kilmartin, Argyll. Proceedings of the Society of Antiquaries of Scotland (hereinafter P.S.A.S.), 109, 104-11.

Beveridge, E. (1903). Coll & Tiree: their prehistoric forts and ecclesiastical antiquities. Edinburgh.

Beveridge, E. (1911). North Uist: its archaeology and topography. Edinburgh.

Burl, H.A.W. (1971). Two 'Scottish' stone circles in Northumberland. Archaeologia Aeliana, 49, 37-51.

Burl, H.A.W. (1976). The stone circles of the British Isles. New Haven & London.

Burl, H.A.W. (1979). Rings of Stone. London.

Burl, H.A.W. (1980). Science or symbolism: problems of archaeoastronomy. Antiquity, 54, 191-200.

Burl, H.A.W. (1981). "By the light of the cinerary moon": chambered tombs and the astronomy of death. In C.L.N. Ruggles & A.W.R. Whittle (eds.), Astronomy and society in Britain during the period 4000-1500 BC, Oxford (B.A.R. 88), pp. 243-74.

Burl, H.A.W. (1982). Rites of the Gods. London.

Burl, H.A.W. (1983). Prehistoric astronomy and ritual. Aylesbury.

Campbell, J.L. & Thomson, D. (1963). Edward Lhuyd in the Scottish highlands, 1699-1700. Oxford.

Campbell, M. and Sandeman, M. (1961). Mid-Argyll: a field survey of the historic and prehistoric monuments. P.S.A.S., 95, 1-125.

Carlson, J.B. & Chamberlain, von del (eds.) (1985). Proceedings of the first international ethnoastronomy conference. Washington DC (2 vols., forthcoming).

Cooke, J.A., Few, R.W., Morgan, J.G. & Ruggles, C.L.N. (1977). Indicated declinations at the Callanish megalithic sites. Journal for the history of astronomy, 8, 113-33.

Cowie, T. (1979). In Discovery and excavation in Scotland, 1979, 28-29.

Crawford, O.G.S. (1933). Iona. Antiquity, 7, 453-467.

Curtis, G.R. (1979). Some geometry associated with the standing stones of Callanish. Hebridean Naturalist, 3, 29-40.

Freeman, P.R. & Elmore, W. (1979). A test for the significance of astronomical alignments. Archaeoastronomy, no. 1, S86-96.

Hawkins, G.S. (1963). Stonehenge decoded. Nature, 200, 306-8.

Hawkins, G.S. (1973). In Discovery and excavation in Scotland, 1973, 13.

Hawkins, G.S. (1983). Mindsteps to the Cosmos. New York.

Hawkins, G.S. & White, J.B. (1966). Stonehenge decoded. New York & London.

Heggie, D.C. (1981a). Highlights and problems of megalithic astronomy. Archaeoastronomy, no. 3, S17-37.

Heggie, D.C. (1981b). Megalithic Science. London.

Henshall, A. (1972). The chambered tombs of Scotland, 2. Edinburgh.

Krupp, E.C. (ed.) (1977). In search of ancient astronomies. New York.

Leach, E.R. (1954). Primitive time-reckoning. In C. Singer, E.J. Holmyard & A.R. Hall (eds.), A history of technology, Vol. 1, Oxford, pp. 110-127.

Leach, E.R. (1961). Rethinking anthropology. London & New York.

Lockyer, N. (1909). Stonehenge and other British stone monuments astronomically considered (2nd edition). London.

McCluskey, S.C. (1977). The astronomy of the Hopi Indians. Journal for the history of astronomy, 8, 174-195.

MacKie, E.W. (1974). Archaeological tests on supposed astronomical sites in Scotland. Philosophical transactions of the Royal Society of London, A276, 169-94.

MacKie, E.W. (1975). Scotland: an archaeological guide. London.

MacKie, E.W. (1977). Science and society in prehistoric Britain. London.

MacKie, E.W. (1981).   Wise men in antiquity? In C.L.N. Ruggles &
    A.W.R. Whittle (eds.), Astronomy and society in Britain during
    the period 4000-1500 BC, Oxford (B.A.R. 88), pp. 111-52.

Mardia, K.V. (1972). The statistics of directional data. London.

Martin Martin (c. 1695).   A description of the Western Isles of
    Scotland. Edition edited by D.J.Macleod, Stirling, 1934.

M'Laughlin, T. (1865).   Notice on monoliths in the Island of Mull.
    P.S.A.S., 5, 46-52.

Moir, G. (1980).   Megalithic science and some Scottish site plans:
    Part I. Antiquity, 54, 37-40.

Moir, G. (1981).   Some archaeological and astronomical objections to
    scientific astronomy in British prehistory. In C.L.N. Ruggles &
    A.W.R. Whittle (eds.), Astronomy and society in Britain during
    the period 4000-1500 BC, Oxford (B.A.R. 88), pp. 221-241.

Neave, H.R. & Selkirk, K.E. (1983). Nearest-neighbour analysis of the
    distribution of points on a circle. University of Nottingham
    Research Report 05-83.

Orr, J. (1937).   Standing stones and other relics in Mull. Trans.
    Glasgow arch. soc., 9, 128-34.

Patrick, J.D. (1974).   Midwinter sunrise at Newgrange. Nature, 249,
    517-19.

Patrick, J.D. (1979). A reassessment of the lunar observatory hypoth-
    esis for the Kilmartin stones. Archaeoastronomy, no. 1, S78-85.

Pennant, T. (1774).   A tour in Scotland and voyage to the Hebrides,
    1772: Vol. 1. London.

Pennant, T. (1776).   A tour in Scotland and voyage to the Hebrides,
    1772: Vol. 2. London.

Ponting, M.R. & Ponting, G.H. (1981).   Decoding the Callanish complex
    - some initial results.   In C.L.N. Ruggles & A.W.R. Whittle
    (eds.), Astronomy and society in Britain during the period 4000-
    1500 BC, Oxford (B.A.R. 88), pp. 63-110.

Ritchie, J.N.G. (1971).   Excavation of a cairn at Strontoiller, Lorn,
    Argyll. Glasgow arch. journal, 2, 1-7.

R.C.A.H.M.S. (1928).   Inventories of ancient monuments, 9: Outer
    Hebrides, Skye and the Small Isles. Edinburgh.

R.C.A.H.M.S. (1971).   Argyll: an Inventory of the ancient monuments,
    1: Kintyre. Edinburgh.

R.C.A.H.M.S. (1975).   Argyll: an Inventory of the ancient monuments,
    2: Lorn. Edinburgh.

R.C.A.H.M.S. (1980).   Argyll: an Inventory of the ancient monuments, 3: Mull, Tiree, Coll and northern Argyll. Edinburgh.

R.C.A.H.M.S. (1984).   Argyll: an Inventory of the ancient monuments, 5: Islay, Jura and Colonsay. Edinburgh.

Ruggles, C.L.N. (1981).   A critical examination of the megalithic lunar observatories. In C.L.N. Ruggles & A.W.R. Whittle (eds.), Astronomy and society in Britain during the period 4000-1500 BC, Oxford (B.A.R. 88), pp. 153-209.

Ruggles, C.L.N. (1982a).   Megalithic astronomical sightlines: current reassessment and future directions. In D.C. Heggie (ed.), Archaeoastronomy in the Old World, Cambridge, pp. 83-105.

Ruggles, C.L.N. (1982b).   A reassessment of the high precision megalithic lunar sightlines, 1: Backsights, indicators and the archaeological status of the sightlines. Archaeoastronomy, no. 4, S21-40.

Ruggles, C.L.N. (1983).   A reassessment of the high precision megalithic lunar sightlines, 2: Foresights and the problem of selection. Archaeoastronomy, no. 5, S1-36.

Ruggles, C.L.N. (1984).   A new study of the Aberdeenshire Recumbent Stone Circles, 1: Site data. Archaeoastronomy, no. 6, S55-79.

Ruggles, C.L.N. & Burl, H.A.W. (1985).   A new study of the Aberdeenshire Recumbent Stone Circles, 2: Interpretation. Archaeoastronomy, no. 8, forthcoming.

Ruggles, C.L.N. & Norris, R.P. (1980).   Megalithic science and some Scottish site plans: Part II. Antiquity, 54, 40-43.

Ruggles, C.L.N. & Whittle, A.W.R. (eds.) (1981). Astronomy and society in Britain during the period 4000-1500 BC. Oxford (B.A.R. 88).

Scott, J.G. (1955).   The excavation of the chambered cairn at Brackley, Kintyre, Argyll. P.S.A.S., 89, 22-54.

Scott, J.G. (1975). In Discovery and excavation in Scotland, 1975, 12-13.

Scott, J.G. (1976). In Discovery and excavation in Scotland, 1976, 15.

Scott, J.G. (1977). In Discovery and excavation in Scotland, 1977, 7.

Scott, J.G. (1978). In Discovery and excavation in Scotland, 1978, 22.

Scott, J.G. (1979). In Discovery and excavation in Scotland, 1979, 32.

Scott, J.G. (1980). In Discovery and excavation in Scotland, 1980, 30-31.

Simpson, D.D.A. (1967).   Excavations at Kintraw, Argyll. P.S.A.S., 99, 54-59.

Smith, R.A. (1872). Descriptive list of antiquities near Loch Etive, Argyllshire: Part I. P.S.A.S., 9, 81-106.

Smith, R.A. (1874). Descriptive list of antiquities near Loch Etive, Argyllshire: Part III. P.S.A.S., 10, 70-90.

Stukeley, W. (1776). Itinerarium Curiosum, Vol. II. London.

Tait, D. (1978). A map of the standing stones and circles at Callanish, Isle of Lewis, with a detailed plan of each site. Glasgow.

Tedlock, B. (1984). Zuni sacred theater. American Indian Quarterly, in press.

Thom, A. (1954). The solar observatories of Megalithic Man. Journal of the British Astronomical Association, 64, 396-404.

Thom, A. (1955). A statistical examination of the megalithic sites in Britain. Journal of the Royal Statistical Society, A118, 275-95.

Thom, A. (1966). Megalithic astronomy: indications in standing stones. Vistas in astronomy, 7, 1-57.

Thom, A. (1967). Megalithic sites in Britain. Oxford.

Thom, A. (1971). Megalithic lunar observatories. Oxford.

Thom, A. & Thom, A.S. (1978a). Megalithic remains in Britain and Brittany. Oxford.

Thom, A. & Thom, A.S. (1978b). A reconsideration of the lunar sites in Britain. Journal for the history of astronomy, 9, 170-79.

Thom, A. & Thom, A.S. (1979a). Another lunar site in Kintyre. Archaeoastronomy, no. 1, S96-7.

Thom, A. & Thom, A.S. (1979b). The standing stones in Argyllshire. Glasgow archaeological journal, 6, 5-10.

Thom, A. & Thom, A.S. (1980a). A new study of all megalithic lunar lines. Archaeoastronomy, no. 2, S78-89.

Thom, A. & Thom, A.S. (1980b). The astronomical foresights used by Megalithic Man. Archaeoastronomy, no. 2, S90-94.

Thom, A., Thom, A.S. & Burl, H.A.W. (1980). Megalithic rings. Oxford (B.A.R. 81).

Thom, A., Thom, A.S. & Burl, H.A.W. (1984). Megalithic rows (provisional title). Oxford (B.A.R., forthcoming).

Thom, A.S. (1981). Megalithic lunar observatories: an assessment of 42 lunar alignments. In C.L.N. Ruggles & A.W.R. Whittle (eds.), Astronomy and society in Britain during the period 4000-1500 BC, Oxford (B.A.R. 88), pp. 13-61.

Thorpe, I.J. (1981).   Ethnoastronomy: its patterns and archaeological implications.   In C.L.N. Ruggles & A.W.R. Whittle (eds.), Astronomy and society in Britain during the period 4000-1500 BC, Oxford (B.A.R. 88), pp. 275-288.

Thorpe, I.J. (1982).   On megalithic astronomy (Comment). <u>Current anthropology</u>, <u>23</u>, 220-221.

Thorpe, I.J. (1983). Prehistoric British astronomy - towards a social context. <u>Scottish archaeological review</u>, <u>2(1)</u>, 2-10.

Turton, D.A. & Ruggles, C.L.N. (1978).   Agreeing to disagree: the measurement of duration in a southwestern Ethiopian community. <u>Current anthropology</u>, <u>19</u>, 585-600.

Urton, G. (1981).   At the crossroads of the earth and sky. An Andean cosmology. Austin, Texas.

Williamson, T. & Bellamy, E. (1983). Ley lines in question. Tadworth, Surrey.

Wood, J.E. (1978). Sun, moon and standing stones. Oxford.